FRANK PORTER GRAHAM

A Southern Liberal

WARREN ASHBY

FRANK PORTER GRAHAM

A Southern Liberal

JOHN F. BLAIR, PUBLISHER
Winston-Salem, North Carolina

Library of Congress Cataloging in Publication Data

Ashby, Warren, 1920–
    Frank Porter Graham, a Southern liberal.

    Bibliography: p.
    Includes index.
        1.   Graham, Frank Porter, 1886–
2. North Carolina—Biography. 3. Legislators—
United States—Biography. 4. United States.
Senate—Biography. 5. College presidents—
North Carolina—Biography. I. Title.
F259.G7A83   328.73′092′4 [B]   80–23370
ISBN 0–89587–009–6

Acknowledgments

This recounting of the life of Frank Porter Graham is the result of the cooperation of many individuals and institutions. Some persons, especially university colleagues and other friends, who provided generous assistance of various kinds during the years the book was in preparation will unavoidably remain unnamed. I trust that they know of my gratitude. I must mention however, with continuing appreciation, persons and institutions who gave specific assistance beyond that recorded in "Sources."

Financial support which made possible the basic research and writing came from three sources: a grant from the Field Foundation and its secretary, the late Maxwell Hahn, who through the years have been good friends of the South; several grants from the Research Council of The Woman's College, now The University of North Carolina at Greensboro; and a grant from the Frank P. Graham Fund, especially created by Fred W. Weaver, then vice-president of the University of North Carolina. While at the time I expressed appreciation to Fred Weaver and asked him to convey my gratitude to the fund's contributors, I did not know who the persons were until the writing was completed: Kemp D. Battle, Mrs. Laura Weill Cone, Reuben B. Robertson, Otho B. Ross, Mrs. Charles W. Tillett, A. Lee M. Wiggins, and Francis E. Winslow.

There can be no better place to work than the Jackson Library of the University of North Carolina at Greensboro. The Southern Historical Collection and the North Carolina Room, both of the Wilson Library in Chapel Hill, provided essential materials. It is always a joy to enter those libraries and to work with those librarians.

Special assistance in typing drafts of the manuscript and in organizing materials was given by Paul Ashby, Margaret Bostian, Carrolton Johnson, Alice Lutz, Judy McDowell, and Joan Steele.

A seminar which I taught in "Biography" at the Residential College of the University of North Carolina at Greensboro used an early draft of the biography as a case study. The students in the mid-seventies found Frank Graham a strange person from a strange era, but the sensitivity of their insights into and criticisms about my theory and practice of biographical writing were important to me at a crucial stage. I learned much from Owena Alston, Cecelia Babb, Deborah Everett, Martha Hyatt, James Heilman, Lynette Lucas, Jean Shaw, and Ramona Stone.

A number of persons have read the manuscript in various drafts and have given me the benefit of their detailed and varied criticisms: Allen Ashby, Kemp D. Battle, Albert Coates, Richard N. Current, Joanne Daniels, Joseph Herzenberg, G. Maurice Hill, Robert B. House, Charles M. Jones, Fred W. Morrison, William Pruitt, Louise Smith, George B. Tindall, Fred W. Weaver, Emily Wilson, Louis Round Wilson, and Francis E. Winslow. Both the most severe and the most encouraging criticisms came from members of my family—Helen, Allen, Paul, Ann, and Craig; but, as they should know, I am daily indebted to them (as to Debbie and Ashby Lee) for what is far more important in life than reading and criticising a manuscript. I learned, sometimes painfully, from every one of the critics though I did not always agree with them. Nor, even after arduous efforts, have I been able to achieve the many ideals of biographical writing they have taught me.

No author could be more fortunate in his editors. Rick Mashburn, with painstaking care and an eye for style, not only helped reduce a lengthy manuscript to manageable size but, in the process, assisted in bringing order to complex material. John Fries Blair, with an insistence upon accuracy of fact and expression, has provided exacting standards of excellence. The curiosity of the former, the knowledge of the latter, and the love of both for the history of the period brought to greater clarity important facts and subtleties. George McDaniel has been of indispensable assistance with the notes and index. Virginia Ingram has given both professional and personal care to the book design and the collection of photographs.

With the assistance of so many persons, including those listed in the "Sources," I am tempted to say that any limitations in the book surely must be the responsibility of others. Unfortunately, the inadequacies are mine. Those inadequacies give me the hope that others will explore further the inexhaustible materials for a period and a life important in Southern, American, and world history.

At the beginning of the notes to each part, the books and other materials relevant to that part are identified. But other persons and writings that have deeply affected my biographical perspective also require mention. The interest in social and individual history was stimulated by a great teacher, H. Richard Niebuhr, especially through his distinctions of inner and outer history and his scholarly work relating social event and intellectual response. The study of eighteenth-century moral philosophers, particularly Adam Smith and David Hume, of Ernst Troeltsch, and, to a lesser extent, of Karl Mannheim and Erik Erikson, have provided clues for understanding how reason, emotion, and society interact in human experience. In addition, a long-term project of my own in writing a history of Western ethics in which the attempt is made to relate social factors and individual experience to moral theories has provided ways to understand the content and sources of Graham's life. Some books and articles about the writing of biography have also been helpful, though, it should be noted, this is a field of criticism which to date is largely untouched by excellence. The writings I have found beneficial include Catherine Drinker Bowen, *Adventures of a Biographer* (Boston: Little, Brown, 1959) and *Biography: The Craft and the Calling* (Boston: Little, Brown, 1969); James L. Clifford, ed., *Biography as an Art: Selected Criticism* (New York: Oxford University Press, 1962) and *From Puzzles to Portraits: Problems of a Literary Biographer* (New York: Oxford University Press, 1970); Philip B. Daghliam, ed., *Essays in Eighteenth Century Biography* (Bloomington: University of Indiana Press, 1968); John A. Garraty, *The Nature of Biography* (New York: Alfred A. Knopf, 1957); Oscar Handlin, "The History in Men's Lives," *Virginia Quarterly Review* XXX (1954):4; André Maurois, *Aspects of Biography* (New York: D. Appleton, 1929); Harold Nicholson, "The Practice of Biography," *American Scholar* XXIII (1954):2; Marc Pachter, ed., *Telling Lives: The Biographical Art* (Washington, D.C.: New Republic/National Portrait Gallery, 1979), especially the articles by Leon Edel, Alfred Kazin, Doris Kearns, and Barbara W. Tuchman; Mark Schorer, "The Burdens of Biography," *Michigan Quarterly Review* I (1962):4; F. B. Tolles, "The Biographer's Craft," *South Atlantic Quarterly* LIII (October 1954):4.

Every person who enjoys biographies has favorites; and various biographies have, in various ways, offered suggestions and provided models for writing. But one single-volume biography deserves mention since it has provided standards of scholarship and style that have often been both inspiring and challenging: Benjamin P. Thomas, *Abraham Lincoln: A Biography* (New York: Alfred A. Knopf, 1952).

I am especially indebted to the late Fred Weaver, Louis Round Wilson, and Al Lowenstein, and to Albert Coates and Charles M. Jones, for many conversations, criticisms, and suggestions and for their encouragement through the years. Their contributions to North Carolina, the South, and the nation have been incalculable; and my many debts to them, far beyond their assistance with this book, are more than they can have known or I can repay.

Finally, I am grateful to Frank Graham for the freedom and information he gave to me, without any overt encouragement, in the writing of this biography. He would have appreciated the fact that so many persons contributed to the work and would have thought of it as democracy in practice. It was my decision, with which he concurred, that he would not read any portion of the writing until after it was published; so it cannot be known how he would have responded to the interpretations.

Graham would have recognized the ironic appropriateness, though irony was far from his nature, that a biography of Lincoln set the standards for that of a Southern liberal. He was far from being alone in his time as a Southern liberal. He was as much the heir as the developer of Southern liberalism, just as he was as much created by as the creator of a free university. He early placed himself in that tradition of liberalism which, though often concealed, runs throughout the history of the South. And he placed himself, too, in the line of American liberals.

At the present time there is an eclipse of liberalism in the United States and in all Western democracies. To understand Frank Graham's life and activity in the context of his society should provide some comprehension of the travails of liberalism in the South and of its traumatic history in the first three-quarters of the twentieth century in America. And, however it is written, to read that life aright may offer clues for the fate and prospects of democratic liberalism in the future.

WARREN ASHBY

Contents

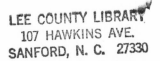

FRANK PORTER GRAHAM

A Southern Liberal

Part One

Years of Preparation: 1886-1920

1

The Door Opens

Call not thy wanderer home as yet
Though it be late.
Now is his first assailing of
The invisible gate.
Be still through that light knocking. The hour
Is thronged with fate.[1]
—George William Russell (1935)

IN HIS EARLIEST VIVID MEMORY HE WAS LYING ON the front porch at home. It was a warm June night, the fireflies scattered the dark with bits of light, and seemingly not far beyond the fireflies, the stars lit the sky. The two visitors who had laughed during supper now talked earnestly with his father. Lying behind their rhythmically rocking chairs, he could not make out what they were saying, but some words he heard: "schools" and "children," "teachers" and "North Carolina" and "Chapel Hill." They were familiar words in his home. Then, when he was drowsing, he heard one speak about staying up all night, talking by a "light that never was on land or sea."

"A funny light," Frank thought. At that moment he rolled toward the visitor in the chair or the chair walked toward him or perhaps both moved toward each other. The rocker came down painfully upon his foot. It was for a five-year-old boy a memorable summer evening.[2]

On that night in 1891 Alexander Graham, the superintendent of the Charlotte Public Schools, was entertaining Edwin A. Alderman and Charles D. McIver. Alderman and McIver, driven by a dream for the education of all North Carolina children, were traveling into each of the one hundred counties in North Carolina to hold teacher training institutes. Alderman, as neat and polished as his exact figures, told of how in the first year he had traveled 3100 miles, taught more than 3600 teachers, and addressed more than 35,000 citizens. McIver, in his early thirties still the robust Scot farm boy, told of how they had persuaded the legislature to give them four thousand dollars for the institutes, which would instruct teachers in the methods of education and inform the people of the need for public schools. And together they told Mr. Graham, who at forty-six was an elder mentor, of the night two years previously they had spent talking about what they would do with their lives in public education. "As I think of it today," said Alderman, "the grim old room in the inn at Chapel Hill and the silent watches of that night are lit with the light that never was on land or sea."[3]

Others joined them in their enthusiasm for education. Indeed, in the last two decades of the century many of the finest university graduates went not into law or business or medicine but into teaching. In 1882 Alderman, as historian of his class at the University of North Carolina, had reported at the commencement exercises that, of the nineteen graduating seniors, eight planned to be lawyers and only one a teacher; but by 1891 thirteen of the nineteen graduates had entered teaching. The enthusiasm for serving human need was contagious.[4]

Born in 1844, Alexander Graham had given himself to the same cause in the seventies. He had left teaching to serve in the Confederate Army. After the war he went to the University until his third year, 1868, when the school was forced to close. Though lacking a degree, he became principal of an academy in Bladen County, and in 1871, on the recommendation of a Chapel Hill classmate, Frank Porter, he went to New York to teach in the Anthon Grammar School on Madison Avenue. While there he studied law at Columbia University, receiving the LL.B. degree in 1873. Porter, after graduating from the Yale Law School, had returned to North Carolina to practice. Participating in the organization of public schools in Fayetteville, he recommended that Graham be made superintendent. Thus it was that Alexander Graham in 1878 became the superintendent of one of the first graded public school systems in North Carolina.

In 1875 Alexander Graham married Katherine Sloan. Both husband and wife were of Scotch-Presbyterian ancestry; their people, in the eighteenth century, had been among the first settlers in North Carolina along the Cape Fear River. Graham, combining a love of history with a wry humor, frequently told of how the English king invading the Highlands gave the individualistic Graham clan an ultimatum. The choice was either to migrate to the New World or to die. "The clan," he reported, "debated heatedly in their Highland home all night which alternative to take before leaving for Carolina."

Though they were alike in their ancestry, Alexander and Katherine Graham were strikingly different in bearing and temperament. He was tall and straight; and to the children, both his own and all schoolchildren, he was firm—even stern. There was no question about his devotion to education and schoolchildren. He had a familiar habit of catching up with a boy on the street, locking arms with him, and asking, "A-boy, what's your name? Who's your daddy and where do you live?" There was also no doubt about his forgetfulness. Once he disciplined a group of schoolboys by locking them in a toolshed and then dismissed them from his mind. When they had not returned home by dark, their parents began an anxious search. Schoolmates reported what had happened to them.

Although he was noted for a far-off look and the continual whistling of a couplet, Mr. Graham was not an impractical man. When an architect who was authorized to present alternative plans for a school inadvertently left among the papers his plans for a hospital, Mr. Graham noted the ample office and lavatory space, the bay window on each floor, and the modern heating. He selected the hospital plans for the graded school.

He and his wife had nine children, of whom the sixth, born October 14, 1886, was named Frank Porter after the friend who was both lawyer and teacher. Katherine Graham was slight, only five feet tall; but she was large enough to love not only her own children but the neighbors' as well. The Graham house and yard was a home for the neighborhood. The fact that the school superintendent lived there did not keep them away; the fact that the superintendent's wife lived there brought them to her porch, where there were rocking chairs and a swing to ride; to her living room, where there were books to read; and to her kitchen, where "the biscuit drawer" was filled daily with homemade bread and cookies and was open for all.[5]

When Frank was four years old, the Grahams moved to Charlotte, a city of eleven thousand. His father had become superintendent of the two schools: the white grammar and high school, which went through the tenth grade and had five hundred pupils, and the Negro school, which had three hundred.

Charlotte was becoming a modern city. On the direct line of the railroad from Atlanta to Washington, and with five busy cotton mills, it was also becoming a center for transportation and industry. Streetcars were introduced in 1887, and two years after the Grahams arrived, the horse-drawn cars were replaced by electric. A rare trip downtown was a treat to remember, whether on the open cars of the summer with seats facing the street or on the enclosed cars of the winter.[6]

A quarter of a mile down the newly macadamized road from the Grahams' house was the white school and the superintendent's office. Some of the Charlotte streets and some of the county roads were being hard-surfaced, but most were still dirt. While their father, in dignity, walked the macadam road to his office, his children generally took the shorter route across the fields.

Although both electricity and the telephone had come to Charlotte, neither was known for years in the Graham home. Frank had to join the others in bringing in wood for the fires and water for the kitchen.

The Grahams overflowed their two-storied, four-bedroom brick house, where life was, for the most part, simple and joyous. The children never heard their parents quarrel. Quiet indignation they saw in their mother, and a Scotsman's anger in their father, when they or others gave cause for it; but because of his authority, Alexander Graham did not have to shout, and because of her temperament, Katherine could not.

Morning began early. Mr. Graham asked the newsboy to ring his bell when the paper was delivered so that he might read the news while it was still fresh. About five each morning, summer and winter, while the household was still quiet, he read the Charlotte paper. In winter he started the fires and read in the living room. Shortly thereafter his wife was in the kitchen preparing for the day. The family ate breakfast together, and it began, as did all their meals, with a simple grace, sometimes spoken by the children in unison, sometimes said by their father. For the most part, religion among the Grahams was not discussed, and prayer was largely a personal matter. But religion was present: the serious intellectual quality from Alexander Graham; the sensitive moral quality from Katherine.

The living room, with bookshelves on two walls, was one of the favorite rooms in the house. As soon as Frank could read, he began to take books off the shelves; and often, on an afternoon or evening, while his father read his favorite newspaper, Josephus Daniels'

Raleigh *News and Observer,* Frank would lie on the floor with a book open before him. In reading sessions that were the beginning of his love of books, a frequent companion was Katherine Cramer, the daughter of a neighbor who was a wealthy Charlotte industrialist.

Katherine was two years younger than Frank. He liked her partly because she liked books, but mainly because she was a good baseball player. As soon as he could hold a bat, baseball was Frank's first love, and to be a champion player, his great ambition. All the neighborhood gang gathered in the large Graham yard, Negro and white playing together until they were thirteen or fourteen. There were trees aplenty to climb or, at twilight, to play hide-and-seek among; but best of all was the open field where they could choose sides for a game of baseball or Indian bat. Though small, Frank was a quick and good player, but he was not as good as his older brother Archie, whom he idolized. (Archie was later a professional baseball player before practicing medicine in Wisconsin.) The world of competitive sports became a passion for Frank. A primary organizer of the sandlot games in his neighborhood, he decided that since he was going to be an athlete, he would not smoke or drink, not even coffee or cola. He was something of a favorite among friends, and he was also clearly favored by his older sisters at home. As Frank idolized Archie for his athletic ability, his sisters idolized Frank for his boyish ideals and success in school.[7]

For eight months of the year most days were spent in school or church. The Grahams were loyal Presbyterians. One of the stronger denominations in Charlotte because of the Scottish population, the Presbyterian churches had more of the white businessmen and educational leaders than the other churches. With, in addition, three Presbterian colleges in the area, Davidson, Queens, and Presbyterian College, the church, for all its Protestant conservatism, had a dignity and intellectual quality. The Calvinistic theology baked by the Southern sun, particularly the emphasis upon sin, was never assimilated by young Frank; but he was seated in the family pew Sunday after Sunday, morning and night, and lived with Presbyterian parents who took their religion not literally but seriously. The mysteries and assurances of religion captured his imagination. The Calvinistic religious intensity and moral drive early became a part of his life.

School was his natural habitat. He was on good terms with teachers, because he usually led the class in grades, and with classmates, because of his modesty and friendliness. Anne, the Negro cook in the Graham household and the confidante of all the children, thought at times that the teachers did not treat Frank as they ought. He would tell Anne about his grades when she asked; and she did, regularly. When she kept hearing the same grade over and over, she went to Mrs. Graham deeply troubled: "Miss Katherine, don't you think Frank's teacher ought to give him 101 sometimes, just to encourage him?"[8]

His first teachers taught him the three R's and the enjoyment of school. Later, when he was in the seventh and tenth grades, two teachers made imprints upon his habits of mind. Both were Renaissance men in their range of interests, and their different methods met the exact needs of the growing boy. When Frank was twelve, William Gilmer Perry, a graduate of Davidson College, lured him into an excitement with science and, particularly, history and poetry. Perry believed in memorizing, and he had something, too, of the poetic approach to history. During the year he led Frank to a history book, *Greek and Roman for Boys*; at the end of the year he gave his pupil another, *Historical Boys*. Both books had a profound effect. When Frank was sixteen and in need of intellectual discipline, J. A. Bivens taught him mathematics, geology, and English literature. Mr. Bivens had been unable to attend college, but he had a zest for learning and inspired many of his students to continue their education. He had also mastered his subjects; he brought to the students a demand for mental rigor as well as enthusiasm.[9]

Much of Frank's experience in school was reinforced by his father, not simply because he was a superintendent of schools, but because of fervor for education and love of history. As a small boy Frank accompanied his father to meetings at which Alexander advocated public education, an entirely new idea in some sections. They were not always polite gatherings: independent farmers and store owners, short on money and long on self-reliance, frequently hurled the epithets of "radicalism" and "socialism" at those who advocated spending public money to build schools. Traveling by buggy into rural communities, Frank saw his father stand up to many an irate Southerner.

"Do you honestly believe in taxing the rich man to educate the poor man's children?" one incredulous Carolinian asked him.

"I believe in education of all the children, and that's what we have to do," Mr. Graham responded firmly.

"Well," the questioner continued with greater disbelief, "you sure don't mean to tell us the white man should pay for the colored children."

Mr. Graham wavered not a moment, and the answer, as the principle, was the same: "I believe in education of all the children."

Alexander Graham's own education, like that of so many others his age, had been interrupted by war and limited by an impoverished land. Living in a disorganized society, he saw that the hopes for North Carolina and the South depended upon the education of its children. And he was both North Carolinian and Southerner through and through.[10]

Frank's father and uncles had fought in the Confederate Army. They did not speak much about those hard years; yet to the impressionable boy their very silence was testimony to a heroic past and to the modesty of great men, which, he was convinced, his uncles and father were. Once Frank asked his Uncle Archie if he had any first-hand impression of General Lee in the war. His uncle said, "Yes," then was strangely silent; so Frank refrained from asking any other question. Later the simple story came out that when the tides of the Confederacy were ebbing, his uncle was asked, as J. E. B. Stuart's courier, to go to Lee to inquire how he was doing. Lee, with quiet dignity, said, "Tell General Stuart I am well and getting along as well as could be expected."

Although the war was not much discussed, it was a part of the silent past extending into the living present. It helped produce a sense of participating in history. In many, that awareness led to a nostalgia for the past and created the era of the romantic fanciful novels of the South. In others, of whom Mr. Graham was one, the historical awareness led to a commitment to the future and spawned the great era of North Carolina education. Frank's father was deeply interested in history, particularly that of his own state, of the South, and also of the nation. There was frequent historical talk at the dinner table. Repeatedly mention was made of the Mecklenburg Declaration of Independence, which good Charlotte citizens were convinced antedated the Philadelphia declaration. In fact, on a glorious day in 1902, the robust Theodore Roosevelt spoke from the rear platform of his train to the cheering citizens of Charlotte: "Someone has just now asked me what I think of the Mecklenburg Declaration of Independence. Here in Charlotte was made the first Declaration of Independence ever made in the United States." Later Alexander Graham wrote a historical pamphlet citing evidence for the priority of the North Carolina assertion of freedom.[11]

In the spring of 1903, when Frank was sixteen and in the final grade of the Charlotte High School, he had measles, which settled in his eyes and forced him to drop out of school. Although he did not complete the last two months of classwork, he received his diploma with the others. Not only did his teacher find that he had passed when his grades for the year were averaged, despite the time he had missed, but special examinations showed that he had mastered the courses.

During the summer his eyes gave great trouble, and he was afraid that he could not go away to school in the fall. The fear became a certainty when, early in September, he developed a hernia from a sandlot football game.

His mother was constantly present during the serious periods of his illnesses, nursing him back to health and protecting him from the exuberance of others in the family, as she did when any of her children were sick. He was closer to his mother that year than at any time since he had entered the first grade. Her quiet ways and inclusive love had long since affected his life, but at sixteen and seventeen he was enabled to sense the deeper roots that were the source of her spirit. Her open attitude toward life and her love of people were contagious.

When he had sufficiently recovered, he found a job as bookkeeper for the Charlotte cotton market. Until the end of the buying season in October, he weighed the cotton and mingled with farmers, Negro and white, as well as with his fellow workers. When that job ended, he became responsible for the newsstand at the Central Hotel. Working at the crossroads of a growing town and meeting all sorts of people, he learned about his small community and the people in it.[12]

There had never been any question in the Graham family that the children would go to college; nor had there been question that the boys would go to the state university. Since Frank had missed a year of school, his father decided in the spring of 1904 that he could profit by one more year of preparatory work before starting in the University at Chapel Hill. Plans were made for him to attend his Uncle John Graham's Warrenton Academy. For the

seventeen-year-old boy the summer of 1904 was an end and a beginning: he shared life in the household with brothers and sisters, worked at the Central Hotel, carried newspapers, played baseball in the familiar field on late afternoons and Saturdays, read and conversed with friends on the front porch, and all the while anticipated life in the Warrenton school. He had studied in medical encyclopedias all he could find about hernias; and, as an operation seemed the only cure, he spoke to his mother about having one. There was, at first, hesitation; but, as he recklessly continued the summer activities, the hernia gave increasing trouble. Late in August it was decided that an operation was necessary, even though it would mean a late departure for Warrenton.[13]

He underwent the surgery, and shortly before his eighteenth birthday, the five-foot-four, ninety-pound boy left home for Warrenton, which was located in the north central section of the state, ten miles from the Virginia border. Arriving late at the school, Frank quickly established himself as a good student, and later, despite his size, as a good—and certainly an enthusiastic—athlete.

Both John Graham and the private Warrenton High School had had remarkable educational histories. John, the younger brother of Frank's father, had left home in 1863 at sixteen to join the Confederate Army. In the Graham household there was no great fervor for the war. When he or his brothers returned home on leave, their father, the owner of a few slaves and modest property, would admit openly willingness to give up slaves and property if only the war were over and all the sons could be safely home.

John was unable to attend college; but his intellect and character were such that when the Rev. C. M. Cook of Warren County was seeking a family tutor, a friend said, "Get John Graham and your problems will be solved." When he was eighteen, the self-taught young man began an educational work that would occupy him for more than half a century, first as private tutor, then as teacher in two schools that he founded, both of which burned to the ground. In 1898 he became head of the Warrenton Male Academy.

The Warrenton Academy, founded in 1786, nine years before the State University opened, was one of the two oldest academies in North Carolina. Its basic aim was to prepare men for public life by giving the necessary foundation for the professions; its method was a strict classical training. John Graham, sharing this view, reorganized the academy as a co-educational high school. He was dedicated to education for any child who would exert the necessary effort, but he was scornful of slovenliness and waste, and would remark on occasion that state schools were fine things except that they spent more money on bricks than on brains and allowed children to elect subjects before they had any minds to elect with. His reliance was upon Latin, Greek, and mathematics. His ardor for learning made him an admired teacher.

Others in the family—John's wife, "Miss Frankie," and their daughters and son—shared the responsibilities for the school, so at times it was called "the Graham school." The Grahams lived in a commodious ante-bellum residence to which they had built an annex with a dining room. The dining room on the first floor was also used for a study hall. On the second floor was a dormitory, and in the backyard another dormitory. The school had well over fifty boarders, with as many day students. The pupils walked to classes held in the weather-beaten schoolhouse three blocks from the home; and there, as the highlight of the day, they would clatter into the large central room for assembly and would feel the moral force of their headmaster. Many who lived there were to say later that in the Graham home they had touched true greatness. There, if anywhere, civilization was in the making.

The daily round of duties was simple; so, too, were the pleasures, whether on the playground, in the dining room and dormitory, or in evening conversation, song, and play around a warm fire. To test the mettle of youth there were football, baseball, and some years, in midwinter months, ice-skating on nearby ponds. There was also the commencement debate, which was one of the major events of the school year. The teacher of English, Mr. Will Graham, selected the debaters, assigning two to a side. In the spring of 1905 he was faced with an obviously insoluble problem. There were three boys who were clearly the best in the school, and there was no doubt they would be chosen: Frank Graham, young Hardy from Arizona, and Kemp Battle from Rocky Mount, Frank's closest friend. No fourth speaker could match them. When the fourth was selected and it was known to everyone that he was not equal to the others, there was curiosity as to how the teams would be matched. Frank went privately to Mr. Will, asking that he and the fourth boy form a team because, he claimed, their weaknesses and strengths would complement each other. His request was granted, and as anticipated, the two were soundly trounced.[14] Frank left the school in June not only academically prepared for the University but with his Uncle John's example impressed upon his life and his uncle's oft-repeated encouragement reverberating in his mind: "Do pray, boys, push up!"

2

A Breath of Freedom

*I have an ideal for this University. My desire
would have it a place where there is always a
breath of freedom in the air . . . .*[1]
—EDWIN A. ALDERMAN (1899)

DURING THE SUMMER OF 1905 FRANK WAS AGAIN
home in Charlotte, sharing the life of his family, working in the
garden, carrying newspapers, playing baseball, and wandering the
streets of the town and countryside with friends. In the evenings
he frequently listened to his older brothers and father talk about
the University. He looked at the yearbooks, noting especially the
records of the athletic teams, and he read and reread the college
catalog. He went so far as to memorize the full names of the sopho-
mores, juniors, and seniors in the back of the catalog, beginning the
lifelong habit of calling people by their first, middle, and last
names.[2]

As the day approached when Frank was to leave home, all was
not yet in readiness. Although the catalog reported that the total
expenses at the University averaged only $265.25, his father was
becoming more and more worried about where to find the money.
It was difficult enough to raise a family on a school superintendent's salary, let alone put the children through college. At last
it was certain there was no other alternative. Much as he disliked
borrowing, on September 9, the day before his boy was to leave, he
went to his neighbor, Stuart Cramer, and asked for a loan. The
personal loan was made immediately and graciously. Without it
Frank's dreams of college might have vanished.[3]

Dreams of youth are often brighter than the reality that appears,
but it was not so with Graham's image of the University of North
Carolina and Chapel Hill.

It was not that Chapel Hill was a thriving community. The
charter of 1789 had forbidden locating the University within five

miles of any town where court was held; and it had been established in a grove, by open fields and forests, at the intersection of two frontier highways near the center of the state. In 1905 the town had fewer than one thousand inhabitants; the closest city was Durham, twelve miles away, with a population of ten thousand.

The wagon bringing new students and their baggage the one mile from the station went down the wide dirt main street, with Chapel Hill dogs barking at the turning wheels, past the frame stores and livery stable. Frank's first glimpse of the University was from the street, past two ramshackle inns at corners of the campus, through the hardwood grove, to South Building. A few minutes later he, with his baggage, was deposited at Old East, the first building to be erected at a state university in the United States. His room was on the third floor; and looking out the window, he saw, below, the historic Old Well, on which President Alderman eight years before had squandered two hundred dollars to change a drab booth into a lovely structure modeled after the Temple of Love at Versailles. Directly across the road was the dyed-stucco-wash South Building, where Alderman had added a touch of beauty by reproducing over its main entrance a detail of the doorway of Westover-on-the-James.[4]

It was mainly a man's world to which he had come. All the faculty were male, all the activities were organized for males, and though there were a few women enrolled, the students were treated like men. The pervading note was struck in the first assemblies. "I do not emphasize the negative virtues of the boy but the positive virtues of the man," said Professor Edward Kidder Graham on September 17. Frank heard his cousin, an admired English professor, say that the greatness of a college depends upon meeting the needs of the people and the time it serves, providing civilization with guidance and a way through its problems, and equipping students to be representative men in their era. Then, when the students, new and old, were caught up in his idealism, he made the meaning personal: "Your own success here and your greatness as a college student depends on your ability to train yourself through your quiet days of study in those qualities that will be demanded of this representative man in the world in which you are preparing to take your place." There were, he thought, four important qualities the student should achieve: first, he should learn to do promptly, pleasantly, and with accuracy every task to which he has obligated himself; second, he should test for himself what he is told, bringing to his work lively curiosity and original interest; third, he should receive from "the master spirits" standards of behavior and judgment that mark a true gentleman; and finally, understanding that he does not live alone, he should know himself as a member of a society to which he owes duties no less than to himself. Students, Frank among them, were inspired by his concluding hopes for the University:

> This college should be and can be the most conspicuous achievement of this people. It can be more influential in making actual the dormant and inactive ideals of the State than any institution in the world has been—more serviceable, more admirable—a genuine triumph of youth and self-mastery, efficient training and self-government.[5]

President Venable had spoken to the new students two days previously. A scientist with an international reputation, Venable had published widely and was president of the American Chemical Society. With high standards of academic achievement, he was patiently, quietly, building a faculty of dedicated, able men; but he held himself aloof, and he was not an eloquent public speaker. Yet in the directness of his speech there were ideals of what the University should be in the state and what students should be in the University, "a strong, self-respecting, self-governing body of men, too clean and true to stoop to petty and unworthy things—men, who, having learned here life's meaning, shall go forth to service."[6]

The words at the beginning of Frank's university life were full of meaning by themselves, but they were far more impressive because of the spirit of the place, and especially because of the respect the older students had for Venable and their admiration and love for Edward Graham. Frank was at home in the university that, throughout the year, regularly advertised itself in the student newspaper as

> The Head of the State System of Education: The university stands for thoroughness and all that is best in education and the moulding of character. It is equipped with 15 buildings, new waterworks, central heating, electric lights. Eleven scientific laboratories equipped for good work. The faculty numbers 67. Students 667. Library of 42,000 volumes. One librarian and four assistants. Fine literary societies. There is an active YMCA conducted by the students. Scholarships and loans for the needy and deserving.[7]

Though in general true, the advertisement did not reflect accurately the campus lights or mention the walks. On the first of October there appeared an editorial in the student newspaper, the *Tar Heel*: "There are just two questions we have never been able to answer satisfactorily. The first is, What is life? The second, Why are students forced to stumble about dark landings and darker stairways? Loss of time, risk of injury and invariable loss of religion results from each venture outside one's room at night."[8] What lights there were went off at midnight. As for the campus walks: "I have ridden the roads of our poorest western counties in the wettest months," wrote a student. "I have travelled bad highways when they were at their worst, and lo, nowhere, have I seen excuses for walks as exist [on the campus]." Near Old West, he continued, one could manufacture mud pies; the path from the library to Main Street would be a disgrace to the poorest farm in North Carolina. Worst of all was Main Street itself.[9]

But it was not always night on the campus nor always raining; and in the fifteen buildings under the oaks, situated in a square less than a thousand feet in each direction, the university faculty and students came together daily in face-to-face, living relations. A hundred feet to the north of Frank's dormitory was Alumni Hall, where students went for most of the classes; to the east a hundred feet was New East, where on the top floor the Philanthropic Literary Society, to which Frank belonged, had a large room with portraits of distinguished graduates on the walls—senators, governors, physicians, clergymen, lawyers, educators—and where each Saturday night more than 150 students gathered to engage in debate. To the south across the road was the library, already too small for the forty-two thousand volumes and still famous for the remark of General Sherman that he had the most educated horses in the Union since, when they had been in Chapel Hill, they had spent their entire time stabled in the University library. Behind the library was the new gymnasium, which had the only good showers on the campus, and beyond, in the open field, there were tennis courts, a football field, and a baseball diamond. Less than a hundred feet from Old East was South Building, with its few administrative offices, classrooms, offices for the YMCA, and the belfry from which clanged the hours of the day. Hard by South was Gerrard, a small auditorium where most formal events were held. Farther to the west was Memorial Hall, originally an auditorium seating twenty-five hundred, which had been used for years as a gymnasium and during the time Frank was a student at the University was unused except for the commencement exercises. Still farther west was Commons Hall, where Frank went with two hundred other students three times a day for meals at a cost of eight dollars a month. Directly west from his dormitory beyond the Old Well was Old West, another dormitory, and New West, a classroom building, which housed the Dialectic Literary Society. Diagonally to the northwest was Person Hall, which, having begun as a chapel, had become the chemistry building.

To a college student the dormitory room was home. There he kept the pictures of his family and girl on his desk, there he wrote his letters home, there he tried to study, and there he slept and dreamed and talked. For the latter purpose college men often formed small, tightly-knit groups; and so it was with those who organized the Pin-Point Discussion Club, especially Frank, Kemp Battle, Francis Winslow from Hertford, and Charles Tillett from Charlotte. Thomas Wolfe, who after four years of loneliness in Chapel Hill graduated from the University a decade later than Graham, described a favorite pastime:

> With great energy and enthusiasm they promoted the affairs of athletic teams, class politics, fraternities, debating societies and dramatic clubs. And they talked—always they talked, under trees, against the ivied walls, assembled in their rooms, they talked—in limp sprawls—incessant, charming, Southern talk; they talked with a large easy fluency about God, the Devil, and philosophy, the girls, politics, athletics, fraternities and the girls—My God! How they talked![10]

It was not all talk for Frank. His first year he was on the class baseball team. The second year he was elected president of his class, which brought him into close working relations with John J. Parker, president of the Honor Council. The second and third years he was on the scrub baseball team. His one great moment of fame on the team occurred in a game with Lafayette when, in the last inning, Carolina tied the score and got the bases loaded with two out. The coach motioned to Frank who, surprised, grabbed a bat with the determination to hit the ball out of the park. As he approached the plate, the coach stooped, put his arm around Frank's shoulder, and asked, "Do you understand the situation?"

Frank nodded. "Then, little man, whatever you do don't you dare hit at that ball!" The Lafayette pitcher, unable to find the pitching zone on the undersize boy wearing an oversize uniform, threw four straight balls.[11]

The third year he received the honor of being elected by the Phi Society to participate in the important Sophomore-Junior debate. He was class historian and was assistant editor of the *Tar Heel*, the student newspaper.[12] Most important, in the spring of his junior year he was elected to Phi Beta Kappa, having received A's in all courses except philosophy, English, French, and public speaking. Francis Winslow beat him for first place by one fiftieth of a point. Kemp Battle came in third. That ranking was an indication of how they had spent most of their time when they were not talking.[13]

Edward K. Graham was the best teacher that Frank had. (As Frank was to say later, the best he ever had.) And so it was for Frank's closest friends. There were others who said the best was the philosophically bellicose "gadfly of Chapel Hill," Horace Williams. Williams was, Frank thought, an excellent professor, but their two minds did not mesh. Except in the widest sense, Frank had no real love of philosophical ideas. His interests moved toward languages, with eight full-year courses in Latin, Greek, German, and French, and toward literature, in which he had five full-year courses.[14]

It was through literature that Ed Graham inspired him. He was a thorough, exacting, logical, and inspiring teacher; and his idealism, combined with his ability, made an indelible mark upon his impressionable younger cousin's life. A survey of English literature and courses in Shakespeare and the Romantic poets gave Frank a sensitivity to the finest reading; a course in composition gave him standards for his own writing. Ed Graham taught him the ideals of orderly arrangement, thoroughness, and clarity.

There were other great teachers, too: in mathematics, Archibald Henderson, with intellectual interests ranging far beyond mathematics; in Greek, William Stanley Bernard, with sensitivity for the music and grandeur of the Homeric hexameters, and Eben Alexander, former American minister to Athens, who helped revive the Olympic games; in English, C. Alphonso Smith, with feeling for the great orations; in geology, Collier Cobb, with lore of the land brought close to home in the description of Chapel Hill as a volcanic eruption from the seabed of the Triassic age; in chemistry,

Francis Preston Venable and Charles Holmes Herty, with their thorough, scholarly, scientific ways. To Frank they were a noble company of professors and men who could be put up against any group of professors in any university in the country.[15]

Frank spent his summers in North Carolina. Almost as soon as each college year was over, he went with the delegation from the University to the YMCA Southern College Conference near Asheville. More than three hundred students from white colleges throughout the South came together to discuss the practical problems of running a student organization and to enlarge their vision of the world. Christian optimism and liberalism were in the air. "The evangelization of the world in this generation" was the oft-repeated theme. To men who used the phrase, to John R. Mott, Robert E. Speer, Sherwood Eddy, and W. D. Weatherford, it did not mean a doctrinaire evangelization, but education, medicine, and agriculture in other countries, and good race relations in the South; it meant the possibility of all people in all nations having the kind of life they saw democracy in America achieving, a kind of life enlightened by a Christ who was no shadowy figure in an ancient land but was a living presence. The Southerners who gathered in the mountains of North Carolina, Frank Graham among them, were determined to remake the world.

After the conference was over at the end of his freshman year, he joined thirty others in climbing Mount Mitchell. It was a challenge to physical stamina; it was, for the nineteen-year-old youth inspired by the conference, something of a symbol of the challenge awaiting him in life. With a guide and two packhorses they left Black Mountain in early morning for the twenty-mile hike past Gray Beard and Pinnacle, and they reached the top in early evening. The crowd slept huddled together under an overhanging rock; and in the morning, from the highest peak east of the Rockies, they saw the sunrise.

When the conferences were over, Graham went home full of talk. He discussed his ideas, especially with his mother, who was coming to mean more and more in his life. The summers were also a time for renewing old friendships and making a little money. He got such jobs as he could, at the hotel newsstand, carrying papers, and collecting back debts for *The Presbyterian Standard*.[16]

In the summer of 1908 he took a good look at himself and a long look at the University. For three years he had worked hard at his studies, though, obviously, he had had his fun, too. But the year ahead would be strenuous outside the classroom as well as in: the past spring he had been elected president of the Senior Class; he was editor-in-chief of the *Tar Heel*; he had been elected president of the YMCA, the most active student organization in the University. Any one of the three responsibilities would have been enough. Each had its own obligations; each would bring him into the center of campus causes; and each would force him into relations of trust with students, some of whom, he knew from past experience, would have a tough time.[17]

On one late August evening he walked down the tree-shaded street to see an older friend, Otho Ross, who was a young physician in Charlotte. Together they sat on the porch and talked, pleasantly interrupted by neighbors who passed by waving greetings to both. They talked about earlier times, about their University, from which Ross had graduated, about professors and mutual friends, about the year ahead for Frank, and about Ross's work. Otho told of a patient who worried him greatly. The man's problem was not really physical, and the young doctor was perplexed in not knowing what he could do to help. Frank listened sympathetically, and when the story was over, there was a long silence. Finally, Frank said, "You know, Otho, I think a man could do anything in the world for another person if he just loved him enough."[18]

In his senior year Frank roomed in "the Houseboat," a small two-room cabin so named because it was generally surrounded by water. There was no water in the house, however; the residents had to go to the gym for showers. The onerous duties of keeping the rooms passably clean and sufficiently warm with a small wood stove were shared by the four roommates, John Wesley Umstead, a Methodist who had plans for overseas work; Henry Plant Osborne, an Episcopalian in pre-law from Jacksonville, Florida; Thomas Joseph McManis, a Catholic in electrical engineering from Buffalo, New York; and Frank. The fact that there were two Republicans (one a Yankee) and two Democrats added to the liveliness in the Houseboat.[19]

That year Frank's grades suffered: six B's, three C's, and a D. Shortly after the term began, he was elected president of the Phi Society. There were some minor administrative details, but the office was more honor and pleasure than labor. Debate was an important activity in the college. Graham found it deeply satisfying to chair a Saturday night debate in which six to ten men participated, to join in intellectual argument about serious matters (all the debates had as topics political and economic issues of the moment), and to observe the dignity with which students could engage in public conversation. The debates took place in a gracious room where the portraits of bewhiskered Southern gentlemen on the walls gave an awareness of being a part of an on-going history.[20]

Satisfying, too, but far more difficult, was the work as editor of the newspaper. Operated freely and entirely by students and sponsored by the Athletic Association, the *Tar Heel* was published each week, usually in a four-page edition. The editor was responsible for both news and editorials, and even had to join in the work of printing and distribution. The news ran mainly to athletics, to debate, to the YMCA, and to special events. And the editorial page, Graham felt, had the obligation of keeping the University honest and alive. Frank thought it his responsibility to arouse enthusiasm when there was listlessness and to provide dignity when there was defeat. Following a football pep rally at which the faculty stirred the students from their lethargy, he wrote flamboyantly:

> The student body has now found that which it had lost: college spirit. The awakened college spirit means games fought harder and games won. To express it in a paraphrase, Let us be spirited and the spirit that lies in our Varsity, sleeping but never dead, Shall rise in majesty to surpass our own.

That weekend Carolina was defeated 31–0. Frank, the head cheerleader, rallied the yells to the last play of the game. The following week he editorialized, "Virginia showed Carolina how to win but Carolina showed Virginia how to die."[21]

The next week he resigned as editor. Overwork and weak eyes had taken their toll, and physicians had ordered him to give up his duties on the newspaper.[22]

It was as president of the Senior Class and of the YMCA, two of the most demanding posts in student life, that Frank gained experience in democratic life and leadership. The former position made him president of the Honor Council, with its responsibility for upholding the honor system. Established in 1875, the honor system had at first applied only to cheating on examinations; then it had come to apply to additional matters of academic honesty; and gradually, as the students claimed more and more freedom to govern themselves, it was extended case by case to other areas of student life. Precise areas of authority had not been delegated to the students, but there were those on the faculty, such as Ed Graham and President Venable, whose ideal was for student self-government. With their implicit encouragement, students clamored for greater freedom and responsibility; and the Honor Council, on its own initiative, judged cases involving drinking, hazing, and gambling, as well as cheating.[23]

Eugene E. Barnett, graduate student and executive secretary of the YMCA, also encouraged the moral responsibility of students, and it was Barnett who was the general behind the famous "Battle of Cemetery Ridge," in which the assault was lead by Frank Graham. Some entrepreneurs from Durham, engaged as business managers for the world's oldest profession, saw the possibilities of securing trade among the university men and so imported two women to Chapel Hill. They let it be confidentially known that on two nights a week, in the quiet, comfortable grass-plotted cemetery, the women's services would be available for a fee. Business seemed to flourish; what had begun as confidential became a matter of campus gossip and, since the business was a menace to both the morals and the health of the students, a matter of some campus concern as well.

Student leaders, led by Barnett and Graham, planned a campaign to capture the men. Volunteers were organized and informally deputized by the town's lone policeman, "Jug" Whitaker, so named because he was the landlord of the village "jug." The volunteers, accompanied by the policeman, advanced to arrest the disturbers of the university peace; but when they reached the cemetery, Jug said, "My jurisdiction stops here," and he refused to go farther. Eagerness for victory was too great to stop the deputized students. As they fanned out, creeping among the tombstones, resistance was encountered; shots were fired by the enemy, one of the bullets piercing the hat of a crusader, Henry Johnston. In the melee the men escaped, but the women were caught.

President Venable was informed that the Battle of Cemetery Ridge had ended victoriously, that the enemy was routed or captured. He called Judge James C. McRae, dean of the Law School, asking him to become prosecutor, and Algernon Barbee, justice of the peace, asking him to hear the case immediately. By eleven-thirty Squire Barbee convened court for a preliminary hearing. Because the news had spread through the campus, boys in all sorts of dress and undress crowded into the justice's office until it was necessary to close the door. On one side was President Venable, giving his benign presence to the proceedings; on the other was Judge McRae, adding his dignity with a masterful handling of the case. Seated in the window, Dave Murchison, a freshman, called out the testimony to the crowd outside. Students in the street cheered each step in the proceedings with shouts of, "Hey, Ven! Dust the dirt off the knees of your britches." The two women were bound over to a higher court, but since the procurers were not apprehended, the women were subsequently released.

Debate raged for months as to whether General Graham's charge had been a moral victory. John Umstead, who had declined to participate in the campaign of Cemetery Ridge, later reported ironically as class historian, "The glory of 1909 lies in the stand she took on college morality."[24]

The work of the YMCA was time-consuming, and into his duties Frank put great zest. The Y had recently moved into a new building, which had immediately become the center of student life. In 1909 there were 260 active members in a student body of 767. There were regular meetings two nights each week; faculty and speakers from outside the University addressed one of the meetings, which had an average attendance of over one hundred. The Y published the student handbook, the college directory, the university calendar, as well as a Bible study prospectus and occasional pamphlets. Bible study enrolled 350 students, who met regularly at noon on Sunday (in his last three years Frank taught one of the classes), and mission study enrolled 125. During Frank's presidency students from the Y sponsored seven rural Sunday schools, to which, whatever the weather, they walked each Sunday an average of seven miles to teach the children.[25]

The most memorable event of Frank's final year was the address by Woodrow Wilson, then president of Princeton University, on January 19, 1909, the birthday of Robert E. Lee. Frank arrived at Gerrard Hall early and found it packed. He went to the gallery, where Dave Murchison, who was seated immediately above and to the right of the rostrum, motioned for the president of the Senior Class to sit on his knee. For more than an hour while Wilson spoke, Frank sat there; never once did Murchison ask him to move; never once did it occur to him to do so.[26]

Wilson began informally:

> It is all very well to talk of detachment of view, and of the effort
> to be national in spirit and purpose, but a boy never gets over his
> boyhood, and never can change those subtle influences which have
> become a part of him, that were bred in him when he was a child.
> So I am obliged to say again and again that the only place in the
> country, the only place in the world, where nothing has to be ex-
> plained to me is the South. Sometimes after long periods of absence
> I forget how natural it is to be in the South, and then the moment
> I come . . . I know again the region to which I naturally belong.[27]

Wilson then launched into his subject, Robert E. Lee, beginning
with a quotation describing Lee that was fixed in Frank's mind
immediately and permanently: "a celebrated American general in
the Confederate service."[28] The fact that Lee had become a national hero, he said, meant that the nation had become unified; so the
future would lie with those men who would devote themselves to
national thinking. And "the nation which denies itself material
advantage and seeks those things which are of the spirit works not
only for each generation but for all generations, and works in the
permanent and durable stuffs of humanity."[29]

Wilson was a great orator. Every word, every inflection, every
gesture, was perfect; nothing was wasted. As he reached his climax,
there erupted the Calvinism bred in him as a boy, which had
matured into a democratic idealism and the desire to be sacrificed
for a cause:

> There is nothing so destructive as selfishness, and there is nothing
> so permanent as the work of hands that are unselfish. . . . A quiet
> company of gentlemen sitting through a dull summer in the city
> of Philadelphia worked out for a poor and rural nation an immortal
> constitution, which has made statesmen all over the world feel con-
> fidence in the political future of the race. They knew that human
> liberty was a feasible basis of government.[30]

It was obvious to the alert audience that he was about to conclude, and Frank felt that Wilson was speaking directly to him:

> I wish there were some great orator who could go about and make
> men drunk with this spirit of self-sacrifice. I wish there were some
> man whose golden tongue might every day carry abroad the golden
> accents of that creative age in which we were born a nation; accents
> which would ring like tones of reassurance around the whole circle

of the globe, so that America might again have the distinction of showing men the way, the certain way, of achievement and confident hope.[31]

After the hall became empty and silent, some of the students, Frank among them, went over to the Y, as they often did after an intellectually exciting evening. As they talked late into the night, buoyed by their enthusiasm, it became clear what needed to be done: they nominated the president of Princeton University for president of the United States. He was elected by acclamation.[32]

Students at Chapel Hill in the first decade of the century made a great impression upon their teachers. Late in 1909 Edward K. Graham spoke of the "prophetic intentness of the Southern student." Graham was obviously speaking of students he taught, his younger cousin included:

> His attitude is almost too serious we are sometimes surprised into thinking. The product with which we have to deal is eagerly curious to find out what we have to offer and rather nervously anxious to apply that something to a civilization that he is vividly conscious demands of him an unusual contribution.[33]

What was it that Ed Graham thought the University had to offer youth? A high education, a masterful efficiency, a wide view that would enable the Southern student to meet his responsibility "for leadership in a section potentially great enough to compete with any civilization in the world."

It was surprising to no one, then, that when Frank Graham made his Class Day address as Senior president, his theme was "The State and the University," a consideration of "the bearing of the life into which we are going upon the life from which we are going." Nor was it any surprise that President Venable thought so highly of the address that he had it printed in pamphlet form and circulated in the state.

In the address Graham reviewed historically the relation of the state to education and of the University to the state, finding nobility in both. But with the relations of the legislature to the University there was much to be desired, since the average state university received an appropriation of $200,000 annually while North Carolina was given only $75,000. Such inadequate support, the class president asserted, was not an expression of the attitude of the state, but the result of a misunderstanding by some people who had an erroneous opinion of the University's religious influence, a lack of knowledge of the athletic attitude, and a misinterpretation of the University's general spirit. If only the people could understand the University, they would support it enthusiastically. He then spoke of each basic misunderstanding in detail, insisting that the University in its deepened spiritual life and high honor standards should receive full encouragement from the churches; in its attempt to develop amateur athletics according to standards set by leading American universities it should have the support of all. "The University is the state's own creature, the people's University, the head of their public school system. With the realization of this great fact of relationship, with the removal of all prejudice and unfounded antagonism will come a new era for the University of North Carolina."

His final words were to remind fellow students about to be graduated of the history of the University, the devotion of the faculty, the friendships formed during four years of life there, and the hopes for the University's future:

> In the making of this greater university, Fellow Classmates, it is our duty and our privilege to have a part. . . . If we leave our university with the determination to serve her nothing will become us like the leaving. Who of us is not eager to have a part in this great work? . . . This ardent impulse to serve her will with the passing of the years be deepened and solemnized into a patriot's duty, for the cause of North Carolina is the cause of the University and the cause of the University is the cause of North Carolina.[34]

Kemp Battle and Charlie Tillett wrote in the college yearbook, *The Yackety Yack*, descriptions of "The University Man"; and they might well have been thinking of their best friend as they wrote. "He must ever in a conflict of duties," said Tillett, "seek to distinguish the highest call and obey it whether it means the sneer of a friend or the scorn of an enemy. Fair-mindedness must be the key-note of his character." And Kemp Battle commented:

> The University Man must be broad in his views, noble in his feelings, just and honorable in his dealings. It is not enough that he be great as an individual; he must be true and faithful in his relations to others. Firm in his friendships, loyal in his affiliations, high-minded in his citizenship, the true University Man fearlessly and resolutely exemplifies in his daily life those noble and manly virtues which his Alma Mater has inculcated into his very nature.[35]

Beside Frank's picture in the yearbook there was the quotation, "A man to all the country dear." Below that was incidental information, "Age 22; height 5 feet 6 inches; weight 125. Law." There was a lengthy account of his student activities, then his names and analysis:

> Frank, Laddie Buck. Everyman's friend, confidant and playfellow. Couldn't do what he is supposed to do tomorrow if he were to live his whole life in one day. No settled tradition in the college can be carried through without him, no new movement can be successful without him at its head. And, curiously enough, with the burden of a college upon his shoulders he bears it without losing himself in it all. Out of it all he comes a little worn, but still the same good fellow of his lazy, less-occupied days.[36]

In 1909 Frank began law school at the University. If not a wasted year, it was a year of marking time, particularly in academic work. He had drifted into law. Having responded to the repeated calls to save the world and serve the needs of his time, he was ready for service in general, but there was nothing in particular that he could decide to do. His closest friends planned to become lawyers. Under their influence, although he could not really envisage himself in practice, he went with them to law school.

The school was meager both in building and in personnel. The classes and library of less than a thousand volumes were housed in the building where Sherman's horses had been stabled; and the faculty consisted of three persons, two of them teaching for the first time and one of those never to teach again. There was little that was intellectually exciting about the work. Following his cousin's dictum that a university man should do promptly and with accuracy everything he has obligated himself to do, Frank studied hard and completed the year's courses satisfactorily.[37]

He was elected president of the Athletic Association, and he gave full support to the sports program. ("Chief cheerer Graham," said the *Tar Heel*, "has been going out to the athletic field every afternoon to lead the cheering on the side-lines.") He had a Bible class for football players on "The Life of Paul," of whom he made a hero, if not a track-star athlete. He wrote for a Charlotte newspaper. And he introduced, with Kemp Battle, a resolution to strengthen the Student Council. The resolution revolved around an important conflict of interests between students and faculty. The Honor

Council, of which Graham continued to be a member, suspended a student for cheating, reheard the case, and sustained its earlier decision. The suspended student appealed to the faculty executive committee, which, influenced by a local clergyman, reinstated him. The entire Student Council resigned, determined to force the issue of authority and freedom. There were mass meetings demanding student self-government and *Tar Heel* editorials criticizing as authoritarian the faculty action. The students were not satisfied with President Venable's attempt to show how students and faculty worked cooperatively in disciplinary problems. A committee was appointed, including Graham, to negotiate with the faculty and take the matter to the Board of Trustees. The committee drew up a compromise agreement, which was adopted, officially designating the Honor Council for the first time as the student governing body with disciplinary powers but also recognizing an individual student's right of appeal to a faculty committee to be selected by the students. It was a long step forward in democratic student life, and by it Frank gained an expanding faith in the democratic rights and responsibilities of students.[38]

If neither the study nor the activities were fully satisfying, the deepening friendships were, and personal relations meant the most to Frank that anticlimactic year. He lived with Francis Winslow, Kemp Battle, and Charles Tillett in the home of Edward Graham, the professor for whom all four had the greatest admiration. The very inadequacy of their law course drove them into a greater companionship with each other and a more sensitive appreciation of the Grahams, who had been married the previous year. Their respect for Professor Graham was matched by their regard for his wife Susan; the two were the most intelligent and cultured human beings the four young law students had ever known. The students received in the Grahams' home a lasting education in gracious, civilized living. To the Grahams' home came visitors of all sorts— renowned guests at the University, professors, and students, including Mrs. Graham's spirited younger sister, Mildred Moses. On one occasion Miss Moses inadvertently left her overnight bag in Durham, and since there was no regular transportation and Frank lacked the money to hire a rig, he walked the twenty-four miles for the suitcase. It was an expression of courtesy and of fondness for Mildred Moses. But the fondness was one he had for many young women. Whenever he visited Mildred, a student at the North Carolina College for Women in Greensboro, it was also a visit to Laura Weill (Frank's competing writer for the Charlotte paper) and to other college girls as well.[39]

When, at the end of an indifferent year in law school, Frank was invited to teach English in Raleigh, he accepted immediately. He could look back to his five years at Chapel Hill with gratification; he had accomplished much and had begun a lasting love affair with the University. But in observing his friends, he might also have recognized that, at twenty-three, he had missed much that young men and women normally experience in growing up.

Unlike most of his college mates, certainly unlike his closest friends, he had no specific vocation; he did not know what he wanted to do with his life except to give it away. To what? He had no idea. His friends were headed somewhere. To be sure, some of them had shifted course in midstream, as had Winslow, who had begun in medicine but changed to law. But Frank had never had a clear course to shift: he had not begun college heading anywhere, during college he had not decided what life-work to enter, and he left law school for high school teaching with no clear sense of direction except to serve mankind.

The moral skepticism and relativism so typical of the young in every age and the normal gnawing religious doubts never touched him. Nor did he ever experience fundamental conflict with his parents: there was never any youthful rebellion against parental authority or parental attitudes and values. He was much given to idealism and was inclined toward a Puritanism in morality. Encouraged by others, he became something of the self-appointed custodian of the morals of men, as in the Battle of Cemetery Ridge. In personal life, too, the Puritanical was obvious. He still kept his vow not to smoke or drink and to avoid any habits that would weaken his moral and physical fiber, even though these promises had been made with the ambition of becoming an athlete. In religion, as in morality, there was never any fundamental conflict. He was singularly free from theological cant, since he considered the doctrines of religion relatively unimportant. The religious spirit, however, was clear and personal in him.

His naiveté was known to all. It was parodied in "Absurdity in One Act," a play published in the college yearbook. The scene is laid in the Houseboat, and Umstead is pictured "sitting on the edge of the bed (Frank's bed) sobbing gently, and wiping his eyes on the foot of the sheet (Frank's sheet)." As the drama unfolds, Umstead explains the reason for his grief: "Last night was my night to undress Frank and put on his little night shirt and hear his little prayers and put him to bed. And just as I got his little pants off and put on his little 'nightie' (sobbing louder) Plant came in and knocked me down and heard his little prayers and kissed him good night and tucked him in bed (wailing)." Beneath such laughter at Frank's naiveté there was respect for the innocence that could not be destroyed by experience of evil and complexity, since it was based upon the counter experience of integrity and simplicity. He trusted himself and was convinced, without question, that others were basically trustworthy.[40]

3

The Discovery of History

*The nation which denies itself material advantage
and seeks those things which are of the spirit
works not only for each generation, but for all
generations, and works in the permanent and
durable stuffs of humanity . . . .*[1]

—WOODROW WILSON (1909)

THE RALEIGH HIGH SCHOOL, WHERE GRAHAM
began teaching in 1910, was a two-storied brick building with wide
steps leading from the dirt street up to the columned portico. It had
a faculty of twelve, and a student body of 250 in its four grades, with
a normal graduating class of thirty. Graham's first encounter was
with the steps and with a strict mathematics teacher. On his first
day, before meeting any of his colleagues, he dashed up the stairs as
usual, two at a time, and as he reached the top, he was startled by an
authoritative female voice: "Boy! Come down here and walk back
up like a little gentleman." There was no alternative; he did, and
that afternoon at the first teachers' meeting, he was formally introduced to the voice.

Her mistake was not surprising. Even the students considered
him boyish (some confessed they felt older than their teacher), and
the boys on the football team were soon calling him Frank. As assistant coach of football and coach of baseball and debating, he
became close friends with many of the boys, and the friendship
was marked by an easy informality. When walking home together
they would part at the corner, and he would normally turn around
to toss a rock as a farewell gesture. One afternoon his aim was off.
A pupil had to have his head sewed, and the young teacher dipped
into his meager salary to pay the bill. But the students, too, were a
danger to life and limb. In football practice the coaches scrimmaged
with their state championship team, urging the boys to play their
hardest. Late in the season, as Graham made a beautiful end run,

the 120-pound teacher was tackled by the 190-pound student full-back, and the two crashed into a fence. Graham was on crutches for weeks.

The boys rarely met a teacher with such a sense of sportsmanship and confidence in them. In a crucial football game the quarterback caught a punt far upfield. The referees disagreed as to whether he was outside when he caught the punt. Graham went onto the field and asked, "Walter, was your foot outside or inside?" The player's answer settled the matter: "It was outside." When the baseball team came up against a rival pitcher who was unable to run because of a broken toe, Graham refused to let his players bunt. He also had strange ideas that exasperated the boys, such as his refusal to allow them to eat ice cream on the day of a game, or the require-ment that debaters and baseball players alike lie with a newspaper over their faces before a contest to relieve their eyesight, or his warnings about the bad effects of Coca-Cola. But for all that, they cherished his friendship; and when Graham organized the Sun-day Boy's Club, those in his classes readily joined him in afternoons of serious discussion and long hikes through the woods.[2]

Frank Graham had long known that he liked athletics and young people. In Raleigh he learned that he loved to teach. He quickly gained a reputation as a tough teacher, one who was thorough in his work, demanding much from his students, and who, at the same time, seemed to enjoy teaching. The "Last Will and Testa-ment of the Class of 1911" included this item:

> We do will to Prof. Frank P. Graham the sole right to divide, classify and separate into their elements, any and all things what-soever, provided that he will in the future make judicious use of this privilege and abandon the merciless course he has hitherto pursued.[3]

Strangely enough, this "merciless course," consisting of parsing sentences and analyzing paragraphs, led Frank farther into his love of history. He had not taken a single course in history at the University; but in teaching English he chose to analyze Edmund Burke's speech, "Conciliation with America." As he worked over that masterful prose with his high school students, he began to un-derstand the time and the mind of Burke. Something in that British statesman aroused Frank's interest in history and supported his fascination with contemporary events. He had enjoyed history as he had heard it from his father and high school teachers, and he had for years read daily newspapers and the leading journals of opinion: Walter Hines Page's *World's Work*, Lyman Abbott's *Outlook*, Hamilton Holt's *Independent*. Now the past and present began to fuse.

Early in 1911 Frank received a letter from Eugene Barnett, who had left the University YMCA in 1910 for work in China. Writing enthusiastically about life and challenges in China, Barnett urged Graham to accept a teaching position then open at Hangchow College. Frank responded by reaffirming his interest in missions, "especially in China at a time critical with the opportunity of the centuries." He pondered the decision for a month, then wrote the trustees of Hangchow declining the position because, as he explained to Barnett, his interest in China and missions "does not make up my life passion."

Almost a year later, February 17, 1912, he confessed that

> The chief interest in my life—and its intensity grows every month—is the question of labor and such related questions as private property. Where it will take me I do not know but I do know that it has me. Sometimes I think the whole scheme of things is wrong and should be turned upside down. Then I remember that the present civilization and its institutions are a growth through the slow centuries and that their further advance must be through evolving growth. I know next to nothing about the whole question but my religion, temperament, and historical perspective preclude my being a nihilist. Though I can't be an anarchist I may be a socialist. At present I have a socialistic bent which will mean at least an interested scrutiny of socialism. I am reading the life of Christ and find him radically socialistic. Yet he was supremely individualistic. A socialistic individual![4]

His "chief interest" had developed rapidly while he was teaching in Raleigh. He enjoyed teaching but felt he wasn't doing a third of what he ought to do. "I earn my salary but I often fear that I do little more." A return to law school, for all his open doubts about the law itself, seemed to be the next step. He did not intend to become a lawyer; his interest simply demanded a knowledge of law. "My life's chief interest and life purpose are fixed," he wrote in 1912, "but the channel of expression is to an extent uncertain. I am going slow—thinking—working and it will all break clear in time."

There were other interests pulling him back to Chapel Hill. There was the university village itself which, from the first moment he arrived in 1906, had cast its spell over him as it did over count-less others. His life would be bound intimately to the place: it was home. There were also the ideals of the University, especially those ideals enunciated by Edward Graham, who had such a profound influence on his younger cousin's life. The ideals included the aim of education as the development of cultured democratic citizens who would serve their society and the belief that the state university was the chief instrument for realizing this aim in the lives of its students.

But most of all there was the interest in Mildred Moses. The fact that he had first met Mildred in Ed and Susan Graham's gra-cious home, and that he often saw her there, added greatly to his interest in returning to Chapel Hill. He continued to see her as often as he could. There was no doubt in the minds of his closest friends, and certainly none in his, that he had fallen in love. The friendship developed, the love deepened. At least it deepened on Frank's side, for he asked her to marry him. Mildred refused. (One of Frank's closest friends, although Frank didn't know it at the time, had also proposed to Mildred and had also been rejected.) It hurt deeply; but with his ebullient spirit he recovered and he and Mildred remained close friends throughout his life.[5]

Graham decided to attend the Democratic National Convention in the summer of 1912 before returning to Chapel Hill in the fall to continue his work in law. The Democrats were to meet in Balti-more the last of June. The Republicans, in Chicago, had renomi-nated conservative William Howard Taft. Theodore Roosevelt, attempting to defeat his successor, who was destroying a progressive Republican program, had stormed out of the convention "like a bull moose" to organize a third party. The main contenders for the Democratic nomination were Champ Clark of Missouri, speak-er of the House of Representatives; Governor Clyde Harmon, former member of Cleveland's cabinet; Oscar Underwood, Demo-cratic House leader; and Governor Woodrow Wilson, who less than two years before had been a political unknown. William Jennings Bryan, three times defeated for the presidency, would be on hand to battle for righteousness. It promised to be a typical, roaring Democratic convention.

Frank arrived the night the convention opened, found a room across the alley from the Convention Armory, and before the week was out, had to borrow money for food. In the five hectic days, crowded among the straw-hatted men and a few bonneted women, he rubbed shoulders with the great and near-great and tirelessly cheered his candidate, Wilson, until he was nominated on the forty-fifth ballot. It was the victory of a man who had told his manager, "No deals."

A month later, after Graham had returned to Charlotte, he read avidly Wilson's lengthy acceptance speech, and its Presbyterian idealism struck home.

> Men are instruments. We are as important as the cause we represent, and in order to be important must really represent a cause. . . . We represent the desire to set up an unentangled government, a government that cannot be used for private purposes. . . . It is a great conception, but I am free to serve it, as you also are. . . . No man can be just who is not free.[6]

After he completed his second year in law school, Frank Graham was admitted to the bar. Something of his indifference to law and his uncertainty about his future was manifest in his immediate acceptance of the position as secretary of the University YMCA when it was offered to him. The position was normally held by a graduate student. Graham did not enroll in graduate school, but he did take a course in American history under J. G. deRoulhac Hamilton.[7]

He entered the work of the Y with enthusiasm. The organization had inspired him as a college student, both in its work on campus and in summer conferences. Hour after hour was spent in counseling students, finding a way to help this one stay in college, persuading that one to change his course of study, talking with another about moral issues. The program of the Y, already complex in its services when he had been president four years before, had grown steadily. During the time he was secretary, it expanded further. Graham was particularly interested in broadening the program with Negroes. W. D. Weatherford had written *Negro Life in the South,* around which study groups had developed throughout the region, and the University Y had in 1911 initiated a modest work with Negroes. But under Graham's leadership there were night schools in arithmetic, English, history, spelling, writing, and debating, in which Graham joined students in teaching. Under the leadership of Mrs. Edward K. Graham the Y helped sponsor a home improvement contest in the Negro community. In the white community there was a night school, a boys' club, Sunday school classes in a number of churches, and a Boy Scout troop.[8]

On campus the Y was engaged in countless activities, and the executive secretary necessarily had a hand in them all. In addition to educational programs and classes, it continued publication of the student handbook and sponsorship of the book exchange and the lost and found departments. Graham had to work closely with all the officers and committee chairmen. During the year 1914-15, for example, he met almost daily with young Bob House, treasurer of the Y, to go over the accounts; at the end of the year they had vouchers for every penny that had gone through the books.[9]

The major program sponsored during his term was a lecture series by John R. Mott, the international Christian leader, whom the *Tar Heel* repeatedly identified as one of the "six most conspicuous men in the world today," along with Woodrow Wilson, Theodore Roosevelt, George Bernard Shaw, Andrew Carnegie, and David Lloyd-George. For three days in February, 1915, Mott spoke to student assemblies on social needs, especially in Asian and African countries, and he expressed his optimism that Christianity and democracy would meet the twentieth-century challenges.

In late 1914 the History Department was understaffed. When Dr. Hamilton, head of the department, asked Graham if he would teach a course in American history, he accepted immediately. The *Tar Heel* in March described the results:

> Last week some forty men who are taking history und— we mean with Mr. Frank P. Graham met in the Di Hall and as nearly as possible reproduced the famous Hayne-Webster debate in the 31st Session of Congress. Frank Graham "Calhoun", occupied the chair as President of the Senate. The fifteen freshmen who had divided the Hayne speech among themselves sat on one side of the Hall; the fifteen young Websters on the other. Mann of Connecticut, Taylor of Missouri and all other details necessary were present.
>
> The meeting began at 2:30 and was two hours short. When the President of the Senate announced the vote at the end of the debate and the Senate solemnly adjourned and immediately was transformed into a group of laughing, excited and pleased young Americans the Spirit of History and Joy of Learning rose from the corner of the Hall and slipped out together arm in arm with a happy smile on their faces. Now if somebody does not just come along and try to make a "system" out of it![10]

Graham had found a way to make history come alive for students, but as the year progressed, he became aware of the serious gaps in his knowledge. If he intended to consider teaching history, it would be necessary to study the subject seriously. In 1915 he decided to go to Columbia University with the idea of returning to Chapel Hill to teach.

With determination to master the subject, he worked hard at Columbia, taking courses with William A. Dunning in Civil War and Reconstruction; Herbert Levi Osgood in Colonial History; Henry Rogers Seager in economics; and James Harvey Robinson in the History of the Intellectual Class. All, he felt, were good professors and good courses; but Robinson impressed him most both as a professor and as a man. Robinson presented the history of ideas from Greek to modern times, revealing interrelations between ideas and the other aspects of history. In manner he was candid without being offensive, stating radical views in such a way that the wrath of the ultra-patriotic groups was not aroused. As a Southerner Graham recognized the significance of manners, that it was not merely what a man said that was important but also the way and spirit in which he said it.

Frank received his master's degree in June, 1916, having written his thesis on Carl Schurz and the Liberal Republican Movement of 1872. It had been a strenuous year. Staying in New York through all vacations in order to study, he had compressed into nine months a graduate program that generally took longer. Immediately after graduation he took a job in the American History Room of the New York Public Library, working with documents that required the steady, exhausting use of his eyes. Plans for the future were not clear. Perhaps he would return to Columbia in the fall, as his professors had urged, to continue work toward a doctorate. Perhaps he would return to Chapel Hill to teach. Neither plan worked out: at the end of the summer his eyes could no longer stand the strain, and for a long time he feared that they had been permanently injured or, worse, that he might become blind.[11]

Graham had to give up his work in the library as soon as his vision became too blurred for the job. Uncertain which way to turn, he remained in New York until, after examining alternatives —all equally discouraging—he decided to visit for a while with his older brother Archie, who was an eye specialist in Minnesota. At first Frank was told that he must not read at all if there was to be any prospect of regaining the full use of his eyes. During the long winter evenings his brother and sister-in-law often read the daily paper aloud. During the days in the small town Frank spent most of his time out of doors in the snow, walking in the woods and skating on the lakes. In the wooded country he became interested in lumberjacks and logging camps, so his brother arranged a weekend with an outfit working on Sturgeon Lake. On Sunday morning, the day after Frank arrived, a big stranger speaking Finnish tried to hold a meeting but was run out of camp. The manager, taking Graham aside, explained, "He's an agitator; he's stirring up trouble for us. He's probably connected with those radical IWW's." When Frank went back to the bunkhouse, the lumberjacks gave him a different story: "He was a preacher, not talking any radical talk but just trying to preach the gospel to us." To the young observer, the conflict of interests and the failure of communication were all too obvious.

One afternoon he set out alone for a walk through the white countryside and across the wide lake covered with snow. The day before, he had watched teams of horses drag great tree trunks across the lake, so he knew it was safe. But he hit an air hole where the ice was thin and, in the sub-zero weather, broke through the ice. His overcoat spread out as he went down. Struggling onto the cracking ice, he crawled back to where it was thicker, then hobbled back to the camp. Water and clothes were frozen solid to his body. The lumberjacks, knowing immediately what had happened to their inexperienced visitor, refused to let him get to the fire, gradually eased off his overcoat, and warmed him bit by bit. "The last fellow who took a walk alone on Sunday came up in the spring," they told him. And one roustabout with a Maine accent added, "Now here I've been in this camp for months and taken no bath yet; and our visitor goes and takes a bath the second day he's here!"[12]

Even in the snow-packed, silent north woods there was no stilling of the war storms that swept across the Atlantic from Europe. Three weeks after Frank nearly disappeared through the ice, news came of President Wilson's address to the Senate on January 22, 1917, outlining the essential terms of peace in Europe. The President, considering himself "the only person in high authority amongst all the peoples of the world who is at liberty to speak and hold nothing back," dealt directly with the problems of war, insisted that the United States had to play a responsible part in the making of peace, and expressed the hopeful belief that he was speaking for the friends of humanity in every nation, including those who had no voice to speak their real hearts. When Graham, whose eyes were nearly back to normal, read his hero's words, he was deeply moved. Wilson told the senators:

> I am proposing that no nation should seek to extend its polity over any other nation or people, but that every people should be left free to determine its own polity, its own way of development, unhindered, unthreatened, unafraid, the little along with the great. . . . I am proposing government by consent of the governed; freedom of the seas. . . . and moderation of armaments. . . . These are American principles, American policies. . . . They are the principles of mankind and must prevail.[13]

Frank, responding to his leader, went to the Army recruiting offices in Duluth. He was turned down: too short, too thin, poor eyesight. He went to the Navy recruiting station. It was the same story. He couldn't do anything about his height, but at least, by a steady regimen, he could get his weight back to his normal 125 pounds. After a month he returned to the recruiters. When the Army and Navy rejected him again, he tried the Marines, but without success. In a nation where so many men were reluctant to leave home for military service, it was discouraging to be rejected.[14]

On April 2 a burdened, determined President again went to Congress with the "distressing and oppressive duty" of asking for a declaration of war against Germany. Every word Frank's idol spoke about "making the world safe for democracy" or the "fiery trial and sacrifice ahead of us" carried a personal message to the young teacher who had been rejected by all the armed services:

> It is a fearful thing to lead this great peaceful people into war, into the most terrible and disastrous of all wars, civilization itself seeming to be in the balance. But the right is more precious than peace, and we shall fight for the things which we have always carried nearest our hearts, for democracy, for the right of those who submit to authority to have a voice in their own governments, for the rights and liberties of small nations, for a universal dominion of right by such a concert of free peoples as shall bring peace and safety to all nations and make the world itself at last free.[15]

Moved by such idealism, Frank decided that the least he could do was to try again. He continued the discipline of exercise and a diet of milk and rich foods, and ounce by ounce he gained weight. Determined to be accepted by the Marines, he wrote to the Secretary of the Navy, Josephus Daniels (who, when appointed, had asked Graham to join his staff), and requested a letter of introduction to the recruiting officer. Letter in hand, he returned to Duluth and showed the Marine sergeant the encouraging note from Mr. Daniels.

"You've been here before," said the officer resignedly. "Well, let's look at you again."

Frank's height was the same; his weight was up a few pounds; his eyes could make out the larger letters. "Now this week," the sergeant told him, "the Marines have let down the bars because we are short on men. We are waiving one or two defects just to get our quota. We'll try you."

It was almost as hard to stay in the Marines as to get in. Frank was herded off with a group to League Island, near Philadelphia, for basic training. Soon he was at work building roads, painting houses, and marching with an eighty-pound pack on his back. His record book had been lost; and when he was reexamined a month after entering service, it was evident that he was not up to Marine Corps standards. "This fellow can't take it," Graham heard the major telling his associate surgeon. "How did he get in here anyhow?" The associate and Graham looked at each other with the surprised recognition of two former Carolina students. The associate turned back to the major: "I dare you to get out there and wrestle with him." With a long line waiting, there was no time for such a test. "You vouch for him? You say he can take it?" the major asked, and stamped "passed" on the new record book.

He was at last a private in the First Regiment, hoping and expecting to be sent, after early training, overseas. Word came that the Second Division in France was not at full strength and that the First Regiment, then at Quantico, was to sail for Europe. The men were rushed to Philadelphia, where there was unexplained delay after delay. Then the rumor leaked out about a bold plan. The American, British, and French fleets were to be combined to smash the Keil Canal in the expectation of bringing the war to an earlier end. The First Regiment, it was said, was being detained to become the Marine advance guard. Next the story sifted down that the British had vetoed the battle plan. The marines in Graham's 87th Company of the First Regiment became stevedores in Philadelphia.

Frank had hoped to get to France with the remote possibility of joining his brother Dave, who was also in the Marines. On June

10, 1918, there came news of the crucial Battle of Belleau Wood. A few days later the Grahams in Charlotte and Frank in Philadelphia received word that Dave had been killed. Now, more than ever, Frank knew he had to get to the front. When he learned that Secretary Daniels had received requests for him to go with a chaplain's staff or with the YMCA, he turned the opportunities down abruptly. He accepted an appointment to officer's training school in the hope that this might land him in an overseas outfit. He became a second lieutenant in a regiment that was assigned to attack the fortress of Metz; but, though their chief officers were already overseas, the regiment had not yet embarked when the armistice came.[16]

Mustered out in the spring of 1919, he had spent almost two years of—what? Of service to country, of sorts, he thought. Dave Graham had been killed in France, and Edward K. Graham had died of influenza in Chapel Hill. Graham felt that he had not given enough. Yet he looked to his life as a Marine with pride and humor. After all, he often remarked, "George Washington reached the height of his career when he crossed the Delaware River, and Robert E. Lee when he crossed the Potomac. Well, during the great World War I crossed both the Delaware and the Potomac Rivers."[17]

Once out of the Marines, Graham turned his thoughts again to Chapel Hill and to teaching. Since he had left the University almost four years before, he had no claim upon it. But the University had a claim upon him. Chapel Hill was the one place he wanted to be. So when an offer came from the new president, Harry Woodburn Chase, to become the University's first dean of students, Graham readily accepted.[18]

Chase, an educator's educator, was elected president of the University on June 17, 1919, when a favored candidate, R. D. W. Connor, was ruled ineligible because he was secretary of the Board of Trustees. The new president was temperamentally cautious in his approach to problems but at the same time was abreast of the latest developments in higher education. He recognized the havoc that war had done to the University's spirit, and he saw the desperate need for rebuilding that spirit in the returning veterans and new students. Chase had learned that American universities were establishing administrative offices dealing with student affairs. One of his first decisions, then, was to appoint a dean of students who would work with students in extracurricular life, making that life the fullest possible education in what it meant to be a responsible human being. Frank Graham was Chase's first choice for the new post; and in September, 1919, the new dean began work. In many ways he was an ideal choice: his enthusiasm for the University and sense of its traditions, his vigor, his genuine friendships with students, and his ethical standards and religious loyalties all made it obvious that he, if anyone, could strengthen student morals and morale. There were 1350 students when Graham returned as dean in 1919; there had been 880 when he left in 1915. Though by comparison the University seemed crowded, it was not too large for an alert, active administrator to be able to deal personally with individuals. Graham worked in just that way, on a person-to-person basis.[19]

The new office also demanded the organizational ability of an administrator. But Graham did not see himself in that role; at the end of one year as dean, he was pleased to relinquish the office and to return, as assistant professor, to teaching history.[20]

Part Two

Time of Trials: 1920-1931

4

The Discovery of a Cause

*Few who consider dispassionately the facts of
social history will be disposed to deny that the
exploitation of the weak by the powerful ... has
been a permanent feature in the life of most communities that the world has yet seen.*[1]
—R. H. Tawney (1922)

IN SEPTEMBER, 1920, GRAHAM EAGERLY RETURNED
to teaching. For eleven years, ever since he graduated from the
University, his life had been erratic. He had found his chief interest
to be a study of labor and man's economic needs; he had discovered
history as the best way to develop his primary interest. All the
while he was looking for a specific cause.

University teaching, Frank well knew, might become such a
cause. It seemed a perfect combination of college students, history,
and serious study, all in Chapel Hill. That was part of the difficulty: it was perfect in pleasure; and for a young Southerner and
Presbyterian who, like Woodrow Wilson, was intoxicated with the
spirit of self-sacrifice, there was something that made him uneasy
about too great a pleasure. With a sensitivity toward the events in
western history and the movements of the people behind them, he
hoped to communicate to his students the sweep of history and the
meaning of living responsibly in it. But to be a professor was not
enough: beyond the walls of a classroom or the limits of a campus
he sought a more inclusive cause.

A cause came for a crowded six months in the postwar campaign
for education in North Carolina. At noon on September 27, Graham received an urgent request to attend a meeting later in the day
in President Chase's office. Chase had that morning received a
letter from the ardent educator Louis R. Wilson, librarian and
alumni editor, urging that he start a campaign to build a first-rate
university, and Chase had acted with unusual administrative haste.

Three days previously Wilson had been stirred by an editorial, "The Thing We Lack," in the *Greensboro Daily News*. The editorial began sharply, "The government in North Carolina is the cheapest in the United States because it is next to the most worthless." The thing that the state lacked was leadership:

> Consider all the agencies of leadership, and see how few of those are really trying to lead, rather than truckling to prejudice, to vanity, and to ignorance. . . . To increase the numbers of this small class, to strengthen their hands—this is the service that North Carolina needs. But to perform it requires boldness, as well as skill.[2]

Wilson had brooded over the editorial all weekend, and on Monday morning he had placed on Chase's desk the editorial and an accompanying letter which said, in effect, "This means you!" He urged the president to begin a campaign to secure sufficient funds for the higher education of youth who, graduating with increasing numbers from the high schools, would otherwise be denied a college education.[3]

Wilson to Chase to Graham. It was Wilson who, because of his concern through the years for educational quality and liberal social leadership, saw the dynamite in the editorial; it was Chase who, in calling a meeting, lit the fuse; it was Graham who exploded with faith in the ability of the University to lead, insisting that the university of the people must work through the people and for them. When, at the afternoon meeting, Graham proclaimed his belief that the University alumni were the key to the future, the others present—Lenoir Chambers, director of the news bureau, Ralph Rankin, alumni secretary, W. S. Bernard, professor of classics, Francis Bradshaw, dean of students, Charles Woollen, business manager, in addition to Wilson and Chase—agreed with him. But what could the alumni do? Graham, typically, was for sending a telegram immediately, within the hour, calling selected leaders to an emergency meeting. Chase was hesitant, whereupon Wilson, noted for his deliberateness but desiring immediate, drastic action, diplomatically suggested that he, Chase, and Woollen withdraw because they "might be overly cautious." The remainder of the group then delegated Graham to draft a telegram, which Chase, with some doubts, signed. That evening selected alumni in all sections of the state received urgent invitations to come to Chapel Hill.[4]

Forty-three alumni arrived at the University the following Sunday and met in "the Coop," a cramped, worn, students' boardinghouse that was witness to the truth of the reported needs. There were 1,547 students and 264 rooms in the University; so, though crowded three and four to a room, the students bulged out of the dormitories into unregulated quarters over stores and in private homes. The colleges of the state had that summer refused entrance to more than 2,300 applicants. There were not enough classrooms, laboratories, and libraries, and those that existed were poorly equipped. As for the faculty, the University had scarcely enough money to keep the professors it had, let alone secure the new faculty essential for increased numbers of students. "Nothing short of a revolution in higher education will handle the situation in North Carolina," said President Chase. Graham called for immediate action:

> If the issue be the privilege of the few as opposed to the rights of all we shall join the fight there. If the issue is taxes, we shall call it taxes and not beat around the bush of expediency. . . . If it is a question of the exemption of property or the redemption of youth, North Carolina will vote for her youth. . . . Suffer the youth of North Carolina to come into the colleges and forbid them not, for of such is the Kingdom of tomorrow.

By the time the meeting adjourned at one o'clock in the morning, the alumni had passed resolutions calling for a vigorous statewide campaign.[5]

Chase was the official leader of the campaign, working with the trustees and making major addresses; Wilson was the propagandist, using the pages of the *Alumni Review* and soliciting press releases from qualified writers with knowledge of the educational needs; Graham was the director of the campaign. It was his conviction that to be successful the movement had to belong not to the leaders or alumni, but to all the people of the state. It existed not for the University alone, but for all educational institutions.

He saw his first venture into a public campaign as a battle for the existence of the University and the future of the state. It soon became known as the "Twenty Million Dollar Bond Issue," since that unprecedented figure was the amount of the total requests for permanent educational improvements. The president wavered momentarily in mid-campaign when in December a leading financier and member of the state Budget Commission, James A. Gray, requested that the University have faith in the commission's forthcoming recommendations. Chase consulted Graham and Wilson about the momentous question: Wouldn't it be more practical to ask for a realistic amount for permanent improvements rather than for the twenty million, with $5,500,000 requested for the University alone? The emphatic answer of both was that the real needs of the University and the necessity of keeping alumni interest alive demanded an all-out campaign. More than that, since Gray's letter implied that the Budget Commission was evidently not granting the full amount, they urged that the trustees be called into a special session to give full support to the total requests. Infected by their enthusiasm, Chase called a meeting for December 30; and the board endorsed the full request of $5,500,000 for the University from the bond issue.[6]

It was well that it did so. Within two weeks the report of the Budget Commission was made public: $990,000 for permanent improvements at the University; and instead of twenty million dollars for all state institutions, less than five. Now the issues were joined; and Graham, seeing the conflict as a war to make North Carolina safe for democracy in education, addressed his communiques "To the Men on the Firing Line," asserting that "Every hour is a fighting hour. The fight is for nothing less than the greatness of North Carolina." He urged supporters to "shell the woods and let the bricks fly for youth and the commonwealth," and he signed his reports, "Yours with joy for the fight." The "shelling" and "bricks" were public meetings and letters to members of the legislature.

The alumni in Hillsboro sent telegrams urging support for the program to every alumni association in the state and to thirty-five hundred individuals. Luther Hodges, a young textile executive later to be governor, organized a county-wide meeting. Citizens in Greensboro raised thousands of dollars to help defray the expenses of the campaign. Graham had a hand in those developments and more; in ceaseless travels throughout the state and by written appeals, he secured the support of the Federation of Women's Clubs, the Parent-Teacher Association, labor unions, and civic clubs, as well as ministers, educators, and other community leaders. Nor were the students forgotten: he urged high school and college students to pass resolutions and to write letters to their representatives;

and the University students, in particular, played a prominent role in the campaign through student publications, mass meetings, and appeals to their home communities. Graham secured the appointment of a senior, John Kerr, as chairman of the student committee and worked closely with him, even writing a sample letter to go to community leaders, which young Kerr used without changing a word.[7]

A new governor, folksy, blunt, tobacco-chewing Cameron Morrison, took office in January; and before he was settled in, Graham sought his support in the education campaign. Morrison's governorship coincided with a widespread progressive era in Southern politics. Though the movement for social justice was muted in North Carolina and the South, it was a period when the states fought for industry, roads, and education.[8] Morrison was ready for Graham. Deep in the battle for a fifty-million-dollar bond issue for roads, he privately expressed some misgivings about the education campaign; but when the needs were made evident, he boldly supported the twenty-million-dollar request in addition to the road program.

From every direction the campaign focused upon the legislature and the totally inadequate recommendation of the Budget Commission. Graham organized a militant delegation of more than five hundred persons from all parts of the state. Led by Alfred M. Scales of Greensboro, they descended upon the legislature in February. "To the Men at the Front," Graham wrote a week before the attack, maintaining his military metaphor, "The last charge is about to be made. . . . Down the fighting ranks of North Carolina soldier to soldier, the word is passing, 'Forward with Scales to Raleigh!' All aboard! Your local train will sound the zero hour. We're off! Let's go."[9]

Under the pressure of the attack, the legislature yielded, but not entirely. The legislature, maintaining it could not commit permanent improvement funds for longer than the budgetary biennium, appropriated more than six million dollars to the education program, including a grant of nearly a million and a half dollars to the University. Faced with only this limited victory, Governor Morrison reached an agreement with legislative leaders that if the funds appropriated by the 1921 General Assembly were well spent, then subsequent assemblies would be pledged, by a gentlemen's agreement, to grant the total twenty million.[10]

The dormitories and classroom buildings that would transform the campus into a modern university were assured. As if to symbolize the triumph, the University was admitted in 1922 as the twenty-fifth member of the Association of American Universities, of which only two were in the South.

It was a victory. Frank Graham had played a key role in it. But so, too, had Wilson, Chase, Morrison, and—fully as important as any of these—the thousands of persons, known and unknown, who had fought for the youth of North Carolina. In the six-month campaign Graham had given many public addresses; but mainly he had worked behind the scenes, eliciting help from others who believed in democratic institutions. The campaign had confirmed his faith that in a democratic society the people would respond to a worthy cause. Confirmed, too, was his way of working with people.

During the six-month campaign Graham continued teaching four courses in history and often worked sixteen hours a day. He had always stayed busy, but previously it had been at his own pace, with ample time for leisurely Sunday afternoon walks, unhurried reading, or conversation with students and colleagues. The rambles were over.

As the teaching continued into the 1921 academic year, Graham began to feel that something was missing in his life. Part had to do with his preparation, the fact that his training in history had been so limited. He had taken only one course at Chapel Hill, and his one year of graduate study, five years before, had not been in the European history that he was teaching. He needed further study. But it was not the academic hunger that gnawed at him most. It was the deeper need for self-discovery and for a cause worthy of his life. More and more he was discovering that his chief interests were identified with the needs of North Carolina and the South. He would seek, then, the best place in the country to understand those needs. In September, 1921, Graham left for the University of Chicago to study with William E. Dodd, a North Carolinian and the first historian in the country to devote all his time to courses in Southern history.

In Chicago, Graham worked with four professors, each in his own way a master: Ferdinand Schevill, who taught Renaissance history; Andrew Cunningham MacLaughlin, who taught constitutional history; James Westfall Thompson, who taught medieval history; and William E. Dodd. The most important of the quartet

FIGURE 1. Frank Porter Graham with his parents, Alexander and Katherine Sloan Graham. *North Carolina Collection, UNC Library*

FRANK PORTER GRAHAM, Charlotte, N. C.

A man to all the country dear.

Age 22; height 5 feet 6 inches; weight 125. Law.

Di Society; Y. M. C. A.; Golden Fleece; Gimghoul; Odd Number Club; Cosmopolitan Club; Mecklenburg County Club; Secretary W. H. S. Club; Class and All-Class Baseball Team (1); Scrub Baseball Team (2, 3); President of Class (2); Soph-Junior Debater (3); Class Historian (3); Assistant Editor-in-Chief of *Tar Heel* (3); Secretary of Phi Beta Kappa; President of Y. M. C. A. (4); Editor-in-Chief of *Tar Heel*, Fall Term (4); President of Class (4); Secretary of Modern Literature Club; Chief Cheerer (4); Editor of YACKETY YACK (3).

Frank. Laddie Buck.

Everyman's friend, confidant, and playfellow. Couldn't do what he is supposed to do to-morrow if he were to live his whole life in one day. No settled tradition in college can be carried through without him, no new movement can be successful without him at its head. And, curiously enough, with the burden of a college upon his shoulders, he bears it without losing himself in it all. Out of it all he comes a little worn, but still the same good fellow of his lazy, less-occupied days.

Frank P. Graham

FIGURE 2. Senior class picture in the 1909 *Yackety Yack*.
North Carolina Collection, UNC Library

FIGURE 3. Frank Porter Graham, right, as a student at the University of North Carolina with friends.
North Carolina Collection, UNC Library

FIGURE 4. Edward Kidder Graham, cousin of Frank Porter Graham, served as University librarian and professor of English before becoming president of the University in 1915. *North Carolina Collection, UNC Library*

FIGURE 5. Former Presidents of UNC, Francis P. Venable, left, Edwin A. Alderman, and Kemp Plummer Battle, right, at Edward K. Graham's inauguration as President in 1915. *North Carolina Collection, UNC Library*

FIGURE 6. Freshman baseball team, 1906, with Frank Porter Graham seated front left.
North Carolina Collection, UNC Library

FIGURE 7. Francis E. Winslow
North Carolina Collection, UNC Library

FIGURE 8. Charles W. Tillett, Jr.
North Carolina Collection, UNC Library

FIGURE 9. The *Tar Heel* Staff. Frank Porter Graham, center, served as Editor-in-Chief of the *Tar Heel* during the fall term of his senior year.
North Carolina Collection, UNC Library

FIGURE 10. Kemp D. Battle
North Carolina Collection, UNC Library

FIGURE 11. John W. Umstead, Jr.
North Carolina Collection, UNC Library

FIGURE 12. The YMCA building dedicated in June, 1907, where Graham spent much time during his student days and later as Secretary. *North Carolina Collection, UNC Library*

FIGURE 13. The YMCA Cabinet. Graham, center, was president of the University YMCA during his senior year. *North Carolina Collection, UNC Library*

Figure 14. Graham as a Marine in the first World War.
Southern Historical Collection, UNC Library

FIGURE 15. The president's house in Chapel Hill, Graham's first home since leaving that of his childhood. *Southern Historical Collection, UNC Library*

FIGURE 16. Dr. Graham welcomed students into his home. *North Carolina Collection, UNC Library*

for Graham was Dodd, with his love of the South and democracy. "Democracy," Dodd wrote to a friend, "is the only thing in this world worth fighting for." His heroes were Jefferson and Lincoln and Wilson; and, like them, he had a passionate faith in the common man, believing in man's abilities and rights. His lectures were informal and often obviously poorly planned, so that frequently at the end of an hour Graham would look down at a noteless page. The magic of Dodd was in his personality, in the passion and pathos of one who still lived the tragedy of Southern history and who had a firm grasp on the present because of his unique grasp on the past.[11] All of this made a deep impression on Graham.

There was one thing more: Dodd was convinced that history could not be understood without a full appreciation of economic factors. Everywhere, in all ages, he saw the continuing battle between property rights and human rights, between monopolistic interests and the common man. This had been implied in Graham's expression of his "chief interest" in labor in 1912. This was what he had seen in the campaign for education in 1921. This was the key.

There was time that year for the development of friendships with other graduate students, both men and women. In particular, a close bond grew between Graham and Mack Swearingen, an unsophisticated twenty-year-old Mississippian; and together they shared friendships with other graduate students. Graham, Swearingen, and two women students, Vera Largent and Geneva Drinkwater, often went to concerts and plays together; they went on carefree outings to the Dunes; and on one occasion Schevill took them to see Babe Ruth play ball. Best of all, from Graham's standpoint, they talked, and since most of the talk was about history, they educated each other.

Almost every afternoon Graham went to the gymnasium for a workout. He hinted once that the daily exercise was more than a matter of physical health. No friend of Graham's, not even in college, reported that he had ever introduced talk about sex, but his closest friends knew that he was as normal in his feeling toward girls as any of them. Swearingen, convinced that his older friend was as chaste as a park statue, once brought up the subject. Graham said simply that when the pressures got dangerously strong, he would exercise to the point of exhaustion and thus keep his physical desires under control.[12]

In mid-July, just at the completion of the first summer session at Chicago, Graham returned to his room in a boardinghouse, where all year he had lived alone, to find all his belongings stacked outside the door and a stranger settling in his place. He had forgotten to tell the landlady that he would attend the second session. Lugging suitcases, bundles, and packages, Graham trudged over to Swearingen's one-room, single-bed, one-window apartment near the University. "I've come to live with you," he said when his surprised friend, sixteen years his junior, answered the door.

"But you can't stay here," Swearingen answered in despair. "There isn't room enough for me and you know my bed won't carry double."

"We can manage. Besides, what else can I do? Where can I put my stuff down?"

Down the stuff went; and for six weeks the two squeezed in and out of the one-room apartment. Swearingen was cramming for his master's examinations and completing his thesis, so during the day Graham left him to study in solitude. But as soon as the light went out at night, Graham crowded with his host on the only bed, and the talk with his captive audience would begin. Always the animated conversationalist, Graham's talk for a brief time each night was enlivening. But Swearingen, pressured by work, would soon yearn for sleep: "Frank, I have an eight-o'clock class, can't . . . " only to be interrupted with, "I know, but I haven't finished yet. Listen." Swearingen would listen until he fell asleep, only to be awakened by a hand on his shoulder and a voice in the dark. "You can sleep some other time; did you hear what I was saying about Dodd's new idea about Calhoun?" "No, can't you tell me tomorrow?" Silence, then the voice in the dark, subdued, "That's just the trouble with the world; people don't talk enough, they don't communicate." Again stillness, then: "You think your class is more important than talking, but it isn't. There's nothing more important than communication. That's the whole trouble with the world. We don't communicate enough."[13]

Graham was at Chicago with a purpose. Generally he was pointed toward a doctoral degree; specifically he desired historical knowledge and insight that would enlighten his understanding of North Carolina. Ceaseless, serious study and the sharing of ideas with others were of the greatest importance. When he found a problem that was his own, he set a task for himself and did not rest until the problem was solved, the task completed. But when he had to complete a general assignment requiring an indefinite, long-range organizational procedure, he would either be late in completing the work or else turn in a lengthy, incomplete paper.

When MacLaughlin explained with his usual clarity the constitutional questions involved in the Virginia and Kentucky Resolutions against the Alien and Sedition Laws of 1798, he paused to say, almost as an aside, that it was widely believed Virginia had actually armed because of the resolutions but he wondered whether this was true. For Graham it was a personal challenge. He disappeared into the library and was scarcely heard from for more than six weeks; and the further he dug into the problem, the more difficult it became until, working through original sources, he found the answer. MacLaughlin had forgotten about the question when Graham dropped on his desk an eighty-page paper showing that Virginia had, in fact, armed at the time. The maneuver was not in support of the resolutions, however, but in response to the threat of a slave insurrection. MacLaughlin was delighted, and he urged that the paper be published or perhaps become the basis for a doctoral dissertation. But Graham had completed his self-appointed job. He did nothing else with the paper except lose it.[14]

Graham's indifference to scholarship that was not definite and humanly relevant was a factor in his turning away from a doctoral program despite the pleas of his professors. For he had found an idea that had clarity and human significance: the importance of economic factors in Southern history.[15]

He was able to pursue that idea when, unexpectedly, in April, 1923, he received an "Amherst Memorial Fellowship for the Study of Social, Economic and Political Institutions, and for Preparation for Teaching and the Ministry." Graham had not applied for the fellowship. He had been nominated by Dodd and supported by his other professors as well as by many colleagues in Chapel Hill. At thirty-six he was older than most Amherst Fellows, who were expected to "possess qualities of leadership, a spirit of service, and an intention to devote their efforts to the betterment of social conditions."[16]

Graham decided to spend the first year of his fellowship studying economics; and the best place for such study, he thought, was at the new Graduate School of Economics of the Brookings Institution in Washington. Walton Hamilton, famous as a teacher for his penetrating economic analyses, his moral conscience, and his stimulation of independent thinking, was leaving Amherst for Brookings. There was the further obvious advantage of living for a year in the nation's capital, where he could be a close witness of government at work. In September, 1923, Graham left Chicago. He had completed sufficient courses for the doctorate; perhaps in Washington he would find a dissertation topic to his liking and return to Chicago in 1924 to complete the requirements for the degree.

For the next nine months his life moved between the Brookings Institution, where he roomed and studied, and the Library of Congress and Capitol across town. At Brookings his entire formal study was with Hamilton, whose life work centered around the epigraph of his earliest book, "To hold the balance true between the material and the human values of life is the oldest and the newest economic problem." A Southerner, Hamilton was convinced that it was in the economy that there might be built in democratic America the good life for all. Hamilton's ideals, in combination with his scholarship and breadth of vision, appealed to Graham. He read voraciously in the Library of Congress on contemporary economic problems, always seeing them in relation to the South.[17]

It was mainly a solitary life for Graham that year. Occasionally friends from North Carolina would visit him, and together they would go out for dinner and, for entertainment, join in serious conversation. For relaxation he often attended sessions of Congress. He kept in close touch with the University.

Under the impact of what he was learning in the study of contemporary economics, Graham decided not to return to Chicago to complete the requirements for a degree. He was still pursuing the idea of economic forces in history, for every new discovery in the complex, uncertain subject opened up larger vistas. He became obsessed with one problem: the coming of the industrial revolution to North Carolina and the South. How, in the face of the inevitable revolution, which in previous history had produced such dislocation and suffering along with its great values, could the South avoid the mistakes of Old England and New England? This was the question for which he had to find an answer. It was the problem of property rights versus human rights that Dodd saw everywhere in history; it was the problem of finding the true balance between material and human values that Hamilton saw as basic to economics. But it was more than this. It was Frank Graham's problem: "the privilege of the few opposed to the rights of all." To find answers to the problem he had to know more about economic history. The best place for that was the London School of Economics, which had brought together an amazing array of intellectual and moral talent. Frank Graham's discovery of history had led to a discovery of economics; and together, with the love of the South, they led him to England.[18]

Arriving in London in June, 1924, Graham found lodging on a square near the British Museum and the London School. His weekdays and nights were divided between the two; and occasionally, after the British Museum closed at eleven in the evening, he would go to Parliament if it was in late session.

Disciplined in his work throughout the week, Graham kept his weekends free for exploring history in London's streets, attending church, and, especially, joining other students on outings. There were about ten American students that banded together that year, and Graham, older than the others, was looked upon as something of an elder brother. He organized baseball games, chaperoned the girls when necessary, and often piloted the group to his favorite eating place, The Fruit Restaurant, where, in accordance with his dietary principles, the entire meal consisted of exotic fruits supplemented by a variety of nuts. Ever health-conscious and proud of the strength that was out of proportion to his size, he had joined American food faddism, particularly the view that meat should be eaten in moderation. He never achieved sympathy for the British view that neither fish nor fowl is meat; at full-course dinners he would, after the first fish course, refuse any other dish he considered meat, never intimidated by the incredulous eyes of the dignified British waiters.[19]

Friends were welcome at his "digs." Once he was visited by Mack Swearingen, who was in London on a Rhodes Scholarship. While Graham went elsewhere for the evening, Swearingen attended the British Exposition and combined too many rides on the steep roller coaster with visits to the Jamaica Building, where free rum was dispensed. How Swearingen even found his way back to Graham's room was a mystery; and when his host returned, there were agonizing groans coming from the bed and work to be done. "I've cleaned up worse than this in the Marine Corps," Frank said to his humiliated friend. Graham's neighbor dropped by to say, in effect, that if the dying patient didn't succumb soon, he would be glad to kill him for no fee. The next evening, when Graham returned in cheerful spirits from the day's study, he uttered no word of reproach but did suggest that Swearingen write a note of apology to the neighbor. The note was stuck under the man's door; and later in the evening the neighbor came to make his apologies in turn. When he left, Graham commented, "See, that's always the best way. Last night he was not your friend. Now he is."[20]

Graham did not register for credit at the London School of Economics; but perhaps no student ever worked more diligently or absorbed more from professors. Five, in particular, were significant for him: Lilian Knowles, Eileen Power, Harold Laski, R. H. Tawney, and L. T. Hobhouse.

Knowles and Power were the first women teachers Graham had had since his days at Warrenton Academy and were the equal of any of his professors in graduate school. Knowles's subject was the economic development of the British Overseas Empire. As he learned how British capital played a major role in the development of railroads and utilities in India and America, Graham's mind turned back to the economic needs of the South, and there dawned in his mind the concept of federal aid to the economically poor region. Power taught British medieval economic history, and her lectures, showing how modern Britain developed, combined poetry with scholarship. Laski was facile, brilliant, exciting, and outrageously one-sided; but he had a social conscience, and Graham had a weakness for any man with social moral sensitivity. Hobhouse, liberal sociologist with both a philosophical and a historical consciousness, was quietly learned, and he was devastating in his critical analyses of forms of socialism popular among British intellectuals.[21]

It was Tawney, however, who meant most to Graham, through both his lectures and his writings. Forty-five years of age, Tawney was taciturn, with an ironic humor. To Graham he was impressive in his scholarship, which was patient, thorough, and profound. He was even more impressive as a man. His dedicated Fabianism, which advocated the gradual development of socialism, was rooted in careful analyses of English economic history guided by moral concern. In lectures first given in 1922 he hinted at the theme of his life work:

Circumstances alter from age to age, and the practical interpretation of moral principles must alter with them. Few who consider dispassionately the facts of social history will be disposed to deny that the exploitation of the weak by the powerful, organized for the purposes of economic gain, buttressed by imposing systems of law, and screened by decorous draperies of virtuous sentiment and resounding rhetoric, has been a permanent feature in the life of most communities that the world has yet seen.[22]

Tawney's theme, Graham had long since discovered, was exemplified by life in the South, whether in the days of slavery or reconstruction or the newer industrialization. So Tawney was not teaching him anything new but was providing a historical and theoretical framework for understanding. Graham, with his personal indifference to money, agreed with Tawney's judgment that the element in industrial civilization most in conflict with the teachings of Jesus was the assumption that material riches are the major object of human effort and the criterion of human success. As it had been for earlier men, a supreme task of modern man was to strive to build a society in the light of Christian standards. To perform this task, it was necessary that Christians test the changing aspects of society by the insights of their faith, even at the risk of rashness. For, said Tawney, "Rashness is a more agreeable failure than cowardice, and, when to speak is unpopular, it is less pardonable to be silent than to say too much."

Sooner than he then knew, Graham would be challenged to speak.

In mid-February, 1925, Virginia Terrell, a graduate of the North Carolina College for Women who was writing feature articles for the *London Times*, came to her fellow Carolinian with the news that academic freedom was endangered at home. In early February conservative forces had stimulated the introduction in the state legislature of the Poole Bill, which forbade the teaching of evolution in state schools. The fact that five other Southern states had adopted, or would soon adopt, such restrictive legislation was not encouraging.[23]

In North Carolina the controversy had centered for years around William L. Poteat, a biologist and president of Wake Forest College, who as early as the 1880s had espoused the evolutionary theory. Attacks upon Poteat came largely from his fellow Baptists; and, coincident with anti-evolutionary movements across the South, they were intensified in the early 1920s, culminating in the restrictive Poole Bill. Because the bill referred only to state schools, Poteat attended the hearings before the House Committee on Education but did not speak. He gave his full support to President Chase, who led the fight for academic freedom. The bill was defeated in the House on February 19 by a ratio of 3-to-2. But conservativism did not succumb because of that one defeat, and the religious attacks upon Poteat, Chase, and the University continued.

When Graham heard about the controversy over the Poole Bill, shortly before the vote, he was upset. Hastily he wrote an article that appeared in leading state newspapers on March 2, after the vote. He defended Chase and then focused upon the central issue, academic freedom: "The inquisition, the Index and the stake are the unclaimed ancestors of the Poole Bill." He reached into the history of the University to affirm, in words he had memorized:

> It is a tradition of our people that they "would have it a place where there is always a breath of freedom in the air—and where finally truth shining patient like a star bids us advance and we will not turn aside." To preserve this spiritual possession of the people for the inheritance of their children North Carolinians will fight against the false fear of truth and the foes of freedom, whatever be their power.[24]

In the spring of 1925 Graham made three trips across the Channel. The first was with Mack Swearingen to Brittany, where they were joined by Vera Largent and Geneva Drinkwater, the two women friends from their Chicago days, for refreshing walks through the Breton countryside, relaxation on the beach at Roscoff, a visit to Mont-Saint-Michel, and enjoyment of the simple, nourishing food in the small hotel. When the two men took a train, Swearingen was horrified by Graham's Southern gentlemanliness in the rural French province. The train stopped every few kilometers to pick up a passenger or two, usually old peasant women burdened with bundles. When they got on or off, Graham rose from his seat to help, only to be rebuffed by one old Bretonne after another, who snatched her possessions out of his hands, telling him with rough finality, in a language he did not understand, that he should tend to his own business. He was abashed neither by their rejection nor by Swearingen's explanation that peasant women in Brittany, unacquainted with Southern manners, saw his advances in a light entirely different from the one he intended. Remonstrance was to no avail; when he saw old women carrying bundles, he continued to offer help.[25]

Two other trips to the continent were pilgrimages. The League of Nations Association helped to subsidize a week in Geneva, where, with the memory of Wilson still fresh in his mind, Graham looked at the efforts of the young League to create the conditions for peace. And later in the spring he went with Thomas Wolfe to Belleau Wood, where Frank's brother Dave had been killed eight years before and was buried with thousands of Americans who had crossed an ocean "to make the world safe for democracy."[26]

In Chicago and Washington and London, Graham looked back to the South and, far from home, saw North Carolina in a new light. Industrialization was inevitable. The acceptance of that fact and the understanding of the processes of industrialization in other regions would make it possible for North Carolina to lead the way for the South to avoid the fateful errors that both Old and New England had made. The problem was how to build into the new society the democratic life Graham had always advocated. Through the discovery of history and economics, which fused with his earlier religious and moral beliefs, Frank Graham, at thirty-eight, had discovered his own life in the South and a cause to which he would devote that life.

5

History Taught and Lived

*North Carolina and the Piedmont South are fast
making the transition from a dominantly agricultural to a dominantly industrial civilization.
. . . The people of North Carolina have more at
stake in this industrial revolution than in any
event since the civil war.*[1]
—FRANK PORTER GRAHAM (1926)

ON A TORRID AUGUST DAY IN 1925 FRANK GRAHAM
arrived at the Chapel Hill station and took a taxi the remaining
mile to the University. The front campus, the most beloved area of
the University, was as he had often remembered it. But he soon
noted that things had changed in the three years he had been away:
new classroom buildings fronted the south quadrangle, and nine
new dormitories housed increasing numbers of students. The new
buildings were the result of the campaign in which he had worked
so hard.

Walking the familiar paths of the campus, Graham knew that
he was home. The return to his office as assistant professor of history and the greeting of old friends confirmed the fact. Quickly,
naturally, friendships were restored where they had been left three
years before. Like the University, his friends had changed and yet
remained the same.

He, too, had changed, but there was a continuity underlying his
character. For the cause he had at last found in London was a clari-
fication of the purpose that had motivated him for years, certainly
since his student days: to share in building democratic ideals into
the life of the University and the state. In returning home Frank
intended to serve the University as teacher and the state as private
citizen. His desires were simple and intense: to enliven young students through teaching that would stimulate them to think and to
live responsibly in society; to enrich the state through participation

in programs that would emphasize human values in the inevitable transition from an agricultural to an industrial life.[2]

Graham's sense of history had begun long before his journey abroad; but it was studying with historians and reflecting upon life in North Carolina that gave the sensitivity a new sharpness. He had a compulsion to identify the forces from the past that were shaping lives, including his own, in the present; and this knowledge of the past, coupled with a continuing fervent belief in freedom, forced him to try to chart a path into the future. It was this historical consciousness that "Mr. Frank," as he was now called by University students, wanted to communicate.

Scholarly work in the libraries of Chicago, Washington, and London had established a permanent working method for Graham. When confronted with the task of preparing for a class or a major address or when facing a social problem, the first steps would be to the library. There books that provided the historical background for the subject would be listed in a lengthy bibliography. These would be read and assimilated, and a notebook would be filled with quotations, outlines, and personal reactions. There would follow the task of writing, crossing out, and rewriting in longhand. Inevitably the subject would be interpreted historically; and many a brief paragraph would have its origins in hours of reading.[3]

Considered one of the best teachers in the University, Graham believed that students had to educate themselves and each other, so lectures were kept at a minimum. There was considerable discussion; and, as one who enjoyed listening to debate, Graham purposely tried to help students find where they disagreed. The examination was not an occasion for the recital of bare facts but was a learning experience in which the meaning of history should become clearer. At examination time he would write on the board, "Discuss the evolution of revolution from the fall of Constantinople to the fall of the Bastille" or "What are significant relations between the democratic and industrial revolutions?" His type of examination was subject to abuse; and there was a story among students that other members of the history department advocated the use of uniform examinations to ensure that Graham's students would learn dates and names.

Chief among his personal teaching methods was the dramatic reenactment of significant historical events, a method he had used more than a decade earlier. In a popular course, American History, the class lived through the Constitutional Convention of 1787. Each student was given the name of a delegate. It was the student's responsibility to find out everything he could about the sovereign state he came from and the forces he represented, and then to place himself in the position of the delegate. ("So many of your students come over here," the librarian once told Graham, "that I sometimes wonder whether you think the library was built for your class.") To enliven and to clarify the meaning of the debates, Mr. Frank would create functionaries that never, in fact, existed—floor leaders for the Hamilton and Jefferson forces, for example. The instructor would set the stage and provide the running commentary of background information. Always the Constitution was drafted, but only after bitter floor fights, argumentative committee meetings, and political compromise. Indeed, on one occasion representatives of the small states' plan and the large states' plan became so angered that they had to be restrained physically.

Students saw Graham as an exciting but not a tough teacher. One of the members of a class was honored by being assigned the role of General Washington because he had scored the winning touchdown against Duke. And there were times when the classes, upon arriving in the room, found this note on the board: "Mr. Graham is ill. He asks you to appoint a committee and continue the work of the course until his return." When the students reported what they had done, he remarked that the state was not getting its money's worth, since his classes learned more in his absence than in his presence.[4]

His friendship with students was one of the principal reasons for his popularity. Because of his facility for remembering faces and names and his wide acquaintance in the state, many a lonely student fresh from the country would be amazed that not only his crossroads but even his relatives were known: "Are you from Davie County? I know your uncle, and you must be related to Cousin Alex." In class he was formal with the students, addressing each as "Mr." Out of class it was different. The love of wrestling expressed itself through many a half-nelson and twisted arm. And on the days of the student-faculty baseball game, the students would mercilessly hit ball after ball to his outfield in the hope, they claimed, of wearing down his short legs.

Friendliness did not stop with the students. After becoming acquainted with the parents of a student by cooperating with them on a social issue, he wrote:

The two of you explain to me the fine qualities of your boy here. I hope that the University will bring out these qualities in the finest sort of way. Though I have not seen him but three or four times I feel drawn to him and hope that he will feel free to call on me to talk about anything or nothing at any time. If at any time you have any suggestions to make with regard to his interests or reading or his life work I trust that I do not need to assure you that you can trust such suggestions with me. That's what I am here for. It's the biggest job I know.[5]

"It's the biggest job I know." To assist students in the search for meaning and value, to open minds and hearts to the world of the past, present, and future, to develop intellectual and moral methods —in short, to teach history as alive and the individual as important —was a big job. It required about all the available time to prepare classes, read papers, counsel students, and try to keep up with the growing body of knowledge. But that was not enough. If the students were to be taught moral responsibility for society, if the individual student was to be stimulated to participate in social causes, then the teacher had the obligation to live responsibly outside the classroom according to his beliefs.

When the invitation was given to make a major address at the annual Newspaper Institute on January 14, 1926, Graham accepted the opportunity to express his personal views to the gathering of editors, publishers, reporters, and business managers of North Carolina papers. Choosing as his theme "The University and Press," he reviewed the history of both, noting parallels between the two institutions:

The press is a vehicle of information and interpretation between the present world and the people and its influence is immediate. The university is a vehicle of information and interpretation between the past and the people, and its influence is mainly in the future. But the better the press the more it plays its present news against a background of the past with a view to the future. The better the university the more it builds on its past for the understanding of the present.[6]

He suggested that the press and the University had faced three crises since the war. The first two were educational crises concerning the freedom of the public schools to live and grow and the freedom of the University to consider and report scientific data. Both had been won; and, though he did not say so, in both he had played a role. The third was the contemporary social crisis that involved economic and social development. The Piedmont South as a new industrial belt was undergoing transitions greater than at any time in its history. "The mills and factories confront the university and the university is found to be a friend of all those who are working here with capital or industry, brain or hand, to win a larger life for themselves and all our people." The challenge of these transformations was a challenge to study society in order that, together, Southerners might work out in the midst of industrialization the humanization of life. In 1926 Frank Graham had learned and extended the lessons of his professors and his father, of Edward K. Graham and Woodrow Wilson, which he expressed in his own words:

> The chief business of the people of North Carolina is the business of their university. It is her purpose to violate no right, to promote no special interest, to hamper no industry but to study and envisage the whole and various life of the people and help build a nobler and fresher civilization in this ancient commonwealth.[7]

On behalf of that purpose he was teaching at the University and speaking quietly throughout the state. But talk was not enough; there must be action as well. So from late in 1926 through the early months of 1930, Graham engaged in a number of campaigns.

Some of Graham's concerns outside the classroom were directly related to education. In 1926 he was shocked by library and reading statistics he came across: North Carolina, spending a bare four cents per capita for libraries, ranked forty-seventh in the nation (only Arkansas was lower); North Carolina was also forty-seventh in the number of newspapers, magazines, and books read per capita; forty-seven of the one hundred counties had no public library facilities; sixty-eight percent of the citizens did not have access to a public library. For one committed to education, this reading poverty was deplorable. On November 3, 1927, he urged the North Carolina Library Association "to organize, to press the fight and put libraries in those counties." This was the beginning of the Citizen's Library Movement, the first of its kind in the nation. The association immediately passed a resolution endorsing a campaign and, the following March, asked Graham to head a crusade that would have as its aim the creation and improvement of public libraries in every county in the state. Declining to lead the movement, he agreed to promote the program until a director could be found. He spent much of the summer—even while on vacation—writing personal letters asking individuals to join the campaign.[8]

In the fall the letter writing continued, and the public speaking was renewed with increased vigor. Josephus Daniels, desiring to write an editorial about the Citizen's Library Movement for the Raleigh *News and Observer*, requested a copy of a speech; unable to find any, Graham sent a report telling how he had tied the movement for libraries in with the American Revolution in a speech celebrating the Battle of Moore's Creek Bridge:

> In Elizabethtown where people had come to celebrate the battle I had a chance standing there in the courthouse near the Tory hole to draw the line between the Whigs and Tories in our commonwealth today on such issues as the need of an eight month school term and a public library in every county. These issues of 1928 involve the issue of freedom and equality of opportunity which were at stake in 1776. I tried there to identify the cause of the American Revolution as continuing in these present day issues; and of course tried to show the responsibility of the Daughters of the American Revolution in fighting on the same side as the fathers of the American Revolution. . . . Of course you know there are those who would like to use the Daughters of the American Revolution on the Tory side and would try to black-list the Thomas Jeffersons, the Patrick Henrys, the Sam Adams and the Willie Jones of each age. I suggested this as something to be on guard against to vouchsafe the fact that the Daughters of the American Revolution should not become the Daughters of the American Reaction. . . . It is my nature while drawing the line clearly on great human issues, not to attack so much but to build on what is hopeful in any organization.[9]

A director for the campaign was elected in November, but the movement was inactive for a time when the new director, waiting to be instructed what to do, did not develop a program. Graham was disappointed; but despite requests that came to him, he refused to reassume leadership: "However impatient I may get sometimes or wish to recur to my aggressive position and activities of the formative period, I am intent on being a private in the ranks and a follower of our state leaders."[10] He continued to challenge individuals to take responsibility, insisting that "every public library in this state has resulted from the fact that one or two people have taken the lead in working for the establishment of a local public library. The most vital public institutions have come that way."[11]

The governor of the state, O. Max Gardner, was secured by Graham to champion the Citizen's Movement. Hundreds of persons were at work; but no one was more rhapsodic than Graham as to the nobility of the cause:

No American pioneer who ever stood with axe and rifle along the fringe of the unconquered wilderness ever faced an adventure more thrilling than that which calls to us today as we stand with books, ideas, and inquiring minds along the frontier of the vast possibilities of our yet unmastered civilization.[12]

In 1929 the Library Commission announced the organization of thirty-five school libraries and the establishment of one local library, with five new community libraries following in 1930.

The crusade for libraries throughout the state occurred at the same time that, as president of the North Carolina Conference for Social Service, Graham fought battles for human welfare, helped develop a strategy for a workmen's compensation law, and worked for the improvement of industrial conditions in North Carolina.[13]

In the North Carolina Conference for Social Service he had found an organization perfectly suited for the implementation of his own convictions. From its formal organization in 1913, the Conference had been concerned with "human life and the conditions that affect human life in North Carolina." Interested in social legislation, the Conference from 1916 through 1921 had been concerned primarily with public welfare, from 1922 through 1926 with justice and prison reform, and toward the middle of the decade the emphasis had shifted to industrial problems. Thus, at the very time Graham became a member of the Conference, its interest was identical with his predominant concern.[14] Graham was elected to the board of directors of the Conference in 1927. The following year he was elected president; and in 1929, in a move unprecedented since 1914, he was reelected.[15]

Early in 1927 Graham had made an address on "The Old South and the New Industrialism" to the annual meeting of the Conference in Raleigh. Following a historical analysis, he outlined the "hopefully human sounds and signs that send us forward," including advances in public welfare, race relations, roads, colleges, mental institutions, freedom of inquiry, and business methods. Then he turned to the barriers that block progress: economic pressures, the misunderstanding of others through stereotypes, and the mood of reaction throughout the world. Nothing, however, should block the building of a good society. "The chief business of a state is the welfare of the people. The chief business of a people is the equal opportunity of their children. . . . It is through the new industrialism that North Carolina has the opportunity to win the new humanism."[16]

In 1928 the Conference passed a resolution advocating a state institution for delinquent Negro girls. The problems of race had never been a dominant interest of the Conference, though since its founding there had been a concern for the welfare of the Negro, and in 1925 the Conference had passed a resolution for fairness to minority groups, particularly Indians and Negroes. When Robert Hanes, a leading banker in the legislature, castigated the 1928 resolution, Graham responded, "Of course the Negroes have no lobby in Raleigh to make their case, but the case is real in the facts of life and social responsibility."[17]

The North Carolina Conference had for years advocated a workmen's compensation bill. By 1928 forty-three states in the nation had workmen's compensation laws, and all but three of those laws had been passed between 1911 and 1919. In North Carolina, too, there had been concern for the worker disabled in industrial accidents, and in the preceding eight sessions of the legislature, sixteen bills concerning compensation had been presented. None had passed. Many other groups and individuals favored a bill, but they had not worked consistently or cooperatively: the state Democratic platform had since 1913 advocated such a law; the commissioners of insurance and labor began in 1914 to recommend a law in regular reports; and the Federation of Labor began going on record in 1915 as favoring a law. Opposition in the legislature always easily overcame the well-meaning, ineffective proposals for action. There was the need for some agency that could stimulate cooperation among the advocates of workmen's compensation in writing a specific bill. Graham viewed this as the work of the Industry Committee of the Conference, to which he appointed leading industrialists, the president of the state Federation of Labor, professors of economics, and women leaders.[18]

Graham joined the Industry Committee in meetings to study and discuss the details of compensation laws; Harry Wolf, professor of labor economics at the University, was appointed to draft a bill to recommend to the legislature. Graham met many nights in personal conference with Wolf, going over the bill word by word. The bill was then reworked by the committee and proposed to the state legislature. It was substantially like other bills concurrently recommended by representatives of the manufacturers and of labor. With effective support given by Governor Gardner, the most liberal compensation law in the South was enacted.[19]

When he was reelected president in 1929, Graham continued the direction of committee studies, organized college students as a branch of the conference, and developed cooperation with women's clubs. But in the spring, industrial strife exploded into violence in North Carolina, and the driving wedge of his interest turned toward a more solitary crusade in which he felt he had no right to involve the Conference.

6

Industrial Revolution and a New Bill of Rights

*In the face of the marvelous rise on our virgin
soil of the new industrialism, we have been com-
placent and even blind to the human implications
of the consequent rearrangement of our economic
and social structure. Our spiritual adjustments
have lagged far behind the mechanical advance.
We have handicraft ideas in an industrial age.*[1]
—FRANK PORTER GRAHAM (1929)

FOR ALMOST FOUR YEARS FOLLOWING HIS RETURN
to Chapel Hill, Graham had worked quietly, focusing on North
Carolina's transition to an industrial economy. His procedure was
invariably to enlist the cooperation of others and to stimulate them
to act on their own while he remained in the background. He became widely known and respected among liberals in the state, but
he was not a public figure; the causes were not sufficiently controversial, the activities were not sufficiently known.

Events in the spring of 1929 changed all that. There occurred
crises too significant, too emotion-laden, for him to remain in the
background. He was carried into the center of the controversy and
became a focal point for attacks. It began with the depression in
the Southern textile industry that preceded the stock market crash
of October, 1929.

North Carolina, in 1929, was still an agricultural, rural state. It
was, in fact, second in the nation in the number of farms and in
farm population. But this merely served to highlight the state's
urban, industrial transformations. The population had increased
far more rapidly during the 1920's than it had in the nation as a
whole, and the sharpest increases were in the industrial areas of

the piedmont and mountain regions. The trend was unmistakable: North Carolina was moving toward a predominantly industrial society with one-third of its citizens living in urban areas, one-third on farms, and one-third in rural areas but not on farms. From 1919 until 1927, the number of wage earners had increased almost thirty percent, and in the crucial years between 1926 and 1929, sixty percent of all the industrial workers were in textile manufacturing.

In the decade of the twenties there was an annual increase in the number of spindles in Southern mills that paralleled a decrease each year after 1923 of the number of spindles in the North. Half of this Southern growth was accounted for by natural expansion within the region; half by the flight of New England mills to the South.[2] The industry moved south for obvious economic reasons, particularly because of the labor supply, which was, in the words of advertisements in the *Southern Textile Bulletin*, "all American, native white . . . contented . . . English language . . . plentiful . . . cheap . . . faithful and efficient . . . free from outside influences and consequent labor unrest."[3] The average income of the textile worker for 1923 was $644 in North Carolina and $1,025 in Massachusetts. In the North Carolina mills in 1920, nearly seven percent of the workers were fourteen and fifteen years of age; and more than thirty-five percent of the workers were nineteen and under, with several hundred of these ten to thirteen years of age. The normal hours of work were from six to six, five days a week, with an hour for lunch, and six to eleven on Saturday. Families, averaging five persons according to one study, were usually crowded in four-room houses that were clustered on the periphery of a town or strung along a railroad track.

Simple developments during this period had a great effect upon the daily life of the worker. There was a large increase in absentee ownership; thus the personal relations and loyalties that had previously existed between the mill owner and worker began to disappear, with a serious loss of morale on the part of the worker. Even in those industries owned locally, there was the development of "more professional management," which was a euphemism for "the stretch-out," by which a mill worker had to tend a larger number of machines.[4]

These developments were fact and symbol of the new industrialism in North Carolina. Graham saw these events primarily in human terms, and the fact that he was a personal friend of a number of industrialists did not deter him from a felt duty. In February, 1929, he had written letters to state commissioners of labor in nine states, to labor unions, and to agencies of the federal government. He requested information on industrial conditions, arguments pro and con regarding wage-and-hour legislation, child labor, and night work for women in order to build a case for essential reforms of working conditions in North Carolina.[5] He had written, also, his first letter on the subject for the public press:

> In the face of the marvelous rise on our virgin soil of the new industrialism, we have been complacent and even blind to the human implications of the consequent rearrangement of our economic and social structure.... Social justice is yet to be more advanced through the wisdom of enlightened manufacturers, the cooperation of organized labor, and a sensitive public opinion, all behind acts of the commonwealth which shall end the sixty-hour week, the twelve-hour day, night work for women and the fourth grade clause of the child labor law.[6]

Others were making their studies and writing letters, also. The previous year, as an aftermath of a New England textile strike, Communists had organized the National Textile Workers Union and in the organizational meeting had made plans to invade the South. With neat Communist dialectic, the conclusion was reached that "North Carolina is the key to the South, Gaston County is the key to North Carolina, and the Loray Mill is the key to Gaston County." This conclusion was based not only on the wishful thinking of Communist theory and a general knowledge of economic developments in the South. It was founded also upon a knowledge of Gaston County and particular information about the Loray Mill.[7]

In 1929 Gaston County had ninety-nine mills, one-fifth of the textile industry of North Carolina, and was called "the combed yarn center of America." There were only two other counties in the United States with a heavier concentration of cotton manufacturing. Built in 1900, the Loray Mill was one of the largest mills in the country. In 1919 it was sold to a Rhode Island corporation that had seven additional mills in New England and one other in the South. That year a new superintendent was appointed at Loray and was given incentive to decrease costs. The stretch-out began, perhaps for the first time in the South, and within fifteen months the new superintendent had decreased the work force from 3,500 to 2,200 without decreasing production. (During the firings a group of workers paraded down Gastonia's main street carrying a coffin containing a man dressed as the superintendent. The man in the coffin arose at intervals to ask, "How many men are carrying this thing?" "Eight," shouted the paraders. "Lay off two," directed the superintendent. "Six can do the work.") The squeeze was on, for at the very time he was asked to produce more, the individual worker was paid less, some wages moving down from an average of twenty dollars to ten or fifteen per week. The increased work loads and pay cuts hurt, and hurt severely, the individual workers and their families; but more grievous still was the corrosion of morale.[8]

In mid-March, 1929, a Communist, Fred Beal, went to Gastonia and secretly began organizing a union. Careful to avoid emphasis on the Communist affiliation of his union, he was so successful that on March 30 he called a public meeting that was attended by over a thousand people. Two days later, almost all the workers went on strike with demands upon the management that included a minimum weekly wage of twenty dollars, a forty-hour week, abolition of the stretch-out, equal pay for equal work by women and youth, improved sanitary and housing conditions, and recognition of the union. The management of the mill, other mill owners in the community, and civic leaders were dumbfounded. When they learned that the strike was led by Communists, the amazement turned to anger, and the anger soon became a frenzied attack upon the Communists. Beal, from the first, announced that the Loray strike would be followed immediately by a general strike in the county, which in turn would lead to the unionization of all Southern textile workers. Representatives of Communist organizations poured into Gastonia, bringing with them copies of the *Daily Worker* and, what was worse, Northern, even foreign, accents. Delegations of scrawny textile workers, gaunt women, and sickly children were taken to Northern cities to be exhibited as examples of bourgeois capitalism. After a minor struggle between pickets and sheriff's deputies, Governor Gardner was asked by local authorities for assistance. But when National Guardsmen were sent to Gastonia, Gardner was denounced as a "slave-driving capitalist." Within three days the company began to recruit workers from other communities. Strikers drifted back to work, and by April 15 it was clear to all but the Communist leadership that the strike had failed.

The fear, the frenzy, the bitterness, were not allayed on either side. The city council passed an ordinance forbidding street demonstrations; the Communists and remaining strikers reacted with a parade. A mob destroyed the strikers' headquarters, and the mill management ejected the strikers and their families from the company houses. Immediately a tent colony of about fifty families was set up on the edge of town, and an armed guard of strikers patrolled the colony at night. On the night of June 1 the police reportedly received a call indicating trouble at the colony and upon arriving were met by the camp's guard. What followed was chaotic and never became clear, but within moments five persons, including the Chief of Police, were shot. Although it was not known how seriously any were wounded, a mob estimated at two thousand met at the courthouse, and raids were made on the tent colony. Seventy terrified strikers were arrested. The following day Chief Aderholt died, and the local newspaper, claiming that the murder had been planned by the Communists and that other honest persons (including the newspaper editor) were on the blacklist to be killed, set the tone for the community in an editorial, "Their Blood Cries Out":

> The blood of these men cries out to high heaven for vengeance. The community has been too lenient with these despicable curs and snakes from the dives of Passaic, Hoboken, and New York. For weeks and weeks we have put up with insult and injury; we have tolerated their insults and abuses.... And now they have made good their threats of violence.... The blood of these officers shot down in the dark from behind cries aloud. This display of gang law must not go unavenged.[9]

Fifteen strikers, including Beal, were indicted for murder. Public sentiment and legal talent were overwhelmingly against them. The leading lawyer of Southwest North Carolina, Clyde R. Hoey, brother-in-law of the Governor and later governor himself, was retained by the City of Gastonia, as were many of the best-known Charlotte and Gastonia attorneys, to assist the prosecution. The pressures were so great against the strikers that liberal North Carolina newspapers and national journals felt the need to insist upon the rights of the accused to a fair trial. Perhaps the most notable of those who did so was the columnist for the Raleigh *News and Observer*, Nell Battle Lewis, who also sponsored a legal defense fund for the defendants. Graham joined in trying to secure North Carolina lawyers to defend the accused, but the Communist leadership in the North insisted that their own New York lawyers take the case.[10]

The trial was scheduled to begin July 29; and the day before, Frank Graham sent Miss Lewis a telegram for publication in her column:

> Many who deprecate most any killing of a human being will join you in your effort to arouse public opinion in behalf of a fair trial for those accused. Whatever the crime charged and however overwhelming be the opinion against them, they should have in our state their day in court. It is due the commonwealth that their case be fairly and competently presented. We owe it to the most despised of those accused in this case that they be tried by due process of law without regard to their economic or religious views.[11]

After two days of testimony regarding the possibility of a fair trial in Gastonia, the judge rescheduled the trial for August 26 in Charlotte, twenty miles away. On September 7 the prosecuting attorney introduced into the trial a life-sized dummy wearing the clothes and bearing the wounds of the Chief of Police. The Chief's family wept; the courtroom audience gasped; and a juror previously suspected of mental disorder became hysterical. The judge ordered the wax model removed and declared a mistrial.

The mistrial was a sign for citizens of Gastonia to act again. That night a large caravan of men drove through the city and county triumphantly singing, "Praise God from whom all blessings flow." They wrecked the union headquarters and captured three organizers, carrying them into an adjoining county, where they beat and abandoned them. The Communists, desperately trying to rebuild morale, called a mass meeting on the following Saturday, September 14, to listen to the singing of Ella Mae Wiggins and to chart strategy. On the way to the meeting Saturday afternoon a truckload of workers was forced off the highway by a car occupied by private citizens. Shots were fired at the truck; the workers fled across a field; and as she ran, Mrs. Wiggins, twenty-nine years old and the mother of five, was shot in the back. The state now had two murder trials on its hands.[12]

Graham had hoped that, in the trial of the strikers who had allegedly killed Chief Aderholt, economic and religious views would be insignificant. They were, in fact, together with racial views and implied sexual irregularities, the main weapons of the prosecution. At no time was it made clear who had shot Chief Aderholt. A rumor circulated among the mill workers that he was shot by a policeman who coveted his job, and after the trial responsible Gastonia citizens admitted that in the confusion of the melee, he might have been shot accidentally by one of the deputies. After three weeks of testimony, argument, and summation, the jury was sent out, and it returned within an hour with the verdict: "Guilty." A sentence of from five to seven years was given to one defendant, sentences of from twelve to fifteen years to two others, sentences of from seventeen to twenty years to the remainder, including Beal.

Justice following the murder of Ella Mae Wiggins took a different course. Though she had been killed in daylight in the presence of more than fifty witnesses, a Gaston County grand jury failed to indict; and the Governor assigned a special judge and prosecutor to reopen the case. Indictments were brought against five anti-union employees of the Loray Mill; the company furnished bail; the trial was moved to Charlotte; and on March 6, 1930, the defendants were acquitted. A North Carolina newspaperman summarized the trials: "In every case where strikers were put on trial strikers were convicted; in not one case where anti-unionist or officers were accused has there been a conviction." [13]

Graham felt that there were fundamental, lasting issues at stake that should not be obscured by the drama of the trials. Entirely on his own initiative in the late fall of 1929, he drafted "An Industrial Bill of Rights," which he hoped many leading citizens would sign.[14] In the heat of the battle, at the height of feeling, he tried to marshal the forces of reason and good will. Copies of the document were delivered or mailed at his expense with a request that the recipient allow his name to be published with the statement.

The Bill of Rights enunciated four principles Graham considered essential if out of the economic change and industrial conflict there was to emerge "that freedom of personality and equality of opportunity for which this commonwealth was founded." The principles were these: (1) The constitutional rights of person and property, especially the right to freedom of speech and assembly, should be granted all persons. (2) The right of labor to organize and bargain collectively should be assured along with the right of investors of capital to organize. (3) Because of the sickness of the textile industry, there should be a national economic and social study of the industry. (4) There should be a reduction of the sixty-hour workweek, the abolition of night work for women and young people, and the improvement of child labor legislation, with provision for enforcement of these needed social adjustments.

The response to the Bill of Rights was instantaneous. There were many who signed because they agreed with the principles, others because they respected Frank Graham. (A Charlotte physician wrote, "I have been hesitant to sign. However, knowing you as I do, and trusting your judgment, I am going to authorize my signature to the statement.")[15] The pained cries of those bitterly opposed to the statement were shrill, and the objections of those who doubted the wisdom of its publication were muted. "I am hoping," wrote one industrialist, "that you will not in your zeal for a cause which you believe to be true, issue your Manifesto and array one good citizen against another."[16] David Clark, editor of the *Southern Textile Bulletin,* a leading trade publication,[17] began to attack Graham. In November a friend reported to Graham that Clark had agreed to retract an error published in his journal, stating that "Dean Graham" had attended a labor conference, and the friend received in reply a candid note: "I haven't been worried by Mr. Clark's attacks. In fact, as you know, I might have attended the meeting if I had considered it a valuable thing to do."[18] Two months later Clark's attack was renewed when he sent industrialists a copy of the Bill of Rights with an accompanying letter, concluding with a charge against the University:

> Mr. Graham has had no experience either in business or industry, but seems to consider himself as an authority upon all industrial questions. . . . We have no knowledge of the industrial struggle to which he refers. . . . We know of no case in which lawful freedom of speech or assembly has been denied anyone. . . . Everyone is proud of the University of North Carolina, and its able faculty, but it is well known that within that faculty is a small group of radicals who are in an insidious manner, eternally fighting that which they frantically call "capitalism."[19]

Graham was not greatly troubled by the attack. It was open, clear-cut, and extreme. Nor was it difficult to understand the position of those like Clyde Hoey, who agreed that the statement might "readily be subscribed to by practically all of the thinking people in the state" but who refrained from signing because he questioned whether, in view of the Communist involvement, it was wise to publish it.[20] Nor was Graham greatly troubled by letters from stockholders and manufacturers, such as the appeal from the president of one of the largest mills in the state, who felt that in a quiet conversation he could convince Graham "that the manufacturers of North Carolina have the interests of their working people more closely at heart than anybody else in the world."[21]

But it was difficult to read letters from friends who felt that the total economic situation was as serious as Graham thought but who were frankly perplexed about the next steps to be taken. Such a friend was Tyre Taylor, administrative assistant to the Governor, who wrote in confidence for himself and perhaps for the Governor, on February 6, 1930, "I very much fear that we are up against the most serious situation we have had to face in North Carolina since Reconstruction. . . . The economic situation among almost every class is nothing short of desperate." All of this, he admitted, had nothing to do with the question of issuing statements about the rights of labor, but the textile manufacturers felt so near bankruptcy that they were in no mood to reason and would view a statement as an attack. "Human nature must be dealt with wherever you touch this situation and if one is interested in results, rather than in just *taking a stand*, this factor must be taken into account."[22]

Graham was relieved to learn from Taylor's letter that the Governor, despite the desperate economic situation, was going to recommend to the General Assembly a fifty-five-hour week and abolition of night work for women and for those under eighteen. But grave doubts about publication of the statement arose when he read Taylor's comments that reflected the Governor's despair:

> It may be all right to go ahead along the lines you have projected. On the other hand, with conditions as they are, it might be best to follow Governor Gardner's leadership and methods and do what can be done with the cooperation and good will of the owners. . . . I have never met with as much despondency on all sides as now. Of course we shall lower our standards of living and come out on top, but it sometimes looks as if North Carolina may yet have to content itself with another fifty years of mediocrity in everything.[23]

Graham had to reject the doubts about the wisdom of publishing the statement: four hundred persons had signed with the understanding that it would be made public, and Graham could not betray them. Nor was this all. To stop now would be to admit that the statement was radical and irresponsible, when Graham knew, in the words of one of the signers, that "the statement doesn't go beyond the Sermon on the Mount or the Bill of Rights." With the conviction that men would always listen to and could be persuaded by reason, he interpreted the statement in personal letters and in public print. Everything was so perfectly simple and clear. Article One was essentially the American Bill of Rights; Article Two was a statement of equal rights of capitalists and labor; Article Three was intended to bring the help of reason to a whole industry; Article Four was a statement of the most obvious adjustments that were needed. And these several articles were all supported by the Republicans, the Democrats, the Baptists, chambers of commerce, several presidents of the United States, and "industrial, civic, and religious leaders all over the civilized world." And so the letters reasoning with opponents of the statement would conclude: "I feel sure that if you think these propositions over that on second thought you will sign this statement as a matter of fairness and long run common-sense. . . . However, if we continue to differ, let me say for my part that I have the greatest respect for your attitude."[24]

By the time the statement was published in February, 1930, it had the signatures of more than four hundred people, especially lawyers, college professors, newspaper editors, and many women. Graham was relieved, commenting to a friend, "I am glad that this is off my mind. I will be, and have been subject to criticism by both extremes . . . . In my opinion the statement is the essence of our simple Americanism. It is historically based, and, I believe, will be historically vindicated."[25]

Graham's response to the events at Gastonia continued to be voiced after the Bill of Rights was published. When the annual meeting of the Conference for Social Service was scheduled for mid-April in Charlotte, a city still shaken by the two murder trials involving strikers and police, Graham, as president of the Conference, shaped the program. He enlisted the support of ministers, requesting them in advance of the sessions to preach on "The Social Message of Jesus" or "Christian Social Principles."[26] "We are mainly concerned," he urged the clergy, "that [ministers] give a spiritual and human emphasis to the economic transition now in process in the Piedmont South."[27] A week after the five vigilante defendants had been acquitted of the murder of Ella Mae Wiggins, he wrote the secretary of the Charlotte Chamber of Commerce that

there are those, of course, who try to stir up the prejudices and fan the fires of fanaticism, whether they be the Communists with their fallacies and hatred, or whether it be the diehard reactionaries who try to stick their heads in the sand and be blind both to the real teachings of Jesus and the history of the last one hundred years.[28]

In his presidential address to the society delivered April 14, he ignored the advice of those who recommended turning toward other less controversial problems, the sharp emphasis of his thesis being that "the industrial revolution has come to North Carolina. No citizen in this commonwealth is outside the range and consequence of this revolution. Its responsibilities are a part of our citizenship. We are not the people to shut our eyes to the lessons of the written records of industrial history and blindly repeat the economic wastes and human tragedies of a hundred years." The lessons of history, he felt, not only provide guidance in making the necessary adjustments "to the resistless sweep of the industrialization of a rural state," but more particularly teach the spirit in which democratic man must live in a revolutionary age:

> The fear of no economic theory, however fallacious, and of no social philosophy, however hateful, can, I believe, terrorize us into the overthrow of the Anglo-Saxon tradition and the American principle of lawful freedom of speech and assembly which our revolutionary fathers, over a century and a half ago, wrote into the American Bill of Rights. . . . The test of the Bill of Rights is its application to those whose ideas we despise most.
> Americanism, grown on this soil is not a frail plant that must be falsely protected with terrorism by those without faith in the depth of its rootage or the robustness of its timber. Its roots are deep in the teachings of our religion, in the traditions of our race and in the history of our country. Jesus does not teach us to destroy the headquarters of those who agitate in an alien cause. He did not teach them to kill a Chief of Police, answering a call in the line of duty whose first words were those of friendliness. He did not teach us to shoot down on the public highway a woman who attempted to attend a meeting whose principles we oppose. He met fallacy with understanding and hate with his great love.[29]

7

"A Man of Power and Enthusiasm"

All our historic shibboleths about equality of opportunity are tested in their sincerity not on the Fourth of July but when we come to make the budget of the commonwealth. In that commonwealth are white people and black people, tenant farmers and industrial workers, children in the city and children in the country, children of the rich and children of the poor....[1]

—FRANK PORTER GRAHAM (1931)

THREE DAYS AFTER THE INDUSTRIAL BILL OF RIGHTS was published throughout the state, Graham was thrust into a new controversy. On February 20, 1930, the president of the University of North Carolina, Harry W. Chase, resigned, effective July 1, to become president of the University of Illinois. Many of Graham's friends longed for him to become president. It was a controversy all on their side; he refused to be considered for the position. There could be no possible doubt about his determination and desire to remain in the classroom.

The news article that announced Chase's resignation also mentioned persons already discussed as possible successors, among them a number of educational leaders from other universities and three professors in Chapel Hill: R. D. W. Connor, professor in the Department of History; Archibald Henderson, well-known mathematician and biographer of George Bernard Shaw; and Frank Graham. Connor, who had been prevented by a technicality from being elected in 1919, was the leading candidate.[2]

Graham's friends began besieging him immediately. On February 24 William de B. MacNider, research professor in medicine, sought Graham out simply to indicate his support. Shocked by Graham's response that he didn't want the job, MacNider began to cajole, then to argue. He talked about the opportunities for Graham; recognizing that as the wrong approach, he then discussed the needs of the University for a strong leader. Graham listened without argument, repeating over and over again that he didn't want the job. He wanted to teach and he wanted the freedom that goes with teaching.

"All this is beside the point," he added. "The job would never be offered me because of my recent battles. But even if it were, I wouldn't accept."

That was too much for the forthright MacNider. "Dammit, Frank, the University is going downhill fast, the budget has been cut to the bone, and you stand there and tell me you won't help. I don't care what you say, I'm going to raise hell and fight for you to be president."

The threat was a rude blow to Graham. "We've been friends for a long time," he said firmly, "and as a friend I ask you to promise me that you will respect my wishes and won't do anything."

"Frank, you're impossible."

MacNider left in disgust, which during a sleepless night changed into a mixture of remorse, anger, and determination. The next day he wrote a short note:

DEAR DOCK:

I fear you may have thought I talked kinder rough to you yesterday— It was all from my heart through my head. When I feel about a thing as keenly as I do your becoming President I have to talk as I feel. I can't temper it and pussyfoot it. I feel you should do nothing to bind us and make us smart. The least you can do is to give our souls freedom.

Devotedly,
Bill[3]

Three days later Louis Graves, who had married Mildred Moses, to whom Graham had proposed, wrote a lengthy editorial, "The Qualifications of Frank Graham," in the *Chapel Hill Weekly*, concluding that "the trustees should consider themselves fortunate in having the opportunity to choose such a man as President of the University." Graves pointed out: "It is known to all of his friends that Mr. Graham has no ambition to ascend to the presidency. In my quarter of the century I have been acquainted with many men prominent in the public eye, and I have never known another so indifferent to his personal interests or advancement."[4]

The pressure from friends across the state did not cease. At first, Graham replied to each supporter, expressing appreciation for his kindness and adding, "It has been hard for me to run counter to the wishes of my warm friends, but feeling as I do, that my work is as a teacher and as a simple citizen of the state, I eliminated my name decisively so that there would be no complication of the situation."[5]

It was difficult enough to go against the wishes of his friends; but when he received an entreaty from his mother, the conflict between his desires and those of others was almost too great to endure:

> DEAR FRANK,
>
> It would give me and your father a great deal of pleasure if you would allow yourself to be considered as a successor to Dr. Chase. You have spent so much time on your education, and have worked so hard for the university, you deserve it. It would give your father [joy] for this to happen in his lifetime. The University needs you. I was terribly disappointed that you withdrew your name. Anybody has a right to change his mind and I hope you will change your mind. If after allowing yourself to be considered you do not get it, I will feel that you have done your part. I will not worry then about it anymore.
>
> Much love,
> Mother[6]

He was firm in the refusal to be considered. Late in the spring a news report stated, "Since the withdrawal of Frank Graham no other faculty member but Mr. Connor appears to be seriously considered."[7]

In March Graham's physician in Charlotte, Otho Ross, invited a select group to dinner at the country club, and together they decided that the University needed Graham. A short time later Ross met Frank at the Graham family home, and he sat in the breakfast room past midnight trying to persuade Graham to allow his candidacy to be supported. No argument could shake him, neither the presidency as a position of service, the good of the University, the need of the state, nor the honor. Finally, in desperation, Dr. Ross said, "Your two sisters are having a hard time paying off the mortgage on this house on their teachers' salaries. Your increase in salary could help them pay off that debt."

Graham arose and abruptly ended the conversation. "The presidency of the University is not to be talked of in terms of dollars."[8]

When friends in Charlotte continued to act on his behalf Graham demanded that they stop. Almost all his friends agreed that their hands were tied, and one wrote, "I suppose we will have to give you up as hopeless . . . you have opposed your own candidacy at every turn, and it looks like your goose is cooked. . . . You have gone out of your way to block your chances of being elected."[9] Charles W. Tillett, Jr., confidentially reported to Kemp Battle that Graham had no chance of being elected.[10]

Ross and others refused to quit; and late in May, Tillett prepared a two-page mimeographed statement describing Graham's qualifications, arguing that a democracy must use the leaders it has trained.[11] The statement was sent privately to the members of the Board of Trustees. When Graham learned that his friends were developing a delegation to present his name to a committee of trustees, he was furious. On June 3 and 4, less than a week before the new president was scheduled to be elected, he sent identical telegrams to all those involved in the plot:

> See in paper a delegation going before trustees committee to present my name. Please use your influences to stop this. Definitely and conclusively withdrew my name in statement to governor in letter to chairman of trustees committee and in response to alumni trustees and friends and stand on that statement of withdrawal a decision I made when subject was broached to me on two occasions in other years. I can best do my work for the University and the state as a teacher and citizen. Sincerely hope all will unite on Connor who is remarkably equipped to be a strong and progressive leader.[12]

To ensure that he would not be elected, Graham decided to find a board member who would withdraw his name in case it should be presented. Kemp Battle at first refused, but when Frank was adamant, Battle reluctantly agreed. "Well, Frank, since you insist, if your name is presented I will rise and say, 'Mr. Graham has requested that I withdraw his name from nomination.' "[13]

It was not necessary. When the trustees met in Chapel Hill on June 9, a committee reported on a number of qualified persons, and probably because the trustees knew of Battle's promise, formal nominations were omitted. Forty-two votes were required for election. On the first ballot Connor received twenty-six votes, Graham twenty, Henderson ten, and the remaining twenty-seven were scattered among a dozen people. On the fourth ballot Graham received forty-seven, and the election was made unanimous.[14]

A delegation was sent for the president-elect. He was not at home, and it was a half-hour before he was found, walking toward town, oblivious of what had happened. When told of the election, he turned ashen, and he said nothing as they drove back to Alumni Hall. The trustees had gathered outside under the trees; Graham went to the group surrounding the Governor, begged for another ballot with his name withdrawn as he had requested. Governor Gardner, Editor Josephus Daniels, Judge John J. Parker, all towering above Graham, argued with him. Finally, Gardner reported that there were rough financial times ahead, that serious cuts in the University budget were inevitable. In such financial straits, they told him, it would be impossible to secure a qualified outsider, and his refusal to accept the position would reflect upon the University. Just then a friend approached and thumped him vigorously, rhythmically on the arm, shouting, "Be a Marine! Be a Marine!"

More than an hour after the election, the trustees pressed back into the hall, carrying the resisting Graham with them. Graham could not be heard in the rear of the room as he mumbled, "I hardly know what to say. I trust you will believe me when I say I want to remain a teacher. I want Mr. Connor to be president. Isn't there anything that can be done now to make him president and leave me free to go back to the classroom?"

"I don't know of any process by which that can be done," Governor Gardner told him.

"Well, with your help and with the help of God," he began, and slumped into a seat on the front row.

As the trustees filed out, one said to a friend, "That's the sorriest acceptance speech I ever heard."

Later that day, according to the *Chapel Hill Weekly*, Tommy Wright, three years old, went to Graham and said, "My mother says I must stop calling you Frank. What's the matter?"

The following morning Josephus Daniels, originally a Connor supporter, commented editorially in the Raleigh *News and Observer*: "Never before in the State's history has there been a parallel to what happened in Chapel Hill yesterday in the election of Frank Graham as president of the university. It was the commandeering of a loyal son who wished the selection of his friend and who in true humility sought to push aside the honor the trustees pressed upon him."[15]

Although Graham was energetically recruited for the presidency, there were those who were uncertain how capable he would be as chief budget officer of the University. Some worried that his social liberalism would antagonize conservative businessmen and politicians in the state and jeopardize University appropriations. His personal indifference to money and apparently haphazard handling of personal financial affairs caused further concern.

Graham's carelessness with his own money was well known to all his friends. If he was not reminded of money when he left home for work, it was likely that he would not have any. Whatever he made from month to month was never saved but spent; to almost any cause or person in need who made a request, whether through the mail or on the street, he made a contribution. On a number of occasions he signed notes for people associated with the University; and more than once, upon the default of the borrower, he had to pay the debt. He also borrowed to meet his own needs; and when he became president of the University, he owed several friends more than two thousand dollars, some of the loans dating back to his years in London.[16]

The uncertainty and doubt about his capability in managing the financial affairs of the University were soon answered. From the day he took office, money was a central, pervading problem.

The financial crash in the banking houses on Wall Street in October, 1929, had been felt in the administration building of every college and university; but nowhere was the Depression felt more acutely than in South Building and in the dormitories, classrooms, and homes of the faculty at the University of North Carolina. The University had begun only in the twenties to receive appropriations adequate to sustain quality education; but even at its highest appropriation of $894,000 in 1928–29, the expenditure of the University was considerably lower than that of any other of the twenty-nine members of the Association of American Universities. Then the cuts had begun: twenty-five percent in 1929–30; twenty percent the following year.[17]

Within days after Graham was elected president, he was carrying the battle for money to the people of the state. He spent the summer speaking at service clubs, churches, farm associations, patriotic organizations—wherever he could find as much as a Coca-Cola crate to stand on. Again and again he repeated his theme: depressions are temporary; schools and colleges are the permanent sources of economic, social, and spiritual well-being.

We have too much at stake economically to turn backwards. Our currents of democratic faith in the value of every human personality and the equal opportunity for all the children of the people run too deep and strong for us not to go forward in our program of education in a democracy. If we turn back in public education we turn back all along the line.[18]

He was never content to speak only about the University at Chapel Hill. Presidents of other state institutions, including the Negro colleges, which suffered more from the Depression than the white schools, as well as superintendents and principals in the public school system, turned to Graham's leadership with gratitude. Nor did he stop with education, since he believed that the state was meant to serve the welfare and protect the rights of all the people. He was speaking for the whole society when he said, "Budget-making in a depression tests what we really believe in." He might have been speaking for individuals as well. He did speak for his own personal finances; he seldom received any honorarium, frequently not even his expenses, as he drove himself day and night, becoming the person in North Carolina most in demand as a speaker.[19]

Budget battles, however, are not won by speaking to the people at the crossroads and in the towns. The issues of appropriations for North Carolina institutions are fought out first in the Budget Commission, then in the legislative committees, and finally on the floor of the legislature. Failure at any point could be near fatal. The 1931 legislative fight was crucial for Graham not only because, being his first, it would test his ability in dealing with tough-minded legislators, but also because the financial chasm made questionable the prospects for the University, even its survival. Tyre Taylor wrote confidentially from the governor's office on January 3, "It is going to require the last ounce of every energy and influence that the friends of the University can command to save it at this time. I should regard a material cut below this year's operating budget as virtually destructive of the institution's usefulness, at least for many years."[20]

The budget requests had been carefully prepared the previous fall and early winter; the University asked the Budget Commission for $875,000 for 1931–32. The Commission recommended to the Joint Appropriations Committee $573,000, more than $100,000 below the previous year's appropriation. This represented an-

other cut of more than fifteen percent. The battle was joined with
fear for the very life of the University.

Graham was scheduled to appear before the Joint Committee on
January 29. On January 26 he was hit by a respiratory illness that
had been recurring regularly in recent years. His doctor ordered
him to bed. Though running a fever, he insisted on attending the
hearing and left his sickbed to be driven to the capital, thirty miles
away. He requested "a drink" for a stimulant. It was an unheard-of
request, and the effect was such that the comptroller, Charles Woollen, later quipped, "Frank Graham took one cup of coffee and kept
the legislature in session for six months."[21]

At his first hearing he set the pattern for all his presentations to
the Joint Committee. In form, his statement began with specific
facts and figures: figures dealing with past expenditures, the budget
requests, and bureau recommendations; facts interpreting the specific needs and describing the meaning of the budget; and com-
parisons of the budget with those of other universities. Throughout
there were appeals to democratic ideals and the meaning of education, and the statement concluded with an appeal to the deeper
meaning of the budget: "Surely we do not propose to beat down the
University of the people. It would be an impairment of great educational investments and democratic values in State building, without
a parallel in the history of higher education on this continent."

In style, there was a directness in his presentation that contrasted
sharply with the rambling quality of his extemporaneous addresses. No attempt was made to humor or entertain the committee.
Standing (upon the advice of Josephus Daniels) and speaking
firmly, he commanded the attention of the legislators, even those
highly suspicious of his liberal leanings. He was asking the legislators that they do something for their state and, thus, for themselves. The committee responded by recommending $800,000. The
disastrous cut the Budget Commission had made was largely restored, momentarily the University was safe, and the stage was set
for the decisive battle on the floor of the legislature.[22]

Graham was aware that the full force of some powerful business
interests, conservative legislators, and certain members of the Budget Commission would be brought against the recommendation.
He could not participate directly in that debate and decision. The
most he could do was to lobby personally, buttonholing the representatives. He quickly became known as a masterful lobbyist. It was

a new job for him, and it required a change in some of his habits. "Frank Graham still goes about without a hat since he was elected president," the *Chapel Hill Weekly* reported in April, "but his trousers are better creased and his shoes are better polished than they used to be."[23]

On April 1 he learned, with shocked dismay, that a rebellious House committee had attacked the Joint Committee's recommendations. Hurriedly Graham made the call for the supporters of education to attend the committee hearings or, at the least, to write. "Every interest, it seems, has had a lobby in Raleigh except the youth of the state. The real call is not from me but it is from them to you."[24] The call was too late; that committee soon brought in a separate report for $721,000. The budget was being dismembered. The battle was renewed vigorously; and Graham conferred with and wrote to Senate and House leaders, including Speaker Willis Smith, tirelessly pressing essential points. "The University ranks 32nd among state universities in per capita cost to the State, and yet stands near the top of all American universities in standards, quality and spirit."[25] And again: "Restoration of the vigor of an institution is slow and costly. Because a child survived on two meals a day it is not a sound reason to put the child on less food."[26]

On May 28 the legislature passed the appropriations bill, in which the University budget was set at $721,000, but it refused to pass an amendment forbidding the Budget Commission to cut the appropriation later.[27]

The only consolation was that complete disaster had been averted. In relation to original requests and recommendations, the University fared better than did the other state colleges; and all the colleges and public schools fared better than seemed likely during most of the legislative session. But there was one more step for Graham to take. Worried that the Budget Commission would indeed slash the appropriation, he was in Raleigh on May 29 again asking for promises that the base of the funds was secure. A week later, at commencement, he was lionized for having saved public education and the University; and he told the alumni: "We have been assured on responsible authority that the University will actually get the $721,000 which the General Assembly appropriated and will not suffer the horizontal cuts of the past two years."[28]

The worst was yet to come. Less than a month later Graham was stunned by the announcement that monies available for the University had been cut $175,000, a slash of almost twenty-five percent from the appropriations and down forty percent from what it had been three years previously. He immediately requested an interview with the Governor, pleading for a reinstatement of the funds. Unsuccessful, he knocked on the Governor's door repeatedly, asking that at least some of the money be made available. Graham was physically drained but not about to give up. He wrote to Gerald Johnson:

> I am not going to give an inch, and I am not going to let up in the attack. . . . I am going to resist with everything I have got any surrender to the dominant business interests of North Carolina which have adopted the false policy of trying to pinch their way out of North Carolina's critical situation. We cannot pinch our way out. We have got to invest, build, and create our way out. I had another hopeful round with the Governor yesterday. I really sympathize with him in his hard situation, but I am not going to let up one minute on him or the situation.[29]

By the end of his first year as president, Graham was, in financial matters, a magnificent failure. Both at Chapel Hill and throughout the state he was lauded for having saved the University and, more than any other person, for having averted the financial disaster that threatened the schools and teachers. But he had not secured even what those knowledgeable in university affairs maintained was an absolutely minimum budget; and the bottom had not yet been reached. Howard Odum, writing from Chicago to the Governor, pointed out that the University was generally recognized as the chief example of high standards and progress in the state and the South, and he spoke fearfully that a drastic budget reduction would inevitably make the University a second-rate institution:

> I can't conceive of a public that clamored for Graham as president and a board that forced him into the position with promises of enthusiastic support, turning against him in the first critical moment and literally cutting from under him the foundation upon which he must build. That is, they have asked for a home man of power and enthusiasm, and the moment they have him they reduce his chances of success as they have never done with any other man. I just can't conceive of a state meting out this sort of reward.[30]

Though financially crippled, the University at Chapel Hill was able to maintain its strength. It was a sheer spiritual triumph that derived from the response of Frank Graham and other men at the University to the financial disaster. Within nine months after he was elected president, Graham counted more than twenty persons who had received offers from other universities, sometimes for as much as three times what they were making at Chapel Hill, but who had refused such offers because of their loyalty to the University.[31] If, as many expected, these men had allowed the University to go down with the Depression, the state and the South would have been deprived of their most liberalizing force.

Toward the end of the summer of 1931, the budget battle had apparently subsided, and Graham was able to spend two weeks of his vacation at Columbia University preparing for his inaugural address, belatedly scheduled for November 11. He spent his time "reading about experiments under way in the Liberal Arts College, and also reading what Francis Bacon, Goethe, Milton, John Stuart Mill, Matthew Arnold, and many others have had to say about liberal education."[32] For two weeks he was alone with books, and with his beliefs, his memories, and his dreams. Here he could look back to Chapel Hill and the University he loved, back to the state whose despair he shared, back to his past life, back to the past of his South and nation and civilization. And in looking backward he could look forward. What should he say? The obvious subject of the inaugural would be the financial crisis of the University and his insistent belief that if the state expected to have a university, the state would have to pay for it. But, obvious or not, he decided that money would not be mentioned.

The university and the world would be the subject; the university as both teacher and citizen would be the theme; and this subject would be developed by detailed interpretation of the functions of the university, its relation to society, and its use of freedom. The speech began to write itself. He later wrote a friend:

> After having read and jotted down ideas of my own that came in response to my reading, I pushed it all aside and then wrote down whatever there was in me which came from my own studies, thinking and experience during the last ten years. I wrote and rewrote for a week and had to stay up until after three o'clock one morning and four o'clock another morning in order to get what was in me [onto paper].[33]

The most important conviction that he had to get on paper had to do with freedom. For it was freedom that must undergird and permeate the total life of the university:

> Freedom of the university means the freedom of the scholar to report the truth honestly without interference by the university, the state, or any interests whatever. . . . Freedom of the university means the freedom to study not only the biological implications of the physical structure of the fish but also the human implications of the economic structure of society. It means freedom from the prejudices of section, race or creed; it means a free compassion of her sons for all people in need of justice and brotherhood. It means the freedom of the liberated spirit to understand sympathetically those who misunderstand freedom and would strike it down. It means the freedom for consideration of the plight of the unorganized and inarticulate peoples in an unorganized world in which powerful combinations and high pressure lobbies work their special will on the general life. In the university should be found the free voice not only for the unvoiced millions but also for the unpopular and even hated minorities. . . . No abuse of freedom should cause us to strike down freedom of speech or publication, the fresh resource of a free religion and a free state.[34]

The defense of freedom could not be clearer, Graham felt; but as he carefully wrote and rewrote his deepest beliefs about the university and freedom, he decided that something more should be quietly stated. "These conceptions of the various forms of freedom of the university are stated for the sake of fairness," he concluded. "The only recourse for changing such conceptions is to change the university administration. This is not said defiantly but in all friendliness and simply as a matter of openness and clearness."

He had finished the task he had set for himself. On September 10 he returned to Chapel Hill and, for almost two months, was immersed in the work of beginning another year. Working in South Building in rooms used by the presidents and faculty for more than a century, walking the gravel paths of the campus to his home, which had been the president's home since 1907, he was in the place he loved far more than any other in the world. The University and Chapel Hill were his home; he was aware that they were and had been the home for many others. So out of deep personal feeling, he added to the inaugural address a poetic, mystical, idealistic passage: "Out of the past come figures, living and dead, to stand by us in this inaugural hour in the woods where Davie, the founder, stood under the poplar and raised the standard of the people's hope. The lives of the presidents reassure us today in their spiritual presence and power"—and name by name he called the roll of the presidents, identifying the contribution of each to the University.[35]

But, he continued, the University of North Carolina does not exist alone in the state. All colleges, all universities, are in a cooperative endeavor: "Not in antagonism but in all friendliness and rivalry in excellence we would work in this region and build here together one of the great intellectual and spiritual centers of the world."[36]

The speech was delivered on November 11, 1931, the Armistice Day sacred to Graham and his five thousand listeners. The ceremonies took place in Kenan Stadium, a natural amphitheatre set in "a forest like Arden." There was something special about the place, something never to be forgotten, never to be lost:

> Here in Chapel Hill among a friendly folk, this old university stands on a hill set in the midst of beautiful forests under cathedral skies that give their color and their charm to the life of youth gathered here. Traditions grow here with ivy on the buildings and the moss on the ancient oaks. Friendships form here for the human pilgrimage. There is music in the air of the place. Above the traffic of the hour church spires reach toward the life of the spirit. Into this life with its ideals and failures, frustrations and hopes, comes youth, with his body, his mind and his spirit. Great teachers on this hill keep the fires burning, fires that burn for him and that light up the heavens of our commonwealth. Chapel Hill and the University, culture and the commonwealth, research and society, would muster here with great scholars, library and laboratories for the poorest youth the intellectual and spiritual resources of the race and make the University of North Carolina a stronghold of learning and an outpost of light and liberty among all the frontiers of mankind.[37]

The speech lasted seventy-eight minutes. "Tell your friend," President Angell of Yale told his wife, who had been Graham's childhood playmate, "he shouldn't speak so long."[38] But a newspaper reporter noted that "he held that audience in such perfect thrall that not until he had gone a full hour did the people break their cathedral silence." Repeated applause came with his insistence on the freedom of the scholar and the right of speech even on controversial issues.[39]

The inauguration was followed by a formal luncheon with more speeches by presidents of major universities in the country; and later in the afternoon there was a reception for the inaugural audience and the more than a thousand persons who had been in the inaugural procession. Throughout the day Graham was feted. But no words meant more to him or his friends than those spoken in Kenan Stadium by Kemp D. Battle, Graham's University roommate, in the most affectionate speech of the day:

Should this institution, precious to him beyond flesh and blood, maintain its high level of distinction and of service or should it yield to the anemia of undernourishment and sink back into mediocrity and to futile dreams of lost leadership?

On Frank Graham's personality more than on the influence of any other dozen men does the answer to that question depend. I venture to say that the spiritual leadership of this man is the moral equivalent of an unimpaired appropriation.[40]

Part Three

University President and
Southern Liberal
1931-1940

8

At Home in the President's House

Friendships form here for the human pilgrimage.[1]
—FRANK PORTER GRAHAM (1931)

FOR TWENTY-FIVE YEARS FRANK GRAHAM AND HIS possessions had been crowded into single rooms or barracks from Chapel Hill to London. In September, 1930, he moved into the president's home, a dignified, white, Southern-columned house set behind a low stone wall and towering oaks on the northeast corner of the campus. The spaces in and about the house were hospitable: the straight, gravel-packed walk; the wide, gray wooden steps to the spacious porch, which opened into a light-filled entrance hall; the comfortably furnished living room; the dining room with tables and chairs always in order; the immaculately bright kitchen; and beyond the carpeted stairs, the four bedrooms and study. It was a house to live in, his first since childhood.

It was his to share. A younger sister, Kate, who had the Graham friendliness, was hostess until her marriage in June, 1932. She and Graham made all who entered feel at home—servants and governors, students and visiting dignitaries, professors and trustees. The servants, in fact, were like associate members of the family. Hubert Robinson, a handsome Negro with a manner as easy to live with as his drawl, had preceded Graham to the house by two weeks. He was to be a reliable companion, and since Graham never learned to drive a car, he was Graham's chauffeur throughout the presidency. Robinson was so involved during the campaign for funds that it became for him "our fight to save our university"; and that was the way Graham wanted it. Alice Neal was as sensitive and sensible a person as she was a competent cook. On one occasion, left

100

UNIVERSITY
PRESIDENT
AND
SOUTHERN
LIBERAL

alone, she went across the street to the Episcopal Chapel of the Cross for a funeral, knowing what Dr. Frank would have done had he been at home. After the service, on her own, she invited the grieving family from another town to come over to the president's house for rest and food.[2]

Since Graham saw no reason for wasting living space, he let students room in the president's home and even had rooms above the garage made available for impoverished students. His method of finding renters was typically fortuitous. On one occasion he heard that a student with no money for food was wandering about town, so he had Hubert find the boy and feed him. The student who came to dinner stayed two years.

Late in 1931 Graham went to the jail for an older student and made him a guest in the president's home. J. Fukusata had been promised a scholarship by the University in 1917. Unable to leave Japan at the time, he asked the University twelve years later to make good its promise. Admitted to the country as a non-quota immigrant, he was allowed to remain only as long as his college work was satisfactory. Deficient in English, he received "incompletes" in almost every course; then, in view of his failure to meet the legal requirements for foreigners studying in the United States, the immigration authorities took him into custody in order to deport him. He was to have been in custody in Raleigh only one night, but a week passed and word came back to Chapel Hill that he was still in the Raleigh jail. It was at that point that Graham first heard of the case. It was six in the evening.

Graham immediately called Raleigh. No one there had authority to release Fukusata. Graham called the immigration official in Wilmington. He, too, lacked jurisdiction. A call went to the district head in Norfolk. His hands were tied: the law must take its course. Graham was determined that Fukusata should not spend another night in jail, so he called the two North Carolina senators in Washington. They would like to help, but the matter, really, was out of their province. He then talked with the Secretary of Labor, who, like everyone else, was both sorry and helpless: he would put the matter on the President's calendar the following morning. "That's not soon enough. I will call the President now," Graham threatened. "It's against all American principles that that student should even be in jail and I want him out tonight."

"Well," replied the secretary, "if you know how it can be done I'll do it."

Graham knew. He suggested that the secretary wire the United States marshal that Graham would take full responsibility for the prisoner. Graham called Raleigh and asked the marshal to go to the Western Union office to wait for an important message; he called Wilmington and Norfolk to apologize for going over their heads in the matter; and he sent Harry Comer, secretary of the University YMCA, to the bank in Chapel Hill to get one thousand dollars in case bail was required. To make sure the money would be given, he wrote a note to the banker authorizing the bank to withhold funds from his future salary checks. Comer could not get the cash because of the time lock on the vault; he secured a cashier's check but did not tell Graham he had not received cash because "I knew that if the U.S. government could not stop him, no bank safe could, and I didn't want to run all over the state looking for a locksmith."

The two drove to Raleigh. When, shortly before ten, they reached the courthouse and were met by the marshal and the jailer, Graham seized the latter and hurried him up the steps. Comer and the marshal followed more leisurely.

"Is that little man the Frank Graham from Chapel Hill that you read about in the newspapers?" the marshal inquired.

Mr. Comer said he was.

"Are you sure that little guy is him?" the marshal persisted.

Comer said he should know; he was absolutely sure.

"Well," said the marshal, "he may be little, but in something less than four hours he's got the whole damned United States by the tail."[3]

University matters took their toll on Graham's private life. His former mode of life had given him independence and security. Restless and active, he had always worked hard, but his time had been his own. He was a welcome guest in homes throughout North Carolina, and few men have known the love and friendship he received. "Some of us were talking," a friend from student days wrote him, not long before his marriage, "and we were wondering what is this strange charm you work upon our wives?"[4] When he became president of the University, however, the pace of his life quickened. He was no longer master of his time, nor could he as readily visit friends.

Early in the summer of 1931, arrangements had been made for him to visit the Francis Winslows, friends from student days, in their summer cottage on the Atlantic at Nags Head. It would be

102

UNIVERSITY
PRESIDENT
AND
SOUTHERN
LIBERAL

his first vacation in two years. All summer he looked forward to August 1, but the financial problems of the University made it impossible for him to leave on the agreed date. On July 30 he wrote to Frank Winslow that he could not get away:

This just simply breaks my heart. I have been almost living for that Nag's Head trip. After a year's absorption in this present job which takes all of me day and night and not to see the person on the other side of the Chowan River who is also going down on Saturday, simply takes the ground out from under me right now. I must stick here and hold on and do the best I can.[5]

Four days later he wrote to Mrs. Winslow, "Please hold the lady back by the Chowan River and not let her get away or be kidnapped. This is my special and confidential charge to you."[6] "The lady" was Marian Drane, whom Graham had met the previous fall. His own mind was already made up about the cultured, charming daughter of an Episcopalian rector, who was fourteen years younger than he; but he had not confided his firm decision and full hopes to anyone. Not even to Marian Drane.

By August 7 the budget battle was, for the time being, over. Graham was free to visit Nags Head and "the lady" for more than two weeks. Marian was 31 and for years had been hostess in the rectory of the historic St. Paul's Episcopal Church in Edenton, where her father had served. ("They say that having gained experience in taking care of one old man," Graham was to comment later, "Marian married me to take care of another."[7]) The strength of her quiet ways, readily adjusting to other people in her life without loss of her own personality, reflected the life she had known in Edenton. Two years at St. Mary's Junior College in Raleigh, an Episcopal school that combined the Christian, English, and Southern ideals of what a woman should be, had climaxed her childhood and given a sense of sureness in the direction of her life.

The courtship developed as rapidly as the duties of the president of the University would allow; and Graham, though chastened by new responsibilities, particularly the daily burdens of budget cuts, saw to it that the duties allowed much. Marian often visited her sister in Hillsboro, thirteen miles from Chapel Hill. There (where, coincidentally, the large white house with a wide porch was across the road from the small Episcopal church) he came to know what kind of person Marian Drane was. As often as possible he had Hubert drive him to Hillsboro. On at least one occasion he forgot that Hubert was waiting in town and caught a ride back to Chapel Hill. Hubert, perplexed as to what could have happened, waited patiently until a stranger told him he had seen Dr. Graham get into a car and drive off. Similar things had happened before; Hubert returned home. As he entered the house, Alice Neal gave him a warning wink and a nod in the direction of the pantry. He refrained from any outburst. A moment later Graham stepped from behind the pantry door and, grinning, said casually, "Hi Hubert, old boy. Where've you been?"[8]

Not only did Graham have to postpone his vacation with Marian because of university financial crises, but in 1932 plans for their marriage had to be changed three times because he could not escape Chapel Hill. Finally Graham went in desperation to the Governor, who, when told of the wedding postponements because of threatened and actual budget cuts, assured him there would be no further cuts, "at least, not until you are back from your wedding trip."[9]

They were married on July 21, 1932. The postponements had made it impossible to plan a wedding with many friends present, as they both would have liked.[10]

Hubert helped Graham in preparations for the wedding. Hubert bought as usual a new pair of boy's size shoes for Graham and took the order for new suits. Together they stopped on the way to Edenton to buy a wedding ring and in a hotel room went over the wedding service. Marian's father, prepared to perform the ceremony, went into the church at four o'clock. There at the altar were the bride and groom. Looking around, he saw only a sister of Marian's, a sister of Frank's, and Hubert. Dr. Drane was surprised. "Where are the people, daughter?" he inquired. "There are no other people, Papa," she answered.[11]

Following a month-long wedding trip to Canada, they returned to the president's house in Chapel Hill. From that time on Graham depended upon Marian to be and to make his home. She gave to him the love he needed, the companionship he craved. He gave to her the opportunity for both a personal and a social fulfillment. It was a love and companionship shared. Their difference in age was never felt, perhaps because, with his restless idealism, he was ever a youth, and she, having cared for her father, was more mature than her years. In many ways he was the younger and the one who needed to be cared for.

A month after settling together in Chapel Hill, they began the

104
—
UNIVERSITY
PRESIDENT
AND
SOUTHERN
LIBERAL

pilgrimages that would take them each summer to the Outer Banks. There they lived in the two-story cottage at Nags Head that was the closest thing to a home that Frank and Marian Graham ever had. (It, too, was across the road from an Episcopal chapel.)

Dr. Drane had built the two-storied, brown shingle beach cottage in 1908 around a two-room house more than a hundred years old. The foundation pilings had been driven deep into the sand until they reached a solid base. It seemed no storm could destroy them. But the windows and walls and rooms could not be so well protected from the wind and water that sometimes raged up from the South Atlantic past Cape Hatteras. Following the most severe hurricanes, the cottage would have to be swept clean, the furniture refurbished and, at times, the walls rebuilt. Each summer the cottage would be readied for use; Marian and Hubert and Alice would drive down early to clean it and make minor repairs. But some summers, after serious storm damage, they would need the help of others for major reconstruction. The cottage, in the process, grew from year to year. With all the changes there was always a homelike sameness about it. This was a cottage to live in. It was a house where people could leave society and be themselves. There was no telephone. Conversation, books, and newspapers provided the entertainment.

Here, each summer, Marian and Frank came to relax, to enjoy life together in a way impossible the remainder of the year, to share conversation and meals with many friends, particularly the Winslows and Battles, who had cottages on the ocean within easy walking distance. And here Graham came to work. The habits of years could not be changed. Each day he would spend two to four hours at his desk. They had not been married very long when Marian turned to him questioningly: "Frank, they say every man needs to have some hobby. What is your hobby?" He looked up from his book sheepishly, eyeing her over black-rimmed glasses. "I guess my work is my hobby." [12]

But for all its variety, despite the hourly changes of wind and sun and wave and shifting sand that gave to each moment a strong sense of immediacy, there was also another mood cast by sea and shore, a mood of simplicity, of mystery, of depth.

A barrier for the mainland, the Outer Banks stretched precariously down the ocean as though it daily challenged the sea to destroy it. There was something about it that, for Graham, symbolized the modern world. On one occasion the Grahams were forced to flee to higher land to escape the waters of a hurricane, and in the home of a friend they anxiously watched the waves rise toward them. At last Frank thought he noticed the water receding by the kitchen steps. Hoping to find some reassurance from the Negro maid whose judgment he trusted, he said, "Look there, I think that water has gone down a little, don't you?" Without bothering to stop her work, she replied, "It's not those two feet that's troubling me, Dr. Graham. It's those thousands of miles of water that's pushing up against it."[13]

When Frank Graham was married at the age of forty-five, the direction of his life was set, the pattern of his personality was drawn. Marriage might well have shifted the direction or distorted the pattern. Instead, it served from the start to give impetus to his life and clarity to his personality. He and Marian accepted his style of life; and they accepted it without being fully conscious of precisely what it was, for he was not given to introspection, nor she to analysis.

Graham's self-understanding was a felt knowledge. He knew himself to be basically religious, for instance. It was natural and honest for him to incorporate religious language into his addresses, but precisely what he believed he never told anyone, and at the time of his marriage, he had not even told himself. While he regularly attended church (he retained loyalty to the Presbyterian, Marian to the Episcopal Church), he did not pray in public nor readily in private. There was a mystical streak in him, but it was not revealed beyond the advice he gave to students to "follow the light within" or his practice, when faced with a major problem, of arising early for a solitary walk. The religious foundations, while not dogmatic, were secure. Lacking a definiteness in thought, the foundations were definite in feeling and experience.

His consciousness was moral more than religious. The feeling for people was always a feeling for human rights, for whatever makes it possible for one to be a person. This meant a sensitivity to freedom, since without freedom a man could not be a man; and to equality, since without equality a man could not become his best self. Invariably the feelings moved toward "the despised minorities," especially toward the laboring man and the Negro. Graham felt both a respect for and a trust in the individual person. "It sim-

106

UNIVERSITY
PRESIDENT
AND
SOUTHERN
LIBERAL

ply never occurred to him as it often occurs to some," remarked a long-time friend, "that the man he is meeting for the first time might be a complete scoundrel."[14] That respect and trust were paralleled by an expectation of others' moral responsibility and a refusal to encroach upon their personal sense of responsibility. The self-awareness that his best work was with people was manifest in his consciousness that he was able to help people find and develop their own abilities.

He knew full well that he was dedicated to education, to an education of the whole person characterized by the development of social responsibility. And he knew, too, that his life was bound by loyalty to certain institutions and places, to the University of North Carolina and universities generally, to the church and Democratic Party, and to North Carolina and the South. His life was also bound to the traditions of the United States and western history.

His religious convictions and moral sensitivities were qualified by a sense of history. Whenever an issue arose, he found it demanded that he view it historically in the light of the western democratic tradition, and it became natural for him to reach out for the religious, political, economic, and social past that flowed into the present. His feelings were for people and social movements in history, not for ideas and philosophy or sensuous qualities and art. The sense of history became a divining rod for understanding the present, a rod that ever turned toward the most significant movements of the moment.

But his clearest image of himself was as an athlete. Each new challenge called for the sporting blood. He wrote to a defeated candidate in a presidential campaign, "I admire a valiant fighter, a good sport, and a generous loser."[15]

He had a capacity for making friends, so a characteristic feeling of others toward Graham was not first "I like him" but "He likes me." Having discovered in both coaching and teaching that a regard for others drew the very best out of them, he relied upon the loyalty of friends, especially the intimate friends he had known since college days. All his outgoing qualities were paralleled by an inner need for love.

He felt a powerful ambition to do something with his life, to serve a worthwhile cause. This ambition was an aspect of a youthful ardor he never outgrew, and it approached, at times, the desire for self-immolation.

In his view of himself there were no feelings of double-mindedness, no sense of inner tragedy, and strangely for a Presbyterian, no particular consciousness of, certainly no preoccupation with, sin. The humility that was often expressed was never in relation to guilt but to finiteness or limitations. Without guilt as a goad, he retained the characteristic Calvinistic consciousness of destiny and the restlessness that would not let him stop working or cease fighting battles on behalf of a democratic ideal.

Graham's sensitivity to history, his commitment to human rights, and his loyalty to institutions was expressed through his personal and social life. This was true in his relations with students, with friends, and with all those to whom he was connected through many controversies. His election as president of the University in 1930 changed the context for his life. It did not change his nature or essential actions. So, too, with his marriage. Rather than inhibiting, it enlarged the potentiality and scope of his life. The most important single fact about Frank Graham's life after July 21, 1932, was that Marian Graham cared for her husband with a kind of love that enabled him to be the person he essentially was, to become the person he potentially might be. She was always fully aware of what she was doing. "He always did the thing he thought was right," she once said. "I hope I encouraged him to do what he thought he should do." [16]

9

The New University
of North Carolina

*We would work in this region and build here
together one of the great intellectual and spiritual
centers of the world.[1]*
— FRANK PORTER GRAHAM (1931)

FRANK GRAHAM HAD BEEN PRESIDENT OF THE UNI-
versity for less than half a year when, in November, 1930, the
Brookings Institution made a report on the reorganization of state
government, which had been requested by the Governor. Although
the report was not primarily concerned with higher education, it
suggested that the University of North Carolina be consolidated
with State College, thirty miles to the east, and with the North Carolina College for Women, fifty miles to the west. On Christmas Eve
Governor O. Max Gardner announced that the next month he
would recommend university consolidation to the General Assembly. So in the first years of Graham's presidency, when he was preoccupied with budget problems, with his vision of the University's
future, and with personal matters, he was increasingly caught in the
most difficult developments in higher education the state had ever
known.[2]

When the proposal for consolidating three of the six white state
colleges was first made, Frank Graham, along with the faculty at
Chapel Hill, was skeptical of the idea.[3] The University at Chapel
Hill was a university. But this could not be said of the other institutions. There were in both places, of course, good men and women
who had given loyal service to education, but the results of their
work were far from equaling those at Chapel Hill. The much
briefer traditions of both were rooted in vocational education.
Neither had been directed toward becoming a university; one had

been directed toward the technical education of men and the other toward the vocational training of women.

Graham was alarmed at the proposal for consolidation, but by both temperament and training he had long since come to believe that much more could be accomplished by being for rather than against, by accepting and trying to guide the currents of history. He refrained from any reaction until, in informal conversation with the Governor, there was the chance to make his concerns clear.

In early January, 1931, as they were driving together, the Governor inquired about Graham's attitude toward consolidation. When Graham indicated serious doubts and many questions, the Governor said that the other presidents, Foust of the North Carolina College for Women and Brooks of State College, would be for consolidation, that the legislature would undoubtedly vote overwhelmingly for it, and that it would be unfortunate if the University was opposed.

"I am not the one in opposition," Graham continued. "I simply have many questions. One thing I am certain of: if it is not wisely handled, it will split the state wide apart."

The Governor was worried. "How can that be avoided?"

"If it is to be done it ought to be preceded by a careful study of competent people who would be chosen from those who know higher education and are experienced in making studies of the kind needed."

The Governor responded immediately, "Suppose I make that a part of the bill?"

Graham was noncommittal. "That would mean a lot to us," he said.

The conversation with the Governor was reported to the University faculty. Soon thereafter, though there was strong opposition and heated debate, the faculty in the University voted not to oppose consolidation at that time.[4]

In early March the bill began its way through the legislature in a House committee. President Foust was enthusiastically in favor of the proposed bill; President Brooks, surprisingly, was opposed; and Graham described his attitude as "an open mind with a question mark." The bill included, as promised by the Governor, an authorization for the employment of experts. But fearing political control of consolidation, Graham wrote an amendment that would

110

UNIVERSITY
PRESIDENT
AND
SOUTHERN
LIBERAL

make mandatory the use of experts and hinted that they might advise some form of "unified guidance" other than strict consolidation. The amendment was accepted; and the bill creating the three-institutional "University of North Carolina" was passed within the month on March 27, 1931.[5]

The bill specified that a commission of twelve should consider reports from competent experts in higher education and make its recommendations to the new Board of Trustees of the University no later than July 1, 1932. Appointed June 14, 1931, the commission consisted of the three presidents, a faculty member appointed by each of the presidents, and six people named by the Governor. The first major problem of the commission, the selection of the survey committee of experts, fell to Dr. Fred Morrison, former professor at The Woman's College, appointed as committee secretary by the Governor, and to Dr. L. R. Wilson, librarian at Chapel Hill, appointed by Graham.

Wilson and Morrison recommended that Dr. George A. Works, dean of students and university examiner at the University of Chicago, be in charge of the survey committee. Works was appointed by Gardner in October, and two months later he selected as associates in the project Dr. Frank L. McVey, president of the University of Kentucky, and Dr. Guy S. Ford, dean of the graduate school and acting president of the University of Minnesota.[6] For six months the survey committee explored with complete freedom the many angles of the problem. Because of widespread fears that the University in Chapel Hill (which meant Graham, working behind the scenes) might control the report, Dr. Works felt it necessary to state categorically that "no individual or institution has tried to influence any member of this committee at any time."[7]

The survey committee examined the three institutions, considered the needs of the state, and tried to discern what would be desirable in the distant future of twenty-five or fifty years. The major recommendation in the report issued in May, 1932, was that the consolidated University should be centered in Chapel Hill; a woman's college with a simplified organization should remain in Greensboro; but North Carolina State should become a junior or community college, with the schools of agriculture and engineering transferred to Chapel Hill, where they could be developed and supported by strong work in the sciences. The report was received in shocked dismay everywhere except at Chapel Hill and by almost everyone from the Governor down. Not only had Gardner introduced the consolidation proposal in part to strengthen State College, but the bill had specifically declared that the North Carolina State College of Agriculture and Engineering would be at Raleigh. The Governor immediately pledged the outraged alumni of State College that their institution would not be weakened.[8] The commission met with Dr. Works on June 13 and 14, 1932, to consider the report of the survey committee. In its unanimous findings it made no mention of the controversial elements of the report but recommended that the University have a single executive, designated as "Chancellor," to be elected; a single Administrative Council; and one director each of summer schools, extension, and graduate studies and research.[9] (Less than a month later, on July 11, the Board of Trustees decided the term "President" should be used, rather than "Chancellor.")

The difficult details of consolidation were yet to be solved. Brooks and Foust, fearful for their institutions and their positions, were opposed to a single president; and when they lost that battle, they argued that the three presidents could direct the new University until well into 1934, Foust insisting that "it will take ten years or longer to bring about a complete and satisfactory merger."[10] Graham abstained from participating in this controversy. The commission decided that the single executive should be elected by July 1, 1933, and with that decision completed its work, turning the many unsolved problems over to the new Board of Trustees.

Graham had a great sense of relief, for he had feared that decisions might be politically motivated and hastily made. Dynamite was still present; but the commission, at least, shared his view that time and the long-run interests of the state would work the problems out. In writing to the president of the alumni association, he defended the Works report, especially in its consideration of the distant future and the fact that the state could afford only one university of the first rank. "Of course," he concluded, "there are a lot of things that we must have great regard for so that the University quality of our life shall not be lowered in any way."[11]

The three presidents began meeting together, and at Graham's insistence, Foust, the eldest at sixty-six, was made chairman. But if Graham was willing to let time take care of the problems, the new Board of Trustees was not. By midsummer it became evident to everyone that Graham would soon be elected president of the new

112

UNIVERSITY
PRESIDENT
AND
SOUTHERN
LIBERAL

University. There was some consternation in Raleigh and Greensboro. In July David Clark wrote President Brooks, "When Frank Graham becomes president of State College as part of the University . . . we shall be absolutely in [his] power and I see no future for us."[12] Dr. Foust was chagrined, feeling that the decision was unduly rushed. After the board's executive committee unanimously nominated Graham for the presidency, Foust wrote him in early October:

> As I see the matter we are not ready for a complete merger of the three institutions, and no power on earth could force me to accept the chancellorship or presidency of the merged institutions as I now see the situation. It has been my hope all the time that we three presidents could work together for a few years and prepare the way for you to finally be chancellor of the three institutions. . . . If the politicians of the state will not follow the advice of those of us who know most about the institutions, and force a merger upon us when we are not ready for it, it cannot be anything but a failure.[13]

Recognizing that Graham would be elected in November, Foust suggested that Graham refuse the position. Graham had tried following that course once before. He replied to Foust that he had not been enthusiastic about consolidation and had made clear to the trustees that he did not want to be president.[14]

He had, indeed, earnestly pleaded in conversation and letter that another person be found. "My best work," he pointed out to one of his closest friends on the board, Leslie Weil, "is with human beings and not with an organization."[15] He added that he was too close to one of the institutions, that he feared being forced onto the others, and that he felt he had become too controversial. Weil asked a simple question and made a simple observation: "Can you tell me plainly, if you know of a man in this state to whom you would be satisfied to entrust this particular job? . . . I question whether we could find a man of the rare ability necessary who would be fool enough to undertake it for the satisfaction or the monetary reward he could even hope for and would not get."[16]

Blustery Josephus Daniels was more blunt:

> I say to you what I said to you on the day you were first elected president, that it is the duty of every man to serve where those who have the life of the University at heart think he can serve best. . . . the only thing for you to do is to say, "Aye, aye, Sir!" and quit this

business of being over modest. I think a man ought to be humble
before his God and not before anybody else.

Then, knowing Marian Graham, he added, "Show this letter to
your wife and tell her what I say, and say as an elder brother."[17]

It was settled, then. The two words, "duty" and "University"
met once more in Graham's life, and they were words that he
could not resist. He was vaguely aware, when he was elected in
November, 1932, of being placed in a difficult position, not so
much because the consolidation process would be hard, but because he would necessarily be a different kind of president for The
Woman's College and State College from the one he would be for
the University at Chapel Hill. But he was determined that he
would be their president in fact as well as name, that their life
would be his life, and that they would receive as fair a treatment
from him as if he lived on their campuses. In his brief acceptance
statement he expressed his need for the cooperation of all, "so
that we will be free, and fair, and intelligent in the long run
with the best interest of the whole state in mind." (One decision,
immediately made, was to go to each of the other campuses at
least one day every week, but it was not a policy he could long
maintain.) Now that he had been called to a new job, he felt that
perhaps through him the university tradition that he had learned
in Chapel Hill could by natural ways become a fuller part of the
life of The Woman's College and North Carolina State.

With a strong sense of loyalty to the institution of which he was
a part, he had already begun to enlarge that loyalty to include the
other institutions. He had always spoken on behalf of all the colleges and schools in the budget hearings; but even so they had been
other institutions. Now two of them had become intimate parts
of his own family. What was spontaneously said and left unsaid
in a letter to Judge N. A. Townsend, a long-time trustee, revealed
his feelings:

> There is The Woman's College, with its great body of fine-spirited
> and loyal alumnae reaching through all the schools and all the
> counties in North Carolina. It has one of the finest plants of any
> woman's college in America. . . . There is North Carolina State
> College of Agriculture and Engineering with its fine educational
> and public service and its body of devoted sons. It has the oppor-
> tunity to have a part in the further agricultural development of a

114
UNIVERSITY
PRESIDENT
AND
SOUTHERN
LIBERAL

great agricultural state. . . . There is the University of North Carolina, the oldest State University in America. . . . Its traditions make it one of the historic and unique institutions of America. It is a member of the American Association of Universities, of which there are only 29 on the North American Continent, including such universities as Harvard, Yale, Chicago, California, Minnesota and Illinois. The name and prestige of the University of North Carolina will be a great asset to all the member parts of the consolidated university.[18]

The Governor and the legislature had made the decision that there would be consolidation. But Graham was the one who would have to face the tough, irreconcilable forces competing for a place in the sun. His tendency was to refrain from using the legal power he had and from forcing issues or making demands. More could be accomplished by the patient, slower way of education and the democratic process; if true consolidation would come, it must come through people, especially the faculty. He would not be rushed, nor would he be intimidated by the demands for economy. "I am going to go so thoughtfully and carefully and fairly," he told a friend, "that I know I am going to be disappointing to many people who expect miracles overnight. There isn't going to be a great deal of economy in any high-grade sort of consolidation."[19]

When consolidation was first suggested, Graham had insisted that outside experts were needed, since what was essential at that stage was impartial judgment. Now that basic steps had been taken, his first policy in reaching decisions over details was to use inside experts, those within the faculties. His attention was first directed to The Woman's College and North Carolina State, where there was widespread anxiety regarding the future. It was necessary for the administrations and the faculties of the colleges to know Graham and for him to know the colleges. Patiently by example and decisively by act he introduced university structures and standards into the institutions. Instead of following the trustees' authorization to appoint the majority of members of standing committees, he ruled that the faculties should have a major voice; instead of securing outside experts to make recommendations, he created, in both colleges, faculty planning committees; instead of working only with the administrators, he consulted directly with faculty and students and, following the pattern of Chapel Hill, instituted advisory committees elected by the faculty. He was criticized by some of his closest friends for too great a patience, too slow a process, but when he considered a problem ripe for resolution, and not until then, would he deal with it directly.[20]

One of the most difficult of the problems had to do with his lieutenants in the University. For obvious practical reasons, the same board that elected Graham president elected as vice-presidents Julius I. Foust, now sixty-seven, and E. G. Brooks, sixty-one. Both men had given years of service to the state, Foust having been president of The Woman's College since 1907 and Brooks president of State College since 1923. Both men had devoted followers among their schools' alumni. Neither was in the university tradition; in the new challenges each was restricted by his loyalty to the institution he loved.

Graham had seldom met a man he could not cooperate with if only there was dedication to a common ideal. His initial intention, then, was to work with the vice-presidents until each voluntarily retired. It was not long before relations began to go awry, first with Foust at The Woman's College. Foust resented Graham's bypassing him through direct consultation with faculty. A man used to having authority, he naturally found it difficult at his age to be placed, as he felt, under authority. His moods toward consolidation oscillated from the bleakly pessimistic ("It cannot be anything but a failure") to the confidently optimistic ("I am writing to express my thorough endorsement of the way you are handling consolidation"). Again and again he complained that he was being misunderstood or mistreated; again and again Graham replied, trying to mollify his feelings. Others might have told Graham that he and Foust could not work effectively together; but he so detested personal altercations and so feared hurting or being disliked by another person that, if he had this knowledge, he did not act upon it. Then the complaints against Foust began to come from faculty and trustees close to him. Graham had requested that a committee at The Woman's College make recommendations regarding retirement, and the committee reported in May, 1934, that their personal judgment was that Foust should be retired immediately, but their recommendation was that his retirement should be postponed until 1935 because of reaction among the alumnae. At about the same time, the executive committee of the Board of Trustees informed Graham that there were plans to ask for the resignations of both vice-presidents.[21]

Graham, typically, had to speak directly with the person central to the problem. But with his vision for the University complicated

116

UNIVERSITY
PRESIDENT
AND
SOUTHERN
LIBERAL

by the recommendations of others, his own future, and his concern for a colleague, he was, in actuality, insensitive to Foust's situation and feeling. Graham spoke, at first indirectly, about his own father, who had retired after years of public school service and was finding great joy in life. He explained how the time comes when it is best for a man that he retire, and best for the institution too, though this is not because of any fault in the man. He said that he was talking as a friend, merely making a suggestion. Foust was angered; and when he began to feel that it was more than a suggestion, he was more deeply incensed. A man of Lincolnesque stature, he sat rigid. His features and voice were icy: "By whose authority, Mr. Graham, do you say this?" Graham was cornered. He could truthfully tell of faculty and trustee letters; he could report that the responsible committee planned to ask for the resignations. This would only deepen and lengthen the hurt, and it placed ultimate responsibility elsewhere, which was not fair, especially since he personally felt Foust's resignation wise. He replied: "By my own authority, Dr. Foust." Foust resigned, greatly offended.[22]

There was an equally distressing contretemps with Dr. Brooks. In the fall of 1933 Brooks had an unexpected illness on a business trip. Graham visited him in a Washington hotel after the onset, surprised to find that he was still in the care of the hotel physician. Through troublesome arrangements, Graham brought in Dr. Ruffin, a personal friend from North Carolina and a respected physician in the nation's capital. Ruffin soon called Graham aside. "Dr. Brooks is in a very serious condition. He should never hereafter have any strain with any position of worry or executive responsibility. I'm telling you because I don't want to alarm him and I don't want to alarm Mrs. Brooks; but that is his situation."

After Brooks returned to Raleigh, he was confined to his bed for more than three months, thinking all the while that complete recovery was immediately ahead. All that spring Brooks was physically incapable of working more than an hour a day, and this oftentimes had to be at his home rather than at the office. Graham, wanting to be considerate, was perplexed as to what should be done, and the perplexity was compounded by the fact that once more his conception of the university and his personal place within it were involved. It was certainly no time to ask for a resignation. He decided that the humane way was to put it on the ground not of Brooks's capacity to be vice-president, but of the danger, as Dr. Ruffin had said, that the vice-presidency might be to his life. He explained the whole situation to the Raleigh physician, who agreed with Dr. Ruffin's prognosis. "In that case," said Graham, relieved that he could avoid unpleasantness by turning the delicate problem over to someone else, "I would like for you to take this in your hands. You know what a gentleman Brooks is; and I do not want to hurt him more than is absolutely necessary." The physician agreed, and spoke to Mrs. Brooks in preparation for seeing Dr. Brooks. Still thinking her husband would recover, she exploded, "What right have you to speak of his stopping his life's work?" The physician, caught by surprise, stammered, "Well, well, President Graham talked to me about this and . . . ." It immediately seemed obvious to her that it was all a perfidious plot to remove her husband.[23]

Both Foust and Brooks resigned in early June, 1934, and within a month after the two resignations, new lieutenants were appointed at all three institutions. They served first as "deans of administration," later as "chancellors," for as long as Graham was president. Despite their divergencies from Graham in personality as well as in educational and social philosophy, there were logical and complex reasons for the choice of each. Those reasons had to do mainly with practical necessities, with Graham's need for personal loyalty and support, and with his desire to be democratic in the selection process. For practical reasons, it was essential to appoint people already familiar with the work of the three institutions. Walter Clinton Jackson had taught at the College for Women for twenty-three years; John W. Harrelson had taught at State College since 1909; and R. B. House, a graduate of the University, had been executive secretary of the University for ten years. None of the three had a doctor's degree, a lack they shared with Graham. Each had a fervent love for the institution in which he worked. What former Governor Gardner said of Harrelson was accurate for the others as well: "Above all, Harrelson will be loyal to Frank Graham and faithful to North Carolina."[24] Jackson, the most liberal of the three, was active in interracial relations in North Carolina, but he had a more leisurely, less progressive attitude toward social issues than did Graham.

Regarding the appointments at The Woman's College and State College, Graham made a careful survey, talking with faculty, students, and even janitors. ("You get insights about persons from people who are servants and janitors," he said. "They know clearly what kind of human beings they are working with.") At

118

UNIVERSITY
PRESIDENT
AND
SOUTHERN
LIBERAL

The Woman's College the sentiment was overwhelmingly for Jackson: faculty, students, townspeople, and alumnae deluged the president's office with the assurance that if only he were appointed, all would be well; and one janitor, who had prayed about the matter, informed Graham that God wanted Jackson. That made it almost unanimous; and the general support coincided with Graham's personal preference. In the case of Harrelson the support was not so strong, but it was sufficiently enthusiastic that, with assurance of his loyalty, the appointment was logical. At Chapel Hill Graham had inherited House as executive secretary of the University, but they had long before worked closely together; in 1914, when Graham was executive secretary of the YMCA, House had been treasurer. And for the last four years they had worked side by side in South Building. House had, in effect, become an administrative assistant, keeping the store when the president was away, protecting him when he was sick, substituting for him when it was necessary, always with fidelity to Graham. Through the years they had their differences, and there were occasions when Graham overruled House on important points; but no strain ever broke the trust that had developed between them. Though House did not sympathize with most of the president's reform activities outside the University, Graham's confidence in House did make it possible for him to take time from University responsibilities to engage in the battles of democracy.

With the consolidation of the three disparate institutions, Graham was faced with problems of curriculum, personnel, and co-ordination of educational programs. His method was to approach the problems through studies by faculty committees; and the attention he gave to the separate units depended primarily upon the difficulty of the problems encountered.

The initial studies and basic decisions were made at The Woman's College. From the first, he envisioned the institution in Greensboro as a Woman's College of Arts and Sciences that would become second to none in the nation. All his subsequent actions he viewed as steps in that direction.

The first decision early in the spring of 1933 was that, contrary to the practices in certain programs, no men should be admitted to the college. A howl of protest was heard from the City of Greensboro. Letters from the Chamber of Commerce, the civic clubs, leading businessmen, and mothers of college students poured into the president's office. But Graham was adamant in the position that it would be a woman's college.

The dream that it should be a liberal arts college was not in keeping with the institution's dominant tradition or current programs, though there were those on the faculty who were sympathetic to the idea. Through the smooth functioning of faculty committees, Graham was instrumental in reorganizing the curriculum and introducing more required liberal arts courses into the basic studies. In 1934, largely through his efforts and because the college had become part of the University, a chapter of Phi Beta Kappa was established. In 1935 he instituted departments of art, classical civilization, and philosophy "to round out a complete college of liberal arts." After making these changes and a limited number of key faculty appointments, he felt that he had taken as much administrative action as was proper in reaching his goal. This feeling coalesced with his confidence that people at the college would, on their own initiative, develop not merely "a Bryn Mawr or Wellesley of the South but another Bryn Mawr, another Wellesley." Nowhere in the University did he receive more personal devotion than from the faculty at The Woman's College; nowhere did the committees shaping the new University function with more apparent ease and harmony; so it was not surprising that with confidence in the college he turned his major attention elsewhere. Other issues demanded his time; and after the basic decisions were made, The Woman's College was never a major problem for Graham.[25]

That could not be said of the University at Chapel Hill nor of North Carolina State. At Chapel Hill, while there had been bitter opposition to consolidation, once the basic decision had been made, it caused no great controversy except on the one issue of the location of the school of engineering. The adjustments, rather, were psychological, on the part of many professors who believed that the traditions of their university would be diluted by those of two inferior institutions. But life in Chapel Hill after consolidation went on much as it had before. Graham appointed faculty committees which engaged in self-examination. There was the introduction of the General College for the first two years, incorporating more courses in the liberal arts, especially the social sciences. But maintaining and strengthening the quality of the faculty was the principal concern. This responsibility was met not primarily by

120

UNIVERSITY
PRESIDENT
AND
SOUTHERN
LIBERAL

Graham but by the loyalty of men who, at personal sacrifice, stayed by the University through financial privation. Graham played a significant role by his continuing struggle for funds and by eliciting, through personal example, the loyalty of others.

The first appearance of inadequacy struck his office with explosive force when, on June 6, 1933, he received in reply to his request a letter from Randall Thompson, the musician who had recently made a study of music education in American colleges for the Carnegie Foundation. There had been no particular reason for believing that the Chapel Hill department was not adequate, but Thompson's confidential letter destroyed all illusions. The situation was desperate. Thompson reported that he had never met better students than those at Chapel Hill, and "herein lies the gravity of the situation. For if your students were mediocre a mediocre department might take care of their needs . . . in view of the type of students in hand it is reprehensible."[26] There were, he said, some good teachers, but on the whole, the department was one of the weakest in the country. Graham was shocked into action, and while he was making inquiries, three students came to him with charges of incompetence against the department head. The head was called in, the students made the charges in his presence, and Graham indicated that the charges were sufficiently serious to justify releasing him. The professor, enraged, promised to take this trampling upon academic freedom to the Association of University Professors. Graham replied, "Take your case to them and give me just thirty minutes before that committee and I will abide by their decision." He never had to carry through on this promise since, in trying to develop a watertight case, he discovered that the head did not have the degrees he claimed to have and had never even attended the universities from which the degrees had supposedly been granted.[27]

There was another discovery. The original appointment had been made, under an earlier president, simply on the recommendation of the outgoing head of the department. Graham immediately instituted the procedure throughout the University by which the head of a department would be appointed only after a committee, including professors from outside the department, had made recommendations. Through this process the Department of Music was rapidly rebuilt. Graham soon strengthened other departments, especially physics, chemistry, and German.[28]

At the time of consolidation, there were engineering schools at both Raleigh and Chapel Hill; they became the source of a storm that threatened to sunder the University. Into the vortex of this storm were drawn the personal feelings and loyalties of faculties, alumni, and leading citizens. The consolidation commission and Board of Trustees had both aired the problem and then passed it on to Graham, who sat in the eye of the storm.

There were many forces involved, all arising from the Works Committee's recommendation to place all engineering at Chapel Hill. The engineering education survey had been made for the committee by Dr. W. E. Wickendon, prominent engineer and president of the Case School of Applied Science. Works was firm in his report to the Board of Trustees at their first meeting: "In Dr. Wickendon's judgment the outstanding school of engineering in the South is at Chapel Hill. When it comes to sanitary engineering, there is no institution in the United States doing better work. . . . Wipe out the Chapel Hill school of engineering if you choose, but do not transfer it. The people of the state would hesitate a long time before disposing of the outstanding school of engineering in the South."[29] On one side of the battle, then, was the School of Engineering at Chapel Hill, which offered the master's degree in general engineering and the B.S. degree in chemical, civil, electrical, and mechanical engineering. These departments had national recognition and the school a scholarly, crusading head, Dr. H. G. Baity. They had the support of science departments of high quality, faculty members in other fields who were protective of Chapel Hill's priority, and one of the strongest bankers in the state, John Sprunt Hill, who was also a trustee. On the other side were the Governor's ambitions for and promises to State College, powerful agricultural and engineering leaders, influential alumni of the college, a physical plant marked "engineering," and the act of consolidation itself, which had prescribed "that a unit of the University shall be located at Raleigh and shall be known as the North Carolina State College of Agriculture and Engineering of the University of North Carolina." In between these two forces was the fence-straddling resolution, adopted by the Board of Trustees the same day it elected Graham president, stating that "there is no intention to demote any of the institutions to the rank of junior college or to discontinue the Schools of Engineering at Chapel Hill and Raleigh."[30]

122
—
UNIVERSITY
PRESIDENT
AND
SOUTHERN
LIBERAL

More than a year passed before Graham took action. In the fall of 1933 he appointed a commission composed primarily of qualified engineers in the state but including members from the faculties at Chapel Hill and Raleigh, specifying that the group should not be bound in its recommendations by any previous decisions. The appointment to the new commission of persons with opposing views was an expression of Graham's hope that they might reach a consensus where others had failed. He was doomed to disappointment. After exhaustive consideration, the commission voted 6 to 5 that the School of Engineering should be at Raleigh. The minority favored retention of both schools with differing professional and technical emphases. Majority and minority reports were handed to Graham on September 22, 1934.

The commission had decided, but in the absence of a consensus Graham felt that the problem had returned home. Since no authorized body had been able to resolve the problem to his satisfaction, he decided that he would not be bound by the recommendation of any group but, using all available material, would make his own study and reach his own conclusions on the basis of a philosophy of consolidation. For the next eight months he spent many hours in solitary study; and he consulted with the presidents of other universities including Lowell of Harvard, Butler of Columbia, and Angell of Yale. During this period the trustees adopted a principle for the allocation of functions among the three institutions that forbade duplication of curricula on the upper and graduate levels, apparently unaware that this was a contradiction of an earlier resolution that both schools of engineering should be continued. Examining all alternatives in the light of the new allocation principle, Graham reached his conclusion: "By the logic of consolidation, there should be one engineering school and by the principle of the allocation of functions that one engineering school should be at the college of agriculture and engineering in Raleigh." On May 30, 1935, the trustees accepted his recommendation by an overwhelming margin.[31]

The bitterest stage of the controversy began with that decision. There were those at Chapel Hill, and not only the engineering faculty, who felt it was a fatal mistake that might well weaken the sciences and mathematics all down the line. Recognizing that the consolidation of engineering at Chapel Hill was an impossibility, Baity renewed the careful arguments he had made earlier for two types of engineering, with professional and primarily graduate engineering at Chapel Hill, and technical and industrial engineering at Raleigh.

There was much to be said for this position since historically the existing schools had varying emphases on the *why* and the *how* of engineering. The storm increased in its fury in 1936, when the faculty at Chapel Hill voted eighty to nineteen against Graham's position and requested the trustees to keep the school at Chapel Hill. It was the first time a faculty had opposed Graham, and the professors were so sensitive to this fact that they unanimously passed a resolution praising their president for his encouragement of faculty freedom and stating that their difference in no way implied a lack of confidence in his leadership. The rebellion of the faculty was matched by rising opposition in the state.[32]

The antagonists met for the last time before the Board of Trustees on May 30, 1936. After hearing the now familiar arguments, the trustees reaffirmed their earlier decision. The university School of Engineering would be at Raleigh. There was a transfer of some professors to Raleigh; others remained at Chapel Hill, including Dr. Baity, whose work in sanitary and municipal engineering was placed in the School of Public Health.[33]

10

University Crusades and Crises

Without freedom there can be neither culture nor real democracy. Without freedom there can be no university.[1]

—FRANK PORTER GRAHAM (1931)

WHEN GRAHAM WAS ELECTED PRESIDENT OF THE University in 1930, there were still fresh in memory the battles for freedom in which he had been involved: the fight of the University against legislative bills restricting the freedom to teach theories of evolution in the schools; the personal fight of Graham for an "Industrial Bill of Rights." The strongest portions of his inaugural address, therefore, had dealt with the freedom of the University. He stated in detail what academic freedom meant in research, teaching, and the active life of the University in the state; and he was clear about his own freedom as president:

> For the administrative head freedom means to take full responsibility in his sphere and to make decisions in the long run view of all the circumstances, to express views without illusion as to their influence but with some sense of fairness, humility, and tolerance, on those issues that concern the whole people, asking no quarter and fearing no special interest.[2]

As long as he was president of the University, freedom would be a reality for himself as well as for others.

In his struggles for the financial survival and restructuring of the University, Graham had given expression to his ideal of freedom. But the first major tests of freedom did not occur, as expected, over economic issues nor over university consolidation but concerned the more emotional issues of sex, race, and religion. Shortly after Graham's inauguration Bertrand Russell, the British philosopher, and Langston Hughes, the Negro poet, spoke on the Chapel Hill campus and at The Woman's College. Russell, on a lecture tour of the United States to raise funds for his experimental school, had recently published *Marriage and Morals*. The sexual attitudes expressed in his school, writings, and life challenged prevalent social standards. Hughes had been invited to speak at Chapel Hill by the liberal YMCA and a sociology professor. Shortly before his appearance, *Contempo*, an off-campus magazine sponsored by left-wing students, had published some of Hughes's poetry, including "Black Christ": "Christ is a nigger on the cross of the South." It was too rare an opportunity for the anti-Graham forces to overlook. For the first time since he had been elected president, his office and that of the Governor were flooded with mail critical of the University in general and of Graham in particular. "One hundred prominent citizens of North Carolina" petitioned the Governor to forbid "further predatory acts by so-called modern educators." They described Russell's views as "the incarnation of paganism, dressed up in inveigling and seductive non-biblical terms, and properly branded as neo-paganism." Langston Hughes was similarly attacked as being sacrilegious. And Graham, it seemed, was responsible for both at the University. It was those letters, which had begun to arrive in early summer, that crowded his desk when, in late August, he returned from his wedding trip to Canada.[3]

Among those who were critical there were some genuinely concerned for what might happen to young minds unprepared for the sophisticated world. Replying to a parent who wrote of the depravity of modern literature, complaining about obscene passages in Thomas Wolfe, Graham pointed to the distinction between "honest realism and depraved realism." He wrote that "the real basis of our perplexity is the fact that we are living in an age when so many ideas, customs and standards are in flux and transition, and we have not yet evolved a reintegration of our standards and philosophy of life. This is one of the greatest needs of our time."[4]

The main force of the attack upon Graham struck at the opening of the academic year. For a period of about a month, the freedom of the University seemed in real jeopardy. The hundreds of people joining the attack were motivated by diverse interests. Some desired simply to register their protests against the appearance of men such as Russell and Hughes and to suggest that there should

126

UNIVERSITY
PRESIDENT
AND
SOUTHERN
LIBERAL

be a more careful screening of guest lecturers; others wanted a definite restriction upon freedom in the University. Some were critical of liberal professors; others wanted to destroy Graham.[5]

A petition protesting the appearance of Hughes and Russell was signed by more than three hundred prominent citizens in the state and was presented to the Governor. It was reported confidentially to Graham that the author of the petition, obsessed with sex, had made a previous reckless attack upon Florida State College and that officials there had a file about the affair, which Graham might use to silence the critic. Graham refused the material.

"The integrity, the moral autonomy, and the intellectual freedom of this University are going to be preserved with faith and good will," he wrote an Alabama critic in mid-September.[6]

To a minister in Chapel Hill he said plaintively, "It seems sometimes that the more a person or an institution follows in the way and the spirit of Jesus the more that person or that institution is attacked as an enemy of religion and the state. For my little part, I shall not bend to the power of those who make the attack but seek sympathetically to understand them."[7]

To all who wrote him, whether in perplexity, in anger, or in bitterness, Graham replied in detail, always assuming the sincerity and intelligence of the writer, always believing that if the critic could visit Chapel Hill he would see the wholesome spirit of the University, always confident that if he and the critic could only talk together they would find much to agree upon. When the volume of critical mail that came in daily convinced administrators in South Building that the University was in jeopardy, Graham asked his friends to write the Governor and to urge others to do so. He asked that they give their impressions of the moral, intellectual, and spiritual life of the University. "Do not do this," he cautioned, "unless you have the impulse to do it yourself on your own responsibility. Do not urge anybody to do it who wouldn't freely and gladly do it. We want to win this fight, but we want to win it tolerantly, graciously, but decisively."[8] Again he was working behind the scenes; and in his eagerness to believe or make it appear that the support of the University came entirely spontaneously from others, he inconsistently informed a critic, "I, myself, have not said a word and do not especially care for anyone to make any defense whatever."[9]

When the controversy was at its peak, Graham received notification from the American Civil Liberties Union of his appointment to its board of directors. He expressed complete sympathy with the purposes of the union but declined the appointment on the ground that it would be better to concentrate everything on the struggle in which he was engaged, that of preserving the freedom of the University and winning the people's support of that freedom. "It is more important that the University of North Carolina does not yield on any point with regard to the great issues raised at this time of misunderstanding, recrimination, and vicious propaganda."[10]

By mid-October the academic freedom of the University was secure. When the critics learned that the Board of Trustees would take no steps to limit freedom and, on the contrary, were prepared to elect Graham president of the consolidated University, they ceased their campaign, at least temporarily.

But the scars of the battle would not disappear so rapidly. In December Graham urged a member of the board not to resign because of her differences with the administration regarding a socialist on the faculty. The faculty, he reported, "is by and large a very conservative body of men." While it was true that a professor of English was a socialist, Graham said, he had the right to believe and speak his political and economic views.

> I know I am often subject to misunderstanding and even misrepresentations, but I owe it to the great traditions of this University to take the blows as they come and as long as it is my responsibility to hold fast to those principles which are the very intellectual and spiritual stuff of her history and her life. America is in no danger from fascism, communism, or any other ism, just so long as she remains true to those principles for which the American revolution was fought; mainly, freedom of opinion, freedom of speech, freedom of assembly, and equal opportunity for all the people of this country.[11]

The attacks upon freedom were always directly related to finances. The uses of freedom by faculty, students, or visitors such as Russell and Hughes seemed to political friends of the University to come at the most inopportune times in the midst of crucial fights for funds. This was pointed out to Graham by some who threatened to withdraw support and by others who said the University would necessarily suffer financially because of his radicalism. "It may not be good form to mention the fact that the University is dependent for its very existence on the prosperity of the manufacturing and

128
—
UNIVERSITY
PRESIDENT
AND
SOUTHERN
LIBERAL

other industries of the State," one industrialist warned him about his own liberal activities, "and anything done to subvert or imperil the welfare of these industries will necessarily react upon the welfare of the University."[12] The plain fact, as Graham saw it, was that there could never be an opportune time when it would be safe for freedom to operate; each month, each week, was crucial in finding necessary money. And, especially at the beginning of his presidency, there was so little to find.

In mid-September, 1933, a student, appealing for justice, wrote a complaint to President Graham stating that he had been refused admittance to the Medical School because he was a Jew. Graham immediately called the student in and, convinced of his sincerity, dropped pressing University matters to determine the facts in the case.

The facts, he discovered, were plain. Dr. Isaac H. Manning, highly respected dean of the Medical School for twenty-eight years, pointed out that the two-year school consistently found great difficulty in placing its Jewish graduates in a four-year school to complete their training. Facing that difficulty, Manning believed the best solution was a quota by which not more than ten percent of the student body would be Jewish; so for years that had been the practice. To Graham the issue was a moral one: no matter what the hardships might be in placing graduates because of the policies of other schools, the University had no right to bar a qualified student from any course of study solely because he was Jewish. Late into the September nights, he and Manning discussed the issues, the practicality of the policy, and the right of the dean to administer the school against the responsibility of the University to avoid discrimination. When Manning finally convinced the President that his considered judgment in the case would not allow him to change his decision, Graham concluded, "In that case, Dean Manning, I will have to overrule you, and the young man will be admitted to your school."

"Then I have no alternative but to resign as dean of the school."[13]

The resignation had far-reaching repercussions. The *New York Herald-Tribune* praised Graham editorially, and most of the state newspapers supported him.[14] The correspondence that once again deluged the president's office was generally enthusiastic.[15] A number of physicians and Medical School alumni groups complained, but their complaints were primarily on the grounds of loyalty to Manning, hope that he would not be lost to the University, and belief in the autonomy of the Medical School, rather than on open dissatisfaction with the principle of "no discrimination." One month after Manning's resignation as dean, Graham replied to a group of physicians that had criticized him:

> I trust it is not necessary for me to express my deep appreciation of the character and services of Dr. Manning both as head of the Medical School and as an able teacher and a fine person. . . . Dr. Manning and I understand each other and frankly and openly disagreed on a matter of principle and policy. . . . The position I have taken is simply that there shall be no discrimination on a quota basis or any other basis because a boy is of Jewish descent.[16]

Dr. Manning continued as a professor in the school.

Graham's defense of freedom had long since alienated many people throughout the state; yet from the faculty he received strong support, albeit with criticism. At Chapel Hill he was generally recognized as poor at handling details: when confronted with a single, major problem, he could, after careful study, develop clear policies; but in most matters decisions were made on the run and with too great a confidence in the goodwill and judgment of others. Graham was so much involved in so many non-University causes that he rarely achieved that symbol of the effective administrator, a clear desk. Many faculty members resented what they considered his neglect of University affairs, yet they supported him because, with his commitment to a free university, he protected them. He also shared in their poverty. There were times when he viewed the president's main job as that of defender of the faculty. When Governor Gardner once told him of aspersions cast upon some of the professors, Graham bristled. He heatedly defended the faculty, specifically pointing to those who had refused to leave for higher salaries elsewhere and describing the spirit of sacrifice with which continuing salary cuts were accepted. He added, "It is my desire and hope that they will never know their patriotism and loyalty to the University and State have been thus misrepresented."[17] Again and again he had to go before the faculty to explain another cut that required further sacrifices. "He is the only university president I know,"

130

UNIVERSITY
PRESIDENT
AND
SOUTHERN
LIBERAL

commented a professor recently arrived from Pennsylvania, "who can announce a cut in salaries and receive a standing ovation from his faculty."[18]

By the mid-thirties the count of faculty members who had refused offers elsewhere was more than sixty; and the difference between present and proffered salaries was more than a hundred thousand dollars annually. Graham was one with them: he received many inquiries about positions elsewhere (for example, as president of other state universities, as czar of the radio broadcasters, and as a chief official in the Department of Agriculture) but, with one exception, he refused to consider leaving Chapel Hill on the ground that his work in North Carolina was not yet finished. The one exception was, in effect, turned down for him by the Board of Trustees. In October, 1933, when offered a major position in the National Recovery program in Washington, he was inclined to accept. He would have been directly involved with economic recovery, which he saw as the central problem of American and Southern life. He was also pulled toward Washington by great regard for Roosevelt. However, the Board of Trustees urged him not to accept, because he was needed in North Carolina.[19] Again he yielded to the call of duty at home.

It was among students that he always felt most at ease, for he considered himself a teacher. When he said that his best work was with people rather than institutions, the reference was mainly to students. The students responded with the enthusiasm of youth. At the time of the inauguration, an edition of the *Chapel Hill Weekly*, which was edited by journalism students, commented about Graham editorially:

> Recognized as a man, he is realized as a friend. Never too busy to stop for a chat. Always willing to help with a problem. And with all this democracy there is a dignity that cannot be displaced. It is associated with a dynamic force within the man—an unquestionable fire of zeal and enthusiasm for right and justice. Simplicity is a part of him. It is seen in his appearance and the formula of his character. There is no room for vanity.[20]

He enjoyed conversations with students on the campus paths and on Sunday evenings, when he and Marian were "at home." Other ways in which students became close to him were through his encouragement of student freedom, his support of the honor system, his frequent addresses to students, and his enthusiasm for athletics. At one outdoor pep rally, when the cheerleaders began the popular chant, "We don't give a damn for Duke University," Graham leaped to the platform and took the microphone to cry out, "I don't like that cheer." A voice from the crowd shouted, "But we don't give a damn."[21]

Graham's enthusiasm for university athletics was an enthusiasm for fair competition among amateurs. It was ironic that this enthusiasm led to the greatest hostility he had known to that time and to his first major defeat.

In 1930 Graham had been inspired by Abraham Flexner, the renowned authority on universities, who had maintained that "there is not a college or university in the country that has the courage to place athletics where everyone knows they properly belong."[22] The National Association of State Universities had been meeting on the day that the *New York Times* quoted Flexner; and the association had placed the matter on its agenda for the next annual meeting. At the 1931 meeting debate had been lively, but no action had been taken that year or the following three. After the 1934 meeting, Graham, as chairman of the Committee on Group Life of Students, took personal responsibility for the athletic part of the committee's work.[23]

Graham first turned to the detailed documents on athletics in American colleges published by the Carnegie Foundation for the Advancement of Teaching. The study of 112 colleges and universities described the tendency of college sports to become professional athletics.[24] While the report was a detailed analysis of all aspects of college athletics, the section that made the greatest impact upon Graham was "The Recruiting and Subsidizing of Athletics," for it was here, he felt, that the real problem lay. The conclusion of that section came to him as a call to battle: recruiting and subsidizing constitute "the deepest shadow that darkens American college and school athletics. Probably portions of the picture are even blacker than they have been painted." The report maintained that with capable leadership any college or university could solve the problem:

> Experience has shown that, of all who are involved in the evils—administrative officers, teachers, directors of athletics, coaches,

132

UNIVERSITY
PRESIDENT
AND
SOUTHERN
LIBERAL

alumni, undergraduates and townsmen—the man who is most likely to succeed in uprooting the evils of recruiting and subsidizing is the college president. It is his duty to coordinate opinion and direct the progress of an institution. If neighboring presidents are like-minded, his task is a little lightened, but under no circumstances we have been able to discover is it impossible even if he stands alone. It cannot be easy. But such are the position and powers of the American college president that, once having informed himself of the facts, and being possessed of the requisite ability and courage, he will succeed.[25]

Graham accepted the challenge. Here was a cause close to his heart. He had always been a devotee of athletics, but he saw that financial interests, which he believed had too much influence elsewhere, had invaded intercollegiate athletics and were having a corrupting influence upon young sportsmen and sportsmanship.

The next step was to make a study of existing regulations. Graham first examined the policies of the Southern Conference, of which the University was a member, and of the neighboring Southeastern Conference. Then he turned his attention to other schools he regarded highly, which he assumed had come to grips with the problem, to Harvard, Yale, and Princeton and to the large Midwestern universities. Building on what he considered those practices that would ensure the integrity and purity of athletics, he wrote eleven regulations that made athletics an integral part of the university but subsidiary to the basic purposes of higher education. His main rules stipulated that the athlete would receive neither preferential nor discriminatory treatment in financial aid; athletics would be under the control of the academic faculty; athletes would have to provide statements of financial income; recruiting would be strictly limited; no member of the athletic staff would receive remuneration except from his college; athletic accounts would be audited and published; and there would not, under any condition, be post-season contests.[26]

It was clear that these principles would mean nothing until they were supported by the universities and adopted by individual conferences. Aware that there would be opposition, Graham made his battle plans carefully.[27] In his general statement at an early fall meeting of the Board of Trustees, Graham hinted at the policies that were being developed and asked for support in helping to locate intercollegiate athletics in their proper place in higher education. "Is student life to revolve mainly around a circus sub-sidized and brought into the institutions," he asked, "or is it to center around, mainly, the teachers, library, classrooms, laboratories, historic buildings, shrines, and traditions which are a part of the soil, the air, and the spirit of the place?"[28] He was encouraged by the favorable response of board members.

On November 23, 1935, the principles were adopted by the National Association of State Universities and received publicity throughout the country.[29] On January 11, 1936, the presidents of six of the ten institutions in the Southern Conference supported the plan; and two weeks later the University faculty, by a decisive voice vote, also supported it.[30]

There was opposition, however. Alumni associations in ten cities passed resolutions against the proposals; the athletic council of the University of North Carolina rebelled and unanimously fought the plan; three presidents did not attend the meeting to discuss the proposals; and W. P. Few, the president of Duke, announced the opposition of his university and left the meeting early. There was a steady barrage of criticism from sports enthusiasts and Graham opponents. Writers, coaches, students, and directors of physical education all joined in the fray. Many of the coaches declared that it would mean the end of intercollegiate athletics. One sports writer said that the principal argument against the plan was the question, "Why add more rules and more stringent rules when we now have plenty of rules that aren't being obeyed?"

Support in the Southern Conference was undermined by the action of the Southeastern Conference. In November, at the very time when it was clear the Southern Conference would consider restricting subsidization of athletes, the Southeastern Conference had voted overwhelmingly for open subsidization in which athletes who met academic requirements would be given special consideration. The main arguments advanced were that assistance helped worthy young men get a college education and that, since subsidies were inevitable, it was better to bring them into the open.[31]

In the midst of the battle, the issues were confused by a public stand Graham took in relation to the forthcoming Olympic Games in Germany. Disturbed by reports of the treatment of Jews in Germany, he joined in the sponsorship of a Committee on Fair Play in Sports, which advocated that the United States should not participate in the Olympic Games under Nazi auspices if any German

134

UNIVERSITY
PRESIDENT
AND
SOUTHERN
LIBERAL

citizens were barred. This startling position brought its inevitable critical reaction. Graham wrote one of his critics:

> I respect your point of view. I think I might make my point a little clearer by saying that if the Olympic games were held in the South and America prohibited Negro athletes from their participation in the games or handicapped them in preparation for participation, I believe that other nations out of a sense of international or interracial sportsmanship would be entirely justified in not participating in the games. I would myself vote against our own participation on such a basis of discrimination of Negro athletes. The question to me is not a question of international politics but a question of international sportsmanship.[32]

All the forces opposed to Graham's views on athletics and other matters were present at a bitter fight that occurred in the meeting of the Board of Trustees on January 31. Graham went to that meeting hoping for the trustees' endorsement of his plan for university athletics. His opponents were determined that the "Graham Plan" should be destroyed. It soon became apparent to Graham's supporters that if the trustees voted on the plan it would probably not pass. A motion was made and passed to refer the matter to the faculty: "If we can't trust the faculty to control and regulate athletics," firmly insisted Judge John J. Parker, "then we ought to get a new faculty."[33]

The attack by trustees and alumni was indeed venomous. The attackers fell into two groups: those devotees of athletics who genuinely felt that the Graham proposals would weaken and probably wreck intercollegiate sports, and those who were opposed to Graham because of his social or educational policies. There were some, most notably David Clark, who fought Graham bitterly for both reasons. Graham had anticipated opposition, but the frontal attacks caught him by surprise and merely strengthened his resolve. "The present practices," he said, "are so damaging to institutional integrity and student honor that neither my respect for the opinion of others nor knowledge of the strength of the opposition can relieve me from doing my duty."[34]

The following week the faculties at Chapel Hill and State College again endorsed the plan and commended Graham by overwhelming majorities. On the eve of the special meeting of the Southern Conference, the six presidents who had originally backed the proposals announced their determination to stick by the new code. With such forces in favor of athletic reform, victory was inevitable, and the plan was adopted February 8, 1936, by a vote of six to four.[35] The battle was apparently won; but it was, Graham felt, only the beginning. He hoped that university presidents and conferences throughout the country would reform their codes, not merely for the sake of purifying intercollegiate athletics, but to breathe a new spirit into higher education.

The counterattack began as soon as the plan was passed. The greatest means of propaganda were the sports pages of the newspapers, where the sports editors, usually in disagreement with the editorial page, opened their columns to letters and articles disparaging the new code. Writers insisted the plan was autocratic and Graham dictatorial.

Dire consequences were predicted. Said David Clark: "The Graham plan will encourage falsehoods and deceptions and that is about all it will accomplish other than eventually break up the Southern Conference." The coach at North Carolina State said flatly, "Football will be dead in two years." The coach at Duke threatened to ask the conference to police its students, thus implying a subversion of the plan.[36]

Graham's line of defense was his power of moral suasion, supplemented by the endorsement given the plan by such presidents as Conant of Harvard, Angell of Yale, Lindley of Kansas, and Coffman of Minnesota. Indeed, the latter went so far as to say that the plan "constituted the most constructive regulations adopted by any group in the country."[37]

In November Ambassador William Dodd in Berlin scrawled a note to his former student, wishing him success in the athletic battle. He continued:

> There is all over the South an extraordinary development in higher educational life. I have been amazed at the number of liberal scholars and thinkers who have written books and articles the last few years. Several of them seem to me to be at the very front of social economic reform movements in our country. You seem to me to represent them better than any other president in our region or even the whole country. If universities and colleges could devote their energies in the right direction, democracy may be preserved.[38]

Tempests had been brewing in all the institutions of the Southern Conference, however, and they broke at the December meeting of the conference when the University of Virginia, an early supporter

136
——
UNIVERSITY
PRESIDENT
AND
SOUTHERN
LIBERAL

of the plan, announced its resignation unless certain revisions were made in eligibility regulations. Virginia was attempting to build a strong football team, and the absolute prohibition of special aid to athletes made that impossible. One simple word would solve the problem: in the regulation that made faculty committees responsible for seeing that special treatments to students "have not accrued because of athletic ability," if the word "primarily" were inserted after "accrued," the matter would be taken care of. It was done; and the Graham Plan began to dissolve. Even the faculty council of the University of North Carolina voted to accept the modifications of the conference.[39]

Later, at a meeting of the National Association of State Universities, Graham reported on the failure of his reform program. President John J. Tigert of Florida, who had led the fight for open subsidization in the Southeastern Conference, turned to Graham: "I am sorry your noble experiment failed."

Graham responded to the association:

We had a bitter fight in North Carolina and there was practically unanimous opposition. The press, the public, the alumni and the student body joined in opposition to that plan. I am sure the matter is not settled on the present basis, but we were simply defeated on all fronts. Not being dictators we will have to await the democratic process for the next struggle for the same principles in which I believe.

The presiding officer ironically concluded the discussion: "In other words we haven't quite succeeded yet in belling the cat. The next report is Cooperation with Religious Agencies."[40]

In the midst of the feverish battle over the control of athletics, when Graham was being attacked from many quarters, his attitude toward student freedom and responsibility was tested by a freshman at the University. The student, although fearful that his information might be used against the University and its president, had on January 25, 1936, a private conference with Graham in which he produced incontrovertible evidence of the existence of a cheating ring. The racket, headed by a graduate student, had existed for more than two years. Guaranteed grades had been offered for sale in the preparation of themes and even, in some courses, the taking of examinations. A list with the names of more than 150 students who had apparently used the service was discovered. It reportedly included the president of the Senior Class, members of Phi Beta Kappa, and a member of the Golden Fleece, a University honor society. Graham knew that in most universities such a breakdown of an honor system would cause the administration to investigate and dispose of the problem; he knew of specific cases where similar cheating rings had been concealed from the public. The freshman assured Graham that since he alone, by accident, had discovered the racket and since he had taken only two other students into the strictest confidence, it would be a simple matter for the administration to handle the entire matter in secrecy.

"The honor code," said Graham abruptly, "belongs to the students. It is your responsibility. Blow the lid off, if necessary; but get to the bottom of it."[41]

Graham considered the honor code to be the heart of student life, the basis for his trust in students. Though grieved by the revelation of honor violations, he was gratified by the way the students handled the problem. Proceeding carefully, making certain that there was clear proof for every suspension, the Student Council released information to the press, protecting the names of students involved until the council president was himself dismissed. With the disclosure of the cheating ring, the council president confessed to cheating two years previously, and at the insistence of the council, he presided over the session at which he was suspended, voting for his own suspension. Not long afterwards he wrote to Graham, "I am deeply grateful to you for your kindness during those hectic days and I shall always love you for the consideration that you showed me. Although I cannot truthfully say that I always agree with you, I can and will say that in principle you are always correct and that I have never known an individual whose motives were more sincere or unselfish." He concluded by describing dissatisfaction with his new work because it provided no chance for self-expression.[42] Graham replied immediately: "You are making a good fight and you are going to come through all right, I am sure. Keep plugging away and the work in which you will find self-expression and satisfaction will come to you. It may not come just as soon as you had hoped for, but it will come."[43]

To a mother whose son was one of the forty-eight students suspended, he wrote, "I know it has been a heart-breaking experience for you as it has been for all of us. I am writing this little note

138

UNIVERSITY
PRESIDENT
AND
SOUTHERN
LIBERAL

simply to express my deep sympathy and to hope that your boy is stronger today. You must not give up for his sake, and he must not give up for your sake."[44]

Just as the investigations were being completed, Graham spoke to the freshmen on the theme of student responsibility. "Carolina is going to be a more honorable place than ever before from now on," he told them; and he asked those who supported the honor system to stand. In a moment every student was on his feet.[45]

Although Graham had the support of the students, the statewide publicity about the scandal increased the suspicions of many persons about what was going on at their university and, therefore, about Graham. Even the officers of the Alumni Association seemed to join in the opposition when they sent members of the association a trickily worded questionnaire that was clearly designed to defeat Graham's athletic proposals, to increase the power of the alumni, and to keep engineering at Chapel Hill. The sharp-penned professor of writing, Phillips Russell, sent Graham a note quoting Robert Hutchins, "All alumni are dangerous," and remarking, "It must be glorious to have so much unpopularity."[46]

A move to oust Graham was reported in front-page articles in the Raleigh *News and Observer* in late February, 1936. The story received publicity throughout the state and nation, the *New Republic* commenting:

> In recent years the University of North Carolina has moved forward rapidly until it has become, in the opinion of many competent observers, the leading institution of higher learning in the South. This development is largely the work of its president, Dr. Frank Graham, who has a national reputation as an educational executive and as a practitioner of the old-fashioned American principles of freedom of thought and speech. It is not surprising, therefore, the times being as they are, to hear that efforts are being made to oust him from his position because of the very qualities that to many persons seem most valuable.[47]

The impossibility of identifying those behind the "ouster movement" led David Clark to assert that the whole story was "a hoax, deliberately and purposely concocted." But Graham's supporters and, in particular, newspaper editors were convinced that it was no hoax. Ambassador Josephus Daniels' offer to return from Mexico to defend Graham attested to the potential strength of the ouster movement and the fear, held by even the moderates, that it might succeed. Daniels, cagey in his understanding of North Carolina events, wrote on March 4:

> In a period of crisis in North Carolina in 1894 I resigned my position in Washington under Cleveland and returned to North Carolina to take part in what I called the redemption of the state, and we succeeded. In the present situation, when some reactionaries resent your making the University the dynamo of justice and liberalism and democracy, I am ready to come back home and enlist for the war.... I am ready to surrender everything to preserve a free and liberal university. It is a bulwark against Toryism.[48]

Graham was ill with his annual influenza, which had begun on February 11. This time the sickness was more serious than usual, and on March 14, at the direction of his physician, Marian took him to Florida, where they stayed for almost two weeks. When they returned, his desk was piled high with letters of support not only from individuals but from churches that had passed resolutions and from newspaper editorials. He wrote several hundred letters in reply, making no reference to the attacks but expressing his feelings for the University:

> Individuals, presidents, and others, of course are episodes in the high traditions, continuous purposes, and unconquerable spirit of a great institution. With insight and cooperation such as yours the University of North Carolina will hold to its purposes for the development of youth ... and for the creative cooperation of higher education and democracy in the building of the commonwealth.[49]

Though he was not afraid for himself, his friends were afraid for him. Charles Tillett and Kemp Battle put all their talents as lawyers into securing from University officials records and facts for building a defense of Graham. They were reasonably sure the executive committee would stand by him, but they had considerable doubt that the hundred trustees could resist the conservative pressures. Graham developed no defense but made the usual preparations for the board meeting, transmitting the criticisms that had come through his office and listing with factual background the issues on which the board's judgment was needed. But he refused to compromise on the open issues of consolidation and athletics or on the hidden issues of academic freedom and his right as a citizen to express his views. "I have certainly not meant to be dogmatic or unnecessarily stubborn," he told Tillett and Battle, "and I have not

140

———

UNIVERSITY
PRESIDENT
AND
SOUTHERN
LIBERAL

carried on any fight or even made replies. I have simply held the ground on which the University has stood." Others fought and made replies for him. It was well that they did, for following a six-hour debate on May 30, the board upheld his policy on consolidation and refused to consider any other controversial matters. The ouster movement collapsed.[50]

But Graham's activities that had caused the ouster movement did not cease, nor did the opposition to him throughout the state. It was perfectly clear that his liberal economic and social views and his absolutist stand on academic freedom and integrity had offended some influential, wealthy citizens beyond the point of endurance. Certainly Graham's friendship with Roosevelt did not help. For some, "that man at Chapel Hill" was as dangerous as "that man in the White House."

11

Social and Economic Justice

In the face of revolutions, dictatorships, and
catastrophe, America, through the schools, col-
leges, and universities, must learn to be true to
her inner Americanism of freedom of the mind
and equality of opportunity for all people.[1]
—FRANK PORTER GRAHAM (1931)

GRAHAM DID NOT BELIEVE THAT THE ONLY RE-
sponsibility of a university president was to attend to institutional
problems. The controversies in which he had been involved at the
University had not kept him from continuing his interest in social
and economic justice. He had been and remained on the board of
the Southern Summer School for Workers in Industry and, at the
annual banquet in 1932, had emphasized the importance and inevi-
tability of labor organization in the South.[2] In 1933, Roosevelt appointed him vice-chairman of the Consumers Advisory Board,
and he engaged with vigor in New Deal activities, advocating
ambitious plans for nationwide organizations of local consumers'
councils that would parallel the powerful trade associations and
labor organizations.[3] He made a major address in Washington's
Constitution Hall, insisting upon the necessity for economic planning, since there had developed "new autocracies of corporate
industrial power, kingdoms within themselves, which uncon-
sciously and irresistibly encroached on the freedom and security of
the individual in his working life and the equality of opportunity
for millions of people."[4]

He helped make economic adjustments at the local level too.
Joining with others in Raleigh, he was a major force in creating a
farmers' cooperative movement designed to help impoverished

142

UNIVERSITY
PRESIDENT
AND
SOUTHERN
LIBERAL

farmers through mutual aid in their purchases of fertilizers, seeds, and other necessary materials.[5] He appeared before a legislative committee to speak against the Criminal Syndicalism Bill, commenting afterwards, "It may have been that the committee would rather have reported the bill unfavorably than to have to listen to us talk against it."[6] And at home, he gave directives to the comptroller of the University to do everything possible to raise wages of janitors, workers in the laundry, Negro help in general, and all the unskilled workers.[7]

In spite of all of that activity, however, it was his response to a general textile strike that pushed him again into the maelstrom of public controversy. The strike, the most widespread ever known, began September 1, 1934. Of the almost 700,000 textile workers in the nation, 377,000 were on strike; and in North Carolina 71,500 of the 111,000 were out. The demands were for union recognition, collective bargaining, elimination of the stretch-out, and a thirty-hour week with no reduction in take-home pay. Tempers were high; on September 6, eight strikers were killed in South Carolina. In North Carolina the National Guard was patrolling in force.[8]

A former University of North Carolina student, Alton Lawrence, twenty-two years old and the secretary of the state Socialist Party, was arrested in High Point with thirty others on charges of forcible trespass. The Grahams were taking their last, brief vacation before the opening of the University; and Lawrence, in jail, received an unexpected telegram from Pawley's Island, South Carolina: JUST HEARD OF YOUR ARREST. GLADLY GO ON YOUR BOND. CONFIDENT YOU HAVE COMMITTED NO CRIME. The telegram was reported on the front page of newspapers in the state, and the furor began.[9] It was the kind of angry reaction that would not be forgotten. The telegram convinced the reactionaries of what they had suspected all along: "Now that he has bailed out a Socialist, he has shown his true colors," they said. "Obviously he is a Communist or the next thing to it." More moderate conservatives believed the telegram showed that Graham was sympathetic with the irresponsible strikers rather than with the respected mill owners. Even many of Graham's friends who saw the telegram as the act of a president who trusted a former student enough to offer him a simple democratic right wondered why he could not have asked an intermediary to make the bond.

It made no difference that the chief of police refused Graham's offer because the telegram was not a legal document. In an editorial, "A Man Stands Up," the Raleigh *News and Observer* agreed that the police chief was legally correct but stated that "everybody else in North Carolina knows that by telephone, telegraphy, letter, or voice Frank Graham's word is as good as his bond." Pointing to the real danger that the government was more concerned with preserving property than the rights of man, the editorial concluded that liberals "will thank God that the courage of one great liberal gleams in the present darkness."[10] That view was not widely held throughout the state. Nor did the fact that Lawrence's case was ultimately dropped alter the feelings of many outspoken conservatives toward Graham.

Graham also began to take increasingly significant roles in national affairs. Late in October, 1934, Graham received a call from Frances Perkins, the social worker who had become the aggressive Secretary of Labor. She requested, on behalf of President Roosevelt, that Graham serve as chairman of the Advisory Council on Economic Security. She told him that the council, representing management, labor, and the public, was to make direct recommendations to a committee of the President's cabinet charged with the responsibility of proposing specific social security legislation. Graham immediately accepted the position. The first meeting of the council was on November 15, the last on December 15; and in those hectic, crowded days Graham's actions became a part of the many crosscurrents that resulted the following year in a law that would touch directly the lives of millions of American men, women, and children in future generations.[11]

The first hundred days of Roosevelt's administration were over.[12] The nation had never seen anything like the governmental activity of those days in 1933 and perhaps never would again. Roosevelt had sent fifteen messages to Congress, and Congress had responded by enacting fifteen major laws. Most of the laws, hastily passed, were attempts to patch up the crumbling economic structure. Not all moved through the legislative mill with the speed of the first, the Emergency Banking Act, which took only eight hours from its introduction to presidential signature. But that record tells something of the feverish flavor of the time. Even the bill creating the Tennessee Valley Authority, a plan designed not to patch but to

144

UNIVERSITY
PRESIDENT
AND
SOUTHERN
LIBERAL

reconstruct a whole region, was passed in less than a month of congressional debate. Congress, like the country, lived breathlessly from day to day, revived by hope, expectant with action.

The second session of the Congress, beginning in January, 1934, had moved more slowly. Much had been achieved in the first session by efforts to repair the economy, but the poor were still with the country. Recovery had not come from hope and action, and Roosevelt himself seemed to be having second, cautious thoughts. An unemployment compensation bill had been introduced in February, and late in the session an old-age pension bill had been reported favorably by committees in both houses. The initiative had been taken from the President, and apparently feeling that all social security legislation should be coordinated, he began to fear that Congress would create a crazy-quilt of welfare laws.[13] On June 8 he sent a special message to Congress asking for no new laws but urging the harmonization of all pending legislation during the next session. He announced that he was looking for sound means to recommend insurance against social hazards, particularly unemployment and old age, and indicated his preference for a federal-state cooperative program. "Our task of reconstruction," he insisted, "does not require the creation of new and strange values. It is rather the finding of the way once more to known, but to some degree forgotten, ideals and values. . . . Among our objectives I place the security of the men, women, and children of the nation first."[14]

Later the same month Roosevelt announced his plan for developing legislation. An executive order of June 29 involved the unusual creation of a Cabinet Committee on Economic Security and an Advisory Council. The committee, of which Miss Perkins was chairman, was to make recommendations to the President by December 1; the Advisory Council was to "assist the Committee in the consideration of all matters coming within the scope of its recommendations."[15] In addition, the committee was authorized to appoint a technical board, and Edwin E. Witte, long an advocate of unemployment compensation in Wisconsin, was named executive director. His became the impossible task of bringing harmony out of chaos. That he was not entirely successful is evidenced by the hodge-podge bill passed the following year; but in the presence of irreconcilable proposals, ignorance, and political machinations, it was testimony to his skill that any bill emerged. Certainly the gyrations of those months could never again be reproduced.[16]

Because Perkins and Witte considered their first task the establishment of the technical committee, the Advisory Council was not appointed until late October. Graham had been carefully selected as chairman because he was both a Southerner (it was anticipated the greatest opposition would come from the South) and a genuine progressive. But the delay in naming the council meant that it could not possibly have the strong influence upon the cabinet committee that Roosevelt had apparently envisaged. Indeed, the business members of the council came to feel that they were being used for public relations purposes only, and they doubted that it was ever intended that their views should be given serious consideration. Whatever Roosevelt's intentions may have been, Graham and others on the council never doubted that their recommendations would be highly valued.

Graham undertook his responsibilities with enthusiasm. He felt he had finally been brought to the point where he could have a direct share in shaping a national program for human welfare. Suddenly, into a few November days had been brought all his concerns for human beings: the sympathy for the underdog, the concern for the consequences of the industrial revolution, the sensitivity for the plight of the worker, the feeling for the dispossessed and despised, the awareness of the downward pull of poverty. He saw in the battle for social security the most important immediate means toward the renewal of democracy, and he saw a chance that "the old society may yet become the great society of liberty and opportunity, security and happiness for more and more of the people of America and the world."[17]

That, at least, is how it seemed to him when he made a major address on November 14 as chairman of the National Conference on Economic Security. The conference, called by President Roosevelt, was designed to focus attention upon the problems faced by the council. The 150 invited delegates from throughout the country met first at the White House to hear the President set the theme for the sessions.[18] There was complete amazement when they heard him say, "I do not know whether this is the time for any federal legislation on old age security";[19] and not all the adroit interpretations by Secretary Perkins the following day could explain away what he had said. In their addresses both Perkins and Graham left no doubt that this was the time for federal legislation, not alone for old age insurance, but also for unemployment compensation,

146
—
UNIVERSITY
PRESIDENT
AND
SOUTHERN
LIBERAL

security for children and their mothers, and health and disability insurance. Graham proclaimed:

> The human casualty of an industrial society is unable alone to provide for his own security. Labor unions, fraternal organizations, and cooperative societies are necessary. Social legislation is required for minimum wages and maximum hours. But social insurance is indispensable to security against unemployment, sickness and old age. These millions of human beings provide the life and labor necessary to industrial civilization, but our modern civilization with its fragmentary view of human beings and human society, makes but little provision for the security of their labor, sickness and old age.[20]

Graham's task as chairman of the council was two-fold: to express his own views without compromise, and to mediate among the conflicting views so that recommendations might be made to the committee. Although he was successful in the former task, he was unable to reconcile antagonistic positions. The best that could be done was, through a sense of fair play, to make it possible for each divergent position to have representation in the council, before the committee, and subsequently at congressional hearings.[21]

It would not be accurate to say the council "deliberated." The deadline for recommendations and the diversity of opinions made deliberation impossible. There were four sessions of the full council lasting two or three days each, and there were a number of subcommittee sessions. When the council began its work, there were various possible areas of legislation proposed for consideration: old age pensions, old age insurance, unemployment insurance, aid to dependent children, maternity benefits, health insurance, public health, and vocational rehabilitation.[22]

The main attention of the council, as of the committee, was given to unemployment insurance; slightly less attention to old age insurance; and little attention to the other matters. The basic issues before the council, thus, were: What kind of systems shall be established? Where shall the funds be secured? If payrolls are taxed, what shall be the rate? What shall be the benefits? The arguments advanced in resolving these issues were labyrinthine, because any answer reflected both a philosophy of government and complex actuarial estimates; but in general, the basic report of Graham's council was both more consistent and far stronger than either the cabinet committee's recommendation or the act as passed by Congress. On every point at issue, Graham personally advocated a strong program, one that moved either toward complete national control (in the case of old age insurance) or toward setting national norms (in the case of subsidy recommendations for other programs) and one that had a high rate of payroll tax contributed by the employer and a high rate of employee benefits.[23]

The council had little direct influence upon the specific writing of the legislation for a number of reasons, the most important of which were the lack of time in which to arrive at clear decisions and to communicate them to the committee, the preconceptions of the members of the technical and cabinet committees as to what type of bill should be written, and most important, the belief of the President and his cabinet that Congress would not accept a national program. In any case, Graham and the most liberal wing of the council supported the President's legislative proposals at the same time they made clear their opinion that the law did not go far enough in giving essential security to the American people. Graham argued that inadequate legislation meant the law would soon have to be revised.

On February 2 Graham testified before the Senate Finance Committee in the large, bare Finance Committee room. Most of the committee viewed him as an impractical professor. During the first part of the hearing, he gave the audience that impression, too, by being overly apologetic for not being an expert, by becoming confused at the scornful baiting of Virginia's Senator Harry Flood Byrd concerning North Carolina's financial incapacity to participate in any program, and by apparently desiring to make a speech. But under the more friendly questioning of Alabama's Senator Hugo Black, he declared emphatically his position that the financial resources should come from industry and the government, not from the worker, because "unemployment is a matter of industry and the nation, and not the workers' responsibility." He insisted that any program be predominantly national in scope, since "American economic society is national in nature"; and upon the final query of Byrd about what should be done if North Carolina could not financially support a program, he answered firmly, "If there are States who cannot meet this expense the Federal Government has a great national responsibility and should make a supplementary grant-in-aid."[24]

When the chairman inquired if he had a further statement to

148

UNIVERSITY
PRESIDENT
AND
SOUTHERN
LIBERAL

make, he concluded with what some of the senators around the table considered good campaign talk but hopeless idealism. But he meant what he said, and speaking spontaneously, expressed in nine sentences his awareness of the meaning and challenge of American history:

I would just like to say this and then I am through. I think this committee has one of the greatest opportunities of any committee of the United States Senate, that any committee has ever had. With all of us doing the best that we can with what we have we can work out of this present situation.

As I think of it now there are, in one sense, three large periods in American history. Here was a great wilderness, and the Americans with their axes and rifles, subdued that wilderness with initiative, enterprise, courage, daring, and social vision. Then, with scientific knowledge and mechanical devices, we have mastered this great physical continent.

I think today we face, in a sense, a great wilderness, a great wilderness of unemployment, insecurity, desolation and fear. I believe the American people focused today in your councils and deliberative bodies can, in this generation, with inventive capacity and daring, enterprise and social vision, work out social problems and build a cleaner, a nobler, and more beautiful America. That is my faith.[25]

The bill that finally emerged in Congress was far weaker than the one Graham and the Advisory Council had recommended. The employer tax contribution, for instance, was not as high as Graham had advocated. But the act did contain provisions for assistance to states for unemployment compensation and various forms of aid to needy dependent children, to the health of mothers, to the needy blind, and to public health. A national old age insurance was adopted, conditional upon the states passing cooperating legislation. Even the weakened act was a significant step in the United States. It was passed overwhelmingly by both the Senate and the House, and on August 14, 1935, was signed into law by President Roosevelt, who stated that the act was "the cornerstone in a structure which is being built but is by no means complete."[26]

In September, 1936, President Roosevelt appointed Graham a member of a twenty-one-man committee to study vocational education; in April, 1937, the President authorized the committee to expand its considerations to the entire subject of the relationship

FIGURE 17. Dr. Graham as president of the University of North Carolina.
North Carolina Collection, UNC Library

FIGURE 18. Frank Porter Graham and his wife, Marian.
North Carolina Collection, UNC Library

FIGURE 19. South Building with the historic Old Well, the center of the university campus, was adjacent to Old East, Graham's first dormitory. *North Carolina Collection, UNC Library*

FIGURE 20. Mock tombstone erected by supporters of the UNC School of Engineering after its transfer to North Carolina State College. *North Carolina Collection, UNC Library*

FIGURE 21. President Franklin D. Roosevelt, left, is joined by Governor Clyde Hoey, center, and Dr. Graham in Chapel Hill in 1938.
Division of Archives and History, Raleigh, N. C.

FIGURE 22. Dr. Graham, left, with Governor Clyde Hoey and Dr. Walter C. Jackson of The Woman's College in 1939. *North Carolina Collection, UNC Library*

FIGURE 23. Dr. Graham with his former teacher and longtime friend, Ambassador William E. Dodd in 1943. *North Carolina Collection, UNC Library*

FIGURE 24. Dr. Graham receives some sage advice from bandleader Kay Kyser.
Southern Historical Collection, UNC Library

FIGURE 25. Eleanor Roosevelt arrives in Chattanooga, Tenn., to speak at the Southern Conference for Human Welfare in April, 1940. Left to right: Dr. Graham, Conference Chairman; Mrs. Roosevelt; Lucy Randolph Mason, Public Relations Counsel for the CIO in the South; Carl Thompson, Jr., Public Relations Representative for the conference; Dr. Rufus Clement, President of Atlanta University. *Acme Photo, UPI, Franklin D. Roosevelt Library*

FIGURE 26. Dr. Graham visits the Marine base at New River, N. C., in November, 1942. Left to right: General J. C. Smith, commanding general of the post; Dr. Graham; Josephus Daniels; and Brigadier General Allen Hal Turnage.
North Carolina Collection, UNC Library

FIGURE 27. The War Labor Board, Washington, D. C., January 16, 1942. Seated, left to right: Vice-Chairman George Taylor, Chairman William H. Davis, and Frank Graham. Standing, left to right: E. J. McMillan, Matthew Woll, Walter C. Teagle, A. W. Hawkes, Roger Lapham, George Meany, Thomas Kennedy, and R. J. Thomas.
Franklin D. Roosevelt Library

FIGURE 28. The Committee on Civil Rights which met with President Truman in October, 1947. Left to right: Rt. Rev. Henry Knox Sherrill, Channing Tobias, Richard Potter, Rabbi Roland G. Gittlesohn, Francis P. Matthews, Morris Ernst, John S. Dickey (rear), James B. Carey, Mrs. Sadie Alexander, C. E. Wilson, President Truman, Most Rev. Francis J. Haag, Mrs. M. E. Tilly, Boris Shiskin, Dr. Graham, Charles Luckman, and Attorney General Tom Clark. *Associated Press-Wide World Photo, Harry S. Truman Library*

FIGURE 29. Students and townspeople gather in front of the president's home to bid fare-well to Dr. Graham on his appointment as a United States Senator.
Southern Historical Collection, UNC Library

FIGURE 30. A rare time for relaxation.
Southern Historical Collection, UNC Library

between the federal government and state and local education. Graham was the only university president on the committee, and despite the fact that the greatest area of educational deficiencies was in the South, he was one of only three Southern members.[27] Since he had long been an ardent advocate of federal aid to education, seeing in such support the only long-range hope for what was essentially a rural and Southern problem, he studied carefully the material prepared by the staff and wrote many of his own memoranda. He attended most of the more than forty lengthy committee meetings and conferences.

On February 18, 1938, the Advisory Committee on Education made a radical departure from tradition in its report, which advocated federal aid to public schools, to library service for rural areas, and to teacher and adult education. In comparison with other federal programs the financial recommendations were not large, calling for an expenditure of $873,750,000 over a seven-year period to supplement the existing grants of $382,123,000 to the land grant colleges for vocational rehabilitation education.[28]

The specter of federal control arose; but the committee dealt with it forthrightly, pointing out that there was not undue federal interference in the land grant colleges and proposing that the congressional bill specify that there should be state and local control in all essential matters. The committee also recommended that where there were racially segregated school systems there should be an equitable allocation of all federal funds without any cut in the existing state appropriations to Negro schools. In a national radio address Graham emphasized that "Federal aid to education became a historic part of the American system before even the adoption of the Constitution."[29] It had continued not only in agricultural, vocational, and higher education but in aid to states for agriculture, roads, health, research, and social security. "Failure to provide federal aid now for the elementary and secondary schools is a failure of the American system to follow through for the most basic of all our institutions." It would be a failure in equal educational opportunity for all children. Graham, too, wanted local responsibility and authority, but he saw no way out of the Southern, rural educational dilemma of less money and more children apart from a federal program. "Just as within the States children in rural localities can have a fairer educational opportunity only through State aid to the localities so children in the rural states can have a

150

UNIVERSITY
PRESIDENT
AND
SOUTHERN
LIBERAL

more equal opportunity only through federal aid to the States."[30]

As a public proponent of federal aid to education he traveled in 1938 to twelve states explaining the program in more than one hundred addresses. Explanation, he was convinced, would be enough, for once the people understood the need and the proposals, they would recognize that there was nothing un-American or socialistic about the program.[31] A bill based upon the recommendation of the Advisory Committee report was introduced in Congress, but it died in the House Committee on Education, the victim of the continuing fears of federal control of schools.[32] It seemed that the acceptance of the principle of national aid to the public schools would come only in the distant future, if at all. Yet the support of federal aid to education was in harmony with Graham's insistence that the chief concern of the nation was social and economic justice. It was in harmony, too, with his battles for justice closer home, in the University and in the South.

12

A More Democratic South

*In the South two great races have fundamentally
a common destiny in building a nobler civilization, and, if we go up, we go up together.*[1]
—FRANK PORTER GRAHAM (1931)

IN JUNE, 1938, PRESIDENT ROOSEVELT AUTHORIZED
the National Emergency Council, directed by Lowell Mellett, to
make a study of the problems and needs of the South; and he appointed an Advisory Committee on Economic Conditions in the
South to assist with the project.[2] Roosevelt envisioned the study as
the first in a series of regional reports, but no other studies were
made.

The advisory committee, consisting of twenty-two Southerners
of diverse occupations, met July 5 in Washington, with Graham as
chairman. Roosevelt requested that the conferees assist in drawing a
picture of the South "in order that we may do something about it";
for, he wrote, "It is my conviction that the South presents right
now the Nation's No. 1 economic problem—the Nation's problem,
not merely the South's."[3] Graham, along with most of the committee, sadly agreed with this description and was excited by the
hope that at long last the federal government was going to give concerted help to the South.

When the phrase, "the Nation's No. 1 economic problem," was
shouted from headlines throughout the nation, the reaction of other
Southerners varied. Virginia's political leaders were ominously
silent, and Senator Bailey of North Carolina was defensive: "The
South has advanced much in the last twenty-five years," he said;
but the credit for that belonged not to the New Deal but to "our
forefathers who rebuilt the South after the Civil War."[4]

The Report on Economic Conditions of the South was transmitted to the President on July 25, but it was not released until Roosevelt began political campaigning in the South two weeks later.

152

UNIVERSITY
PRESIDENT
AND
SOUTHERN
LIBERAL

Southern governors were generally favorable; many Southerners, however, resented the report. Anti–New Dealers were suspicious of its political motives, considering it "an unnecessary reflection on the region and an obvious groundwork for more 'interference' " from Washington. But since the report had been developed by an advisory committee of respected Southerners, and since its findings were what Southern social scientists had been saying for years, those who saw the South insulted by it were effectively silenced.[5]

A mine of succinct information on life in the South, the report was a factual, and woeful, story of tremendous waste of natural and human resources. "The paradox of the South is that while it is blessed by nature with immense wealth, its people as a whole are the poorest in the country."[6]

The report described the natural resources of soil, water, and land and told how these resources had been abused through exploitation or neglect. With more than a third of the nation's arable land and with two-thirds of the region receiving an annual rainfall of forty inches, it also had sixty-one percent of the nation's badly eroded land and lost three hundred million dollars worth of fertile topsoil each year. Although there were abundant water resources, relatively little use was made of them in terms of transportation, power, fish and game, and health and recreation. Communities throughout the South needed better systems of water supply. Two-thirds of the farming was in tobacco and cotton. The latter was sheer gamble; and each year two million families staked their lives on the cotton crop. While the Southern farmer grew more cotton and tobacco than he could profitably sell, four-fifths of all he ate he did not grow but had to buy. More than half of the farmers were tenants working land they did not own. With a decrease in tillable land, migration increased, taking away from the South many of its ablest people, mainly in the middle-aged groups, and leaving the region to the very old and the very young.[7]

The facts of income, education, health, housing, labor, and the status of women and children were parallel stories. The richest Southern state ranked lower in per capita income than the poorest state outside the region. Industrial wages in the South were the lowest in the country; and with twenty-eight percent of the country's population, its federal income taxes in 1934 were less than twelve percent of the total.[8]

In no Southern state was the average teacher's salary equal to the average of the nation. The region was forced to educate one-third of the nation's children with one-sixth of the school revenues. It was no wonder that, especially in the rural areas, there were overcrowding and short school terms and that only sixteen percent of the children enrolled in school were in high school, compared with twenty-four percent outside the region. And as for higher education, "The total endowments of the colleges and universities of the South are less than the combined endowments of Yale and Harvard."[9]

In health, "The South is deficient in hospitals and clinics, as well as in health workers. Many counties have no facilities at all." More than one-half of all the families, by conservative estimates, had inadequate housing. Child labor was more common than in any other section, and "in a region where workers generally are exploited, women are subjected to an even more intense form of exploitation."[10]

In the important areas of finance and industry, there had never been enough credit to meet the needs of the people and of industry. In 1937, with twenty-eight percent of the country's population, the South contained only eleven percent of the nation's bank deposits; and the expansion of industry, essential to a prosperous society, was plagued by problems of absentee ownership, the high cost of credit and freight rate differentials, and the nation's high tariff policy, which forced the South to sell its agricultural products in an unprotected world market while buying more expensive manufactured goods.[11]

The report was compacted into sixty-four pages. Though it was a startling summary, no summary could do justice to the inescapable but frequently suppressed facts. They spoke for themselves, demanding, pleading with those who loved the South to devise ways to transform the society.

But throughout the statements of resources and needs, the report gave no emphasis to the one fact that had run through Southern history like a scarlet thread, ever entangling, ever inhibiting, ever frustrating the attempts to create a full democracy. It was merely stated, incidentally to the fact that the South had a larger percentage of peoples from early American stock than any other region, that the population was "71% white and 29% colored." The explanation for the omission of analysis of that simple fact was that the report was concerned with economic needs; the deeper reason

154
——
UNIVERSITY
PRESIDENT
AND
SOUTHERN
LIBERAL

was the hope that in the interest of improving the economy, bitter controversy over racial matters might be minimized. It was not to be so; nor did Graham and others expect that it would be so, considering the fact that the biracial structure existed as a challenge and a threat to every attempt to improve Southern life. "In the South," Graham had said openly in his inaugural address, "two great races have fundamentally a common destiny in building a nobler civilization and, if we go up, we go up together."[12]

Graham was one of many people in the South who had long been alert to the facts that the report contained and had worked at transforming the economic and social life of the region. But whenever those people's concerns were expressed, it was always through a homogeneous group: a state organization such as the North Carolina Conference for Social Service, which was still strong in the thirties; a white study group such as the Southern Policy Committee, which since 1934 had, in cooperation with the University of North Carolina, prepared papers on the Southern scene; vocational organizations such as the Southern Tenant Farmers Union, which had fought with courageous leadership for the rights of the dispossessed, and the labor unions, which were usually at war among themselves but were trying desperately to improve the lot of the workers. There seemed to be a thousand and one such groups, many of them suspect by middle-class white standards, and to many of them Frank Graham belonged or gave his support.[13]

But the problems of the South were Southern, and there was no comprehensive regional organization to cope with them. Nor was there any movement that could bind together mill hand and mill owner, sharecropper and independent farmer, college professor and minister and housewife, white-collar worker and blue-collar worker and the many more who worked with no collar at all. Most of all, there was no South-wide organization that brought together Negro and white to work toward common goals.

In July, 1938, when the Advisory Committee on Economic Conditions in the South was meeting in Washington, other Southerners had gathered in Birmingham, Alabama, dreaming of coordinating the efforts of liberals throughout the South and formulating a program of action. They planned a meeting to create a permanent organization. This meeting, convened September 6, consisted of one hundred representatives from seven Southern states, who elected officers and voted to have a South-wide conference in

November. Judge Louise O. Charlton, a United States Commissioner in Birmingham, distinguished for both her charm and her organizational ability, was elected chairman, and three vice-chairmen were named: William Mitch, forceful district president of the United Mine Workers; Sam Roper, president of the Alabama Federation of Labor; and Clyde Helms, a Baptist minister. Other officers included an Alabama congressman, the Birmingham postmaster, a newspaper columnist, and representatives from the League of Women Voters.[14] Frank Graham, who was not at the meeting, was asked to give the keynote address at the Birmingham conference and to serve as chairman of the Thomas Jefferson Award Committee, which was authorized to "choose the Southerner who has done most to promote human and social welfare in line with the philosophy of Thomas Jefferson." He readily acceded to both requests.[15]

Supreme Court Justice Hugo Black was selected to receive the first Thomas Jefferson award; and it was Graham, chairman of the committee, who chose the words from Jefferson that would appear on the award medal: "Equal and exact justice to all men of whatever state or persuasion." Black, the egalitarian Alabamian whose former membership in the Ku Klux Klan had raised a furor when he was appointed to the Supreme Court in 1937, considered the conference and award sufficiently significant to journey to Birmingham for his first public appearance as a judge. In a speech that sang the democratic ideals of Jefferson, he accepted the award "as a symbol confided in me for the many Southerners who stand with Jefferson in the belief that good government must give first importance to promoting welfare and happiness of human beings; all human beings, by insuring equal justice to all and special privileges to none."[16] He brought the delegates and visitors at the conference to their feet.

"Equal and exact justice to all" was the theme of Graham's keynote address before the vast integrated audience in the Birmingham municipal auditorium. He spoke out for "the helpless minorities and the underprivileged majorities," with special emphasis upon the treatment of the Negro as the main test of the genuineness of democracy and of Christianity. Describing the retreat of democracy in the face of the totalitarian powers, he appealed for a greater equality of opportunity for all the children, and this meant, specifically, federal aid for elementary and secondary schools.

156

UNIVERSITY
PRESIDENT
AND
SOUTHERN
LIBERAL

Equality of opportunity in the South also meant new rights for the laboring man, new concerns for the farmer, and a fair treatment of the businessman, all without regard to race or religion. His appeal "for the simple thing of human freedom" was not an appeal for bitterness toward anyone or any group, nor was it a call for revolution. The proposals were for building a new South rather than tearing down an old one, and the methods were those of education and religion and the American tradition. He made reference to the spiritual sung by a Negro choir before he arose to speak:

> "Deep River, My Home is Over Jordan." In the overtones of that song in the South our colored peoples are on the march, "into the promised land." This is their home. White and black have joined hands here to go forward by way of interracial cooperation toward the Kingdom of God. With all the marks that have been placed against us in the South let us prove at this Southern Conference for Human Welfare that we stand for the more helpless minorities and the underprivileged. Let us demonstrate, in our stumbling and defective way that we wish to go the Jesus way, the slow way of education and revelation of the inner life. Let us show that this Conference stands for the Sermon on the Mount, the American Bill of Rights and American democracy.[17]

Birmingham, indeed the entire South and nation, had never seen anything like this conference. Twelve hundred delegates and an almost equal number of visitors crowded into the municipal auditorium. Side by side were Negro and white, businessmen and sharecroppers, ministers, labor union leaders, professors, farmers, housewives. Graham spoke for all of them, and when they thunderously cheered him, they were cheering themselves. As he looked at his fellow Southerners who, he believed, were coming together for a common cause without ulterior motives, it seemed that his dream of building a nobler South was beginning to take shape. As he stood there, encouraged by the enthusiasm, his feelings for the conference were those expressed later by Lillian Smith:

> I want most of all for this Conference to catch hold of men's hearts and imaginations, to give them faith in each other, to break down suspicion and fear. I want it to do this not only by fine words but by fine acts. I want us to show that we believe in the democratic process not only by declaring that we do but by being democratic; not only by talking about men's freedoms and working for men's freedoms but by treating men as free human beings. I want us to

hate the exploitation of his labor. I want us to hold in profound suspicion any act that exploits a human being for a goal no matter how excellent that goal may be. You see, I want us to prove to our country that democracy works.[18]

It was a beautiful dream, and the enthusiasm of Southerner finding Southerner, all encouraged by the idealism of Graham's speech, momentarily made it seem that the dream was becoming real. But the dreamers were awakened the next morning by the coarse authority of "Bull" Connor, the Birmingham police commissioner, who told the group's leaders they should have had more sense than to have a racially mixed conference. "Birmingham has a law, and you segregate or else!" When the word reached the delegates, there was consternation, confusion, and bitterness, for the "or else" was clear: arrest and dissolution of the conference. There were those who loudly insisted that the conference should go on as planned, unsegregated. "If this should mean arrest, so be it. Our consciences will be clear." But the moderates prevailed. "A law is a law," they argued, "and our disliking it does not change the fact. Now that it has been brought to our attention we should obey it; and we can at the same time tell the world of our distaste for it." Sadly, the chairman announced the decision at the next full session. There was a subdued shuffling as Negroes moved to the left, whites to the right. "Bull" Connor's police kept careful surveillance over the plenary sessions thereafter. Eleanor Roosevelt, objecting to the policy, sat with the Negroes. When asked by the police to leave the Negro section, she moved across the segregation line. Members of the conference, unsegregated in the smaller sessions, worked for two days discussing the woes of the South and developing resolutions dealing with a whole range of problems from freight rate differentials to human rights, from education to farm tenancy, from wages and hours for women to prison reform, from social security to world peace, from human rights to the Dies House Un-American Activities Committee. The segregation resolution, mildly worded, referred to "a situation we condemn" and urged that if possible, future meetings avoid a similar situation. This resolution (misquoted in newspapers throughout the entire South), together with the presence of some Communists at the conference, brought the first attacks. The conference was assailed for condemning all forms of segregation and for being controlled by the Communists.[19]

158

UNIVERSITY
PRESIDENT
AND
SOUTHERN
LIBERAL

Graham, who had left the second day to attend an educational meeting in Richmond, read the attacks in the Southern press but was certain they were false. He had been in Birmingham; he knew the leadership; he had set the theme for the conference. Race and Communism were not the issues. The conference was, in his view, the moderate approach of North Carolina enlarged to the entire South. "The resolutions that were adopted," he wrote a critic, "were nothing more than what the Conference for Social Service in North Carolina has stood for for a long time. This Conference has long stood for equal facilities for Negroes and for justice to them with regard to their legal rights."[20] And he pointed out that unsegregated interracial meetings had been held in his own state.

The simple fact of the attacks and the misrepresentation of the stands taken by the conference inevitably determined a fateful decision. Before leaving for Richmond, Graham had been approached about becoming the permanent chairman, and he had refused, insisting that his name not be considered. He was elected despite his request, and when the urgent telegram and telephone appeals reached him in Richmond, he could not turn them down.[21] He had not wanted the job; but once the battle lines were drawn, he was not reluctant to enter the fray. He was willing to work with those "who appreciate the South and can take it on the chin if necessary for the region and the people they love the most."

His refusal to run from a fight was fully expected by those who knew him best. Lucy Randolph Mason, labor leader scion of an old Virginia family, wrote Graham:

> After the attacks on the Southern Welfare Conference were launched, I knew you would feel compelled to accept the chairmanship. You bring to the Conference leadership something that no one else in the South could give. As for yourself, you so evidently have guardian angels who bring you through every attack by those who cannot or will not understand you and your motives, that I believe you will not be hurt by this connection. For years I have known that the South cannot be saved by its middle class liberals alone—that they must make common cause with labor, with the dispossessed on the land and the Negro. At last we have a Southern conference considering human welfare which combines all of these elements.[22]

On the other hand, Mark Ethridge, editor of the Louisville *Courier-Journal*, warned Graham that because of the segregation issue the conference would be widely discredited. "But I still believe," he added, "that it was a good thing to have and that it did a great deal of good." At the same time, Ethridge expressed his view that a regional council would provide the "ultimate solution."[23]

Such a council had originally been proposed by Howard Odum, a professor at the University of North Carolina and a leading Southern sociologist. Odum and Graham shared basic democratic principles; but they were fundamentally different in personality and methods of working. Odum was publicly quieter than Graham and was more conscious of the social complexities. He had created at Chapel Hill a strong program in Southern regional sociology, whose work had been the indispensable basis of the report on Economic Conditions in the South. Odum believed such research should continue and be made more public. At the time plans were being made for the Southern Conference in 1938, he had proposed an alternative Southern organization that would assimilate the moderate Committee on Interracial Cooperation, which had been organized in 1918, and the research-oriented Southern Policy Committee, which had been active since 1935. Odum's proposal, which evolved four years later into the Southern Regional Council, was for a regional group "analogous to our best universities for making more articulate the researches in the universities and for utilizing the sentiment, action and facts gained by all these groups." He encouraged Ethridge to call together twenty-five white Southerners to plan a program that in his view, unlike the SCHW, would have an "enduring structural relation to the whole South."[24]

Graham planned to attend the meeting called by Ethridge for January, 1939. Prevented from doing so by University business, he sent a paper he had prepared on federal aid to education. He was willing to work with the group of reflective, white, Southern liberals, but he had also committed himself to the battle of the more inclusive Conference for Human Welfare. Although he had not been entirely pleased with the Birmingham meeting, he told Ethridge:

> There was much about the Conference that was impressive to me. We should have the historical understanding and the social insight to know that with freedom and democracy inevitably go mistakes of judgment, tactics, and even action. The only way to have a mistake-proof meeting is to make the biggest mistake of all in not

160

UNIVERSITY
PRESIDENT
AND
SOUTHERN
LIBERAL

having the meeting free and democratic. Of course, the safest thing to do, as some people interpret safety, is to take the cue from our vested interests and privileged groups and not have the meeting at all. If we are to promote research with sincerity, we should at least by example teach our young people that they should take research findings seriously, for further consideration and even action.[25]

Graham, then, accepted the chairmanship of the conference solely because his idealism would not allow him to desert his friends or an organization whose principles he believed in, when they came under attack. The initial attacks had come almost before the conference adjourned. They had come not only from Southern newspaper editors, from "Bull" Connor and others in the Birmingham city government, but from Martin Dies, chairman of the Un-American Activities Committee, which had just been established as a temporary investigating committee of the House of Representatives. Dies had announced on November 26, almost before the delegates had left Birmingham, that he had ordered his staff to go to Alabama to "investigate the whole thing."[26] Graham saw nothing to fear in these bitter-end forces if only the responsible leadership of the Southern Conference would stand firm.

During the first months of 1939 Graham held two meetings of the executive committee of the Southern Conference for Human Welfare to plan the program state by state, committee by committee. Because he had not inherited a competent, responsible board, he tried to add strength through appointing into strategic positions such persons as Mark Ethridge, Lucy Randolph Mason, Rufus Clement, who was president of Atlanta University, and Barry Bingham, who was publisher of the *Courier-Journal.*[27]

During the entire twenty months Graham was chairman, until June, 1940, complex social forces swirled about him. For the first ten months, the forces that beat upon the conference after the initial conservative affront were invisible to the public and even largely invisible to Graham. Beginning in October, 1939, the conflicting forces became irrepressible and pounded with ever-increasing fury; the secret strategies pulsed into a tense climax of open warfare at the second Southern Conference in April, 1940.[28]

From his office in South Building, Graham could discern three main groups that were destroying or eroding the effectiveness of the conference. There were, first of all, the conservative social and business interests, which publicly maintained that Communists were running the conference and privately objected to the inter-racial nature of the organization. A leading Southern banker, who was on a first-name basis with Graham, scribbled across an announcement of a conference program: "Frank can find more crack-pot organizations. Where in the hell did he find this one?"[29] Graham had a long familiarity with such people and their attacks, and he knew of but one way to deal with them. "I propose not to run because some groups shout Communist or Negrophile," he told a friend. "Even more important than this is that we be open and candid with both friend and foe."[30]

There was a considerably larger group who in Graham's judgment were essential to the success of the conference—responsible Southern white liberals. Without other groups, the labor unions, for example, or farmers or industrialists, the conference would lack strength; without respected white liberals it could not possibly survive. There were many reasons why, after an initial participation, many white liberals were disaffected. Some felt that they had to withdraw for political reasons. These included such persons as Senator Claude Pepper, Congressman Luther Patrick, Brooks Hays, and Francis Pickens Miller. Miller, a long-time friend of Graham's from YMCA days, had political ambitions in Virginia; and he left the Birmingham conference early when he observed a Virginia Communist present.[31] Other liberals disagreed with Graham that there should be an inclusive, direct-action organization. They insisted that Southern problems could best be dealt with by the type of organization for quiet research and public information that Odum had proposed.[32]

Finally, Graham recognized from the outset that there were a handful of Communists active in the organization. At first he neither knew who they were nor knew that they were particularly respected or powerful. His method of dealing with them was to let them have their say and to try to bring them out into the light of day where they could be opposed openly, in fair combat. To be a Communist was not illegal; and Graham's attitude was based upon his sense of law and freedom:

I do not object to the members of any political party Democrats, Republicans, Socialists, Communists, or what-not coming into an open democratic meeting so long as it is open and above board. I am in favor of the majority who have a decent sense of fair play

162

UNIVERSITY
PRESIDENT
AND
SOUTHERN
LIBERAL

and a Christian sense of ethics and who believe in wise and humane movements for more liberty and democracy in a real American way holding their ground and maintaining their control of the Conference against the devious methods of both Communists and Fascists. I refuse to run in the face of Communist intrigue on the one side or smearing by powerful and privileged groups on the other.[33]

In the fall of 1939 the charges about Communists in the Southern Conference began to come increasingly from reliable sources, and Graham became aware that there were forces that were not acting in the open. He saw that, to meet both the responsible and the irresponsible criticisms, he must learn precisely the number and names of the Communists. The next step was not merely to grant them freedom but to make certain that they operated aboveboard. Then, marshaling the forces of the democratic liberals, the Communists could be defeated openly and decisively.

Graham tried to get the facts. He wrote to three or four who had been charged with being Communists. He told them:

I am not personally concerned with your politics, religion, or economic views. I am concerned that I tell the truth in answer to any question I am asked with regard to my official, in addition to my personal, responsibilities. I am not one of those who think that Communists should not have the rights and liberties guaranteed in the American Bill of Rights. I have taken and will continue to take stands in behalf of the Constitutional freedom and rights of all minorities. I simply wish to have in writing from you a statement on which I can stand in my answers whatever the accurate answers may be. I am always glad to answer any and all questions. The more above board we are and the more light we can have, the more inner-satisfaction we can have, the more influence we can have in the long run.[34]

All those persons to whom he wrote replied readily with vehement denials of any association with the Communist Party.

Graham also wrote to people he trusted, asking them to give him the names of any known Communists in the Southern Conference.

I am not on a witch hunt. I am not asking for hearsay evidence or for anything that you do not know. No doubt a few Communists, in their devious ways, would like to get control of the Conference as a part of an underhanded and even ruthless program. We should give them the fair and open chance of a democratic way of holding our own ground as believers in liberty and democracy. We owe this to the millions of Negroes, under-privileged, and disinherited people all over the South who, through injustice, could become the innocent victims of Communism, Ku Kluxism, or Fascism.[35]

The bits of information he received from these sources added up, at first, to plain facts: there had been five or six Communists at the Birmingham meeting, but they did not control the conference, they had not sponsored it, and they had not been the prime source of the funds. Only one person felt he had sufficient information to provide names. Howard Kester, a Congregational minister, who had fought with the Southern Tenant Farmers Union and who, in those battles, had cooperated with the Communists at the same time he abhorred their views, identified four Communists and two fellow travelers from the more than one hundred persons listed in the conference program. He was careful to point out, however, that "the only positive identification rests securely in the files of the Communist party." Then, after insisting how important it was to know exactly who the Communists were and the devious methods they used in order "to proceed in a very tangled world," Kester added that "the corresponding secretary of the Tennessee branch of the Southern Conference is Opal Lee, or Howard Lee (at times), a not so well known Communist."[36]

Graham was shocked. Less than a month before, in mid-November, 1939, he had appointed Lee the executive secretary of the Southern Conference! After Lee had been suggested for the important position, Graham had checked his credentials. Lee had received high recommendations from many people and clearance from three who Graham thought were well informed and reliable, though one other had warned that Lee's appointment would "surely and disastrously backfire on the Southern Conference" largely because of his personal way of working. The same informant, whom Graham did not know, was convinced that Lee was not a Communist but added that "his politics and beliefs are almost identical with those of the Communist party."[37] In spite of the warning, Graham had appointed Lee, only to learn that it was indeed "a tangled world." The new information provided by Kester meant that Graham would have to take personal responsibility for the development of the second South-wide conference, scheduled for April, 1940, in Chattanooga. The theme of the

164

UNIVERSITY
PRESIDENT
AND
SOUTHERN
LIBERAL

meeting was to be "Democracy in the South";[38] but the vital problem was whether the conference itself was to be democratic.

In January the conservative *Chattanooga News–Free Press* printed a statement by Representative Dies that the conference was being planned by Communists. At the same time a local story reported that the Southern Conference had requested that the conference be closed to the public, including reporters, and that permission be granted to seat Negro and white delegates together on the convention floor. This information, coming from Julian La-Rose Harris, editor of the *Chattanooga Times*, was news to Graham; and he immediately asked Harris, Barry Bingham, and Mark Ethridge, all Southern newspapermen, to meet him in Chattanooga to work out the problems with the city officials. They agreed at the meeting that it not only was undemocratic but would be disastrous to prohibit the press or public from attending the conference, and they quietly persuaded the Chattanooga officials to allow the conference to be unsegregated.[39]

One of the Southern Conference leaders, Clark Foreman, reported to Graham that W. T. Couch, the liberal director of the University of North Carolina Press, had written that he planned to propose a resolution denouncing Russia. Such a resolution, Foreman felt, was completely out of place in a conference devoted to "Democracy in the South." Warning that it could only cause trouble and that he personally would find himself "unwillingly voting with the Communists," Foreman urged that all resolutions be limited to Southern matters. But limiting the freedom to deliberate and debate was foreign to Graham's nature. Furthermore, he had already stated that the conference was opposed to the "undemocratic ways of dictatorships."[40] The day before the conference opened, when Couch told Graham he would not attend because he understood the majority would limit statements to Southern problems, Graham urged him to bring to the Chattanooga meeting his resolution denouncing the Russians.[41]

Couch attended the conference and at the first business session, on April 14, presented his resolution. The Communists, with tactics carefully planned, raised the point of order that since the conference was concerned only with Southern problems, the resolution could not properly be considered. Graham pointed out that in Birmingham German aggression had been denounced and that the South was inextricably involved in international problems,

so he ruled that the resolution was clearly in order. There was a
call for a vote on Graham's ruling; the furor began. One by one
the few Communists tried to control the debate and give the appearance of overwhelming opposition to the ruling. They refused
to yield in debate, and there were fisticuffs as delegates grabbed
for microphones on the convention floor. Graham, irate at the
tactics, pounded the speaker's desk for order and, in the intensity
of the moment, used his black-rimmed glasses for a gavel and
shattered them. When order was resumed and the vote taken,
Graham's ruling was upheld, and the Couch statement was sent
to the resolutions committee.[42]

The Communist bloc was not yet defeated, however. The Communists thought it possible to manipulate two groups that were far
larger than they but lacked a knowledge of Communist tactics: the
primarily religious and largely pacifist group that conscientiously
wished to keep America out of war and desired to focus upon
pressing Southern problems; and those members of the United
Mine Workers who were strongly opposed to Roosevelt's foreign
policy. These could be counted upon to oppose or weaken any
resolution dealing with the international crisis.

The second stage of the Communist strategy was two-sided. They
would work in the resolutions committee to weaken Couch's resolution, and they would conduct a campaign to discredit Graham.
The attacks upon Graham in the conference rooms and hotel corridors were vituperative and bitter. He was a "tool of Wall Street,"
a "lackey of the mill barons"; he was charged with being a pseudo-
liberal, in favor of segregation and opposed to the admission of
Negroes to his own university.

In the committee, the Communists tried to wear down the
members in an effort to destroy or weaken the resolution on Russia.
The committee sessions were interminable. Late one night Graham, who was not on the committee, was awakened by William
Mitch, the chairman, who reported that some of the members,
through disgust and weariness, had left the meeting. Among those
remaining, there was a strong sentiment to strike out all adjectives
in the resolution. It was argued that the wording would be much
stronger with nouns not modified by any adjectives.

"There is one reason and only one reason for that, Bill," Graham
said. "They want to get rid of the word 'Communist' from the
resolution."

166

———

UNIVERSITY
PRESIDENT
AND
SOUTHERN
LIBERAL

"Right," replied Mitch, "and they will get it out over my dead body."

Mitch took the Couch resolution which he and Graham had revised back to the committee.[43] After hours of hammering away, he was able to report it to the conference substantially as it had been rewritten by Graham:

> We deplore the rise of dictators anywhere, the oppression of civil liberties, the persecution of minorities, aggression against small and weak nations, the violation of human rights, and democratic liberties of the people by all Fascist, Nazi, Communist, and imperialist powers alike which resort to force and aggression instead of the processes of law, freedom, democracy, and international cooperation.[44]

Graham felt that the battle was still not over, for he believed determined Communists would make their last play in the floor fight over the resolution. At his urging, the liberals caucused and made plans for confounding the inevitable Communist strategy of monopolizing debate and proposing confusing amendments. When at last the resolution came to a vote, it was passed by an overwhelming majority.

All other matters of the conference, even including a major address by Mrs. Roosevelt, paled in contrast to the importance of the simple resolution of opposition to the dictatorships of Fascist Italy, Nazi Germany, Communist Russia, and imperialist Japan. The small group of Communists had not attempted to control the entire conference but to prevent it from speaking out on the one issue on which they were particularly sensitive.[45]

The Communists' defeat was a vindication of Graham's long-held belief in freedom, his cherished conviction that freedom of speech was a fundamental right, and his belief that the Communists should be brought into the open, since there they could be defeated by the forces of genuine democracy. It appeared an even greater victory for Southern liberalism. The conference had been attacked bitterly by the conservative right outside and the radical left within, but it had not succumbed. The defeat of the Communists in Chattanooga seemed clear indication that the democratic center had held firm. The way seemed open for the responsible persons in the conference to move ahead in the creation of a more democratic South.

Yet it immediately became evident that there was further trouble ahead when the Communists, frustrated by their defeat, introduced a resolution that the Southern Conference favor immediate admission of Negro students to the University of North Carolina. No other university was mentioned: it was obviously an attempt to embarrass Graham. So few were the Communists in the Southern Conference, so ineffectual their leadership, that the attempt was abortive.[46]

The nominating committee of the conference decided to make certain that no Communist or Communist sympathizer would receive a nomination for any post. But the committee could not agree upon a person for chairman; so to provide time to find a successor, it asked Graham to keep the chairmanship of the executive committee. He agreed to hold on until the meeting of that committee in June.

Following the meeting in Chattanooga, Graham was convinced that years of great usefulness awaited the Southern Conference if only good leadership could be found. Eminent, qualified Southerners were approached; none was willing to accept a position with the conference. The noises and bruises of the battle had been too great; the times, particularly with the increasing concern over American involvement in war, were not right. Unable to find adequate leadership and pressured by tasks at the University, Graham reluctantly became willing to accept the advice of those who thought the conference should lie fallow for a while. The executive committee, however, insisted on electing a chairman, and chose the Rev. John B. Thompson, left-wing minister of the Oklahoma University School of Religion. The choice was acceptable to Graham, who believed Thompson to be "a sincerely fine person." But following Graham's term as chairman, the voice of the Southern Conference became more strident. Invective against traditional forces in the South was used for the first time and with increasing frequency.[47]

Barry Bingham was one of those who had become disenchanted with the organization. In May, 1940, he took his concerns directly to Graham. He was troubled not simply by the presence of Communists on the board but by the fact that, like it or not, the nation in its excitement over "fifth-columnists" was in for a period of witch-hunting. Any nonconformist organization such as the Southern Conference was destined for certain trouble. And Bingham

168

UNIVERSITY
PRESIDENT
AND
SOUTHERN
LIBERAL

had strong doubts whether the promise of the group was worth the inevitable trouble or possible personal catastrophes. Prophetically, he wrote Graham:

> You are a man who has a great responsibility and a great work to perform in the South. That work is too important to be jeopardized by your running unnecessary risks with public opinion. I feel you have performed a real public service in keeping the Conference afloat so far, and I know at what sacrifice you have performed that task. I want to say without flattery that you are the best democrat, with a small "d" that I have ever known. Please believe me when I say that I am more concerned for your prestige and the maintenance of your full usefulness than I am for any other factor in this whole situation. The South cannot afford to lose one whit of your leadership.[48]

Graham did not consider resigning from the organization. He considered Bingham's appeal a reason for staying in the Southern Conference. Moreover, the Communists had been defeated in a clear and open battle. Gradually, he had come to believe that "the reason the Conference is criticized is not because it is one per cent Red but that it was fifty per cent Black."[49] As soon as he had sensed this, there was no possibility that he could resign, for although others might recognize it as prudent, resignation would be for him the desertion of fellow Southerners who were trying against odds to create a more democratic South.

Part Four

Triumphs:
1940-1949

13

"The Central Issue Is Human Liberty"

Modern democracies stand face to face today with communist and fascist dictatorships. . . . The stakes are too great, and catastrophic developments are too swift for the universities to stand aside. . . .[1]

—FRANK PORTER GRAHAM (1943)

ON SEPTEMBER 1, 1939, THE GERMAN JUGGERNAUT rolled across the Polish border. Great Britain and France declared war two days later. The United States, prohibited by a prior act of Congress from sending aid to any of the belligerents, was officially neutral. England's voice in Prime Minister Winston Churchill's accent rang in Commons and reverberated throughout the world:

> We shall not flag or fail. We shall go on to the end. . . . We shall defend our island, whatever the cost may be. . . . We shall never surrender; and even if . . . this Island or a large part of it were subjugated and starving, then our empire beyond the seas, armed and guarded by the British fleet, would carry on the struggle until, in God's good time, the New World, with all its might and power, steps forth to the rescue and the liberation of the old.[2]

The New World was not yet ready. The prevailing sentiment was to send help, but not if it meant the risk of war. As the Battle of Britain raged with "the survival of Christian civilization" in jeopardy, more than sixty percent of the American people, according to Gallup polls, were convinced that it was more important to stay out of war than to help England. Supported by a strong minority in the country, President Roosevelt was ready to step forth to the rescue, and following each new disaster in Europe, he adroitly maneuvered to get war materiel—weapons and munitions, planes and destroyers—to England.

Almost ten years before, Graham's inaugural address had begun with a reference to war and the demand that universities help build a warless world; and he had pointed out, even then, that "modern democracies stand face to face with communist and fascist dictatorships." This longing for peace and this implacable hatred of totalitarianism had been reiterated through the decade of the Depression. Both attitudes, he felt, required the same two-fold response: the strengthening of internal democracy, and cooperation among nations. In 1935 at the Williamstown Institute of Human Relations, he had reasoned that American democracy could survive in the world crisis by making necessary political and economic adjustments.[3] Returning to Williams College in August, 1938, to speak on "The Challenge of Totalitarian Dictatorship to Democracy," he had proclaimed that "in America we would seize the hour not for a dictator, and not for war, but to put our house in order according to the intended way of a real freedom and a just democracy." America, then, should lead the way in making the world "safe for differences" by exhibiting free minds and equality of opportunity, since the best way to stand against war and against totalitarianism was to stand for democracy.[4]

All this was changed by German aggression. Now Graham felt it was necessary to oppose. The resolution adopted by the Southern Conference for Human Welfare deploring totalitarianism with its violation of human rights was one expression of that opposition. The resolution was not, however, sufficiently strong for Graham personally; and at the very moment he was helping to steer its passage past the bitter Communists and the reluctant isolationists, there was on his desk in Chapel Hill a letter from William Allen White requesting a contribution to a forthcoming symposium, *Defense for America*. Graham quickly responded, and in the volume published in June he joined others, including the presidents of Harvard and Yale, political analysts, and religious leaders, in saying, "This is our war." Though he was strongly opposed to totalitarianism, he returned to the characteristic tactic of being for rather than against, even, he was convinced, ultimately for the Germans: "We favor immediate aid to the Allies with equipment and supplies because the democracies, with all their own injustices, frustrations and failures give the world's people, including the German people, more hope of the opportunity to struggle for peace, freedom, democracy and humane religion as the basis of them all."[5] Direct aid was not enough; American democracy had to be strengthened within, and a more democratic league of the peoples of the world had to be organized. On June 1, following a visit to the White House at which the President had spoken confidentially of the fearsome developments on the shores of the English Channel and within France, Graham wrote Mrs. Roosevelt:

> When I think of Hitler I almost despair; then I think of our democratically elected leader of the peoples of the world and I have faith and hope again. There has never been such a team as you two in human history. . . . I know the president could voice for the world the deep aspirations of people everywhere for a new international order through a more democratic league of peoples based on principles of justice, freedom, democracy and international law backed up by an international police force.[6]

Reports of the German attack upon England daily disrupted the quiet summer in Chapel Hill, and Graham, like millions of his fellow Americans, watched with admiration the few in Britain to whom the free world owed so much. As he went about the work of the University, he tried to place the events of the moment in their historical setting; and for the convocation opening the 147th session of the University, he carefully prepared an address on "The University and National Defense." While "the case of democracies is not all white and the case for the dictators is not all black," he said, the meaning of the conflict should be clear to all. "Stripped down to the most precious things of the human spirit and to the humane liberties of common men, the central issue is human liberty, the freedom to struggle for freedom and justice in the nations, and the freedom to struggle for the organization of justice and peace in the world."[7]

Graham announced that by action of the Board of Trustees, the University, "a child of the American Revolution," was offering "its total resources to the nation for the defense of the freedom and democracy it was founded to serve."[8]

He would have liked to offer himself in the same way. After a faculty member, a major in the Army, returned for a brief visit to the campus, Graham wrote about how fine he looked in uniform. "The only thing about it was I wanted to get into a uniform just like yours and join you."

Before breakfast on March 20, 1941, Graham glanced at the front page of the Raleigh *News and Observer* and was amazed to see his picture with the announcement that the President had appointed him a member of the eleven-man National Defense Mediation Board. The two-columned story reported that his appointment had also been a surprise in Washington.[9]

It was greeted on the floor of Congress with shocked outrage. Representative Walter C. Ploeser of Missouri rose in the House on April 15 holding in his hand a booklet, "The Fifth Column Against the Dies Committee." He quoted the section stating that Graham had been president of the Southern Conference for Human Welfare, which Earl Browder had identified before the Dies Committee as a "transmission belt" for the Communist Party, and that he was a board member of the "University of Moscow summer school for training students in communism." If the facts were true, Graham should be investigated, concluded the representative, since "he is no man to represent the public on this super mediation board."[10] By the time Ploeser made his attack, however, Graham was already in Washington involved in his first labor case.

Graham's initial knowledge of the National Defense Mediation Board and its functions had been limited to newspaper accounts. The Lend-Lease Bill, symbolically numbered H.R. 1776, had been passed March 11, making the United States the "arsenal of democracy." But labor troubles were crippling the flow of essential goods, and there was a strong move in Congress for the passage of anti-strike legislation. Roosevelt established the Mediation Board, the newspapers had it, to forestall the passage of an anti-labor bill. The board's main purpose was to get the war materials to the front by making certain "that all work necessary for national defense shall proceed without interruption and with all possible speed."[11] But the board was given little guidance and less power. It could work only with those disputes certified to it by the Secretary of Labor, and it was given no enforcement powers—only the authority to mediate and to make recommendations. There were dire predictions of failure by some senators; Arthur Krock's column in the *Times* was headed "A Rocky Path Ahead for Mediation Board."[12]

Graham did not know intimately any of the men with whom he would be working closely in the coming months. The appointments to the board were uniformly hailed as among Roosevelt's best, but there was grave doubt expressed about the wisdom of having a tripartite division of representatives from labor, management, and the public. Representing management were Walter Teagle, chairman of Standard Oil of New Jersey; Roger Lapham, president of Hawaiian-American Steamship Company; Cyrus Ching, vice-president of U.S. Rubber; and Eugene Meyer, publisher of the Washington *Post*. Representing labor were Philip Murray and Thomas Kennedy of the CIO, and George Meany and George M. Harrison of the rival AFL. The public representatives, who would obviously be crucial in the board's work, were Clarence Dykstra, president of the University of Wisconsin and head of Selective Service; William H. Davis, a lawyer who was chairman of the New York State Mediation Board; and Graham.

175

"THE
CENTRAL
ISSUE IS
HUMAN
LIBERTY"

When the board met in Washington for its organizing session on March 24, Graham gained further information about both the seriousness of the situation and the functions of the board. Newspaper headlines told menacingly of the strike called at Bethlehem Steel, which would idle 21,000 workers; of the strike-breaking troubles at Allis-Chalmers, where $45,000,000 in defense contracts were tied up; of the threats by the CIO for a general strike in Chicago; and of the close-down of a Ford plant, which endangered the entire automobile industry. The first session of the board was announced in a story reporting that, since January 1, strikes had been responsible for the loss of a million man-days on Army contracts alone. The total number of strikes and lockouts had risen from 147 in December, 1940, to 316 in March, 1941, and man-days lost because of work stoppages had risen from 458,314 to 1,543,803. A board lacking the authority of initiative and enforcement powers was expected to solve these problems.[13]

It immediately became evident that since the President had not provided principles, the board would have to proceed pragmatically from case to case. It was, in truth, a mediation board; and despite the inevitable friction of personalities and viewpoints, the working relations were unusually harmonious. The effectiveness of this informality is indicated by the fact that in March and April, when the first cases came to the board, all the workers involved in the disputes were on strike, but by October none of the workers in the cases before the board were on the picket line.

No one or two persons were responsible for the board's achievements, and even though the many opinions were signed, individual activity cannot be identified with precision. It was a team effort.

The public members held key positions, however; and it was two of those members, Graham and William H. Davis, who were the effective catalytic agents that made of the board's diverse elements an effective compound. Davis, who became chairman of the board when Dykstra resigned on July 1, was a Maine Democrat with a robust, Whitmanesque love of and confidence in democracy. An aversion to force and an admiration of persuasion were matched in him by a distrust of principle and a devotion to fact. He maintained that too many wars had been fought over abstract principles, and to the last, he insisted that negotiation should proceed pragmatically.[14]

The eight months following Graham's appointment to the board were a period of some of the most intensive and important learning that he had ever known. And the achievements he shared with his fellows on the board matched the learning. "I suppose," he told Southern educators later, "I was the greenest person on the Board. Green people have to learn. . . . I tell you the truth, I didn't then know the difference between a closed shop and a union shop."[15]

Almost all the cases brought to the board involved the questions of union security or wages or both. Graham was especially interested in the former, since for years he had been an ardent supporter of labor unions. That had begun when, as a student of history, he became enamored of voluntary self-government and began to see in history a pattern developing in which the church, the corporation, and the political party—all forms of voluntary organization—had developed and defended human freedom. The newest organ of democracy was the labor union. Without the union, he was convinced, the worker was helpless; with the union, he was free to participate democratically in the struggle for freedom and equality. It was not surprising that many observers feared that Graham might be too friendly to labor.

For hearing individual cases, the board was normally divided into panels of three persons, one representative from labor, one from management, and a public member as chairman. The first case thrown to Graham's panel, on April 1, 1941, involved union status, the case of "Snoqualmie Falls Lumber Company and the Puget Sound District Lumber and Sawmill Workers, an A. F. of L. Union." Snoqualmie Falls was a small company, and Puget Sound a small union; but those lumberjacks in the woods of the Northwest had been on strike for six months. John Steelman of the Conciliation Service said it was the most stubborn strike he had ever known. The issues over union security began to be symbolic of the larger struggle between labor and management. The differences seemed irreconcilable. For Graham, whose work to this point had involved leadership and administration, there could not have been a better, or rougher, initiation into the quiet, stubborn work of a mediator.

When representatives of the union and management appeared before the board panel, they showed not only a deep distrust of each other but an open resentment toward the government's interference in what they considered a private battle. "Here you talk about fighting Hitler and his vicious regimentation," they both said, "and yet you start to fight regimentation by regimenting us, and we just don't like it." The distrust of each other and of the board had to be dissolved. After the panel listened to the disputants through the day, Graham had off-the-record sessions late into the night. He met first with the workers. Noticing North Carolina names among the delegation, he inquired, as any Southerner would, where the men had come from and about their families. For two hours the talk was personal, about the counties in North Carolina where their forebears had lived, about the migrations west, about their schools and churches, their communities and families. As one told of being superintendent of a Sunday school and another of membership on the board of aldermen in his little town, as they talked with pride of the forest where they worked and with reminiscent pleasure of summer picnics, some of the distrust began to dissolve, and gradually Graham came to feel that they might speak frankly about the dispute. He soon discovered that they had not seen the full effects of their strike.

"Now, boys," he said, "just tell me. I know what you said on the record, but just give me the lowdown on this. Here you have been striking for six months. You know what you have done?"

"Don't say what we have done," they interrupted heatedly, the distrust reappearing. "Say what the company has done."

"Anyway, you are a part of the situation and you share the blame. There is a battleship being built in Newport News that may be needed to go into the war. Work is stymied because it needs special wood from the Northwest forests. That is over in Virginia just north of where your people came from. And there is a great airport that is under construction by the army out in your section that has stopped." He continued with a list of crippling effects of their strike.

"Well," they agreed, "that is pretty serious."

177

"THE
CENTRAL
ISSUE IS
HUMAN
LIBERTY"

"It is, and that is the reason—off the record—I want you to give me the lowdown."

"All right, Mr. Graham, we will tell you the truth. We hope we didn't show it today, but we are scared to death. We have struggled and struggled for years to get a union. You know what it was once to join a union, it just meant you lost your job. Well, we've struggled to get this union and we think we ought to have some say-so about the terms under which we work. But the company doesn't want to give us a union shop. They talk about the freedom of the company. Well, we are talking to you about democracy."

They talked until four in the morning. Graham returned to his room in the Washington Hotel and wrote down the things that were on their minds. Heading the list was their desperate desire for the security of the organization they were building.

After another full day of listening to formal charges, complaints, and arguments, Graham asked the employers to meet with him, and suggesting they ought to know better than the workers what was involved for America and the world, he asked if they wouldn't speak their minds confidentially. He listened in amazement to almost the same words the workers had used the night before.

"Mr. Graham, we are scared to death. We are making a stand here for the democratic rights of management to manage. For God's sake, hasn't business got some rights left in this New Deal Era?"

"Well, what are you scared of?"

"We are afraid this union is trying to take over management. You see encroachments going on all over the country. Somebody's got to have the nerve to stand up and fight it out. We have stood for six months, and we haven't given an inch, and we are not going to give an inch. There is too much at stake. Not just the right of the company to mind its business—the right, too, of men not to join a union. We know men who won't have anything to do with that union, and we are not going to force them to join it. We are just not going to do it."

Returning to his hotel room in the early morning hours, Graham listed the major items in management's position. As he reflected upon the two long, informal sessions, new items appeared: the sincerity and, according to their lights, the democratic idealism of both sides. This combination became the keystone of all later negotiations. With sincerity and a degree of idealism, the hardest conflicts might be resolved, he thought. Without those elements mediation was hopeless.

179

"THE
CENTRAL
ISSUE IS
HUMAN
LIBERTY"

Putting together what the union wanted and what the company wanted, he was able to get agreement on a compromise position, "maintenance-of-membership," whereby a man was free to join or not join a union, but once he voluntarily joined was required to remain a member in good standing for the life of the contract. Graham did not know that a similar formula had been used in a few cases by the Labor Board in World War I.

Union security was the most important issue involved in work stoppages. Snoqualmie Falls was the first case resolved by a maintenance-of-membership proposal. A similar solution was used again and again, sometimes by mutual consent of the disputants, sometimes with protest by one side or the other. It did not become a formal principle, since Chairman Davis feared abstract principles, but in 1941 it did become the most effective solvent for disputes regarding union security.

If the formula gave strength to the Mediation Board, it also, months later, destroyed the board. In November John L. Lewis, a bitter foe of the President's foreign policy and a more bitter foe of big mine owners and big steel companies, brought to the board a case involving workers in coal mines owned by the steel companies. In all large independent mines Lewis had fought through to a closed shop. In the "captive mines," those owned by steel corporations, ninety-five percent of the miners were union members, but Lewis wanted the same closed shop principle. Lewis requested, then fumed, then threatened. His foghorn voice bounded off the walls of the hearing room, resounding in headlines across the nation and echoing on editorial pages. Never were the lines more sharply drawn: it was clear from the outset how the labor and management representatives on the board would vote; all the pressure was on the public members. Because the board had in another case recommended a closed shop for a West Coast shipyard, it was anticipated that they would yield to Lewis's demands. "If the Board refuses the miners a union shop," Lewis roared, "the Board is through. The Board chairman, Bill Davis, a fine patent lawyer, is through."[16]

Davis, like Graham, could not be threatened. Unanimously the public members voted against Lewis, insisting that there was no question of union security, since ninety-five percent of the workers were union members, and that a closed shop would force a monopoly upon all mine workers.[17] Lewis raged, calling Graham "that sweet little son-of-a-bitch." The CIO members of the board walked out.[18]

It seemed too late for the forces of democratic mediation, whether within America or in the world. On the morning of December 7, the Japanese Ambassador left a conference at the White House. Later that day, but shortly after dawn, Hawaiian time, Japanese bombers attacked Pearl Harbor.

The day Congress declared war on Japan, an arbitration panel announced that, contrary to the decision of the Mediation Board, John L. Lewis's demand for a union shop in the large steel companies' coal mines had been granted. The National Defense Mediation Board continued to meet, but in the absence of CIO members it was in actuality dead. At the moment of greatest need there was the prospect of the greatest industrial chaos.[19]

On December 11 Germany and Italy declared war on the United States. The President and Congress reacted instantaneously. Now it was a global conflict. On the same day, President Roosevelt called a conference of twenty-four labor and industrial leaders to be moderated by Davis.[20] The President's hopes were that a way would be found through cooperation to ensure maximum production in a free economic system. When the conferees met at the White House on December 17, Roosevelt had been unable to prepare a written statement, but speaking informally, he was at his best.

> We have got to do unheard of things. I have asked you to help win the war, just as much as if you were in uniform. I am going to use a word which none of us likes. The word is "must." I am applying the word "must" to you as individuals, and to myself. A boy the other day was out in a plane. The government did not tell him he had to dive on a battleship and lose his life. That was his "must," young Kelly's own personal "must." And each of you and I, too, have our personal "musts."[21]

Setting a deadline of three days for agreeing upon principles for industrial relations throughout the war, he concluded by reminding the conferees that Congress was poised to pass legislation that would regiment management and labor. "The country is looking to you. I am looking at you. Congress is looking at you. All I can say is God speed your efforts."[22]

Working rapidly, the conferees agreed on three basic points: there should be no strikes or lockouts during the war, all disputes should be settled by peaceful means, and the President should establish a War Labor Board to handle the disputes. On the critical issue of union security, the conference was in irreconcilable conflict, and long past the deadline, Davis reported the deadlock to the President. Industry demanded that the status of unions be frozen for the duration, as it had been in World War I, and insisted that the demands for a union shop were nonarbitrable. The unions felt that something should be given in return for a no-strike pledge, and they believed that if they could not negotiate for union shops during the war, unions would inevitably be weakened.[23]

181

"THE
CENTRAL
ISSUE IS
HUMAN
LIBERTY"

The crucial problem was passed on to the War Labor Board, which was appointed January 12, 1942.[24] Given the duty to "determine finally" all labor disputes that involved the "interruption of any work which contributes to the effective prosecution of the war," the board was also provided with the authority to use "mediation, voluntary arbitration, or arbitration under rules established by the Board."

With half the members reappointed from the Mediation Board, including Davis as chairman and Graham, it was ensured that a policy of persuasion would prevail. In addition, the new board was strengthened by placing the public members on a full-time basis and adding two new ones, Dean Wayne L. Morse of the University of Oregon Law School, and Dr. George L. Taylor, professor of economics at the University of Pennsylvania.[25]

For almost three years Graham held two full-time jobs. He never worked less than sixty hours a week. In addition, he normally spent sixteen hours each week shuttling between Washington and Chapel Hill. He accepted salary solely from the federal government. During the week, he lived in a small room in the Washington Hotel on Pennsylvania Avenue, two blocks from his office at the Department of Labor, which he shared with Morse. He got to Chapel Hill only on the weekends, and not all weekends at that. When he was at home, he had to spend considerable time trying to keep abreast of developments in the University. Wartime transportation was slow and crowded: the Friday night, seven-hour train to Raleigh sometimes took as much as eleven or twelve hours, and there were trips when he had to stand or sit on his suitcase for the long ride south.[26]

The War Labor Board, like its predecessor, was tripartite, with representatives from management, labor, and the public. This division was both its greatest weakness and its greatest strength. The weakness lay primarily in the fact that though there was desperate need for haste in resolving disputes, the divisions on the board meant that the problems were worked through slowly. Throughout the years there was a backlog of cases; by December, 1942, the national board found it necessary to create twelve regional boards, which, like the federal lower courts, processed cases on the basis of the national board's decisions. But even with the delays, the national board, in its four-year history, dealt with almost 20,000 dispute cases; and before the end of the war with Japan, it had resolved 17,087 disputes involving more than twelve million workers.[27]

The board's strength lay in the fact that it was democracy at work, and what was more remarkable, at work during the crisis of war. It was not simply the representation of labor, management, and the public that made this possible; it was also the presence of particular people and procedures. The informality of the earlier Mediation Board was maintained: members were frequently in and out of each other's offices on the fifth floor of the Labor Building, communicating factual details and debating fundamental differences. The debates were strenuous. Dexter M. Keezer, at one time a public member of the board, reported that only rarely was the challenge made to " 'Come outside and finish this!' But it was commonplace to have charges ranging from those of deceitfulness, venality, and vulgar avarice to the relatively mild accusations that one was being willfully and stubbornly obtuse tossed around the board and accentuated by shouting and table pounding. It was even more commonplace to have several members of the board talking at the same time, perhaps in a series of independent parleys cutting across the main thread of discussion." There was frank recognition that the members from labor and management represented more than their personal viewpoints; so "it was not unusual for a member of the War Labor Board to characterize one of his colleagues as bountifully endowed with a large variety of despicable human qualities, and then add blandly, 'Nothing personal of course.' "[28]

The public members of the board were often caught in the cross fire of invectives hurled between labor and management, and at times they had the task of deflecting the verbal assaults to ensure that essential issues should not be lost in attacks and counterattacks.

On more than one occasion, the public members were themselves attacked, and if necessary, they could—except for Graham—respond in kind.

At the conclusion of a dissent in a decision that had been against labor, the members representing the unions made a serious charge against the public members: "This decision of the majority adds another to the list of the decisions of this Board which have been determined not on the basis of merit, but rather by that attitude of individuals and government agencies who dominate the actions of the public members of the Board." Davis, Taylor, Morse, and Graham, all men with independent minds, were indignant. Davis, as chairman, was incensed because the charge struck at the heart of the equitable operations of the board; so he prepared a sharp statement, signed also by Taylor, which struck back at the critics: "The last paragraph of the dissenting opinion, filed by certain American Federation of Labor members, evidences an irresponsibility which is entirely unworthy of the labor movement which they represent." Wayne Morse was not satisfied with that statement. The AFL members, he felt, had made "an unwarranted and unjustifiable attack upon the integrity and judicial independence of the public members of the Board." In a long reply opinion, he pushed the labor representatives into a corner, insisting that "if there is a scintilla of evidence which supports the charge," they had an absolute obligation to make that evidence known; if not, the labor members should resign. Graham was also concerned about the attack because it challenged the foundations of the democratic process and the integrity of board members. He, too, had to answer, but refraining from joining in counterinvective, he made a simple affirmation: "The people who control the votes of the public members of the National War Labor Board are the American people, who through the Congress and the President of the United States, have determined the limits of the national stabilization program in the interest of all the people of our nation at war." [29]

Although Graham was unwilling to defend himself openly, if another person were unjustly attacked, he could speak sharply. In another dispute, when Graham reached a decision similar to previous rulings which Morse had made, Cyrus Ching, a genial and six-foot-five company vice-president remarked laconically, "I see Frank Graham has gone to bed with Wayne Morse." Graham heard rumor of the remark and felt that his colleague's honesty was being

183

"THE
CENTRAL
ISSUE IS
HUMAN
LIBERTY"

questioned, since Morse had voluntarily disqualified himself in the case. The members coming to the board meeting knew that something was troubling Graham, and when Chairman Davis, in keeping with the procedure, asked Graham to read the opinion, he arose at the head table, obviously agitated, and said, "Mr. Chairman, I am not ready to read. A grave injustice has been done to Mr. Morse. He refused to let me read opinions he had written in similar cases. Whoever made that remark about us will either have to apologize or knock me down." There was an embarrassed silence; then Ching, almost twice the size of Graham, puffed his pipe, took it from his mouth, and said softly, "Frank, I made that remark but you know I didn't mean anything. Your decision is your own. You can sit down."[30]

A British visitor who attended one of the hearings could not believe what he had seen. Shaken by the experience, he asked one of the members, "Was I being had on when I was told that your Board is like the Supreme Court, that it makes decisions from which there is no appeal?" Assured that such decisions were made, he exclaimed, "Then, I say: why don't you behave like the United States Supreme Court?"[31] The answer was that the Supreme Court would not behave the way it did if the opposing lawyers, after heatedly presenting a case, sat behind the bench to vote on the judgment. Moreover, the board was not alone a judicial agency; in a fundamental sense it was also a legislative body creating labor law and an executive body issuing directives both to the regional boards and to the litigants. It was a strange way of proceeding; and everyone familiar with the division of powers prescribed by the American Constitution could have seen clearly that it could not possibly work.

Yet it did work. There were spiritual factors brought by Davis and Graham from the Mediation Board, factors shared with other members, that were indispensable. Most important were the confidence in democracy, the belief in persuasion, and permeating all else, the trust in people.

Working relations were informal and often seemed chaotic. It was the kind of situation in which Graham loved to work and in which he was at his best. For he could deal directly with everyone from the secretaries to the chairman of the board. It was much the way he had run the University, always leaping from crisis to crisis, always on the move.

But for all the spontaneity of the work, there was a clear pattern to Graham's activity that derived both from his democratic social faith and from his conversation and study into the late night hours. On the one hand he was convinced that the organization of workers into responsible unions was an essential next step in the history of democracy, and on the other hand he knew that democracy moved by compromise. The unions did have the right, he was convinced, to some kind of security. But management and the individual worker also had rights: the one, freedom to manage the industry, and the other, freedom to refuse to join a union.

Some of the earliest and most difficult cases were centered upon the irreconcilable conflict that had destroyed the Mediation Board and had split the President's conference. In the deliberations of the board, Graham joined the others in frank debate; then, when in key cases the board voted, usually eight to four, for the maintenance-of-membership principle he had stumbled on in the Snoqualmie Falls dispute, he wrote the major decisions. Within six months, adding a bit here, modifying there, the board had adopted what amounted to a policy. Thus Graham was able to write into his opinion in a dispute involving the Humble Oil Co. not only that the War Labor Board had a maintenance-of-membership policy, but that in 291 cases prior to February, 1944, it had decided 271, involving a million and a half workers, in favor of such a plan.[32] The policy was later described as one of the most creative and enduring achievements of the war administration.

In writing the most significant opinions in the development of a War Labor Board policy on union security, Graham was giving effective expression to specific beliefs regarding the rights of the working man, beliefs he had first clearly formed in the mid-twenties in England and first clearly expressed in the "Industrial Bill of Rights" in 1929. In a brief opinion written June 5, 1943, he gave expression to another human rights problem that would increasingly concern him and, in a brief time, would engulf the nation: the rights of the Negro.[33]

In a unanimous decision involving an oil company in Texas City, Texas, the board directed that "the classification 'colored laborer' and 'white laborer' shall be abolished. All workers affected shall be classified as laborers and shall receive the same rates of pay for that classification regardless of color."

As the only Southerner on the panel participating in the case,

185

"THE
CENTRAL
ISSUE IS
HUMAN
LIBERTY"

Graham asked and was assigned to write the opinion. It consisted of six paragraphs. The first two contained the decision and specific justifications for it. The last four were an expression of his faith in which he used phrases from his past:

America, in the days of its infant weakness the haven of heretics and the oppressed of all races, must not in the days of its power become the stronghold of bigots. The world has given America the vigor and variety of its differences. America should protect and enrich its differences for the sake of America and the world. Understanding religious and racial differences [makes] for a better understanding of other differences and for an appreciation of the sacredness of human personality, as basic to human freedom. The American answer to differences in color and creed is not a concentration camp but cooperation. The answer to human error is not terror but light and liberty under the moral law. By this light and liberty, the Negro has made a contribution in work and faith, song and story, laughter and struggle which are an enduring part of the spiritual heritage of America.

He emphasized that there were no more loyal citizens than the Negroes who came to the defense of America "in the spirit of Dorie Miller of Texas, the Negro mess boy, who, when the machine gunner on the *Arizona* was killed, jumped to his unappointed place and fired the last rounds as the ship was sinking in Pearl Harbor."

He presented the thesis that the Negro had made more progress in less time in the United States, in spite of slavery and discrimination, than any race in human history; but it was not enough. "Slavery gave the Negro his Christianity. Christianity gave the Negro his freedom. This freedom must give the Negro equal rights to home and health, education and citizenship, and an equal opportunity to work and fight for our common country."

Finally, he stated that America and the Negro needed each other:

The Negro is necessary for winning the war, and, at the same time, is a test of our sincerity in the cause for which we are fighting. More hundreds of millions of colored people are involved in the outcome of this war than the combined populations of the Axis Powers. Under Hitler and his Master Race, their movement is backward to slavery and despair. In America, the colored people have the freedom to struggle for freedom. With the victory of the democracies, the human destiny is toward freedom, hope, and equality of opportunity and the gradual fulfillment for all peoples of the noblest aspirations of the brothers of men and the sons of God, without regard to color or creed, religion or race, in the world neighborhood of human brotherhood.[34]

187

"THE
CENTRAL
ISSUE IS
HUMAN
LIBERTY"

Wayne Morse was not on the panel that made the decision, but he took the unusual step of requesting that his concurrence in the opinion be placed in the record. Almost two years later, serving his first term in the Senate, Morse made reference to the opinion "written, in my judgment, by one of the twenty-five greatest living Americans. I say it is one of the great decisions in the annals of American law."[35] During the war, the Office of War Information broadcast Graham's opinion on the rights of the Negro to Europe, Africa, Australia, and Asia as a statement of fundamental American philosophy.

Graham wrote seventeen opinions, which was far fewer than any other major public member of the board. Serving only two years, Morse wrote well over one hundred; Taylor, over seventy; and Davis, though responsible as chairman for the board's operations, wrote thirty-seven. Even members who served half the time Graham did, Lloyd K. Garrison, Dexter M. Keezer, Lewis M. Gill, and Edwin E. Witte, wrote more opinions. Graham's method and purpose in writing opinions, as well as the subject matter of most of the disputes he handled, largely account for these differences.[36]

Though his opinions frequently employed phrases used in addresses as early as the mid-thirties, each was completed only after lengthy study and deliberate writing. The self-imposed requirement of study was derived from his ideal of research and also, since he came to the board with less practical experience in economic problems and industrial relations than did other members, from his need for accurate information. In preparing the opinions, he did not dictate or use a typewriter; he wrote, usually in the quiet of early morning hours, in his square-lettered hand, which was illegible to everyone but his secretary and his wife. He wrote and rewrote every page, frequently with as much scratched out as retained.

The essential problem he returned to again and again was how to state the democratic faith in the context of the particular issue and the war crisis. Unlike Davis, who felt that each case should be decided afresh with no attempts to develop a policy, Graham devoted his entire work on the board to shaping his democratic liberalism into general policies relevant for particular issues. His absolute certainty that the history of democracy was the history of free men forming their lives through self-organization developed into the maintenance-of-membership policy; his absolute faith in "all men as brothers and sons of God" became "equal pay for equal work."

While Graham was interested primarily in the underdog, in the rights of union security and the rights of the Negro, there were far more disputes centering upon other factors, such as grievance procedures, seniority rules, discharge, and contracts, in which he had less interest. There was the whole host of problems involving wages and fringe benefits with which he had even less familiarity. Though he participated and voted in the disputes involving these issues, he rarely wrote an opinion dealing with them.

In the spring of 1945 a Johns Hopkins professor wrote a careful evaluation of the significance of the board. "Barring a few exceptions," he stated, "it has maintained harmonious labor relations. And it has also succeeded in stabilizing wages." Pointing out that the board had contributed to a more rational pattern of industrial relations by its emphasis on such policies as maintenance-of-membership, equal pay for equal work, and partially eliminating the prevalence of substandard wages, he concluded that "even if the Board should go out of existence, its influence will be felt a long time in the future. Many of the policies developed by the Board will prove to be eminently useful as a starting point and, in some instances, as a permanent framework for the development of democratic industrial relations."[37]

While Graham was working without letup, Justice Felix Frankfurter once heard rumors of another call to service overseas. In scrawling hand he wrote Graham:

> I want to congratulate you on the quiet effectiveness with which you secured adoption of your 48 hour coal-digging adjustment. You are one of those rare men who care passionately about furthering justice with complete indifference to that childish consideration of credit.
>
> Which leads me to say something I hope you won't deem officious. For it's not my business, but does concern public welfare. I have heard rumors that efforts are afoot to entice you away from your present job for labor among to-be-liberated peoples . . . . But

if it's all one 'front'—and rightly—as the president says, what is the sense of taking a key man from the U.S.A. and putting him into Patagonia? It not only has no sense—it's close to being irresponsibly wicked. For you are a key man (to put it mildly) on the most delicate sector of the 'home' phase of the war. For the country's sake, don't go.[38]

189
"THE
CENTRAL
ISSUE IS
HUMAN
LIBERTY"

During the years Graham served full time on the War Labor Board he saw Marian and the University only on the weekends. He kept in touch with University problems through the administrative staff. Most of Graham's concerns were for the Chapel Hill campus, but no major decision was made in any of the units without his concurrence and usually his active participation. Running the University was left to individual faculties and departments and fell more and more into the hands of others, particularly the chief administrative officers at each of the three units and William Carmichael, who was appointed controller in 1940 and had an aggressive and loyal ambition for the University.[39]

The task of directing the University during wartime was complicated by the fact that while civilian enrollment decreased (from 3,663 to 1,387 at Chapel Hill during the four years from 1941 to 1945) more than 20,000 men attended the University in special training programs. Since these students used the resources of the University, including the faculty, their presence required painful adjustments.[40] But Graham had offered the University to the nation, so the adjustments were made in good spirit, even though, as he wrote a friend, "We are running a two ring circus."[41]

There were complaints from North Carolina against Graham. As early as July, 1942, after serving on the War Labor Board for only six months, Graham had received a letter from Professor William deB. MacNider maintaining that he was needed at the University for guidance and constant counsel. "It is important for us to know more of you here at home," MacNider told him.[42] Graham was troubled. If a devoted friend and ardent supporter could feel this way, then how much stronger must be the feelings among others! But the decision and promise to serve the country had been made; he could not suddenly renounce a commitment. The dissatisfactions in the University, especially at Chapel Hill, grew with each month until in the spring of 1944 the faculty unanimously adopted a statement that Graham's absence "has retarded unduly and inevitably the administration of affairs" and that the faculty members "lack cohesion and direction."[43] It was partially in response to this discontent that Graham, in a lengthy ten-year report to the trustees, included detailed statements by the three deans of administration, which appeared to indicate that the University in its multifarious activities had not suffered unduly because of his absence. Graham, who earlier in the year had started giving one-third of his time to the University, reported that he had conferred with Chairman William Davis of the War Labor Board about returning to full-time service at the University, but that Davis had asked him to continue on the board with the present schedule.

> I have no illusion as to my indispensability. The Board's maintenance-of-membership policy, now in jeopardy, is basic to the national effort toward both maximum production and minimum inflation. Since this part of the Board's policy has, by a division of work, been assigned to me, it is only fair to the work of the War Labor Board that, with your approval, this matter of my early return be timed in accordance with the judgment of the Governor, the Executive Committee, the Chairman of the War Labor Board, and the president who made the appointment.[44]

His explanation did not satisfy the trustees. As a body and individually, they continued to urge him to resign from the War Labor Board or, at the least, to give more time to the University. "I do not think . . . if it came to choosing between the WLB and the University, that you should quit the University," Charles Tillett wrote on June 3. "I think that you could calm the whole thing down by spending your time continuously at Chapel Hill for the next few weeks and thereby give your faculty members an opportunity to come to you and tell their troubles to you." Tillett had been shocked by the fact that when he had talked with one department head about his problems, Graham's name had not even been mentioned! "I do not think he would be satisfied to moan on any shoulder of less dignity than the one belonging to the president."[45]

The situation did not get any better during the summer, and on October 2 the Board of Trustees requested that Graham return full-time to the University. He wrote his letter of resignation to the President on October 9, but it was not accepted. Roosevelt requested that he remain on the board at least half time until the war with Germany was over or until leaving would not impair the work of the board. Graham acceded to the request (as did Davis and Taylor, whose resignations had also been refused). The University board, deciding that half a loaf was better than none, concurred in the decision. Yet the restiveness on the faculty and among some trustees was not entirely allayed.[46]

191

"THE
CENTRAL
ISSUE IS
HUMAN
LIBERTY"

The war with Germany ended May 8, 1945; the war with Japan, August 14. Graham's resignation from the War Labor Board was accepted as of December 31, 1945. Before his work was completed, however, he was appointed in November by President Truman as chairman of the Oil Panel Fact Finding Committee. To settle the inevitable postwar industrial disputes, Truman planned to appoint a number of fact-finding groups; and since the first major dispute came in the oil industry, that panel was to be the pilot group.[47]

Graham's three-man committee worked through the Christmas holidays, handing their report the second week of January to Secretary of Labor L. B. Schwellenbach, who commented on January 12, "Representatives of both sides have expressed appreciation of the care, patience, and fairness with which the procedures have been developed and the hearings conducted. I am sure that the procedural pattern which the Board developed will prove helpful in the future to other fact-finding boards."[48]

Graham had served on the War Labor Board since its beginning, indeed, since the beginning of its forerunner, the National Defense Mediation Board, which had been established in March, 1941. With the job done, he could at last return to the University full time.

14

A People's Movement for Medical Care

The people's movement rolled on in gathering power from the mountains to the sea. Petitions by the people from all parts of the state, mass meetings of the people, the uprising of communities, columns of news and editorials of support east and west, signboards along all the highways told in facts and figures the needs of the people for doctors, nurses and hospitals here and now.[1]

—FRANK PORTER GRAHAM (1953)

EIGHT DAYS AFTER GRAHAM COMPLETED HIS WORK with the War Labor Board, there was the first meeting of an important committee he had been instrumental in establishing, the "National Committee for the Medical School Survey."[2] For more than ten years Graham had fought intermittent battles for medical education in the University; and two years previously he had played a role in proposing a comprehensive state health program. In 1946 the national committee set the stage for a complex drama.

During the same period Graham was deeply involved in other matters. After returning full time to Chapel Hill from Washington, he devoted his major attention to the University. It was not only a period of readjustment and the creation of new academic departments—City Planning, Mathematical Statistics, Radio and Communications, and Religion at Chapel Hill and an Institute of Statistics at Raleigh—but it was also a time for finding money to meet expanding or new needs.[3] Sometimes the money came with simple action on Graham's part: once, when informed that through an oversight in Washington the bill for GI university housing might become void without the presidential signature, he called

John Steelman, University alumnus and special assistant to the President. The bill was signed immediately.[4]

193

A PEOPLE'S
MOVEMENT
FOR
MEDICAL
CARE

Other monies came with more activity. John Motley Morehead, chairman of the board of Union Carbide, noted that there were only five major planetariums in the nation and none in a university, so he informed Graham in 1946 that he would give two million dollars to his University for building a planetarium. The money was accepted immediately; the details took weeks to work out, and Graham alone negotiated with Morehead.

The liberal Democrat and the conservative Republican, recognizing that they were poles apart in politics, got on well with each other. Morehead noted at one point that Graham did not receive the salary he deserved and offered him a personal gift of $10,000. Graham refused. As they continued to talk money, Morehead told Graham, confidentially, of other millions he planned to give the University. When Graham pointed out that he was president of other colleges as well as the one at Chapel Hill and that they also had their needs, Morehead replied, "Mr. President, I am talking about my University at Chapel Hill. This is my life."

Together the seventy-seven-year-old philanthropist and the sixty-year-old university president walked about the campus to find a location for the planetarium. Again and again Morehead rejected available sites because, as he repeated, "My Chapel Hill is not in that direction." Finally they came to a satisfactory spot on the edge of the old Front Campus. "There," Morehead said, "is where I want the planetarium to be."

"There it shall be," replied Graham.[5]

In 1947 the legislature was lavish with money, not so much in appropriations for maintenance as in funds for capital improvements. In maintenance, the budget was increased fifty percent over that of the previous biennium, which made it possible for the first time in twenty-seven years to develop a new salary scale. The new scale, unfortunately, was still in the lower category according to the annual survey of faculty salaries by the American Association of University Professors. With the capital improvement funds Graham and the entire administrative staffs inherited new work that would go into the construction of libraries, dormitories, dining halls, and academic buildings on all three campuses. The greatest single expenditure, almost one-third of the total, went to the expansion of the medical program at Chapel Hill.[6]

The medical program had been approved by the North Carolina General Assembly on March 28, 1947. On that day Graham was able to see the results of more than a decade of work toward a comprehensive program of medical care for the University and the state. The medical care bill authorized the establishment of a four-year medical program and the building of a hospital in Chapel Hill, and the creation of hospitals and health centers in counties and cities throughout the state. It was the most ambitious state program since the educational and good roads campaigns in the early twenties. Like those campaigns, it had been a people's movement; so, while not a single senator dared vote against the bill, mutterings were heard, and one irate legislator complained to his colleagues, "Where the money came from to carry on this gigantic campaign I do not know, and I doubt if you know."[7]

Graham was one of the few who did know. The greater marvel was not where the money had come from but how and why the people had come. For the ambitious medical program was not the work of any one man or any small group of men. It was the result of the patient labors, the refusals to be discouraged, and the sacrifices of many. Victory depended upon those with dreams, such as William MacNider, internationally known for research in pharmacology and known in Chapel Hill for his humanity; FDR and the curmudgeon Secretary of the Interior Harold Ickes; Governor Melville Broughton, with his sympathy and statesmanship; Dr. Paul Whitaker, Dr. William Coppridge, and other physicians dedicated to the medical profession. To name a few is unfair, but to name all, impossible. In any case, Graham was not responsible for the triumph, although he had been continually involved in the battles that led to the ambitious medical program. As he sat in the gallery of the legislature on the day of victory, it was not difficult to remember some of those battles.

Graham's first major involvement in the medical program was the fight in 1935 to save the two-year medical school at the University.[8]

Teaching in medicine at the University had begun in 1879. In 1896 the modest and inadequate program had developed into a two-year school, which in 1898 had been admitted to the Association of Medical Colleges. The school had a number of distinguished scientists. Graduates of the program completed the last two years at some of the best medical schools in the country; and most of them, more than from all the other schools in the state combined, returned to North Carolina to practice medicine.[9]

195

A PEOPLE'S
MOVEMENT
FOR
MEDICAL
CARE

On September 15, 1935, the Council on Medical Education and Hospitals of the American Medical Association passed a resolution stating that "after July 1, 1938, the Council will no longer publish a list of approved two-year schools." With the power to control the number of physicians in the country through the accreditation of medical schools, a committee of the American Medical Association had moved to destroy the two-year medical schools at Chapel Hill and at nine other universities. When MacNider heard the news, he was furious; and when he passed the news to Graham, the crusade started. Together they decided to take on the monolithic AMA committee. Both attended the meeting of the Association of American Medical Colleges, which convened in Toronto on October 28. Graham, unable to participate in the floor debates, lobbied continuously in the corridors for a resolution supporting the two-year schools.

Dean William Pepper of the University of Pennsylvania pointed out in the meeting that a third of the students received during his deanship had come from Chapel Hill, that they had done as well as the students who had finished the first two years at Pennsylvania, and that, though some became leading physicians in Philadelphia, more than sixty percent returned to North Carolina to practice. "I am not theorizing," he said. "I know what I am talking about. I want these two-year medical men at the University of Pennsylvania." He made the motion that the two-year schools be considered on their merits. The vote was unanimous, and the first battle was won.[10]

The second step was to secure a resolution from the National Association of State Universities, which met in Washington on November 21. Five of the two-year schools were represented at the meeting, but Graham was the only person present who had attended the Toronto session. He made certain that a disinterested president introduce a resolution endorsing the Toronto action and stating, not requesting, that the association's views would be represented at the next meeting of the AMA Council on Medical Education. Again, the resolution passed unanimously. The second battle was won.[11]

The first two battles were mild preliminaries. The essential fight was in Chicago at the meeting of the AMA Council in December. Graham directed the strategy. MacNider analyzed the place and value of a two-year school in a university, and George Thomas, president of the University of Utah, showed that in a region of a half-dozen states unserved by a four-year school, the two-year program at his university was indispensable. Graham marshaled the basic arguments: First, the universities needed the two-year schools, since they made a contribution to both the colleges of arts and sciences and the graduate schools. Second, the four-year medical schools, because of their high mortality the second year, needed the two-year schools. Third, the medical profession needed the two-year schools, since the schools enlisted some of the best science students. And fourth and most important, society needed the two-year schools because of the maldistribution of physicians, who were concentrated in the cities and woefully lacking in the rural areas.[12]

The AMA Council voted to rescind its previous action and to approve each two-year school on its merits. When the meeting adjourned, the chairman of the committee, Ray Lyman Wilbur, president of Stanford University, put his arm around Graham's shoulders and leaned over to say confidentially, "Well, you gentlemen have won your reconsideration, but my advice to you is that you get your house in order and prepare the way for the expansion of your school into a four-year medical program."[13]

Wilbur's advice caused Graham to give further thought to the meaning of his experiences of the previous year in serving as chairman of President Roosevelt's Advisory Committee on Social Security. Both in that committee and in congressional hearings, he had been stunned by the bitter, absolute antagonism of the American Medical Association toward social security. On the other hand, within the inner circle of the government, he had heard considerable talk about federal support for a public health program. Three years before Roosevelt characterized the South as "the nation's No. 1 economic problem," Graham had seen it as the nation's dominant health problem; in all that vast area of need there was not one school for the training of public health personnel. In 1935 he made the secret commitment to himself that a school to serve the region should be located at Chapel Hill. Then he went after the money.

The purse strings of the Public Works Administration, in the second year of granting funds for public projects, were controlled by crusty Harold Ickes, Secretary of the Interior; so Graham went to him and also persuaded influential friends in the government to approach him. The University received a grant in 1935. A building to house the new School of Public Health and the two-year medical school was completed the following year. In September, 1936, Dr. Milton Rosenau, the recently retired director of the School of Public Health at Harvard, began work at Chapel Hill.

197
——
A PEOPLE'S
MOVEMENT
FOR
MEDICAL
CARE

In May, 1937, Governor Hoey appointed a committee to make a recommendation regarding medical education; and it reported the following year, favoring a four-year school at Chapel Hill. The proposal was killed before reaching the floor of the 1939 legislature.

In the spring of 1938 the business manager of the University, Charles Woollen, asked Graham informally what his attitude would be toward receiving a large grant from a North Carolina family on condition that the third and fourth years of the medical school be in one of the larger cities in the state. As far as Graham knew, the question was purely hypothetical, but the answer, that he would oppose the acceptance of a grant under such conditions, was direct and unalterable. The matter was never pursued further. Graham was reminded of the conversation when, the following summer, the announcement was made that the Bowman Gray family had awarded a grant to Wake Forest College to build and endow a four-year medical school in Winston-Salem. The men in the Gray family, the father and the two sons, had all graduated from the University at Chapel Hill and were closely related to its history.[14]

Graham decided that he would do nothing more about a medical school until the professionals most concerned, that is, the physicians in North Carolina, exhibited a readiness. For a long time all was quiet. Then, in December, 1943, upon hearing that five past presidents of the North Carolina Medical Society were preparing to present a recommendation to Governor Melville Broughton that involved the University, he went to see the Governor the day after Christmas. It was a Sunday evening, Graham was on his way back to War Labor Board work in Washington, and the two talked earnestly until time for his train. Broughton was beginning his final year as governor and was looking for something unique by which to make a notable contribution to the state. He accepted the idea of a medical program with enthusiasm, and arrangements were made to present proposals to the January meeting of the University Board of Trustees.[15]

The Governor's medical program was carefully planned. On

January 31 he proposed to the University trustees the expansion of the two-year medical school and the creation of a hospital and medical care program for the entire state. Broughton emphasized that "the ultimate aim of this program should be that no person in North Carolina shall lack adequate hospital care or medical treatment by reason of poverty or low income." Though only the medical school was the immediate responsibility of the trustees, they approved the entire plan unanimously.[16]

Responding to the enthusiasm of the trustees, the Governor appointed a fifty-man Hospital and Medical Care Commission to make a study of need and proposals for remedy. Clarence Poe, editor of *The Progressive Farmer*, was named chairman. The commission spent eight months in amassing data which showed that the average national ratio for physicians in 1940 was 1 per 790 people, while in North Carolina it was 1 per 1,554, in rural areas 1 per 3,613, and among Negroes 1 per 6,916. Having demonstrated the great need, the commission issued a call for more doctors, more hospitals, and more health insurance. It recommended a comprehensive plan including a four-year medical school with a teaching hospital (it was not specified where the school should be), loan funds for medical students, improved opportunities for Negro students, the construction of county and community hospitals and clinics, state aid for the care of indigent patients, increased appropriations for public health work, and state stimulation of insurance plans. The commission was especially concerned with working where the need was greatest, which, it specified, was among the poor, the tenant farmers, and the Negroes.[17]

As soon as the commission's report was published, Dr. Paul Whitaker, president of the North Carolina Medical Society, began a campaign to enlist the support of physicians throughout the state. He traveled at personal risk (because of a serious heart condition) to most of the meetings of local medical organizations, urging their adoption of the program. Fifty-five of the sixty-five societies approved the complete plan, and an additional eight approved it in part.[18]

Committees from the Medical Society met in lengthy sessions with the governor's commission, with Graham sometimes present, to write a bill for the legislature. Almost one year to the day after Broughton first presented proposals to the University trustees, a committee including Graham went to the office of the new governor, Gregg Cherry, to secure his approval of the program. Although they knew that Cherry was conservative, they expected his agreement, since in his campaign he had made a forthright statement endorsing the Broughton program. It was not generally known that Graham had written and persuaded Cherry to make the campaign statement.

199
—
A PEOPLE'S
MOVEMENT
FOR
MEDICAL
CARE

After formalities, the Governor's first words were startling. Obviously something had gone amiss. Cherry spoke generally to the delegation, stating that the plan seemed too large, that he could not subscribe to it. "But," he said, turning to Graham, "I think the state may need the four-year medical school; and I believe I could recommend that to the legislature. If you will drop the other parts I'll give you the medical school."

Graham answered quickly, "Governor, I appreciate your trust in the University and in me. But I am for the whole program."[19]

The members of the delegation left despondent, knowing that there was no chance for a comprehensive medical program in the legislature at that time. They would have to rescue whatever bill they could and start again to push for their goals. The bill that worked its way through the legislature called for the creation of a medical care commission that would make a survey of needs in each county and would be responsible for any hospital building program. It also called for a contribution from state funds for indigent patients and for the expansion of the medical school of the University after the location for the school was determined. One of the key legislators refused to support the bill unless a committee of experts from outside the state made a study and recommendation for the medical school. Graham, negotiating on the bill, accepted the legislator's proposal and wrote a new section specifying that no action should be taken regarding the medical school until a survey was made "by the Rockefeller Foundation or some other accredited agency." The provision became crucial.[20]

When Graham saw that the Governor would not fight for the comprehensive program and that the legislature would go no further than authorizing the University to develop a four-year medical school, he was convinced that there was need, once again, for the people of the state to act. He went to see former governors (beginning with Melville Broughton), newspapermen, leaders of women's and farm and labor organizations, educators, and social workers. The North Carolina Good Health Association was organized to advocate state assistance for building hospitals and rural health centers, loan funds for students who would practice in rural communities, aid for the indigent sick, a University four-year school, the study of medical education for Negroes, and voluntary insurance plans.[21]

For the next year the association flooded the state with a massive publicity campaign. W. D. Carmichael, university controller, secured funds from some of the leading industrialists to underwrite the campaign, and Graham scoured the state, making addresses and organizing local committees to get support. Billboards espousing the program appeared on all major highways, advertisements were placed in local newspapers, and spot announcements resounded from radios. Kay Kyser, the popular band leader and graduate of the University, became an enthusiastic supporter, stumping the state.[22]

During the time the people were being aroused, the battle was developing more quietly in another sector. The Governor appointed a new commission, replacing Poe as chairman with James H. Clark, who was not known to be favorable to the total plan. The appointment to the commission of some who were opposed to the program and others who were lukewarm made it seem that the Governor was attempting to modify the proposals. The commission was responsible for bringing in proposals, but a fight within the commission was inevitable.[23]

The Rockefeller Foundation refused to make the required study, as did every other group. At the urging of Graham, Rockefeller officials expressed willingness to sponsor an independent committee. The seven-man National Committee for the Medical School Survey held its first meeting January 8, 1946, electing as chairman W. T. Sanger, president of the Medical College of Virginia. Dr. Whitaker, chairman of the state commission's Committee on Medical School Expansion, secured an agreement from Graham that the National Committee should survey not just the location of the medical school, as had been authorized by law, but the need for the school as well. The proposal was risky, for the committee might well decide that a school was not needed, but it was the only way Whitaker could find to reopen the possibility of developing the comprehensive program.[24]

Most of the National Committee members worked diligently at their task, and on July 1 the committee recommended that a four-year school of medicine with a teaching hospital be established on the campus of the University at Chapel Hill as a part of an integrated health program at the University and throughout the state. The committee stated that the medical center in Chapel Hill should be "integrated effectively and continuously with a state-wide network of hospitals and health centers." The final recommendation, "that the University of North Carolina develop a philosophy of medical education, research, and medical care which will make it a service facility for the whole state," reflected the committee's meeting with Graham and their confidence in him.[25] ("Your president is quite a guy," a nationally known physician from Harvard told Whitaker as they left a conference at the University.)[26] Frank Graham's dream that the University should be for medicine in North Carolina what it was for education, the apex of a system nourished by and nourishing the life of the people, was thus written into the report; and Edward Kidder Graham's affirmation that the boundaries of the University campus were the boundaries of the state was reaffirmed.

201

A PEOPLE'S
MOVEMENT
FOR
MEDICAL
CARE

The committee was not unanimous. A stinging minority report was written by Victor Johnson, secretary of the AMA Council on Medical Education, and Graham L. Davis, who for fifteen years had been assistant director of the Duke Endowment, which had done yeoman work in North Carolina in health and other fields. Opposed to a new medical school, particularly if it should be in Chapel Hill, they were convinced that the two fine schools at Duke and Wake Forest could meet the growing needs. Moreover, they felt that the proposals were overly ambitious.[27]

Before the next battle could be fought within the commission, there were critical days in Washington when the entire North Carolina program hung in the balance. The comprehensive plans depended upon the enactment of the federal Hill-Burton Bill for hospital construction. The bill had passed the Senate easily the previous December with the requirement that the federal government provide one dollar for every dollar of state or local funds. So Graham, confident that the bill would pass the House, was responsible for making major sections of the National Committee recommendations contingent upon its passage.

There was some nervousness in North Carolina circles when in midsummer Congress moved toward adjournment. On July 20 Frank Graham received a call from Senator Lister Hill of Alabama saying that his bill was in real trouble. It was blocked in the House Rules Committee. The chairman of the committee was Representative Bayard Clark of North Carolina. Hill reported that he could not do anything with Clark and asked Graham to fly to Washington to see if together they could pry the bill out of the committee.

As soon as Graham reached the Capitol, Hill left the Senate floor to explain the gnarled situation. Clark was strong for the bill with the full fifty-fifty appropriation principle; Republicans, joined by conservative Democrats, were either entirely opposed to the bill or opposed to the liberal federal payments. Clark was unwilling to yield. Hill suggested that if Graham could persuade Clark to compromise, the bill might get out of the committee and pass the House. Perhaps any formula cut might be restored in the Senate-House Conference. "I put Representative Clark in your hands," he told Graham.

When Graham consulted with Clark, pointing out all the ramifications of failure to pass the bill, Clark promised to report it. He pleaded with the Rules Committee to report the bill out with a one-to-two formula, one federal dollar for every two local dollars. The bill passed in the House; and in the conference the formula was changed to forty-sixty. The battle was not yet over, for whenever Representative Bulwinkle, the North Carolinian who was handling the bill for the conference committee, tried to call it up in the House, he was frustrated by requests for a quorum call by Republicans opposed to the bill. The House was within three days of adjournment, and it seemed likely that the bill would be defeated by a procedural form of filibuster. Senator Hill urged Graham to see Bulwinkle to find some way, any way, to get the bill through Congress. On July 30, in an adroit move, Bulwinkle moved that the bill be sent back to conference. When the Senate conferees reported the next day to their colleagues that no compromise agreement could be reached, the Senate voted to accept the one-to-two House measure. Congress adjourned two days later. The following week Graham received a letter from Senator Hill thanking him for saving the hospital construction bill.[28]

Meanwhile, serious opposition to the program had arisen from three sources. Some dominant financial interests were concerned with the tax burden: "North Carolina needs a medical school," said one of the state's leading financiers, "like I need three legs." More serious opposition came from physicians, primarily those associated with the Duke Endowment, who feared what another school might do to medical work in progress. A third force of vociferous individuals was not opposed to the medical school but wanted it located in the city where they lived.[29]

203

A PEOPLE'S
MOVEMENT
FOR
MEDICAL
CARE

On August 9 Whitaker's committee recommended that the commission request the General Assembly to appropriate funds for a four-year medical school and teaching hospital at Chapel Hill, which would be related to hospitals and health centers throughout the state. "The Committee would like to emphasize the fact that no state-supported medical school has undertaken the role which the National Committee has recommended for the University of North Carolina."[30]

The debate in the commission was intense and, at times, bitter. With the certainty that the commission could not reach a unanimous report, there was a drive by the minority to postpone a decision in the hope of modifying the proposals. The determined Whitaker, armed with material provided by Graham, demanded a vote on his committee's resolution. He won, thirteen to four.[31]

Within the state, the final battle shifted from resistance to the total program to opposition to the medical school and its location in Chapel Hill. If the proponents could be set to quarreling among themselves, the opposition felt, the entire program might be destroyed. The quarreling began. Two of North Carolina's larger cities, Charlotte and Greensboro, made concerted drives to secure the school, and from the latter there was a conditional offer of large sums of money from the Moses Cone estate for relocating the school. The offer was tempting not just to powerful financial interests in the state but to some of the top administrative leaders in the University.

Seven years before, Graham had unknowingly turned down millions of dollars because of his personal conviction that a state school of medicine should be an integral part of the state university. Now the question arose again, somewhat complicated by the fact that one of the University campuses was in Greensboro. To test his convictions, he decided to talk with the three men in the nation most knowledgeable about medical education: Abraham Flexner, who had written influential studies on medical and university education; Alan Gregg, director of medical sciences for the Rockefeller Foundation; and Ray Lyman Wilbur, long an AMA leader.

Flexner was particularly receptive because his daughter admired

Graham's controversial democratic stance. "If I could do something for you," he told Graham, "it would be very pleasing to her."

"I am not asking you to do anything for me," replied Graham. "I'm just asking your advice. Should a medical school be part of a university? Or, if you had big money given to you on condition that a school should be pulled away to a big city, would you take it?"

"Well," Flexner responded emphatically, "I'll answer that question pretty quickly. If they give you fifty million dollars turn them down. That's my answer. Make the school a part of your university. You'll have rough going for a while, but you know there are other generations coming; and you should build with a long future in mind."

Gregg was similarly positive. "We've been studying that problem for some years, and my advice, unhesitatingly, is that your medical school should be at Chapel Hill." The fundamental reasoning of both men was identical: the medical school should be in the same community as the basic sciences of physics, chemistry, botany, and zoology, as well as the social sciences, in order that the fields might influence each other through research and interchange of ideas.

Wilbur, working against time on his autobiography at Stanford, at first said he would be unable to see Graham; but finally, succumbing to persistent requests, he agreed to a brief conference. "But," he remonstrated, "I don't know why you want to fly across the country to see me for fifteen minutes." Graham made the flight.

Pleased with the views of Flexner and Gregg, he approached Wilbur differently: "Dr. Wilbur, do you recall telling me in Chicago more than ten years ago to prepare for a four-year medical school? Well, I bring you your baby." Hastily Graham told of the developments; and he asked Wilbur, on the basis of his previous advice, to write a letter supporting the proposed medical school and, on the basis of his experience in Stanford, advocating the location of the school in Chapel Hill. Though enthusiastic about the school, Wilbur was only mildly concerned with its location, but he acceded to both requests. Graham considered the fifteen minutes worth the seven thousand miles.[32]

But Wilbur did not tell Graham about an action already taken outside the state by the Council of Medical Education which might destroy plans for the medical school. A report in the *AMA Journal* opposed, in general, the establishment of new four-year medical schools. Later, an article by Victor Johnson and others mentioned Alabama and Utah as states where it seemed advisable to expand two-year schools into four-year schools and pointed at North Carolina in concluding, "Unfortunately, this cannot be said of certain other basic science schools."[33]

205

A PEOPLE'S
MOVEMENT
FOR
MEDICAL
CARE

What had not been made public was the council's conditional action at a meeting in Denver not to approve the proposed four-year school at Chapel Hill. Dean Reece Berryhill heard the news the last week in August, and he rushed the word to Graham, who was recovering in a Durham hospital from an operation.

"Well," said Graham, "this is the first I have heard of it. Did they give you any notice of the meeting?" "No." "Did they give the North Carolina Medical Society any notice of the meeting?" "No." "Well, how did they make a decision and not even give us a hearing?" "He said some members of the National Committee were present," reported Berryhill.

But when Graham learned that those present at Denver were the two who had opposed the report, his temperature, already 102 degrees, jumped. Marian was alarmed, but he was not to be calmed. As soon as Berryhill left, he called Victor Johnson, the secretary of the council, who sounded surprised. "Oh, I'm always glad to hear from you, Dr. Graham."

"I want to ask you some questions, Dr. Johnson. Your council had a meeting in Denver and you took action about our school. You're secretary of that commission. I did not receive a notice from you of that meeting."

The voice on the line was incoherent. Graham, in the rush of ire, gave no time for further response.

"Our North Carolina Medical Society received no notice. The University didn't, the medical profession didn't, the commission didn't, the Medical Society study committee didn't, the National Committee didn't."

"Oh," Johnson interrupted, "some members of that committee appeared."

"Yes: the minority. Doctor, the people of the United States are probably not interested in whether we have a four-year medical school at Chapel Hill, but they are greatly interested in fair play. As soon as I get out of this hospital I am going to Washington and though I don't like the headlines I am going to get on the trunk lines of every news service in this country and I am going to tell the American people what you have done."

"Ah, Mr. Graham, you wouldn't do that, would you?"

"That's exactly what I am going to do."

There was consternation in the voice. "Well, wait a while. There's some misunderstanding here. Perhaps you don't know that Dr. Wilbur presided at that meeting."

"And perhaps you don't know," countered Graham, "that I have a letter from Dr. Wilbur endorsing our medical school."

The voice was weak with surprised disbelief. "You have?"

When Graham got back to his desk October 1, he found assurances from the secretary of the council that there was no reason for him to go to Washington.[34]

Still the opposition pressed the fight, determined to defeat the program in the 1947 General Assembly.

A new Fact Finding Committee of North Carolina Physicians hit the front pages of the newspapers February 3 with the claim that two-thirds of the physicians in the state opposed the plan. The basis of the claim was a secret ballot among doctors. But Josephus Daniels pointed out that while two-thirds of those voting opposed the four-year school, only slightly more than half of the physicians in the state had voted.[35]

A large delegation composed of the state's leading citizens appeared before the legislative committee and made the request for forty-eight million dollars to be spent in five years, less than half to come from state funds. When opponents argued that "the problem in the state is not so much the need for new doctors, but the distribution of doctors," L. P. McLendon, a University trustee, replied that he did not know about the figures quoted from the AMA which pointed to no need for new doctors. "But," he added, "I do know that this group was convicted in the Federal Courts of being a monopoly. The trustees of the University are not interested in the glorification of the University. But they are interested in making the University the people's University."[36]

When, on March 28, 1947, Graham sat with his friends in the gallery watching the senators complete passage of the bill, he knew that he had had his part in the long campaign for a comprehensive medical program that would provide better health care for the people of the state.

15

Independence
for Indonesia

In this truce and in these principles, the people
of the Netherlands, the people of the Republic
and all the people of Indonesia have, under God,
a rendezvous with a larger destiny of creative
cooperation in a time and in a world of need of
the best which these historic peoples can give
together.[1]

—FRANK PORTER GRAHAM (1948)

ANOTHER ACADEMIC YEAR BEGAN IN THE MIDDLE
of September, 1947. The freshmen arriving early gave, as always,
new life to the campus. The faculty rekindled the spirit of the University in many an office and laboratory, in the library and Y Court.
The veterans, in larger numbers than the previous year, promised
new maturity, new seriousness, and new problems. There were
more than seven thousand students at Chapel Hill alone, almost
four times the number enrolled four years earlier.

The Grahams had returned to tree-shaded Chapel Hill from
Nags Head on September 2, and early the following day Graham
was in his office in South Building.[2] For the second time in seven
years he was beginning a university year without the responsibilities of a major government appointment. It was not that there was
any less work nor that he was isolated from social and political
problems. But professionally, he did not have to be torn between
official Washington and Chapel Hill, so it would be possible to
give single-minded attention to the problems of a postwar university. Those were enough to occupy a man's mind.

Then the invitation came. The last week in September Graham
received a call from Washington. Secretary of State George Marshall wanted him to become the United States representative on a

three-man United Nations Committee of Good Offices to negotiate in the dispute between the Netherlands and the Republican forces in Indonesia, a dispute that threatened to erupt again into warfare that might well engulf the West. Graham was interested and, pressing for information, was reminded that almost two months earlier the Security Council of the United Nations had adopted a United States resolution calling upon the two forces to "cease hostilities forthwith and to settle their disputes by arbitration or by other peaceful means."[3] The resolution provided no guidance for handling a dying colonial empire and the birth of a new nation. The promised cease-fire had not been kept, so on August 25 the Security Council had established a committee "to tender its good offices to the parties in order to assist in their pacific settlement of the dispute."[4] The United States, moving cautiously in the dilemma between the need for a strong Europe, which consisted of colonial powers, and the need to keep true to traditions of the American Revolution, had its way in the establishment of a three-member committee. Each disputant selected a nation to serve on the committee, and the two selected nations chose the third. The choices were no surprise: the Netherlands selected Belgium, the Republic of Indonesia selected Australia, and Belgium and Australia selected the United States. That the committee was important was clear; how it was to function was vague. Since the infant United Nations had not yet resolved a major dispute, it moved cumbersomely, cautiously, without describing the specific responsibilities and procedures of the committee.[5]

Events moved rapidly for Graham, however. A reluctant University Board of Trustees granted him an indefinite leave, and he was formally appointed by President Truman on October 1.[6] With that matter settled, Graham's first steps were to the library, where he scoured the shelves for books that would teach him something about Indonesia. His final week at Chapel Hill was given to the feverish work of clearing his desk of university affairs and to reading, late into the night, about the people and problems of a land halfway around the globe.

Indonesia, he discovered, was the sixth-largest country by population in the world, its seventy-seven million people living on more than three thousand islands between Australia to the south, the Asian mainland to the north, and the Philippines to the northeast. Stretched across the shortest water route between Asia and Europe, it was also, in the air age, a major thoroughfare for intercontinental plane travel. Here were the island of Bali, with its ancient and gracious culture; the Spice Islands, which lured the explorers of the sixteenth century to the East and to America; Borneo, still largely virgin land, the third largest island in the world; Sumatra, a thousand miles in length lying across the Straits of Malacca from Malaya; and Java, one of the most thickly populated regions of the world with more than a thousand people per square mile—slightly smaller than North Carolina, but with more than twelve times the population. The land was rich with rubber, rice, sugar cane, palm oil, tobacco, coffee, tea, cinchona, petroleum, tin, and bauxite; the surrounding seas teemed with fish; but the average Indonesian's income was less than twenty-five dollars a year.

The people of the islands had absorbed wave after wave of invaders, each invasion leaving threads of its life woven into the many-textured history. There were, in addition to the primitive faiths of the aborigines, three major religions, the Moslem, the Hindu, and the Christian, with more than nine-tenths of the people Moslem. The islands had had centuries of slowly shifting empires until, in modern times, the Portugese, the British, and the Dutch had fought for the rich spoils, and early in the seventeenth century, the Netherlands, in its Golden Age, had conquered the islands. For three centuries Indonesia was the major part of the Dutch overseas empire. It had become "home" to many Dutch, some of the families having lived there for well over two hundred years. The wealth of the country went to Holland or into the pockets of the Dutch Indonesians; and by the mid-nineteenth century, Dutch reformers had begun to protest the treatment of the Indonesians, and the Indonesians had picked up the theme. Movements for freedom gained strength in the twentieth century until the Japanese conquest in 1942.

When the Japanese were driven out, and before the arrival of the Allies in force, an Indonesian Republic was proclaimed on August 17, 1945, by Akmed Sukarno, the revolutionary spellbinder, and Mohammed Hatta, the revolutionary administrator. The Republic included Sumatra, Java, and Madura, with the expectation that it would expand to incorporate all of Indonesia. For more than a year there were, between the Dutch and the Republicans, negotiations and breakdowns in negotiations that always threatened to explode into full-scale warfare. In February, 1946, the Dutch called for the creation of a "Commonwealth of Indonesia," which would be "a partner in the Kingdom," but the Dutch made no mention of the Republic and refused to recognize its authority. It seemed obvious to the Republican leaders that the Dutch were willing to have a free Indonesia only as long as the Dutch were in control.

Finally, in November, under the negotiating pressure of the British, the Dutch and Indonesians met at the mountain resort of Linggadjati and initialed agreements pointing toward the independence of Indonesia. The two governments would cooperate "in the formation of a sovereign democratic state on a federal basis to be called the United States of Indonesia." A number of nations, including the United States and Britain, immediately gave de facto recognition to the Republic. But because of differing interpretations of the agreements, the implementation was thwarted; and on July 20 the Dutch began warfare euphemistically referred to as "police action." With superior mechanized weapons, the Dutch advanced quickly into Republican territory. The Republicans, driven from all major cities, retaliated with the desperation of men fighting for freedom. The outlook was for a brutal conquest to be followed by years of guerrilla warfare. And if any other nation intervened, as appeared inevitable, the world might be shaken once more by war.[7]

For a year and a half the United States, torn by its conflicting loyalties, had been instrumental in preventing the United Nations from taking action. Lake Success, the temporary home of the United Nations, did not seem an appropriate name to many observers, who freely predicted that if it acted in regard to Indonesia the way the League of Nations had acted in regard to Ethiopia and Manchuria and Spain, it would soon go the way of the League. To such observers it seemed fearfully symbolic that the room in which the Security Council met had no windows. In the summer of 1947 there was no alternative to action. The council approved an Australian resolution for a cease-fire, which had been softened in tone by the appeals of the United States delegate, Herschel V. Johnson, who fifty years before had been a boyhood friend of Graham's in North Carolina.[8]

By the time Graham had completed his preliminary reading, his views of his ultimate, general aim were formed; indeed, they had been formed long before he had begun his study, as long ago as his teaching of American history and his devotion to the ideals of Wilson. His inclinations were that Indonesia should ultimately become a free and independent country. The determination was confirmed in his choice of an assistant, Henry Brandis, professor of law at the University, who had been one of Graham's students in American history. Graham's long-term belief in a free nation was strengthened by his conversation with Josephus Daniels, who again and again during World War II had written that a primary goal of the war was the granting of independence to the colonial peoples of the world. On October 4, the eve of his departure, Daniels took Graham aside and said, "Frank, you have always believed in the freedom of the individual and the self-determination of peoples. I hope you can do something in Asia in regard to those principles of the American Revolution."[9]

Although Graham was personally determined to work for the independence of Indonesia, he wanted to be fair to the Netherlands as well and to fulfill his obligations to the United Nations and the United States. This meant that while the ultimate end was freedom, freedom might not be the immediate goal. The means to the final goal, the processes by which freedom would be negotiated, were supremely important. His first loyalty was to the United Nations, since the Committee of Good Offices was a creation of and was responsible to the Security Council. The United Nations Charter referred to the "rights of self-determination"; so his personal goal and that of the United Nations were in accord. The determination to be fair to the Netherlands was aided by the fact that the Linggadjati Agreement, formally approved by the Dutch, had pledged the independence of the Indonesian peoples.

The only real problem, then, had to do with the attitude of the State Department and the degree of freedom it would give Graham to negotiate. Any concerns on these points were dispelled by the two days he spent in conference in Washington before proceeding to the United Nations. It was clear that the State Department was divided within itself between the Far Eastern and the European desks, though, on balance, the more experienced and influential officers were inclined toward furthering the interests of the United States in Europe. Graham felt that this division gave justification for independence of action. In the conversation with Marshall, his attitude was confirmed when it became clear that the secretary considered him, although a representative from the United States, basically responsible to the United Nations. Moreover, clear hints came that Graham had been chosen for the job, in large part, because Marshall anticipated and shared his long-range views on self-determination. On the final evening in Washington, after two days of intensive briefings, Graham and Brandis had dinner with Dean Rusk, the director of United Nations affairs for the State Department; and across the table the three Southerners compared notes on the Indonesian crisis as it related to the world situation.[10]

The following day, in the office of Secretary-General Trygve Lie at Lake Success, Graham met a second member of the committee, Paul Van Zeeland, former prime minister of Belgium, who though formal in approach, soon became impressive because of his moral rectitude.[11] Later in the week, as Graham and Van Zeeland flew from New York to San Francisco, Graham read about Indonesia most of the way and thought of how he was flying that day the distance from the northern point of Sumatra to the southeastern tip of the Indonesian archipelago. It was, indeed, a great land to which they were going. And it was far away: from San Francisco two thousand miles southwest to Pearl Harbor; then two thousand miles, still southwest across the blue Pacific, to the International Airport on Canton Island; another two thousand miles to Noumea, New Caledonia; and then the final leg of fifteen hundred miles to Sydney. Arriving in Sydney on October 19, they met Justice Richard C. Kirby of the Australian Supreme Court, who completed the membership of the three-man committee.

From the first, Graham and Kirby hit it off. Kirby shared the as-yet unspoken aims of Graham. His sense of law complemented Graham's sense of history, and his sensitivity to details harmonized with Graham's sensitivity to people. The entire committee worked with concord despite differences in views. They were civilized men who, as Van Zeeland said, believed that "moral force is enshrined in the United Nations, for the strength of the United Nations is its moral power"; therefore, none of the three underestimated "the moral forces and their effect upon the most concrete realities."[12]

In its original conception, the Committee of Good Offices was strikingly like the tripartite War Labor Board: the rival powers had selected nations that would represent their views, and those two nations had selected the "public member"; and as in the case of the Labor Board, it was the third member who had the most significant role to play. Having learned from his mediation experience, Graham urged in the preliminary meetings in Sydney that the committee proceed, insofar as possible, with informal and frequent meetings, and that, to make for maximum independence, the members view themselves not as representatives of individual nations but solely as representatives of the United Nations. Each would maintain contact with his own nation, and through Van Zeeland there would be special entree to the Dutch. It was decided, further, that the chairmanship would rotate each week and that any action the committee might take would have to be unanimous.

This last decision was, all three recognized, exceedingly dangerous, for it gave any one of the members a veto power; but with the moral character of the three men and their single-minded determination to find a solution, it gave impetus to their work. The committee had received no clear directives; it was to create its own procedures and goals. This provided them with independence to maneuver, independence not only from their own foreign offices, but from the Security Council as well. Indeed, at a critical point, when the Republic of Indonesia requested that a matter be referred to the Security Council, the committee refused. "Work can best be carried out if the parties do not request the committee to refer particular matters to the Security Council."[13] The request was never repeated.

The limitations within which the committee had to work appeared crippling. As members of a committee of good offices, they had no power to arbitrate or even to mediate, they could not make formal recommendations except as requested, and they were unable to make public any suggestions made to the disputing sides. These disabilities were only the beginning. The committee had to wait in Sydney until they were invited by both parties to come to Indonesia. In so doing, they were stepping into the midst of a civil war in which they were supposed to induce the warring peoples to reach an agreement acceptable to each other and to the United Nations.[14]

The invitation came; on the following day, October 25, the committee members flew the twenty-four hundred miles across the Australian continent to Darwin. The next morning they left to complete the eighteen hundred remaining miles to Batavia. Five hundred miles across the Timor Sea, Graham had his first sight of the southernmost tip of Indonesia, the Lesser Sundra Islands. Then, flying alternately over the Indian Ocean and islands large and small, he could recognize Sumba, Sumbaya, Lumbok, then famed Bali, and finally Java. Flying at ten thousand feet, he could see on the six hundred miles of the northern coast of Java the lush green vegetation of forests, of rubber and coffee plantations, and of rice paddies caressed by the white waves of the Java Sea. For centuries Indonesia had been called "the emerald girdle." Flight in an airplane confirmed what men with imagination had lovingly seen.

Far below the plane in which three men and their aides traveled in comfort, Dutch and Indonesians were fighting each other, not for this island only, but for all of the islands and for more: for the honor of the Netherlands or for freedom. The Indonesians for centuries had had a saying, *tanah air sita*—"our earth and our water." Through the years of Dutch rule the pride of that phrase had been suppressed in their lives. Now it was recalled, and the phrase was repeated in cities, villages, and countryside. And Graham, with his dedication to the continuing revolution for independence in his own country and the world, could well understand what men meant by their faith in their freedom.[15]

Arriving in Batavia, a city of more than a million on the northwest coast of Java, the committee members and staff were given comfortable rooms in the Hotel des Indes, and they set to work. The first problem had not been anticipated: meeting with the Dutch officials in Batavia and then with Republican leaders in Djokjakarta, 250 miles to the southeast in the hills, they could not even find a place to bring the parties together. It was not that the Indonesians and Dutch refused to speak with one another, but they would not agree to any conference held on the other's territory, not even if the conference location was alternated, because that would imply that the territory rightfully belonged to the other. For more than a month there was an impasse on this issue, and there were no meetings.[16]

Not all of November was lost, however. The Committee shuttled back and forth between the Dutch and Republican centers, and subcommittees of the staff were appointed to consider military, economic, and political matters. Most important, the members of the two delegations came to know and gain a measure of confidence in Van Zeeland, Kirby, and Graham. Simply learning the names of the chairmen of the delegations—Amir Sjarifuddin for the Republic, Raden Abudlkadir Widjojoatmodjo for the Netherlands— was a major task for the committee members. In addition to the two chairmen, the chief men with whom the committee negotiated were Hatta and Sukarno for the Republic, and for the Netherlands,

H. F. L. K. Van Vredenburch and General Hubertus J. Van Mook, one of the most enlightened of the Netherlands' officials, who from the start had both earnestly sought peace and had faithfully carried out The Hague's orders for military action.[17]

At first the Dutch looked askance at Graham but had great faith in Van Zeeland. Later, seeing the relations between the two men, they came cautiously to accept the American. The Indonesians, on the other hand, were suspicious of Van Zeeland throughout and were never able to overcome their fears that he was on the Dutch side of the dispute. Kirby and Graham, especially the latter, were thoroughly accepted by the Republican leaders. Part of their acceptance of Graham derived from his geniality, which was so like the Indonesians' open cordiality, and part derived from his size, for at five feet four and a half, he was one of them. President Sukarno at five feet eight was tall standing beside him. Although some in Indonesia referred to Graham as a "Western Imperialist," most felt in him a sympathy for their cause. Sukarno even invited him to speak at a school on the subject of "Independence for Indonesia," but Graham refused. "It would not be proper," he said, "since as a member of the United Nations Committee I cannot make any public statements on the subject; but as a teacher of history I could address the students on 'The American Declaration of Independence.'"[18]

On November 1 the Security Council at Lake Success had passed a resolution renewing the call for a cease-fire in Indonesia. Throughout the month the Dutch steadily pressed attacks on all fronts, and toward the end of the month it became clear that unless the committee could get the parties together around the same table, there was no hope for ending the war. Each delegation continued to refuse to meet on soil occupied by the other side. The situation appeared hopeless; there was no other soil on which to meet. It occurred to Graham that a neutral ship in the Batavia harbor might provide the solution. When his colleagues approved the idea, he called General Marshall in Washington, received the promise of a ship from the U.S. Navy ("But one without guns," requested Graham), and made the offer to the two sides. On December 1 the first problem was solved when all agreed to meet on a troop transport provided by the United States, and on December 8 the first meeting was held under a canvas awning on the forward deck of the U.S.S. *Renville*. The Indonesian delegation was seated at one table, the Dutch at another, and the Committee of Good Offices in between. Crowding the deck were assistants, newspapermen, photographers, and a detachment of U.S. Marines, not for protection but to add official dignity to the meetings.[19]

At last the warring sides had been brought together. At the first meeting on the *Renville*, there were the usual expressions of goodwill. Two days later, however, the Dutch representatives insisted that until the cease-fire was settled, there could be no basis for political discussions. The Republican delegates countered that unless the political issues of independence were settled concurrently with plans for the cessation of fighting, negotiation would be useless. Beneath the divergent views was the history of deep mutual distrust and continuing mutual fears. So sharp was the tone of the opposing statements that Graham suggested that the statements not be made public, in view of the disastrous effect they might have upon future talks. The negotiations, he proposed, might begin with the Linggadjati Agreement; so from December 11 to 19 committee members met separately with the two delegations. The prospects were unpromising. The delegates continued to differ in their interpretation of what had been agreed upon at Linggadjati.[20]

The war continued. Each day brought in reports of new advances by the Dutch forces, new charges of atrocities committed by both sides. Politically, the Dutch sponsored a new committee for the creation of a United Indonesia, and plans for a new state were formed in West Java, which had formerly been under Republican control. The urgency created by the moves was underscored by the arrival in Batavia of Prime Minister Louis J. M. Beel of the Netherlands, who stated in a radio address that the United States of Indonesia, that is, the Dutch-sponsored government, would have to take form without delay. "It would be most regrettable, if this appeal," he continued ominously, "this last appeal, were not understood." Van Zeeland, just back with inside information from Brussels and The Hague, convinced Graham and Kirby that with the Dutch stiffening their attitude, the committee must make a "last vigorous effort" to get the Security Council's cease-fire resolution implemented. Failure to do so would be catastrophic on all sides: it would likely mean the end of the Republic; it would be a dangerous failure for the United Nations; and while the Dutch had overwhelming military power for a quick, temporary victory, it would mean the continuation of interminable warfare. Van Zeeland suggested that the committee clarify the resolution by making its own proposals for a cease-fire. Graham, with his eye ever on the political principles and possibilities, drafted a message that was accepted by the committee on December 25. The following day it was transmitted informally to the warring sides, since the committee could not make formal recommendations.[21]

The proposals, which came to be known as the "Christmas Message," began with a statement of fact and moral appeal characteristic of Graham. It cited the Security Council's resolutions in August and November and the work of the committee in doing everything it could to break the deadlock, and continued:

> Today, 24 December, on the eve of Christmas, the symbol of peace on earth, no concrete solution has been given by the parties either to the overall problems, or to the immediate problems of effecting a cease-fire. . . . The mission, the responsibilities, and the possibilities of this Committee are restricted within the limits of "good offices." The main responsibility—the primary and the final responsibility—is and must remain with the parties concerned. . . . The Committee now invites the parties again to reconsider, immediately, the whole problem with greater realism, with reciprocal toleration, and with renewed emphasis on all the human aspects of the dispute.[22]

There followed suggestions regarding a cease-fire and the political issues. The former seemed at first a clear defeat for the Republic, since instead of forcing the Dutch back to the military positions of the previous summer, it was based upon the existing battle lines; but the Dutch, through Van Zeeland, had made it clear that they would not withdraw a single soldier from their front lines. Other cease-fire proposals regarding demilitarized zones and trade were favorable to the Republic; these proposals were included, even though they were contrary to the wishes of the Dutch. The statement underscored the fact that both sides claimed they subscribed to the Linggadjati principles, which Graham summarized as "independence of the Indonesian peoples; cooperation between the peoples of the Netherlands and Indonesia; a sovereign state on a federal basis, under a Constitution which will be arrived at by democratic processes; and a union between the United States of Indonesia and other parts of the Kingdom of Netherlands under the Crown." He added eight new proposals for a political settlement, reiterating that all parts of the Christmas Message "constitute one integrated, balanced whole which the Committee considers essential to the lasting settlement of the dispute."[23]

The Republic accepted the message. The Netherlands agreed to the cease-fire proposals but demanded that the committee withdraw the political principles, both because it disliked the principles and because it viewed the role of "good offices" as meaning that the committee had no right to make even informal political suggestions.[24]

With the response to the Christmas Message there began two weeks of feverish activities by all parties to the dispute, in Washington and The Hague as well as in Indonesia. Graham, knowing that it was "now or never," applied all the pressure at his command upon both the Republicans and the Dutch to reach an agreement: the pressure of personal moral persuasion, of democratic idealism, of political argument, and when these appeared insufficient, the pressure of possible economic and political reprisals.[25]

On January 2 the Dutch made their first political proposals since summer. Rejecting the committee's suggestions and right to make suggestions, they had nevertheless been stung into reaction by the Christmas Message. The pressures on the Dutch to reach a political settlement were obviously at work, for eight of their counter-proposals were based upon the committee's message. But there were differences of great significance in the Dutch draft. There were no references to the Republic by name; there was no guarantee of United Nations participation and observation during the transition period; there was insistence on maintaining the advanced military line and the right to stimulate new states in Indonesia. These proposals were sent to Republican authorities as final and not open to discussion. The informed United Press correspondent in Batavia sent out his story on January 9: "Full-scale resumption of shooting war between the Dutch and Indonesian Republic before the end of the month was freely predicted by both sides tonight. The deterioration has been so rapid that observers expect the work of the Security Council's Committee to reach its climax in the next four days."[26]

Graham was ill in his hotel room. Weakened by a tropical stomach disorder, he was under the care of a physician. During a previous sick spell of Graham's, a conservative member of the American consulate in Batavia, fearful of Graham's democratic sympathies, had communicated with the State Department, trying to have him returned home; and now, at the most critical juncture in the negotiations, Graham was apparently immobilized. He believed, everyone believed, that unless the committee took some further action, all would be chaos in Indonesia. Yet, what action could the committee take, since the Dutch had insisted that the committee had no right to make even informal proposals?[27]

Graham called Henry Brandis to his bedside, and together they reviewed the situation. The Dutch had issued an ultimatum that the Republicans could not possibly accept. One thing alone could prevent renewed fighting: the introduction of principles into the negotiations that would ensure the democratic development of an independent Indonesia. Since arriving in Indonesia, Graham and Brandis had frequently talked late into the tropical nights about the problems of independence, and again on January 9 they talked about the essential democratic principles. Those were principles that, twenty years before, instructor and student had discussed in an American History class as they had imaginatively given shape to the United States Constitution. Finally, Graham suggested that Brandis write, on his own from their conversations, an additional set of principles he considered indispensable for resolution of the dispute. As Brandis left the room, Graham lifted himself to his elbow and said, "Henry, bring your statement to me in the morning, and I will see what I can do with it."

Brandis worked into the night, and in the morning he handed Graham a scrawled draft with six new principles: the Republic, mentioned by name, would be a state within the United States of Indonesia; all states would have fair representation in the new country; upon the request of either party, the United Nations might continue to assist in adjusting differences; the people of Java, Madura, and Sumatra would decide by free elections within a year whether they wished to be part of the Republic or form some other state; a convention to draft a constitution for the new country would be convened through democratic principles; states would have freedom to ratify the constitution or to negotiate special relationships with the Netherlands and the United States of Indonesia.

The draft contained ideas Graham and Brandis had discussed together and was just what Graham wanted. Still running a fever, he met with Kirby and Van Zeeland. They agreed to the new statement, but since the committee could make no proposals, they did not see how it might be presented to the Dutch. "Perhaps," said

Graham, "they can be presented in some other way. I will see what I can do."

Prime Minister Beel of the Netherlands and his party were to leave the next morning for The Hague. Attending the late afternoon farewell tea in their honor, Graham took occasion to inquire whether he might talk with them informally ("Nothing official, of course") before they left Batavia. He was taking a last, desperate gamble. They agreed to his request. Immediately after the gay chatter of the party, the Dutch delegation and Graham withdrew to a conference room.

"I am quite aware," he told them, "that in your judgment—which I respect—the committee is not to make any proposals; and I do not intend to do so. But I do have an informal memorandum of principles written while I was ill by my deputy assistant, Mr. Henry Brandis, which I thought you might want to see for whatever value it might have for you."

He handed the paper to the man seated by him, and it was passed around and read. There was nothing more Graham could say. There was nothing more he could do. The silence was finally broken by General Van Mook, the loyal Dutch soldier who had conscientiously worked for an Indonesian settlement: "It seems to me that this paper should be sent to The Hague." Beel responded, "I'll take it with me."

That was it. Graham returned to report to Kirby and Van Zeeland what had happened, and then got a direct line to the State Department. He refused to speak with anyone except Secretary Marshall, and he explained the situation to him. Graham's desperation underscored his insistence upon the critical nature of the choice facing the Dutch. "Mr. Secretary, isn't there something you can do to persuade them to make a wise decision that we might continue the negotiations in good faith? It is up to you. Without you there can be no settlement." Marshall promised to do what he could.

Graham and the other committee members left the next morning for Kaliurang, a mountain retreat outside the Republican center of Djokjakarta, where they were to discuss in detail with the Republicans the ultimatum previously made by the Dutch. The committee was not free, obviously, to mention the six additional principles. Step by step the conferees went over the proposals, the committee members interpreting and pointing out, wherever possible, their long-range advantages to the Republic. The fact that the

Republicans did not immediately and indignantly reject the demands is testimony not only to their understanding of their precarious military and political position, but also to their respect for the committee and to the pressure of moral suasion and practical argument that Graham brought to bear upon them.

On January 12 the miraculous word reached Kaliurang from The Hague: the Dutch accepted in toto the six additional principles. Without making any counterproposals, without knowledge of whether the Republicans might have accepted their proposals, they had made a surprising about-face. Perhaps the precise pressures, hidden in the files of the State Department and in the mind of George C. Marshall, seemed indeed persuasive.

The committee was now free to introduce the new principles to the Republicans, and Graham, in particular, was free to bring whatever further pressure was required to reach an agreement. At that point, personal confidence in him, as well as the absence of any realistic alternatives, turned out to be sufficient.

There had been times when the entire negotiations had appeared to be seconds from disaster, but after January 12 they were certain to succeed. On January 17 Kirby, Van Zeeland, and Graham witnessed, on board the U.S.S. *Renville*, the fruits of their labors: Raden Abdulkadir Widjojoatmodjo of the Netherlands and Dr. Amir Sjarifuddin of Indonesia signed the truce agreement containing the Christmas Message principles basic to further political discussions and the additional Brandis-Graham principles for negotiations toward a political settlement.[28]

The three members of the Committee of Good Offices agreed that Graham should be responsible for the report to the United Nations; so the day after the signing of the Renville Agreement, Kirby left for Australia and Van Zeeland for Belgium. Graham stayed in Indonesia, and for three weeks he worked on committee details, met informally with Dutch and Indonesian leaders, and prepared a statement for the Security Council. He then met with President Truman at the White House and flew to New York, where he joined Van Zeeland and Kirby for the Security Council debates, which began on February 17 and lasted two weeks. When Graham presented the report, he addressed the Council for an hour and a half, reviewing the history and culture of Indonesia and the struggle for independence, providing a detailed report of the committee's work, and concluding with praise for the Dutch and In-

donesian people, seeing in the history of both, woven together, hope
for the future:

> Long the haven of refugees from despotism in Europe, Holland
> has been the dauntless champion of freedom and tolerance in criti-
> cal times of tension and conflict. The people of the Netherlands,
> with their stubborn dykes and generous blood, have written some
> of the most heroic chapters in the history of liberty. A little land
> but a great people!
>
> By the blood of the sons of Netherlands, who, in the Second
> World War, died for the liberation of Indonesia; by the blood of
> the sons of Indonesia, who struggled and died in the heroic Dutch
> underground for the freedom of the Netherlands; . . . by the needs
> of the world and the responsibility of the Security Council, the truce
> must be kept and the political principles must be fulfilled in the
> freedom, independence and the cooperation of these two great
> peoples in one of the great commonwealths of free and equal na-
> tions of our modern world.
>
> In this truce and in these principles, the people of the Nether-
> lands, the people of the Republic and all the people of Indonesia
> have, under God, a rendezvous with a larger destiny of creative
> cooperation in a time and in a world of need of the best which these
> historic peoples can give together. May they not fail mankind in
> this desperate hour.[29]

Following briefer statements by Kirby and Van Zeeland, Sastroa-
midjojo, speaking for Indonesia, recognized that "the Committee
has already achieved the first significant success in the history of
the United Nations." High praise was bestowed upon the committee by most of the member states, but not by all: the delegate
from Colombia was critical of the committee; the representative from the Ukranian States of the Socialist Soviet Republic
thought the committee should be renamed the "Committee of
Good Offices for the Netherlands Usurpers"; and throughout the
debates, Andrei Gromyko of Russia castigated the imperialists.
Critical of the committee for operating independently, he maintained that the Renville Agreement and the report constituted "one
of the most shameful documents ever prepared under the auspices
of the United Nations." The report was accepted, with commendation to the committee members, by seven votes and four absten-
tions.[30]

All who approved the agreement recognized that it was the
beginning and not the end of negotiations toward an independent

Indonesia. The agreement, in fact, did not differ significantly from the Linggadjati principles; but those principles were no longer in force, and the Renville Agreement, having stopped the warfare, brought the United Nations to a dispute for the first time as a signatory. Even before Graham made his final report to the United Nations, when he had met with the President at the White House, Truman had said:

> In bringing about a truce agreement for the cessation of hostilities and in helping to formulate basic political principles of freedom, democracy and independence for the sovereign United States of Indonesia in equal partnership with other parts of the Kingdom of the Netherlands you and the committee have had a profound influence in putting into practice the ideal of world law and order.
>
> The effectiveness of United Nations machinery as demonstrated by your work has given new hope to those who have faith that by such democratic processes this ideal can be realised.[31]

Thenceforth, the Netherlands and the Republic of Indonesia had to contend not merely with each other but, by mutual agreement, with the United Nations as well. The United Nations was now thrust into the center of resolving the complex, passion-ridden problems in the dissolution of colonialism and the development of an independent nation.

Graham left the council chambers in the center of the sprawling converted wartime factory building at Lake Success and took the night train for North Carolina.[32]

16

Civil Rights and Communism

I have been called a communist by some sincere people. I have been repeatedly called a tool of imperialism by the radio from Moscow. I shall simply oppose Ku Kluxism, imperialism, fascism, and communism, whether in America, Indonesia, or behind the iron curtain.[1]
—FRANK PORTER GRAHAM (1949)

PRESIDENT TRUMAN APPOINTED GRAHAM TO A Committee on Civil Rights in December, 1946. The report of the committee, "To Secure These Rights," was presented to the President on October 29, 1947. Graham, one of the two Southerners on the committee, was not present at the presentation. He was in Indonesia. But he had attended most of the ten lengthy sessions of the unprecedented committee and had worked faithfully with the other fourteen members—businessmen, lawyers, government officials, churchmen, labor union leaders, and educators—and with the staff, headed by Robert K. Carr, professor of political science at Dartmouth.[2]

The basic recommendation of the committee, which had on its membership only two Negroes, Sadie T. Alexander and Channing Tobias, was "the elimination of segregation based on race, color, creed, or national origin, from American life."[3] Specific programs were proposed to achieve that goal. A study, essential as background for the recommended program of action, centered upon the American heritage of freedom and equality, the ways in which practice denied that heritage, and the responsibility of government for the civil rights of its citizens. Graham had long been personally familiar with the inequities imposed daily upon Negroes and other minorities, but he was shocked by the array of facts shown in the study. There were overwhelming, discouraging statistics on discrimination in the safety and security of the person, in the denial of voting rights, in the repression of freedom of speech and conscience, and perhaps most distressing of all, in the denial of equal rights in employment, education, housing, health, and access to public services and accommodations. Graham agreed with the committee's thesis that "separate but equal" was an impossibility, since segregation "brands the Negro with the mark of inferiority," and that "we have a moral reason, an economic reason, and an international reason for believing that the time for action is now." He agreed, too, with many of the specific proposals for action, most of which were directed towards the South: that the governmental machinery for protecting civil rights should be strengthened, for example, and that the poll tax as a requirement for voting should be abolished.[4]

While approving the basic recommendation for eliminating segregation, he disagreed with the methods suggested by the committee, since those methods relied exclusively upon governmental force, upon legislative and executive action. Graham was absent from the meeting in which governmental regulation through federal grants-in-aid and a program of fair employment practices were discussed, but when he saw the specific recommendations imposing federal compulsion, he quickly wrote a dissenting minority statement. Written at the final meeting of the committee in September, the statement expressed his views, consistently held throughout the years, that

> the best way ultimately to end segregation is to raise the educational level of the people in the states affected; and to inculcate both the teachings of religion regarding human brotherhood and the ideals of our democracy regarding freedom and equality as a more solid basis for genuine and lasting acceptance by the peoples of the states.[5]

His racial attitudes and actions reflected his belief in education and religion, and in law as a complement to both. Education, he felt, increasingly provided the knowledge that enabled people to get along with one another. Religion provided the motivation of good will for making improvements in social rights and relations. And law necessarily set the limits and the context for all social action. Where necessary, Graham would strive to change the law, as he did in his equal rights decisions on the War Labor Board; but as long as the law was duly established, he would abide by it.

These beliefs he thought typical of a Southerner; and he was convinced that if other Southerners understood his views, they would agree with him. It was clear that his attitudes toward racial questions were rooted in his personal relationships: he was open and friendly with individuals, and the status of the individual, Negro or white, seemed to matter little. At the same time, however, he accepted social conventions and did not go out of his way either to meet or to avoid Negroes socially. Graham, like most Southern liberals of the day, had not made any frontal attack upon segregation.

Permeating all Graham's racial activities had always been a dominant sense of equity and justice. In his early years at the University, both as student and as secretary of the YMCA, he and many other Southern college men and women had promoted educational and self-help programs among Negroes. In the campaign for education in the early twenties, he had made requests for Negro schools; but significantly, Negroes were not included in any numbers in the campaign battles. In 1928, when a Negro, inadvertently invited to the annual meeting of the North Carolina Conference for Social Service, said he would be delighted to attend, Graham, as president, insisted that he and any others be made welcome but also agreed they should be seated in the rear of the room.[6]

During the thirties most of Graham's racial activities had been in the context of education. They had developed naturally, since he was the president of the University, which he thought should give leadership to all public education in the state, both Negro and white. Whenever he appeared before the Appropriations Committee of the legislature, he carefully included Negro schools and colleges in his appeals for funds. This led to many conversations with Negro educators, including the director of Negro public schools in North Carolina, N. C. Newbold. The presidents of Negro institutions in the state, both public and private, turned to him for assistance. His services on the board of a church-related Negro school, Palmer Memorial Institute, were such that in April, 1934, the president, Charlotte Hawkins Brown, wrote him: "There isn't a word in the dictionary that would convey to you the depth of appreciation I feel for what you did for us. I have just thanked God again and again for you, a brave, fine, strong courageous young man of the white race whom God is using to bring about better understanding, sympathy and active good will."[7]

There were racial activities in the thirties that were not related to education, however. He had attended the 1938 meeting of the Southern Conference for Human Welfare in Birmingham and had joined others in acquiescing in "Bull" Connor's demands that the meeting be segregated. Earlier that year he had publicly advocated a fair trial for a Negro accused of murder, and this had brought on him the wrath of many whites as well as a letter from the editor of the Negro *Carolina Times*: "Such men as you keep the fires of hope burning in the breast of the southern Negro—hope for a measure of justice and fair play."[8] The demand for a fair trial, like his defense of a University professor who had eaten with a Negro Communist, was not in Graham's mind so much a racial matter as a simple question of legal justice. But so tangled had race always been with every facet of Southern life that his straightforward stands for justice gave him the reputation of being pro-Negro. In his own mind he was not so much defending the rights of Negroes as the rights of individuals.

In 1938 Pauli Murray, originally a North Carolinian but at the time a resident of New York, applied for admission to the Graduate School of the University of North Carolina.[9] Although she had no particular claim upon the University, Graham wrote her in detail, stating his view of the facts: the state constitution requiring segregation was the law until overruled by the United States Supreme Court; recent decisions of the court required equal educational opportunities; there was the necessity of obeying both state and federal constitutions either by adequate provision for education in Negro institutions or by changing the state constitution by referendum. But a referendum, he pointed out, would be the most unfortunate thing that could happen. Therefore, within the limits of legal responsibility, he had pledged the cooperation of the University in moving toward more adequate education for Negroes in the segregated schools and colleges. "This may seem to you to be an inadequate and minimum program," he told Miss Murray, "but it is going to take the cooperation and the struggle of us all to bring it to pass. The present alternative is a throwback against whose consequences we must unceasingly be on guard in the best of both races, who after all go up or down together."[10]

Walter White, executive secretary of the National Association for the Advancement of Colored People, wrote Graham of his personal admiration for the directness in Graham's reply to Miss Murray: "Its spirit is magnificent not only in what it actually says but in what, knowing you as I do, I can read between the lines."[11]

On December 12, 1938, the Supreme Court in *Missouri* v. *Gaines* ruled that since the State of Missouri did not provide a law school for Negroes, Leroy Gaines had the right to a professional education at the University of Missouri. There was a stirring in the administration buildings of Southern state universities, and a number of university presidents wrote Graham inquiring about the situation in North Carolina.[12] His reply was immediate: the Constution of North Carolina required separation of the races; the Constitution of the United States, as interpreted by the Supreme Court, required admission of Negroes to state universities or equal provision at Negro institutions. As an official of the state, Graham felt that both requirements had to be satisfied.[13]

In North Carolina a start had been made. Prior to the Missouri decision, Graham had advocated and helped develop a plan of cooperation between the University, Duke University, and the North Carolina College for Negroes for the purpose of aiding Negro colleges with professional and graduate education. Also in advance of the court decision, the Governor had appointed a commission to study the whole matter, and Graham believed steps were in process to equalize professional and graduate training for Negroes. There was also some talk of the development of regional schools. In any case, action was needed. To President H. C. Byrd of the University of Maryland, Graham wrote, "I think that we ought to go at this in a substantial and thorough going way to see to it that a good step is taken forward in behalf of the educational opportunities for Negroes."[14]

In March, 1939, Graham joined with Frederick D. Patterson, president of Tuskegee Institute, and Rufus Clement of Atlanta University in inviting a select group of presidents of Southern public and private colleges, white and Negro, to meet at Howard University to discuss graduate and professional education for Negroes.[15] Walter White of the NAACP, a representative from the General Education Board, which had long been concerned with Negro education in the South, and the United States Commissioner of Education were also present at the meeting. The discussion began on the basis that the Gaines decision was the law of the land. The consensus of the meeting, as reported by Graham, was that there should be a "pooling of all possible resources through cooperation of Negro and white institutions, in making increasingly adequate higher education for Negroes on the graduate and professional levels."[16]

In the early forties, when applications came from North Carolina Negroes for admission to the graduate school, Graham advised the University Board of Trustees to admit the students, since on the basis of the Gaines decision, the courts would ultimately rule in favor of their right to admission. The prevailing view of moderates on the board was that both Graham as president and they as trustees were officials of the State of North Carolina, and therefore, no matter what their personal opinions might be, they were honor bound to keep the laws of the state regarding segregated education. Indeed, they insisted, so clear was the moral responsibility to let the law take its course that neither Graham's recommendation nor their advice should be incorporated into the board minutes, lest Graham's recommendation be construed as an attempt to abrogate state law. Graham became persuaded that the board members were correct and did not insist upon his recommendation being recorded. But his acceptance of his role as a government official who had to act strictly within the limits of recognized law made him increasingly sensitive to the intensifying Negro demands for moral justice and ever more aware of changing court decisions.[17]

Graham's concern for civil rights was not restricted to those of Negroes. In 1942, the United States government's policy of relocating Japanese-Americans disturbed him deeply. The relocation, carried out by Earl Warren, then attorney general of California, forcibly deprived citizens of their property, removing them from their homes into inland concentration camps. Graham did not know about the military necessity of the action, but he instinctively recognized that to deprive any American citizen of his property or freedom without due process of law, even in wartime, was a travesty upon the democratic ideal. In May, 1943, a letter came from a former North Carolina professor, Howard K. Beale, informing Graham that the Navy had cleared The Woman's College for Japanese-American students but had not cleared Chapel Hill, and that the administration at the Woman's College would not accept the students.[18] Graham soon replied:

> I talked to Dean Jackson and encouraged him to accept the Japanese students. I gave him the example of the decision of the University of Chapel Hill, and suggested he was free to go ahead without action of the Board of Trustees.[19]

The decision of the University at Chapel Hill to which Graham referred—his decision—was that Japanese-American students should be accepted. If the Navy had not cleared the matter, Graham felt, it was only because the Navy did not know that he had had prior experience with officers of the federal government and with Japanese students. When an application came to the University from a young Nisei woman only to be rejected by the Chapel Hill administration and faculty in formal vote, Graham, in a rare action, overrode the decisions of dean and faculty and, on his own authority and in the face of hostile pressure, admitted the Japanese-American.[20] It was the least, he thought, he could do.

Following his War Labor Board decision in which the board unanimously ruled for the first time in American law that "the classification 'colored laborer' and 'white laborer' shall be abolished,"[21] Graham made a number of radio broadcasts to servicemen overseas. He was especially pleased to receive responses, such as one from a soldier in Europe: "I am an American Negro. That fact will explain why I was rendered so happy by the broadcast in which you took part. Men like yourself with ideas as you expressed them keep alive in American Negroes their faith in white Americans, and keep constant their loyalty to the only country we love. May your tribe increase."[22]

In 1944 Graham made a broadcast with Pauli Murray, who six years before had raised the question of integration by applying for admission to the University. Following Graham's unexpected response to her application, the two had developed a correspondence in which, though they disagreed, mutual frankness elicited mutual trust. They met for the first time in a Washington broadcast studio. Afterwards Miss Murray wrote Graham:

> It was such a joy to broadcast with you the other night—and for so many reasons. One of the men in the WINX broadcasting station asked my Aunt Pauline if she were Mrs. Graham? So mother's way of kidding me was to say I looked so proud sitting up there by my "Uncle Frank."[23]

In the same letter Miss Murray, who had received a fellowship for the study of law at Harvard, inquired whether the University of North Carolina could make use of some land near Chapel Hill that her family had inherited sixty years previously from their white ancestors, whose only descendants were Negro.

Later in the year the Supreme Court ruled 8 to 1, with Justice Roberts dissenting, that Negroes could not be barred on account of race from the democratic primaries in Texas. Graham penned a note to Frederick Patterson, the president of Tuskegee: "The decision of the Supreme Court is a fine thing. . . . It is remarkable that the thing was written by a Kentuckian and the dissenting opinion by a Pennsylvanian."[24]

In December, 1945, student leaders from the white North Carolina colleges met for the ninth year in the state capital, using the resources of the state government to debate and vote upon bills in a model legislature. A bill inviting students fom the Negro colleges to send delegates in 1946 was adopted 110 to 48. Introduced by a University student, the bill was backed by most of the Chapel Hill delegation and, in the minds of state officials and citizens, was associated at once with University radicalism. Thad Eure, North Carolina secretary of state, requested a special conference with the total student assembly. "I am fearful," he told them with fatherly advice, "that you may be jeopardizing the beautiful picture toward which we are moving." The students listened, some applauding, some hissing, as he spoke of the good race relations in North Carolina. When he referred to the possibility that the General Assembly might forbid future student sessions and that the appropriations to the University might be curtailed, one student blurted out, "To hell with the University appropriations." The secretary's appeal for the students to "go slowly," his advice that they "might find it beneficial to move with a little more care," fell upon deaf ears. They had no intention of rescinding their action.[25]

Once more passions arose among white North Carolinians. The demands that the president of the University do something about the irresponsible students increased in fury until Graham felt it necessary to release a public statement defending academic freedom.[26]

> We always have, and I trust, as a simple part of the traditions of our people, always will stand for the decent and responsible freedom of the students, as well as other people, to express their conscientious opinions, vote their honest convictions, and take positions on public issues, including controversial, unpopular views.[27]

Underscoring the fact that for years churches and civic groups in North Carolina and other Southern states had sponsored interracial meetings, he stated his agreement with the views of the students. "It is to them anomalous sincerely to hope to organize an international assembly of the people of all nations, races, colors and creeds and at the same time in our own State Assembly of youth to exclude representatives of our own Negro colleges."

Elected later to membership on the board of the National Association for the Advancement of Colored People, which was pressing through the courts its fight for equality, Graham wrote the executive secretary, Walter White, "My impulse has been to accept." Two considerations gave him pause: because of his commitments, he had not recently been joining any additional committees; and he felt that he "could serve the general cause better in my present position, and actively, without becoming a member of the Board." He did not refuse outright the election but suggested that someone else be selected.[28]

As a member of the Committee on Civil Rights, Graham was examining the national yet predominantly Southern problem when, in the spring of 1947, he was approached by leaders of the Fellowship of Southern Churchmen, a regional interracial group, which was confronted with a local problem. The fellowship, cooperating with students, had secured the use of a University auditorium for a benefit recital by the Negro artist Dorothy Maynor. In the twentieth century there had never been a public unsegregated concert in Chapel Hill; so there was the delicate problem of how to announce that there was to be no segregation at the recital. The sponsors, wanting to protect the University president, had prepared a vague publicity statement that merely listed Negro colleges among the institutions at which tickets were being sold. When Graham was shown the news release, he shook his head, said, "That won't do," turned the page over, and wrote, "Miss Maynor is a most distinguished artist of a people long distinguished in music and warm melody which comes from the soul of a people. Members of both races are invited to hear her. Except as to the price of tickets, seating will be without discrimination in line with the practices of interracial assemblies long observed here and in many other communities in Southern States."[29]

There was ambiguity in the words "here" and "many other communities." By the mid-forties a limited number of Southern communities were holding unsegregated meetings, but normally they were in Negro institutions or liberal churches. The "here" had to refer to several churches in Chapel Hill and to professional meetings at the University where attendance was by invitation; there was no long-observed practice of unsegregated public assemblies at the University. The sponsors of the Maynor concert still had their anxieties, but all went smoothly and without incident.[30]

All did not go smoothly for Graham with the sixteen-page report released June 16, 1947, by the Committee on Un-American Activities of the House of Representatives. The report concluded that "the Southern Conference for Human Welfare is perhaps the most deviously camouflaged Communist-front organization." Graham was cited as one of the organization's major leaders: "Frank P. Graham, head of the University of North Carolina, was the first chairman of the Southern Conference for Human Welfare and today remains as its honorary president. He is not a Communist and no doubt on occasion has had some differences with the Communist Party. He is, however, one of those liberals who show a predilection for affiliation with various Communist inspired front organizations." There followed a list of twelve "peace and democracy committees" with which, the report asserted, Graham had been associated.[31]

The day the House Un-American Activities report was made, Representative Folger from North Carolina made a speech in the House in which he gave

> testimony to the patriotism, the high character and the splendid worth of Dr. Frank P. Graham. I say without hesitation, mental reservation, or secret evasion of mind he is one of the outstanding men of the nation. He is not a communist, nor a fellow-traveler, nor a communist sympathizer.[32]

Other Southerners were on their feet. Representative John Rankin of Mississippi said that all the members from North Carolina did not share Folger's illusions about Graham, "neither do the white people throughout the South and the better elements of the Negroes of the South share that illusion." And E. E. Cox of Georgia added that if "Dr. Graham is not a communist or fellow-traveler he performs like one."[33]

Graham was faced with the necessity of defending, if not himself, the Southern Conference. But that was what he had been quietly doing ever since he had ceased to be chairman of the conference in June, 1940. He had continued to associate himself with it and for several years had served actively on the executive committee, attending meetings when possible, corresponding with members of the staff and committee, attempting to keep the organization free from Communist domination, and securing funds from foundations to keep it alive. At the 1942 meeting he had received the Thomas Jefferson Award, which he had presented four years previously to Hugo Black. He was not present at the executive board meeting that year, however, and he could hardly believe the reports of Roger Baldwin, executive secretary of the American Civil Liberties Union, who commented that

> the leaders of the Conference do not appreciate the risks they run in collaborating closely with fellow-travelers identified with the Communist Party movements and prefer to shut their eyes to those risks rather than make an issue of excluding political intruders.[34]

Graham was adamant in the belief that if the genuine liberals stuck by the Southern Conference, they could defeat any Communists or fellow travelers in any fair and open fight. He had taken a position and he was unable to retreat from it, even though most of his friends had, one by one, drifted away from the organization or resigned in indignation.

In the spring of 1945 Graham was the major speaker at a Southern Conference meeting in New York honoring Eleanor Roosevelt, who had been a patron saint since the early days in Birmingham.[35] In March, 1946, he was surprised when one of the founders of the Southern Conference, Judge Louise Charlton, resigned because of the Communist issue and wrote him, "I have lots of additional reasons for resignation but I am afraid if I set them down my language would violate the postal laws and regulations."[36]

Throughout the forties Graham was deluged with inquiries about the Southern Conference. He answered each one personally: "I wish to assure you that as far as I can humanly know the Southern Conference for Human Welfare is not a Communist organization. In its origin, intent, and program, it is American and committed to the principles of the American Bill of Rights."[37] He then described his own position and activities in opposition to totalitarianism, white primaries, and the poll tax, and his support of federal aid for education and medical care, farm cooperatives, collective bargaining, and minimum wages. These stands, he thought, coincided with those of the Southern Conference.

The charges that the Southern Conference for Human Welfare was a Communist-front organization were not as threatening to Graham as the continuing attacks upon him for tolerating, even encouraging, communism at the University. These attacks had begun even before he was elected president and had continued, intermittently, through the thirties. Then, in 1940, they were renewed with increased virulence in North Carolina and were soon being repeated in the United States Congress.

On August 12, 1940, David Clark, editor of the *Southern Textile Bulletin*, addressed a civic club in Charlotte, making a claim that was given publicity throughout the state:

> The University of North Carolina is the only Southern institution at which there appears to have been a drive for converts or definite contacts with the Red Movement in the United States. In recent years the University of North Carolina has stood alone in the South as a haven for Reds and fifth columnists.[38]

It was clear to Clark that Graham was responsible for this alarming state of affairs; for while 85 percent of the professors were reliable, "the radical group, under the protection of President Frank Graham, have made Chapel Hill a haven for radicals and fifth columnists."[39]

The address was part of a complex pattern of attacks upon and defenses of Graham. In May, 1940, Tom Pridgen, staff reporter for a Charlotte newspaper, made an intensive investigation of communism in the University and Graham's radicalism, concluding, in a series of documented articles, that the charges lacked foundation in fact.[40] The attacks did not stop. At the June meeting of the Board of Trustees, members complained about the deplorable situation. "Our University," said Thurmond Chatham, later to be a congressman, "is regarded as radical rather than liberal. I do not like some of the atmosphere and as a trustee I want to protest against it."[41] The same month, at a meeting of the Alumni Association, the criticisms were felt to be so important that a newspaper editor, Lenoir Chambers, publicly interviewed Graham about communism at the University. Graham admitted that communism was taught in courses, as it was in any great university, but denied that there was any indoctrination or that there were Communists on the faculty. He was not as certain when asked whether there were Communists among the students.

I couldn't say about that absolutely. I have asked the students, not by way of inquisition but by way of information, because I consider that there are some here, and the students say three or four. To be safe I would multiply this by two—so you might say a dozen more or less. If this were so, we would give them the protection of the American Bill of Rights so long as they obey the law, were desirable citizens, and did their work.[42]

No unbiased study was ever made of communism at the University, so it is uncertain whether Graham was accurate in his figures. It was generally recognized on the campus that there were Communists among the students and townspeople; and some persons thought, though it was not generally believed, that there were Communists on the faculty. Many persons supposed that the center for University Communist activities was a bookstore adjacent to the campus; and this supposition was given some credence a decade later when an informant told a Senate subcommittee that Communists planned to use a small printing press in the store to "flood the South with literature."[43] While the flood never developed, there were some leaflets circulating on the campus and in the state. One of the people responsible for the activity was a student, Junius Scales, who in 1939 privately told his mother that he was a Communist. (When he returned to the University as a graduate student in 1946, after serving four years in the war, he publicly avowed his Communism and was openly recognized as the chairman of the party in North Carolina. Scales later was the first person to go to prison under the 1940 Smith Act, which forbade advocating the overthrow of the government by force.)[44]

In 1941 the charges about Graham's Communist affiliations reached the United States Congress. On November 3 Leland Ford, a representative from California, arose to use words that would later become familiar in anti-Communist crusades: "I hold in my hand the documentary proof of Frank P. Graham's affiliation with the following front organizations of the Communist Party." He listed ten organizations to which Graham allegedly belonged.[45]

During the war the charges about Graham and Communism were relatively quiescent. Then came the House Un-American Activities Committee report in 1947, which revived the issue. Graham was assisted in his defense of the Southern Conference for Human Welfare by a careful study by Walter Gellhorn, professor of law at Columbia University. Gellhorn did not attempt to appraise the

Southern Conference but to evaluate the report denouncing it. His analysis concluded:

> That report is a document which discredits its authors rather than the organization it sought to destroy . . . . The principal effect of the committee's probes has been the unwarranted discrediting of genuine liberals who have been earnestly and sincerely seeking needed reforms, particularly in the field of labor, monopolies, and race relations.[46]

While the attacks upon Graham continued, the next, and most serious, attempts to discredit him occurred in early 1949. They began with a series of seven broadcasts by the conservative news commentator, Fulton Lewis, Jr., who charged that Graham was not a safe security risk with atomic secrets.[47] The occasion for the charge began when, in October, 1946, Graham was elected the first president and chairman of the board of the Oak Ridge Institute of Nuclear Studies, which was sponsored by fourteen Southern universities. William G. Pollard, a physicist on leave from the University of Tennessee to help develop the project, was elected executive director in February, 1947. Pollard had been instrumental from the beginning in shaping plans for the institute. His drive and Graham's decisiveness account largely for the direction the institute took in its first two years. In addition to maintaining the original purpose of making atomic energy facilities at Oak Ridge available to the scientific staffs of Southern universities, the institute expanded into atomic medical research, the American Museum of Atomic Energy, and graduate studies.[48]

More than two years after Graham had become involved in atomic energy activities, the Atomic Energy Commission released information that he had been granted "complete security clearance" enabling him to continue his participation in the institute. "His career as a leading educator and prominent public figure in the South has, it appears, been marked by controversy, engendered in part by his active role in championing freedom of speech and other basic civil or economic rights." The commission admitted that his views had led him to ally himself with many suspect persons and organizations throughout the nation, but it felt that "the specific purposes for which he had these associations were in keeping with American traditions and principles" and the associations had in no way impaired his integrity or independence. It was affirmed that he had been found, without qualification, to be "a man of upright character and thorough-going loyalty to the United States."[49]

The decision ended a long, secret debate over Graham, a debate of which even he was unaware. He had not appeared for a hearing before the commission, its security board, or a staff officer. The significance of the clearance became obvious only when Fulton Lewis reported on January 12 that Graham had been cleared by the commission against the recommendation of its own Security Advisory Board, headed by former Supreme Court Justice Owen Roberts, and its staff security officer, Rear Admiral John Gingrich.[50]

Since Graham had become front-page news with Lewis's broadcast, he telegraphed a detailed defense to Lewis, describing the stands he had taken against totalitarianism and for the democracies and listing the many domestic programs he had supported, especially those related to the South. Stating that he was active in the Americans for Democratic Action, which refused membership to Communists, he affirmed that he had followed the major policies of Woodrow Wilson and Franklin D. Roosevelt. "I do not now renounce any stand I made for human freedom."[51]

The week previously the administration at Chapel Hill had refused use of University buildings for an address by John Gates, secretary of the Communist Party, who at the time was under court indictment.[52] In his telegram to Lewis, Graham made reference to the action, which had stirred dissent among students and faculty, who later arranged for Gates to speak on a public street off the campus.

> While personally holding that a membership in the Communist Party is not per se proof of an individual's crime against the government, I uphold Chancellor House's decision to follow the ruling of the Attorney-General in the interpretation of the state law to deny the use of a state building to a man under Federal indictment on the grounds of his being involved in a conspiracy to overthrow the government by force. I uphold the right of the twelve members of the University faculty to declare against the indictment.[53]

President Truman defended Graham with feeling and indignation at a news conference on January 13.[54] On the same day, trustees of the Sidney Hillman Fund, named after the liberal labor leader, announced that the first grant of $1,000 would be awarded to "Frank Porter Graham for selfless public service."[55]

But knowledge that the security board of the Atomic Energy Commission had recommended against Graham's being given clearance was too much for some members of Congress, in both the House and the Senate. On February 3, Representative F. Edward Hébert of Louisiana thought it "disgraceful that a man in so great a position should so conduct himself that he cannot be trusted in any situation involving his country" and insisted that Graham had no right to remain head of the University of North Carolina. Representative Rankin interrupted to assert that the worst had not been told: there were Communist organizations in the student body of Graham's university. "Of course," said Hébert, "Dr. Graham could be fooled once. After all peace and democracy are alluring words. But Dr. Graham is not a simple-minded man. And what must we say when we find him in half a dozen similar organizations? Did the commies fool him six times in a row?"[56]

On March 3, two Southerners in the Senate carried on a more restrained colloquy. In reply to a question by James O. Eastland, also of Mississippi, Senator Spessard Holland of Florida spoke of Graham's attainments, adding that "he is regarded as ultra-liberal, as on the 'pinkish' side, as not at all conversant, in a sound way, with the traditions of the South.[57]

> Mr. Eastland. I am not trying to disparage Dr. Graham in any way; but would the Senator say that Dr. Graham represents the viewpoint of the South?
> Mr. Holland. My answer is that he does not represent what I think is sound southern philosophy and the southern approach to racial questions.

The Senator from Mississippi was not satisfied. He wanted to know whether Graham was a "representative Southerner."

"From that standpoint alone," said Holland, "my answer would be 'No;' but I think he has done much good work, and that he is so recognized. My observation of educators leads me to believe that we cannot apply the same standards to them that we apply to other people. They are inclined to be idealistic."[58]

It was against that background that Graham embarked on his political career.

Part Five

The Hazards of Politics:
1949-1950

17

Southerner and Senator

America and the other democracies must rely more upon the ideas of freedom and the practices of democracy than on economic and military power. The freedom and dignity of the human being, democratic ideals and moral idealism are the ultimate weapons in the global struggle against totalitarian tyranny.[1]
—FRANK PORTER GRAHAM (1949)

IMMEDIATELY AFTER LEARNING OF THE DEATH OF new North Carolina Senator J. Melville Broughton on March 6, 1949, Governor Kerr Scott, staunch Presbyterian farmer, began collecting the names of possible appointees to the Senate. There were many claimants for the vacancy, and the list, which Scott carried in his coat pocket, grew rapidly to more than fifty names before he showed it to Jonathan Daniels, sharp-penned editor and member of the Democratic National Committee. When Daniels pointed out that Frank Graham's name was missing, Scott paused thoughtfully, relit his cigar, and asked, "Would he take it?"

"I don't know," replied Daniels. "If you want him you can ask him."[2]

Shortly thereafter, in one of his rare evenings at home, the Governor turned to his wife. "Miss Mary," he said affectionately, "I want you to listen to this list of people I'm considering for senator and tell me what you think." He read in his country drawl, and the room was quiet until he reached the name Frank Graham. "You can stop right there," Miss Mary said. "So far as I'm concerned, that's it."[3]

So far as Kerr Scott was concerned, that was it, too; but not so far as Graham was concerned. When Daniels, as the Governor's emissary, sounded Graham out, the response was "No, absolutely not; I'm president of the University." Daniels conveyed Graham's refusal to the Governor, and there began the battle between two strong Presbyterian-minded men, which, the Methodist editor soon saw, could be won only on Presbyterian terms.

Daniels and the Governor returned to the president's home in Chapel Hill for dinner and, after the dishes were cleared, sat around the table arguing earnestly, the quick-tongued, impetuous Daniels knowledgeable through his years of service to presidents, the slower, cigar-paced Scott forceful with the determination of a man who knows his mind. Graham insisted that he wanted to stay in the University. At sixty-two he had few years of service left, and he needed to get the University in shape for a successor. Finally, having run out of patience and knowing that any other man on the list in the Governor's pocket would grab the appointment, Daniels banged the table and said in his intense, gravelly voice, "Frank, why can't you see that it's your duty to accept? The North Atlantic Treaty has to be ratified. Bricker and his fellow-isolationists are riding high in the Senate. Your state, your country, your commander-in-chief need you there. It's your duty." It was a telling point; so the discussion turned to foreign affairs and the Senate.

"Well," said Graham finally, "I don't like to leave Chapel Hill, but if, after we meet with the chancellors, I can be assured the University will be taken care of, I'll go."[4]

At a dinner meeting of the three faculties of the University on March 22, the Governor, who delighted in surprises, nonchalantly concluded a speech, "While I am on my feet I want to make an announcement. The next senator from North Carolina will be Dr. Frank P. Graham." There was professional pandemonium in the dining room in Chapel Hill and, the following day, diverse reactions across the state: never had a political appointment been more surprising, never had one been received with more jubilation by liberals or with more criticism by conservatives. And many on the faculties who had at first rejoiced that their president would be in the Senate, shortly began to have grave forebodings both for their university and for Graham.[5]

The day after the appointment, Senator John W. Bricker of Ohio arose in the Senate. "Mr. President, I note from the morning press that we are about to have a newly appointed Member of the United States Senate, Dr. Frank P. Graham. I wish to invite the attention of the members of the Senate to some very pertinent facts." The facts had to do with what Bricker considered the sus-

FIGURE 31. Frank Graham with his wife, Marian, in 1949.
National Archives, Washington, D. C.

FIGURE 32. Senator Graham discussing campaign with members of his staff.
Division of Archives and History, Raleigh, N. C.

FIGURE 33. Graham spent many hours in hotel rooms working on his campaign.
Division of Archives and History, Raleigh, N. C.

FIGURE 34. Senator Graham on the campaign stump for election to the U. S. Senate in 1950. *Southern Historical Collection, UNC Library*

FIGURE 35. Senator Graham sometimes spent thirteen to seventeen hours in the June heat meeting with crowds of people. *Southern Historical Collection, UNC Library*

FIGURE 36. Senator and Mrs. Graham on primary day.
Division of Archives and History, Raleigh, N. C.

FIGURE 37. The Mobilization Committee of the National Security Resources Board meeting with President Truman in January, 1951. Left to right, seated: Stuart Symington, President Truman, Mrs. Anna Rosenberg. Standing: William Green, Albert J. Hayes, Hershel Newsome, Dr. Graham, James Patton, Otto A. Seyforth, Marion B. Folsom, Murray Lincoln, and George Mead. *Acme Telephoto, UPI, Harry S. Truman Library*

FIGURE 38. Dr. Graham in Anchorage, Alaska, for a labor-management conference, January, 1951.
Southern Historical Collection, UNC Library

FIGURE 39. Congressman Thurmond Chatham congratulates Dr. Graham after he is sworn in as head of the Defense Manpower Administration, March, 1951, with Secretary of Labor Maurice Tobin, left, and Mrs. Graham, right.
Southern Historical Collection, UNC Library

FIGURE 40. Dr. Graham was appointed by the Security Council as UN representative for India and Pakistan, March 30, 1951. *United Nations*

FIGURE 41. Headquarters for the
United Nations in New York.
United Nations/SAW LWIN

FIGURE 42. Dr. Graham, right, United Nations representative for India and Pakistan meets
with Trygve Lie, U. N. Secretary-General, June 1951. *United Nations*

FIGURE 43. Dr. Graham meets with the press in Karachi, June 1951.
Southern Historical Collection, UNC Library

FIGURE 44. Dr. Graham meets the Prime Minister of Pakistan, Liaquat Ali Khan, June,
1951. *United Nations, (from Government of Pakistan)*

picious procedures of the Atomic Energy Commission in finally granting clearance to Graham, and he concluded by reading into the record the analysis of the Southern Conference for Human Welfare by Paul Crouch, who was considered an authority because for eighteen years he had been a member of the Communist Party. Quoting Crouch, he read:

> Although I have the highest respect for Dr. Graham his record of collaboration with the Communists should not be overlooked.... There are few liberals of his type, and the Communists usually take full advantage of them. The majority of my associates in the party leadership regarded such people with secret contempt to be used until the revolution and then cast aside or liquidated.[6]

It was an ominous beginning for a senatorial career. The senior senator from North Carolina, Clyde Hoey, symbolizing in his cutaway coat the near opposite of Graham in political and social philosophy, requested that the Senator from Ohio yield the floor and said, indignantly, "I cannot remain silent when these suggestions or insinuations are made against the loyalty of Dr. Frank Graham." Hoey agreed that Graham had been careless in association with certain organizations. "That very criticism has been made in North Carolina; but there has never been any suggestion that he is not loyal and no one who knows him would hesitate to trust him."[7]

As soon as Hoey had finished his five-minute statement, Senator Morse arose to suggest that perhaps he knew Graham more intimately than any other member on the Republican side of the aisle, and he talked at length of their association on the War Labor Board. He spoke with obvious feeling, his words, as his manner, sharply honed:

> I meant it sometime ago when on the floor of the Senate I said that if I had to name the 25 greatest living Americans, I would include within the 25 the distinguished president of the University of North Carolina, Dr. Graham, and I would place him exceedingly high on the list. The tribute that I now pay him, no man has the right to pay to any human being, unless he knows the man so intimately that he can be sure that the characterization of Dr. Graham I now state is a justified tribute. I say that Dr. Graham is one of the most Christ-like men I have ever met. To associate with him, to observe his courage, to watch his great intellect in operation, to experience the inspiration of his moral leadership makes one

feel truly humble. It strengthens one's faith in men to know there
can live a man in these days as devoted to Christian principles. . . .
I want to say I care not what board raises questions as to the loyalty
of Frank Graham. Small though in stature he may be, he is a giant
in loyalty. . . . I could not sit here in silence and fail to pay this
respect.[8]

Other senators joined heatedly in the discussion. The Vice-President had to remind the galleries that it was against the rules to make any demonstration, when applause greeted Senator William E. Jenner's remark that it was common knowledge Graham was soft on Communist-front organizations, but that he "would rather see a man with his weaknesses in the United States Senate than to see him have a clearance with the Atomic Energy Commission." Senator McCarthy, who had recently shocked the nation with his charge that the State Department was filled with Communists, took the floor to attack the Atomic Energy Commission.[9]

As the debate continued, it was Senator Pepper of Florida who introduced the subject of Senate tradition. Quoting the Senate rules that "no Senator in debate shall, directly or indirectly, by any form of words impute to another Senator or to other Senators any conduct or motive unworthy or unbecoming a Senator," he commented:

It is a strange and uncharacteristic lack of cordiality and reciprocity for the Senator from Ohio, if I may say so without violating the rule, to attack by imputation and insinuation the patriotism of a man named to the United States Senate who has not had the privilege of presenting his credentials to this body, and does not have the opportunity to castigate as false what may be said by those who would impugn his loyalty. I have been in the Senate only a little more than 12 years. But, I have never yet seen a similar spectacle.[10]

When Frank Graham read the *Congressional Record* for March 23, he was reminded of his earlier encounters with Congress: his appearances before committees dealing with social security, federal aid to education, and other matters; his correspondence and conversation with many senators and congressmen he counted as friends; the previous attacks made upon him in both houses. In the late thirties and early forties the attacks had been from Dies, Ploesser, and Ford. Following a lull during the war years, it had been in 1947 Rankin and Cox; in 1948, O'Daniel in the Senate and Rankin again in the House; in 1949, Hébert and Rankin. Then, only three days before the Senate seat to which he was to be appointed became vacant, Senator Holland had agreed with the attack by Senator Eastland that Graham was not a representative Southerner.

All this had struck Graham as ridiculously unbelievable, not even worth replying to, and he felt that accusing him of disloyalty to the South was the most fantastic charge of all.

On March 27 the Grahams had their last traditional Sunday "open house." It was a spring afternoon in Chapel Hill, with temperatures in the eighties. The shrubs were in fresh flower, and grass, bush, and tree were in new, light green. The afternoon sun mingled with the sounds of birds and cars and human voices to brighten "the Southern part of heaven." More than fifteen hundred students and townspeople strolled past the stone wall and up the walk by the budding lilacs, to be greeted by Dr. Frank and Mrs. Graham. Tirelessly the two joined in the gay yet nostalgic chatter; and at one point, Graham stooped to greet the youngest guest, a child crawling on the floor. At the height of the gathering, he was asked to speak to the crowd, and stepping to the porch, remarked:

> As I said to the Governor, this has been the most difficult decision of my life—to leave this place, these institutions and these people which have been a part of my life for over forty years. I feel that we will take with us your understanding, your thoughts and your prayers. Mrs. Graham and I thank you from the bottom of our hearts. Good bye to all of you.[11]

The university band began the college anthem, and the Grahams joined in singing the stately tune followed by the rousing "I'm a Tar Heel born, I'm a Tar Heel bred, and when I die I'm a Tar Heel dead."

Fearing that he might slight someone, Graham did not invite anyone except members of his family to the ceremony in Washington. But friends followed him there, and on March 29, North Carolinians almost filled the galleries in what observers said was the largest attendance ever seen at the swearing-in of a new senator.[12] Neither they nor he knew at the time how strikingly similar essential elements in his personality were to those of the institution he entered.[13]

Described by Gladstone, the prime minister of England, as "the most remarkable of all the inventions of modern politics," the

Senate was, as its name literally means, "an assembly of old men or elders," and Graham, at sixty-two, joined the majority who were over sixty years of age. Consisting of ninety-six senators, each of whom ran his own show, it was an institution with a living spirit. These men, bound by the ties of continuity, had a strong pride in their nation and in their body as responsible for its life. They were jealous of the Senate's responsibilities and rights. Written into their manner, as well as their rules, was a respect for each other and a sense of decorum. No matter how strongly partisan they might be, or how vociferous, they were men who accepted dissent and who lived daily in the necessity of compromise; and among the best of them, there was an ability to maintain friendships across the lines of political disagreement. The presence of continuing history pervaded the Senate chambers, and with history there was a respect for tradition and a certain order of life and manners. Most striking of all, yet hidden from view, there was in the life of every conscientious senator an ever-present tension between conscience and fact, ideals and realities, what is morally right and what is politically possible.

All these characteristics can be used to describe Graham. His friends and his enemies generally thought he lived by his conception of what was right, with little concern for the practical ("a starry-eyed idealist," many enemies called him); but it was not so. The ethical, rooted in a religious spirit, was dominant. Of that there was no doubt. But always the sense of the moral was focused upon what could be done, and then there followed the effort to do it. Mistakes and failures he had known; but tracing them back to their roots, he could see that they had come not because of an indifference to what was practical, but because, concerned most with what was moral, he had examined the possibilities with other persons and had misjudged their commitments to the goal or his own administrative abilities.

But the point at which the personality of Graham and that of the Senate fused most perfectly was in the idea of an institution. For the Senate Graham entered was an institution, "the only thoroughly successful institution which has been established since the tides of modern democracy began to run," as Sir Henry Maine described it. Like any living institution, the Senate was more a conserving than an innovating force. Graham's friends and enemies alike were conscious of a certain democratic radicalism, but they usually failed to recognize that there was, throughout his life, a strong conservative streak in his deeply pervasive loyalty to institutions. With Graham's abiding historical consciousness was the awareness that, in all apparent innovations, he was discovering and conserving the best in man's past. His life was always open to expansion into new and more inclusive institutions.

Never, perhaps, has a new senator revealed to his colleagues more quickly and convincingly that he was a "Senate man." Following Vice-President Barkley's administration of the oath, Senator Hoey had hardly ushered Graham to his desk when a page brought a note from Senator Arthur H. Vandenberg, for twenty years a senator from Michigan and the ranking Republican member of the Foreign Affairs Committee. Vandenberg wanted to see Graham as soon as possible about an urgent matter. When the debate lagged, they met in the Senate corridor. Senator Owen Brewster of Maine, explained Vandenberg, was outraged at the continuing refusal of the Dutch to abide by agreements in Indonesia; so he had introduced an amendment to the European Recovery Administration Bill stipulating that no funds would go to any foreign government that did not comply with Security Council orders. Brewster and other senators, knowing Graham's work for Indonesian independence, were certain he would support the move; and Vandenberg, opposed to the amendment, wanted to hear Graham's opinion firsthand.

His reaction was immediate. "This is not the time for that amendment, Senator, but it is not the time to defeat it either; and if we can sit down together in privacy I will tell you why." They were closeted the next morning in Vandenberg's office. "If Senator Brewster's motion doesn't pass," said Graham, "the Indonesians and Asians will think we have scotched out on them. If it does pass, the Dutch will be furious, and instead of completing their change of heart, they will revert to their most reactionary policy."[14]

Since his return to the University in February a year previously, Graham had followed the Dutch-Indonesian relations with mounting dismay, for the history had been one of repeated Dutch refusal to implement the agreements made with the Republic under the aegis of the United Nations. By summer all negotiations stemming from the Renville Agreement had broken down, and the hostility and distrust between Indonesia and the Netherlands had deepened. In September the Republic had destroyed a Communist revolt, and

the United Nations Committee had succeeded in reopening negotiations. But there was no progress, and on December 3 Graham,
appointed by President Truman an adviser to the Secretary of State,
had written an urgent letter to Marshall:

> The Indonesian situation requires your immediate consideration.
> To avert another misuse of Dutch military action it is absolutely
> necessary that you at once make the strongest sort of representa-
> tion to the Netherlands' Government. The Dutch policy of break-
> ing off negotiations on the slightest pretexts and the long conse-
> quent delays are nothing less than an economic strangulation of
> the Republic for political purposes.[15]

On December 11 the Dutch had again said further negotiation
was useless; and within a week they had renewed military action,
subduing the Republican capital of Djokjakarta and interning the
political leaders. The United Nations had passed resolutions, but
without avail. On January 10 Graham had written to Robert
Lovett, acting secretary of state, regarding the Dutch defiances of
the United Nations, which "are impairing the democratic foundations of the Western Union, are driving non-Communist Asia away
fom the Democratic West and are strengthening the Communist
drive in southeast Asia." Only the United States' leadership in the
United Nations would be able "to do justice in Indonesia, to save
non-Communist Asia, to save the democratic foundations of the
Western Union and the North Atlantic Pact, to save the moral
foundations of the E.C.A. [Economic Cooperation Administration, formerly the European Recovery Program], and, not least important of all for human freedom, to save the leadership of the
United States in a wavering world." Graham had suggested further
that the State Department consider delaying E.C.A. payments to
the Netherlands until it was assured that the transfer of sovereignty
would be completed during 1949.[16]

In January, then, he had advocated privately that the State Department do quietly what the Brewster Amendment advocated
publicly. By the end of March Graham thought progress was being
made with the Dutch; so when Brewster came to him, the second
day he was in the Senate, to say, "I know the Indonesians are
counting on your supporting me," he replied, "Senator, I can't do
that. I'm for Indonesian self-determination, and for twelve months
I have been for doing what you are now demanding. But I'm
against you now because the Dutch are having a change of heart,

and if we slap them in the face with the money bags of Uncle Sam you know what will happen. They are a proud people." Unable to join sides with either Vandenberg or Brewster, Graham tried to reach the State Department, and when he did, about midnight, he said, "Look. If you don't get something in here better than the Brewster Amendment, I'm going to vote for the amendment; and I'll have to speak to it as well." The next morning Ernest Gross from the State Department appeared in his office, and together they worked out a new amendment. Instead of being a unilateral American action, it worked through the machinery of the United Nations, saying to the Dutch, "We have faith in you," and to the Indonesians, "We are for your independence."[17] Graham took the new proposal to Vandenberg and Brewster, and on April 6 Brewster replaced his original amendment with the motion that one of the conditions for the termination of aid would be if "such assistance would be inconsistent with the obligations of the United States under the charter of the United Nations to refrain from giving assistance to any state against which the United Nations is taking preventive or enforcement action."[18]

Graham was not in the Senate chambers when the amendment was introduced. The previous day Hoey had reported to the Senate that Graham was ill but had prepared a very full statement on the Indonesian dispute. That sixty-seven-page document became the major reference for the floor debate. Its detailed review of the history of the dispute, its denunciations of the repeated Dutch violations of agreement, its insistence that the Indonesian story had its tragic shadows and hopeful lights on both sides, and its appeal, "let us build on good faith and fair hopes wherever we can find them," conveyed to the senators the judicious mind of a new "Senate man." Impressive, too, was Graham's unique way of binding the United States to the United Nations:

> All members shall give the United Nations every assistance in any action it takes in accordance with the present Charter, and shall refrain from giving assistance to any state against which the United Nations is taking preventive or enforcement action. . . . We thus, as far as possible, keep our procedures within the framework of the United Nations in the exact language of the Charter.[19]

When the amendment was passed by voice vote, Graham lay in a Washington hospital.[20] His annual respiratory virus had arrived late that year.

For six weeks Graham was absent from the Senate because of illness. The second week, Marian took him from the hospital to the quiet of her sister's home in Hillsboro and, as in every sickness he had suffered since their marriage, cared for him.[21]

On May 2 he had Senator Hoey place in the record a statement supporting a Federal Aid to Education Bill that passed decisively in the Senate but died in the House. On May 12 he was back in the Senate for the first time since April 1. Refraining from speaking on the floor, he worked on the committees to which he had been appointed and tried to keep up with his correspondence. He fitted well into the relaxed, casual camaraderie of the Democrats. He participated, too, in the Wednesday morning prayer breakfast of some senators from both parties and was quickly accepted for his undemonstrative faith. As ever, a hard worker, he almost never took time off to go to the Capitol Restaurant but rather ate in his office the two sandwiches Marian had prepared for him and drank the usual milk or orange juice.[22]

Graham's first major Senate speech was in support of the North Atlantic Treaty, which had been signed April 4. Senate ratification of the treaty was never seriously in doubt, and his address did not swing any votes; but Graham's address was a carefully reasoned statement of what he believed in: the United Nations, the support of the Atlantic Pact to deter aggression and to build European self-recovery, the inadequacy of the pact without more democracy in the democracies, and the pact as leading toward international disarmament and a strengthening of the United Nations. He bore down hardest on the need for affirmative actions:

> America and the other democracies must rely more on the ideas of freedom and the practices of democracy than on economic and military power. The freedom and dignity of the human being, democratic ideas and moral idealism are the ultimate weapons in the global struggle against totalitarian tyranny.[23]

There followed a list of thirteen feasible measures for strengthening democracy at home, ranging from federal aid to education through decent minimum wages, conservation programs, agricultural parity, cooperative medical programs, and "faithful observance of the laws, without nullification by any state of the decision of the United States Supreme Court, regarding equal suffrage and education in the States as the Supreme law of the land."

Immediately after he sat down, liberal Republican Senator Tobey arose: "Mr. President, I have sat here for the last hour and, in my opinion, I have heard one of the finest addresses it was ever my privilege to hear on the Senate floor. The man who has just addressed us has given us a pattern . . . for America in the great objective and offensive toward world peace."[24]

Democratic Senator Donnell, fearful of the internationalist trend, was not so pleased. He questioned Graham again and again. The exchanges were sharp; and Graham, in the fervor of debate, spontaneously expressed his faith:

> This is what is in my heart: To my mind, in the present world situation of international tension, with the threat of totalitarian tyranny now held in check by the staunch opposition of the democracies, the North Atlantic Pact gives to the world time and some sense of security to do the great things set forth in the charter of the United Nations. It provides time to enable amendments to the charter of the United Nations to be considered, for steps to be taken toward universal disarmament, and to make the United Nations actually what its ideals are.

Repeatedly Graham returned to the theme of the responsibility of the United States to take the lead in strengthening the United Nations. When, on February 2, 1950, Senator Brien McMahon impressed the Senate with a bold peace program, Graham joined other liberal senators in immediate gratitude that "he has thrown out a challenge to the conscience of mankind." McMahon, chairman of the Joint Committee on Atomic Energy, had recoiled from the hell of atomic warfare into which he had been forced to gaze. He informed his colleagues that Russia was not far behind the United States in its destructive power, that it might well incinerate fifty million Americans in a matter of minutes; and he proposed a twenty-five-billion-dollar plan for global economic development in exchange for atomic disarmament.

In spontaneous response to the dramatic proposal, Graham said:

> After the First World War the United States of America rejected the League of Nations and failed the hopes of the peoples of the world. After the Second World War the Soviet Union has by its actions blocked peaceful international procedures in the United Nations, and the Soviet Union has failed the humane hopes of the peoples of the world. Whatever else comes of the bold proposal I hope that it will give momentum to the movement to strengthen the

United Nations by amendments to its Charter designed to abolish the veto, strengthen the World Court, widen the responsibility of the Assembly of the United Nations, and provide for an international police force to prevent aggression and enforce peace in the world.[25]

In the late forties there were more refugees on the roads of the world than at any previous time in the history of mankind; and it was those people who stimulated Graham's first bill in the Senate.

In 1948 the Eightieth Congress had responded to the needs of uprooted peoples by passing a restrictive immigration law. President Truman signed the bill reluctantly, denouncing it as a "pattern of discrimination and intolerance." Shortly thereafter the Displaced Persons Commission charged that the law was "all but unworkable."[26]

In the next Congress, the House easily passed a liberalized bill, but in the Senate it was another story. The obstreperous Pat McCarran, chairman of both the Judiciary Committee and the subcommittee considering the bill, attempted to block by stubborn power any efforts to modify previous congressional action. For a long time he was successful; and it was only the adroit parliamentary moves and the moral determination of liberals, cooperating across party lines, that finally outmaneuvered McCarran and the conservatives. Graham was one of the key people in the strategy, working in the offices and on the floor of the Senate, usually behind the scenes, trying to persuade the lawmakers to enact a new law that would give more hope to the hopeless.[27]

Republican Senator Homer Ferguson of Michigan and Democratic Senator Harley Kilgore of West Virginia were the other two key figures in the long fight. After nine months of intentional stalling by McCarran, the three senators tried to get the House bill before the Senate by asking the Judiciary Committee to relieve the subcommittee of its responsibility. When that failed, on August 24 Graham joined with fourteen other senators in introducing a resolution almost unheard of in the Senate to discharge the full Judiciary Committee from consideration of the bill. It was a clear repudiation of McCarran. McCarran was enraged and announced that he was going to Europe forthwith to study the problem further, supposing that the Senate would not be so discourteous as to violate its own traditions in acting upon the bill in his absence.

But act his committee did; Graham joined others in discharging the subcommittee and then reporting the House bill to the Senate floor. Debate began October 13, in which Graham joined both Democrats and Republicans in speaking for the bill. Graham, although dissatisfied with the House bill, thought that it should be passed and that the Judiciary Subcommittee should press its plans in developing a better bill for the future. "These plans will require many more months for fulfillment," he told the Senate on October 15.

> Meanwhile, time is running out on many thousands of unfortunate human beings uprooted from their homes by the marches and countermarches of the armies of ruthless Fascist and Communist dictators who brought on the Second World War. These human beings, their families and children, innocent victims of dictators, war, and the cruel backwash of war, call to the nations, the churches, and humanitarian agencies for continuing consideration and prompt action to save them from despair, to salvage them from deterioration, and to help them to become productive and loyal citizens. Many thousands will lose out while we wait for a complete over-all report and a perfect bill.[28]

But the Senate, having gone to the momentous length of debating a bill while the responsible chairman was absent, was not ready to affront a colleague further by immediate passage; so a motion to recommit the bill to the Judiciary Committee was passed 36 to 30. Attached to the motion, however, were instructions that a bill should be reported out by January 25, 1950, three weeks after the next session of Congress began.

McCarran was forced to schedule new hearings, but the date required for reporting a bill arrived before he got around to having any. On January 25, the Judiciary Committee reported a bill that was somewhat more restrictive than the House measure. Three members of the committee, Kilgore, Graham, and Ferguson, voted against the recommendation, promising a minority report. The three then set to work, first to shape a liberal substitute bill, then to corral Senate support. Graham, knowing that some members who had voted for the committee report were dissatisfied with their own action, went to them privately and secured from four colleagues statements that they were in favor of a more liberalized bill. Then, while McCarran was holding hearings on the bill, Graham buttonholed other senators, Democrats and Republicans.

By the time debate opened on February 28, there were seven Republicans and seven Democrats who sponsored the minority Kilgore-Graham-Ferguson bill. In his one Senate statement on the bill, Graham said:

> We are given the picture that on the roads of Europe moved long lines of people with their packs, their wagons, their pushcarts, and their babies in arms, making their hopeful pilgrimage to their western homelands after desperate years of war. . . . The United States, as the richest and most powerful nation on earth, while lagging in carrying out its proportionate part of the program of resettlement of these homeless people, wants to do its fair part. The substitute bill is designed to this end.[29]

The debate was long and bitter. Finally, near midnight on April 5, after almost eighty amendments had been offered and disposed of, the Senate voted 49 to 25 to substitute the minority bill for the bill McCarran had reported; then it quickly passed the substitute measure 58 to 15. After the Senate-House conferees reported the resolution of their differences, which was generally favorable to the more liberal Senate version, the bill was approved in both houses and was signed by President Truman, who said, "It is especially gratifying to me that this expression of American fairness and generosity has been brought about by groups and organizations broadly representative of all parts of our country."[30]

Graham was the only one of the senators instrumental in liberalizing the law who was absent when the President signed the measure on June 16, 1950. He was in North Carolina at the courthouse in Lincolnton and in the furniture, clothing, and grocery stores, the shoe-repair and barber shops, and the filling stations of Gastonia, Belmont, and Morganton. It was the final week of a campaign ordeal.[31]

18

Campaign Ordeal

I did what I thought was the right thing. If that will keep me from going back to the United States Senate I don't want to go. I don't want to conceal anything. I don't want to be expedient. I want to be honest.[1]

—FRANK PORTER GRAHAM (1950)

WHEN GRAHAM WAS APPOINTED TO THE SENATE, he announced that he would be a candidate in the special election the following year. Editorial and political consensus across the state was that, as the best-known and best-loved man in North Carolina, he was certain to be reelected. "I don't think anyone can beat him," said the Governor, an astute politician, who would not have appointed Graham in the first place if he had had serious doubts. It was predicted for months that Graham would have no opposition in the May 27 primary. But on January 31, 1950, former Senator Robert Reynolds announced his candidacy and his campaign slogan, "Look Homeward Americans."[2]

Reynolds was no serious worry to the Graham camp. The worries began in February when rumors spread that the conservative moneyed interests were seeking a candidate and that a corporation lawyer, Willis Smith, was seeking money. President of the American Bar Association, Smith was far to the right of Graham. When he filed for the primary on February 25, it was evident that, since neither of the men was a political extremist, the lines might be drawn between genuine conservative and liberal political positions. In such a battle Graham was generally favored to win.[3]

Smith made an astute political move at the outset by trying to preempt the center for himself. "The real issue of the campaign is: do the people of North Carolina wish to go to the extreme right or extreme left with one of the other candidates; or do they wish to go down the middle of the road with us? It is as simple as that."

Smith's problem was to convince enough North Carolinians that Graham was on the "extreme left." Graham was obviously vulnerable on two points in addition to the long antipathy the right had had for him: the House Un-American Activities Committee had identified him as belonging to Communist-front organizations, and he had been one of the two Southern members of the President's Committee on Civil Rights. He was confident, however, that while a simple statement of facts would not allay all fears, it would convince his fellow citizens that he was not very far to the left. The House report had erroneously named some committees he had never joined, and he had never been a member of any committee when it was on the attorney general's list of Communist-front organizations. Though a member of the Civil Rights Committee, he was not at the meeting that had discussed a compulsory Fair Employment Practices Bill, which he had always opposed, and he later wrote the statement inserted in the report: "A minority of the Committee favors the elimination of segregation as the ultimate goal but opposes the imposition of federal sanction."

Nothing could be clearer to Graham than these facts, and he had the buoyant trust that the campaign would be waged on the basis of facts and the candidates' real beliefs. By mid-March a reporter on one of the state's largest newspapers stated that political experts predicted the outcome would depend upon "the vigor and viciousness of the Reynolds and Smith campaigns and Graham's skill at parrying their thrusts." When Smith formally opened his campaign on March 22 in an eastern North Carolina county, he proclaimed, "I do not now nor have I ever belonged to any subversive organizations and, as United States Senator I shall never allow myself to be duped into the use of my name for propaganda or other purposes by those types of organizations. The unwary can do just as much harm as the unscrupulous in the days that are at hand."[4] Shortly thereafter advertisements and cartoons began to flood the state. In a typical cartoon, a policeman was pictured stopping Graham, who was driving on the left side of the highway to Washington near a billboard that advertised, "Frank Graham: Communism, FEPC, Socialism." Officer: "Dr. Graham, you're on the wrong side of the highway—folks in North Carolina drive on the right." Graham: "In Socialist England where I studied, they drive on the left—and that's my pattern!"[5]

From the start, Graham was on the defensive. Try as he would, he could not get a discussion on what he considered the real issues—European recovery, the farm program, assistance to the states for medical programs, aid to education, and a voluntary approach to civil rights. His time was spent in repeated denials that he was radical on Communism or race. Although he was a stalwart defender of others or of principle, even a capable defender of himself when he could act affirmatively, it was out of character for him to protect himself directly. He was psychologically unable to say that the opposition was lying about him, and he seemed to be unable to believe that they were. Nor could he make a defense with a counterattack upon Smith. The issues of the campaign were political, not personal. The only time he mentioned Smith by name was to correct personal injustices he thought had been committed by some of his supporters who had attacked Smith's business practices and low-wage policies as well as the kind of campaign the Smith forces were waging.

Graham had enthusiastic supporters throughout the state, and his campaign staff was competent. He drove the staff to distraction, however, by refusing to let anyone write any portion of his speeches, not even allowing them to reweave passages from old speeches. He insisted upon writing every speech laboriously, as ever, in the square longhand; and as a consequence, he was upon occasion late for scheduled appointments. He was at his best in informal, person-to-person campaigning. In every community he renewed old friendships and engaged in energetic conversation with the voters.[6]

Feeling responsible for Senate duties, he did not begin steady campaigning until the last of April. Prior to that time, he answered more roll calls than he missed. On May 5 he interrupted campaigning to fly to Washington for a crucial vote on the European Recovery Program. It was good for the administration program that he did, since the vote was so close that the crippling Taft amendment to strike five hundred million dollars from the program would have passed had he not been present.[7]

Graham returned to North Carolina May 6 for the crescendo of the final three weeks of the campaign. On May 12 disaster struck. Weakened by the incessant pace of the campaign, enervated far more by the reckless charges being made, he succumbed to pneumonia and for two weeks was unable to appear in public. The disaster was not merely that he was incapacitated for the two most crucial weeks of the campaign. Far more important was the fact that he was unable to return to Washington for debate and vote on a critical issue that politicians were convinced would ensure his election.[8]

Graham's staffs in Washington and Raleigh had developed a plan they hoped would save the day; and liberal senators, both Democrats and Republicans, communicated with Graham, urging him to accept the plan. The majority leader, Senator Lucas, who faced a tough contest in Illinois in which civil rights would be a major factor, had called up a cloture motion to stop debate on the Fair Employment Practices Bill. Since Graham could not be in the Senate when the roll call vote was taken, he was merely to authorize Senator Hoey to say, when casting his vote against cloture, "And if my colleague Senator Graham were here, he, likewise, would vote 'nay.'" According to Hoey, that simple act would mean fifty thousand votes, since it would be a denial that Graham was anti-Southern and for compulsory FEPC.[9]

Allard Lowenstein, the energetic aide who had been a student at Chapel Hill and was devoted to Graham and all he stood for, consulted with a number of senators. Working on his own initiative, Lowenstein was trying to enlist the assistance of senators friendly to Graham. He went to conservative Richard Russell of Georgia, who turned upon him, saying, "Young man, don't you tamper with Frank Graham's conscience. That's what we in the Senate love about him."

Those who set the stage for Graham to declare himself against cloture knew that there was no possibility of tampering with Graham's conscience. But before Graham made a decision, he was besieged with requests from campaign chairmen across the state, who were convinced that this would win the election, that he make a stand against cloture. The hotel room in Raleigh, darkened because of difficulty the sick senator was having with his eyes, became a dramatic battleground between the pulls of politics and conscience. Jonathan Daniels and Jeff Johnson, Graham's campaign manager, pointed to the plight of his supporters and urged that it should not be too difficult to come out against cloture, since he had always been for freedom of speech and against silencing debate. "Yes," he answered, "but I'm against filibustering, too, against preventing a vote by speech that is not debate. Have they had a fair debate yet? I'm not there so I don't know. I don't know. How can I say I would do something if I were there when the simple truth is that without being there I can't possibly know what I would do."

Graham was in anguish. He felt he was betraying all his friends, who were clamoring for him to do what they saw as a simple, uncomplicated act. He saw it as simple and uncomplicated, too, but from the other side: lying on a sickbed in Raleigh, he could not know what his judgment might lead him to do if he were on the Senate floor. And there were deeper sources for the anguish that were difficult to discern. Perhaps he felt that such an act would be self-serving and that he would later find it hard to justify to himself. Perhaps, also, there had long been at the base of his character a touch of the desire for self-immolation. In one of the rare times he sought direct advice, he turned, in the dimness of the hotel room, to Lowenstein. "What would you do if you were in my place?"

Lowenstein knew perfectly well what he would do. But he knew more than that: he knew Graham and his principle of living by one's own conscience. "That's not fair to ask," he responded. "I'm not the Senator. You're the Senator."[10]

Graham decided that he could not honestly ask Hoey to speak for him.

At the same time the campaign on the streets below and in distant towns was feverishly building to a climax. On May 16 there began a series of advertisements in daily newspapers by the "Read the Record Committee for Smith." The records that were presented were those of the House Un-American Activities Committee and a California Joint Fact Finding Committee.[11] Smith underscored his belief in the validity of the attacks by insisting on May 21 that "neither Dr. Graham nor his supporters should object to a full revelation of the leftist movements with which he has been associated in the past and the things he has said."[12]

In the last week of the campaign, Smith's staff sponsored large advertisements that emphasized the racial and Communist issues. Despite the fact that ten members of the Civil Rights Committee wrote letters categorically asserting that Graham had been opposed to compulsory FEPC and had personally written the minority statement, there were advertisements denying that there was any minority statement and quoting the report's advocacy of the compulsory FEPC. (Four days before the election, Smith publicly asserted that he believed Graham had signed the Civil Rights Report without ever having read it; and he later insisted privately that there was no minority statement in it.) Graham was associated with Communism through advertisements quoting the Communist *Daily Worker*; picturing the head of the Communist Party, Earl Browder, in prison; and depicting alleged Communists Paul Robeson and James Dombrowski sponsoring a New York rally for the Southern Conference for Human Welfare. Graham, who had supported Truman, was identified with the left-wing 1948 campaign of Henry Wallace.[13]

A far more potent political weapon than advertisements was the material that circulated privately. In February there had appeared a mimeographed page describing in detail Graham's alleged Communist-front activities. At the bottom of the page were pictures of Negro soldiers dancing and drinking with white women. "Look before you vote," was the plea, "and remember these persons could be your sisters or daughters under such an educational program as Graham advocates. THINK. Your decisions today will reflect in the faces of our children in the generation to come." Although most of the privately circulated leaflets were unsigned, L. A. Tatum, who had attacked the University in the mid-thirties, sponsored a page picturing the thirteen whites and fifty Negroes of the 1868 South Carolina Legislature and inquiring, "Will history repeat itself?"[14]

As the campaign developed, Leroy Jones, a Negro student whom Graham had named as second alternate for an appointment to West Point on the basis of a merit examination, became an issue. On May 6 unsigned leaflets were mailed from Raleigh with Jones's picture and the inscription, "Frank Graham appointed him to West Point. No other southern Senator or Congressman has ever appointed a Negro to West Point." Two days before the election, persons in every section of the state received postal cards mailed in New York:

> Dear Voter:
> Your vote and active support of Senator Frank Graham in the North Carolina primary May 27 will be greatly appreciated. You know, just as we do, that "Dr. Frank" has done much to advance the place of the Negro in North Carolina. The Negro is a useful, tax-paying citizen!
> W. Wite [sic], Executive Secretary
> National Society [sic] for the Advancement of Colored People

Graham was unable to reply in kind. The final political appeal from the Graham forces was an advertisement with a picture of the candidate and a statement:

May our America be a place where democracy is achieved without vulgarity, where differences may be resolved without hate, where we may have majority rule without tyranny. We want an America where respect for the past is not reaction and where hope for the future is not revolution. This is America; God Bless America.[15]

The balloting was the largest in any election in North Carolina. As Graham waited for the returns in the early evening of election day, he was propped up on pillows in his room at the Sir Walter Hotel in Raleigh. By nine o'clock, when the counting gained momentum, he had a large lead. Close friends drifted in and out of the private room with their congratulations, and Graham felt a deep, quiet satisfaction. His belief in the people of North Carolina had been vindicated.

Below in the headquarters room, the predominantly young crowd of students and recent graduates was, as a news reporter wrote, a "study in jubilation." The newsman commented, "There was no liquor drinking in the headquarters room and there were remarkably few traces of whiskey on the breaths of the visitors. It was a modern dry miracle for a campaign headquarters on election night and a personal tribute to bone-dry Graham, whose victory drink was buttermilk."[16]

When the tally was complete, Graham had 303,605 votes, the largest ever accorded a candidate for senator in the state. His vote was 11,269 short of a clear majority: Smith had received 250,222 votes; Reynolds, 58,752; and two other candidates, 5,900.[17] Still, it was an impressive victory. Liberals in the nation breathed more easily; and the *New York Times* commented, "Senator Graham seems to have turned back a resurgent tide of race prejudice. . . . A defeat of Senator Graham would have given encouragement to the forces of reaction in the South."[18]

The Grahams, both desperately needing rest, drove to Nags Head, where the waves ceaselessly rolled in upon the sands and steadily washed away the nightmare of an unbelievable campaign. Even there, visitors could not refrain from expressing indignation at what had happened. The state senator from Dare County told Graham, "I don't know why you don't spit a snake at mention of the opposition."

"Me get mad?" Graham looked across the ocean. "It still seems funny to me to be called a Communist, and I wish I had a recording of the Moscow broadcast that denounced me as a capitalist war monger."[19]

Smith had until June 12 to request a second primary. There was a prevalent feeling that he might recognize a 53,000-vote deficit as too great to overcome; and when many of Reynolds' campaign managers began announcing for Graham, there was further reason for him not to run.[20] At one point, only the earnest pleas of his staff dissuaded Smith from sending a telegram conceding the election to Graham. Then the rumors began: Smith was getting money for a runoff; Smith had sufficient money but was polling his county managers; Smith was awaiting a Supreme Court decision on race as a springboard for a second campaign. All three turned out to be true.

On June 6 the press reported that the Supreme Court, in its last decision of the term, unanimously reaffirmed equal facilities for Negroes in education and transportation and forbade segregation in cases involving the University of Texas, the University of Oklahoma, and the railroads. Graham pointed out in a public announcement that North Carolina was attempting to comply with court rulings, and he expressed gratitude that the Southern attorney generals had used his arguments expressed in the minority civil rights statement in their legal fights against compulsory abolition of segregation.

> I still oppose as I have always opposed, the Federal government forcing non-segregation on states or regions. . . . I reaffirm my oft expressed faith in the North Carolina program of mutual understanding, respect and cooperation between the races, under which both races have made greatest progress in the last several decades of any dissimilar groups in any one area in a like period in human history.[21]

On the same day, paid advertisements on radio stations in Raleigh requested Smith supporters to attend a rally to plead with him to continue the fight, and that evening several hundred people converged on the lawn of Smith's home. "I just might have to go along with you," he told them. The next day he filed a formal request for a runoff. Smith told newsmen he had waited so long because of the belief that the decisive race issue would inevitably lead to the kind of campaign he did not want to take part in. But in examining the returns, he had noted that the Negro vote had gone decisively for Graham, and he saw "bloc voting" as a "threat to the kind of democracy North Carolina has enjoyed over the years."[22]

As the second campaign began, hope was expressed on all sides that the smears of the first race would not be repeated. A moderate newspaper welcomed the runoff as a democratic right but pointed out that "Willis Smith's right carries commensurate responsibility to keep the campaign on a higher level."[23]

For the first week it seemed that the hope would be fulfilled; then with only ten days to campaign, Smith assailed the "utterly fantastic schemes" of the Truman administration and lashed out at bloc voting. He had waited until the Supreme Court decision, he said, to see if his running would "unnecessarily create racial ill will. . . . There have long been people who are constantly on the watch to stir up discord between the races for political reasons, as exemplified by the inflammatory report" of the President's Civil Rights Committee.

Advertisements in newspapers began to appear that contained tables of the voting in six Negro precincts in the state, showing a total of 5,445 votes for Graham and 65 for Smith. "Do you want this? . . . Are we going to throw away the work and accomplishment . . . of all those patriotic men who freed our state from Negro domination?" Handbills carried by Smith workers showed the same statistics with a picture of Negroes campaigning for Graham. A broadside inquired, "Did you know that 28% of the population of North Carolina is colored? FEPC means that you might be working next to and sharing facilities with someone not of your choice. . . . The Southern working man must not be sacrificed to vote-getting ambitions of political bosses." The "Know the Truth" committee sounded the clarion:

White People WAKE UP Before It Is Too Late. You May Not Have Another Chance. Do you want Negroes working beside you, your wife and your daughters in your mills and factories? Negroes sleeping in the same hotels and rooming houses? Negroes as your foremen and overseers in the mills? Negroes using your toilet facilities? Frank Graham favors mingling of the races.[24]

On June 15 Graham's staff learned that the Smith headquarters had reprinted a hundred thousand copies of the front page of a Negro paper, the *Carolina Times*, which carried a picture of Graham with a headline "The Negro Press Endorses Graham," together with the claim that Negro registration was more than one hundred thousand. These were mailed from county headquarters with the assertion that Smith had not injected the racial issue into the campaign. The letter concluded:

> Notice, too, that the Negro newspapers carried editorials, reproduced on the back page of the enclosures, advocating intermarriage of the races and the admission of Negroes to the State's white institutions of learning. Do you want these things to come to pass?

Especially in the mill towns and in the eastern counties, where Negro population was greatest, there was widespread circulation of political material that, with no identification of the sponsor, violated federal election laws. There were handbills saying that a vote for Graham was a vote for mixing white and Negro in schools, circulars with pictures of Negro and white children playing together or of Negroes sitting idly on a porch while white people worked in the fields, and even a broadside that pictured a Negro soldier dancing with a woman who had the superimposed face of Marian Graham. In one county there appeared sheets of paper torn from school tablets with the penciled scrawling, "Do you want your children in the same classroom with the Negro kids?" In another county school buses were stopped and children were given similar warnings: "If Frank Graham is elected, you will be sitting by Negroes in school next fall." The whispering campaign spread.[25]

No candidate in a political campaign can be responsible for all the excesses of his supporters; the enthusiastic admirers of both Smith and Graham went beyond the lines of decorum and, at least in the case of the former, beyond the law as well. For the last ten days of the campaign, both candidates were on the hustings, traveling through the countryside and small towns, shaking hands, making speeches when anyone would stand long enough in the broiling June sun to listen. Smith did not decry the use of racist material. "Do you know what the FEPC would do?" he asked on June 18 in Lumberton as he passed out printed sheets assailing bloc voting and the FEPC. "It would make Mr. Whitley there, if he had a vacancy in his furniture store, hire the first man who presented himself even if he is of the other race. My opponent signed his name to that in that book. It is in my car right there."[26]

On June 20, in a factory, Graham saw a circular, passed around and posted by his supporters, which implied that if Smith were elected, the workers would go back to a fifteen-cent wage. He asked that his aides find out the source of the circular, and when the campaign headquarters reported that it was the work of an independent labor committee, Graham immediately asked that it not be used. "I don't think we'll go back to that no matter who gets elected," he said. Newspaper reporters, dissatisfied with his reasons for stopping the circular, pressed for further explanation, but all they could get was a determined "I just don't want to campaign like that." Though Graham had publicly asked that the broadsides not be used, Smith later charged that the Graham forces were continuing with the biased publicity.

Graham simply did not know how to cope with the charges that were made. On June 20, when he was speaking to workers at the Liggett-Myers factory in Durham, a worker shouted, "Isn't it true that Willis Smith is the biggest liar in North Carolina?" Graham, usually quick with an answer, was hesitant, as though trying to find the right words. The group of workers was silent, expectant. Finally he said, "I haven't said that. I wouldn't say that. No. I wouldn't say that. I'm not saying anything against any human being." Two days later someone wanted to know why Graham didn't "call that feller what he is?" "I'm not attacking anybody," he answered evenly. "If I have to do that to get in the Senate I don't want to go."[27]

Graham, incessantly trying to speak directly to the issues and to answer the questions honestly, seemed perplexed and unnerved by what was happening. Speaking to one group of workers, he said, "It is right strange to see laboring people whom I've worked for for twenty years turn against me." Asked repeatedly about the Negro he had sent to West Point, he replied, "I've seen pictures from the ocean to the mountains of a Negro boy I'm supposed to have sent to West Point. He is not there. He wasn't first. The boy who placed first in that examination is there, and they say he's an excellent student. I wish somebody would get a picture of him. He's a good boy."[28]

Somebody not only got a picture of him, he got the student; and for the last week of the campaign, William Hauser, the appointee to West Point, traveled with Graham. He was often met with surprised stares when the people, especially in the rural counties, were told that a Negro was not at the Academy, and he heard one farmer whisper, "My, ain't he light."

Again and again when someone raised the question of Leroy Jones, the Negro second alternate, Graham explained how, upon advice of Vice-President Alben Barkley, he had given competitive examinations for the Academy and how Jones had come out third, Hauser first. "I want you to know William Hauser, who is now at the Academy. He's a good boy." In one town he was surprised when the crowd applauded. "Leroy Jones is a good boy," Graham continued. "And he's the product of our segregated schools."[29] He told how, when Jones placed third, he had been advised to name only the first-place man and not to mention the two alternates. "I did what I thought was the right thing," he said. "If that will keep me from going back to the United States Senate I don't want to go. I don't want to conceal anything. I don't want to be expedient. I want to be honest."[30]

The burden of the campaign bore upon him. It was not just the thirteen to seventeen hours each day in the June heat and dust, meeting waves of people. It was the same questions that were repeated again and again at every crossroad; it was the attitudes of some people on the fringes of the crowd—the suspicious stares, the turned backs; it was the malicious circulars that friends showed him. It was as though something sinister were swirling about him, something that did not fit into his views of man and of North Carolina.

While race oppressively pervaded the campaign like a heat wave across the Carolina black belt, Communism, too, was introduced into the second primary. "Do you want socialism?" Smith repeatedly asked. "My opponent has stood for everything socialistic that has been proposed by Congress for years."[31] According to a news columnist, hundreds of thousands of reprints of a summary from the *Congressional Record* of John Flynn's distorted treatment of liberals, *The Road Ahead*, were mailed into the state, many of them under the frank of a New York representative, Ralph Gwinn. A more serious threat was a deluge of leaflets quoting specific passages from Flynn's book dealing with Graham. They called Graham "a hooded Socialist . . . who is up to his neck in Communists but manages to conceal his Socialist identity from an uncritical Southern governor." Dr. Marjorie Shearon, a former employee of the National Republican Committee, wrote a pamphlet about Graham and his "Communist" groups that were leading the country to socialism. She told a newsman that almost ten thousand copies had been bought and sent to the Smith headquarters by a Colorado physician and two North Carolina business firms. Two days before the election, Smith's publicity director placed in several state newspapers ads stating, "Frank Graham Joins Another." This "new" radical organization was the American Civil Liberties Union, of which Graham had been a member for years. The ad charged the group's executive director with being an atheist who at one time had been an anarchist, had served a federal prison sentence, and had said, "Communism is the goal."[32]

Both candidates spent the last days in person-to-person campaigning. Marian Graham drove her husband in their Ford, crisscrossing the eastern and southern counties, where Graham, to the surprise of many, had led in the first primary. It was in that rural area with a large Negro population that the second primary might well be decided. They stopped wherever a group was ready to greet them: at country stores, in farmers' front-yard oak groves, at mills, on courthouse steps. Graham campaigned hatless and in shirt sleeves, shaking as many hands as possible, answering the questions directed toward him, and defending repeatedly his position on segregation. "Do you stand for segregation in the schools?" How often would he hear that question? And how could he answer it honestly? To the farmers standing in the shade of a big sycamore, he said, "To break down segregation in the schools would set this state back for years. It would lead to great bitterness. You would find support for the schools languishing. The result would be worse schools for both races." And standing on the porch of a farmhouse, he said to the neighbors gathered under the shade trees, "In North Carolina the white people and the Negro people must live together. . . . It is a matter of generations, not of one generation. These are the things which must work out gradually through the teachings of Jesus."[33]

He felt he had to say it again and again: he was against the compulsory FEPC, governmental control of farming, socialized medicine, legislation to end segregation, and against Communism. But whenever he sensed the opportunity, he spoke of the urgency of world peace and of support for the United Nations.

On Friday, June 24, 1950, the final day of campaigning, he was in the industrial Piedmont. At one crossroads, his caravan drove off inadvertently, leaving him in earnest conversation. He had to hitch a ride to the next stop.

The last city to be visited that afternoon was the furniture and mill center of High Point, where fifteen years before, Graham had come to the defense of the workers and where less than a month before, he had lost to Smith by a three-to-two ratio. As they traveled through the city, stopping on street corners and visiting factories, the supporters in Graham's caravan were silent in disbelief and shame at what was happening. In crowds that were generally small and listless, small children on the sidewalk chanted "No school with niggers, no school with niggers." When Graham approached to shake hands, some workers, looking past him, would ignore his open, outstretched palm. Frequently, when he began to introduce Marian, the people turned aside. Once someone said something audible only to the Grahams and turned his head to spit on the ground.

At the next stop, when Graham and Lowenstein were alone in the back room of a store, Graham looked up, his face ashen, and asked in a hoarse voice, "My God, did you hear what that man said?"[34]

When the votes were counted, Smith had 281,114, Graham 261,-789. Smith's deficit of 53,393 in the first primary had changed to a majority of 19,325. More significantly, while Graham had won in sixty-two of the one hundred counties in the first primary, in the second primary Smith defeated Graham in sixty-one counties. Almost all of the shifts came in the eastern counties where the Negro population was large, the Negro vote small.

At nine-thirty Saturday night Graham walked down the five flights of stairs from his headquarters in the Sir Walter Hotel to the Smith headquarters, into the exuberant crowd, to shake hands with the new Democratic nominee for the Senate. Speaking to Smith's supporters, he said, "I congratulate Mr. Smith on his victory. I have for him every good wish in his high opportunity for service to our state, our country, and the world in this critical time."[35]

Sunday. "I'm so tired," Graham told inquiring reporters, "that I haven't been able to think. That means I am not saying anything."[36]

Monday. At Lake Success, the United Nations, responding instantaneously (in the absence of the Russians from the Security Council) to the North Korean advance into South Korea, called for an immediate cease-fire.[37]

The same day, at Lake Junaluska in the North Carolina mountains, filling a speaking engagement made early in the year, Graham made no reference to the campaign. He called for support of the United Nations in a great moral offensive for peace on all the religious, educational, economic, and political fronts. "The paramount issue for the people of the world is the stopping of aggression, the saving of freedom, the prevention of a third world war, and the preservation of civilization and the people of the earth from their own terrible powers of self-destruction."[38]

Friday. A printed card signed "Frank P. Graham" was mailed to his supporters from the Raleigh post office:

This is America . . .

in spiritual faith and the American dream, America is being made safe for democracy without vulgarity, differences without hate, and excellence without arrogance; where men become brothers in the sight of God and in the human heart; where the opportunities of the children in homes and schools are the chief concern of present progress and the chief hope of a nobler society; where enduring progress in human relations is made through religion, education, and voluntary cooperation in the minds and hearts of the people; and where the struggle for the fulfillment of our historic Americanism is the best answer to fascism and communism in the present global struggle against totalitarian tyranny for freedom and peace in the world.

In this America of our struggles and our hopes, the least of these our brethren has the freedom to struggle for freedom; where the answer to error is not terror, the respect for the past is not reaction and the hope of the future is not revolution; where the integrity of simple people is beyond price and the daily toil of millions is above pomp and power; where the majority is without tyranny, the minority without fear, and all people have hope. This is America, God Bless America!

On the final page he concluded:

Deep in our hearts is gratitude to all of you who fought so valiantly, gave so unselfishly of yourselves, your time, and your energy, who kept the faith and regard the defeat as only a temporary setback in a cause which will surely triumph in the minds and hearts of the people of our great state. The comradeship of this struggle will be a source of faith and hope and a most precious possession all the days of our lives.[39]

19

Beyond Defeat

I have run the risks of taking sides ....[1]
—FRANK PORTER GRAHAM (1950)

WHEN HE RETURNED TO THE CAPITOL THE WEEK following the election, Graham was besieged by senators, both Republicans and Democrats, who wanted him to know how much they deplored the way in which he had been defeated. Most talked with him quietly on the Senate floor; but particularly those who were closest to him—Paul Douglas, Wayne Morse, Hubert Humphrey, Herbert Lehman—went to his office to speak privately of their regrets. It was for such men both a personal and a political loss. They, like many other senators, had come to know and trust Graham and the way he worked. More than this, in the time he had been in the Senate, his reputation for liberalism had been confirmed. According to the analysis of the *New Republic*, there were very few in the upper chamber who voted more consistently for progressive measures; and according to the *Congressional Quarterly*, there were few Democrats who voted more consistently with the party. In the Senate he was what he had always been, a liberal and loyal Democrat.

Ironically, the first vote following his return as a lame duck senator was on the cloture issue. Senator Lucas again called for a vote on limiting debate on the question of whether the Fair Employment Practices Bill should reach the Senate floor. Graham was on record as opposed to a compulsory bill and on record, too, as opposed to a filibuster. When the clerk reached his name, there was a resounding "Nay!" As soon as the roll call was complete, amazed senators rushed to his desk. Republican Irving Ives was the first to reach him. "Why in the world didn't you send word two months ago you would have voted like that? It could have meant your re-election."

"I wasn't here two months ago," replied Graham.

Pressed for an interpretation of why he, a foe of the filibuster, voted with the Southern Democrats and conservative Republicans, he said, "The purpose of the cloture rule is to end a filibuster. There was no filibuster; so I voted against the cloture rule this time."[2]

It was 1950, the year of McCarthy. The junior senator from Wisconsin had stumbled into the headlines with a speech before the Wheeling Republican Women's Club on February 9. He had claimed that he had in his hand evidence that there were 205 card-carrying Communists in the State Department known to the Secretary of State, "still working and shaping the policy of the State Department."[3] What he had in his hand was a letter from a former secretary of state reporting that a recommendation against permanent employment had been made for 284 employees, and that of these, 79 had been separated from the service when the letter was written July 26, 1946, almost four years before. McCarthy, without a prepared address, may have thought he was speaking to Republican women in Wheeling, but when the report in the local paper was picked up by the Associated Press and three days later by the *New York Times*, he became, literally overnight, a national figure. The night after the Wheeling speech, in Salt Lake City, he changed the statement to "57 card-carrying members of the Communist Party in the State Department," and the following night, in Reno, to "57 cases of individuals who would appear to be either card-carrying members or certainly loyal to the Communist Party."[4] Always he had the evidence "in my hand," but he was never clear as to what the evidence was nor consistent as to how many persons there were.[5]

It was all so unbelievable. It was believed.

To Graham, returning to Washington defeated by McCarthy-like tactics, the widespread belief in Joe McCarthy was what was most of all unbelievable. But there was the half-year record since the Wheeling speech: Senator McCarthy entering the Senate chambers with his bulging briefcase ostensibly containing secret documents that proved Communists honeycombed the State Department; Senator McCarthy hurling his charges about the 205, the 57, and later the 81 Communists to audiences across the country. And there was the Senate, often immobilized in dealing with pressing legislation because McCarthy had the floor and had the newspaper headlines. There was the defeat of liberal Senator Pepper in

Florida and Graham's defeat in North Carolina; and there were already present, in August, the rumblings of a McCarthy campaign against Senator Tydings in Maryland. In all those campaigns there were the similar, obviously professionally directed tactics of misrepresentation, of innuendo, of composite photographs. (In the Maryland campaign a faked photograph of Tydings with the Communist leader, Earl Browder, was prepared by McCarthy's staff.)

There was all this to demonstrate that McCarthy was believed. There was all this and much, much more: the television actress who was fired by the sponsor of her serial dramatic program because private groups had asserted that she had once belonged to a front organization; Owen Lattimore, who endured ordeal by slander and, though absolved by the Senate, had a speech canceled with the explanation that "now with the critical condition of this country, anyone about whom there is any question should not be allowed to speak"; the mayor of Los Angeles, who requested citizens to turn over to the police information regarding anyone they thought politically suspicious; the rash of new city and state laws for "internal security." If further evidence was needed, there was the August 28 report of the Senate Judiciary Committee on Senate Bill 4037, "designed to protect the internal security of the United States."[6]

Graham, a member of the committee, joined with Senators Kilgore and Langer in filing a minority report. While approving certain sections of the bill, they said that it was "clearly unconstitutional in some respects, and will be entirely unsatisfactory."[7]

It was the second time in the congressional session that Graham had shared in filing a minority report against a bill sponsored by the powerful, arch-conservative Pat McCarran. The first McCarran bill had been defeated. Perhaps it could happen a second time. The security bill that carried McCarran's name was essentially the same bill sponsored by Representatives Nixon and Mundt that had passed the House in the previous Congress. It was the culmination of a decade of work by the House Un-American Activities Committee; and with the anxieties released by Senator McCarthy's attacks, it was natural that the Senate should press for a security measure. The main features of the Senate bill (1) denied admittance to the country of Communists; (2) tightened the anti-espionage and sabotage laws, making it a criminal offense "knowingly to combine, conspire, or agree with any other person to perform any act which would substantially contribute to the establishment within the United States of a totalitarian dictatorship"; (3) required the registration of Communist and Communist-front organizations, denying members of such organizations federal jobs or passports; and (4) established new passport and visa legislation.

Graham was most fearful of those sections that would limit freedom. Pressed in debate by Mundt, recently elevated to the Senate, and by Senator Ferguson, he expressed his views: "I may say that any suppression of human liberty or repression of human liberty disturbs me, whether it is in this bill or some other bill. I merely start that way. I spent a good deal of my life, if I may say so modestly, fighting for civil liberty for human beings."

Senate liberals (Graham was not among them) worked themselves into a trap by sponsoring as a substitute measure a bill that would allow the President to intern certain persons in time of war or insurrection. The proposal merely established procedures for what every wartime president had done, providing certain rights for the internees. The Senate rejected the substitute bill, and then the conservatives attached it to the McCarran bill. Some of the most liberal senators felt compelled, in that circumstance, to support the Internal Security Bill. Graham was one of only seven senators who, on September 12, voted against the measure.[8]

The fight was not yet over, however. On September 22 President Truman vetoed the bill and returned it to the House and Senate; and he took the unprecedented step of placing on the desk of every congressman a personally signed letter accompanying his veto message. He asserted that Congress had been led

> in cowering and foolish fear . . . to throw away the ideals which are the fundamental basis of our free society. . . . The net result would be to help the communists, not to hurt them. These provisions are not merely ineffective and unworkable. . . . The application of the registration requirement to the so-called Communist-front organizations, can be the greatest danger to freedom of speech, press and assembly, since the Alien and Sedition laws of 1799.[9]

Responsible newspapers and political scientists also attacked the bill. The *New York Times* asserted that it provided "such curbs of freedom of speech and press and political association as to render suspect all but the most orthodox, the most conformist."[10] The

Washington Post added that the bill was "as dangerous to the national security it pretends to protect as to the American tradition of personal freedom it utterly ignores."[11] Shortly thereafter, "informed and impartial persons" viewed it as "an ill-considered statute, many of whose provisions seriously endanger our fundamental freedoms." Zechariah Chafee, Jr., Harvard's champion of civil liberties, wrote Graham, "When the history of our period is written forty or fifty years hence, I anticipate that the multitudes who voted for this bill will be regarded with the same amazement which we now give to the Sedition Act of 1798."[12]

But the kind of report that worried Graham most was the kind that, supporting the bill, appeared in the *U.S. News and World Report*: "If in doubt, don't join!" read the headline.

> Warning to loyal Americans: check your membership cards, anticommunist net might get you if you don't watch out. For the person who wants to keep out of trouble in the future this appears to be good advice: Be very careful about organizations joined. Be equally careful about contributing to organizations.[13]

There could not be, in Graham's view, a more insidious doctrine to teach Americans, particularly young Americans, than to encourage them to stand on the sidelines, refusing to engage in the fight for democracy, because there were risks. In his view, to be human meant to engage in battles for humanity; to be a democrat, to be an American, meant to throw one's full weight on the side of freedom, taking the risks rather than carefully weighing in advance what the personal cost might be. So beyond the fact that he considered some portions of the act unconstitutional was the even greater danger that it would teach Americans, especially the youth, "If in doubt, don't join."

Graham was grateful, then, for the strong veto message; and later, in his final Senate speech, he took fifteen minutes to outline his opposition to the bill and to conclude:

> Repression is the way of frightened power. Freedom is the way of enlightened faith.
>
> The best way to preserve internal security and human freedom and to fight international communism is to make America so free in its basic liberties, so democratic in its equal opportunities, and so deeply spiritual in its meaning . . . that America will become such an example of human freedom, social justice and international cooperation that the American story will reach through the iron

curtain and to people everywhere on this earth with the hope of freedom and peace. . . .

Through faith in God and love of man, may we pray that the light of liberty will yet shine through the iron curtain of men's minds, the warmth of human brotherhood will yet melt away the iron curtain of men's hearts, the people's hope of freedom and peace still fly their flags high in the western world and across the eastern seas, where people of all faiths, races, colors and nations, look up in prayer to the God of us all for one free and federated world neighborhood of human brotherhood.[14]

Congress was not to be stopped in the face of the "dire internal communist threat," however, no matter how emphatic the veto nor how unanimous the security division of the Department of Justice, the Department of Defense, and the Central Intelligence Agency were in opposing the bill. The House overrode the veto within moments after receiving the President's message, and it did so without debate. In the Senate there was an effort to hold off a vote until there could be reaction in the nation to the President's veto. Graham refused to join in the delaying tactics, which were all to no avail. Only five senators changed from support of the bill to support of the President. "I can honestly say," reported Senator Humphrey about his previous affirmative vote, "that I have never been more unhappy in my life. But this is indeed a happy moment, because it is good to be able to vote one's convictions. I join the ranks of free men. I am going to rectify the miserable mistake I made. I am going to join the ranks of those who believe in their fellow man." Quaker Senator Douglas, who said he also felt that in the earlier passage he had made too great a sacrifice of freedom on behalf of security, continued, "The inner voice, which in the long run is our best guide, whispers to me that I am now acting in conformity with the right."[15]

It may have been in conformity with the right, but it was not in conformity with the majority. The Senate, with Graham and nine others opposing, overrode the President's veto. It was another defeat; it was Graham's last vote in the Senate.[16]

Graham's fight against the McCarran bill was reassuring to his liberal friends, as had been his eloquent affirmation, "This is America," which was twice read by other senators into the *Congressional Record*. Both proved that he was weathering the crisis of his defeat for the Senate.[17]

Some of his closest friends sensed, however, despite his silence, that he had been deeply, personally hurt. It was not primarily the tactics of the opposition, for he had met such tactics before. For the first time in his life he, who had been lavished with love, was publicly rejected, apparently hated—and in North Carolina. The hurt was greatest of all because he was rejected by the very people— the textile workers, the farmers and sharecroppers, the small businessmen—for whom he had lived and fought. And it had happened because he was misunderstood. Steadily, throughout the years of battling for human rights, he had been convinced that the positions he took were democratic and Christian, true to the best traditions of America and North Carolina; that if fellow North Carolinians understood the positions, they would see for themselves that it was so.

They had not seen. The defeat had inexorably produced a quiet, personal crisis. There was the obvious crisis as to what a man sixty-three years of age and without financial reserves would do. When reporters questioned him about his plans for the future, he responded, "I'm going to finish my job in the Senate, take a month's rest and then decide." The more intense crisis was inner. The attitudes and beliefs he had tenaciously held had brought defeat. What would happen to them now? It was because of this question that the democratic affirmation and fight against the McCarran bill were reassuring.

After returning to the Senate in July, Graham had participated fully in the work of the Judiciary Committee, in frequent caucuses of the tiny Democratic remnant holding out against the bill, and in debate on the floor. During the same busy weeks he spent many hours collecting material, writing and rewriting statements expressive of his feelings and aspirations. On each of the last three days he was in the Senate, he introduced into the *Congressional Record* an unusual document.

Statehood for Alaska and Hawaii had been blocked in the Senate by party politics; alone among Southern senators, Graham advocated that they be admitted immediately. In the statement he presented September 21, he reviewed the history and resources of the territories, arguing that the admission of both would be "timely expressions of the self-determinations of peoples and for the defense of freedom" with moral democratic reverberations throughout the world.[18]

The following day Graham presented a seventeen-thousand word "Farewell Statement," a factual record of his opposition over two decades to "fascism, communism, imperialism, and other forms of special privilege and totalitarian tyranny."[19] He reviewed in detail the committees he had joined ("perhaps 100 organizations," he said, but that was well over a hundred short), the charge about being on the staff of the summer school of the University of Moscow, and his relation with the Oak Ridge Institute. Of the 159 committees listed by the attorney general as Communist fronts, Graham reported that he had been associated with four for brief periods, years before the listings. His associations with two had been through contributions he sent to hospitals treating the Republicans in Spain and the Chinese who had fought Japan. A third he had resigned from when it became evident that its principal purpose of protecting the foreign-born was subordinated to other interests. The fourth was the sponsorship of a four-day conference held at Tuskegee Institute under the auspices of the Southern Negro Youth Congress. The explanations were clear. The attacks against him that he repeated from Communist propaganda left no doubt that Moscow viewed Graham as a tool of Wall Street. The passage he quoted from his letters and addresses communicated an expanding devotion to democracy over a twenty-year period.

It was an impressive document. But friends found it sadly out of character. The very existence of a farewell statement attempting to straighten the record seemed to confirm the judgments of those who sensed how painful the defeat had been. But if it was in part defensive, there were also other reasons that led Graham to make the "simple statement of facts." It was made, he stated, "in support and appreciation of my colleagues in the Senate who have generously given me their faith and friendship." The concern for friends, which was typical, had two sides. Many of his friends, both in the Senate and out, trusted him without knowledge of the facts about his associations. Such friends deserved accurate knowledge that their faith had not been betrayed, so the document was presented "for reference by those whose own faith needs no statement." There was, however, another subtle way friends concerned him. While he had always acted quietly, neither counting the cost nor caring about credit, he seemed, as he grew older, increasingly to want his friends to know about his battles for democratic causes. Finally, he was fearful that the McCarthy atmosphere, including what had happened to him, might cause free men to become cautious; and he knew such caution would be the death of freedom.

I have run the risks of taking sides in the midst of events which could not wait for certificates of safety and conformity while freedom itself was embattled by fascism, communism, imperialism, privilege and monopoly on many fronts in a fearful world. I would be lacking in candor if I did not express the hope that the present hazard of the smear will not cause any of us . . . [to] stay safely on the sidelines and refuse to take part in the struggles and the hopes of the people for a fairer world.[20]

The last day before the Senate recess, Graham introduced "An American National and International Program,"[21] which would lead to the more just world he envisaged. The national program advocated a strong America in military and economic matters but most of all in the welfare of a free people through development of natural resources, equal educational opportunity for all children, continuous progress in the relations between the races, decent minimum wages and an increase in social security, more adequate medical care, and the provision of a refuge for those left homeless and hopeless by the march of dictators.

Graham stated that America, as the leader of the free peoples, must give greater emphasis to a "strong international program against all dictatorships, all aggression, for better international understanding, and for freedom and peace in the world." Such a program would require three simultaneous advances: (1) cooperation among the free nations, supporting mutual defense and economic recovery in the Americas and Europe, defending the rights of self-determination in West Germany, Berlin, and among the new Asian and African nations, and providing for technical assistance to the underdeveloped areas; (2) reaching through the iron curtain to all people with the word of hope, which could be convincing only if it came from an America that was both a defender of human freedom and a promoter of human welfare; and (3) the resolute support of the United Nations, which among other goals would willingly risk in Korea the disaster of a Dunkirk to avoid the appeasement of a Munich, would work toward international disarmament and control, and would establish an international police force sufficiently strong to resist aggression anywhere. The statement had been many years in the making: it had come from that "light that never was on land or sea." Graham concluded his brief time in the Senate by affirming:

A dynamic, more powerful than the electromagnetic compass, stronger than the power engine, more potential than atomic power, and more fundamental than the controls and hopes of the United Nations, greater than all these, is the moral dynamic of the spiritual revolution in the teachings of Jesus who lived and died that people everywhere might be free and equal in the brotherhood of all men under the Fatherhood of God who "made of one blood all the nations of men for to dwell in all the face of the earth."[22]

The Grahams returned to Chapel Hill shortly after the congressional recess September 24. The month's rest he had promised himself and Marian consisted in large part of making campaign speeches for the Democratic candidates, including Willis Smith. Of the twelve major rallies in congressional districts, Graham spoke at eight, telling "why we should close ranks and unite as a Democratic Party." He was unable to attend the first two, and when he made the major address at the third, in Morganton, his endorsement of the New and Fair Deals and his praise of Truman and Roosevelt were the first times those names had been heard at the rallies.

Sitting in the living room of the small rented cottage in Chapel Hill the night before the election, Graham spoke to Marian and Al Lowenstein of their getting ready to vote a straight ticket the next day. Lowenstein, still rankling from the June defeat, was incensed. "I don't care what you say. No force on this earth could make me vote for that man tomorrow. There's one person in this room who won't vote a straight ticket." Marian spoke softly, "There are two persons in this room who won't vote a straight ticket."[23]

In the morning Graham voted alone in the town hall. It was a cloudless autumn day, the morning temperature in the mid-sixties. He walked back to the cottage, along the neat business street and beside the campus, where the trees aflame with fall color and the students hastening to classes on familiar paths were reminders of the past. Here he had spoken, as a student, of the state and the University; and for more than forty years he had served both. Here he had made friends for the human pilgrimage.

The pilgrimage was not over; yet the doors, all doors it seemed, were closed before him. He felt that he could not stay in Chapel Hill, or even in North Carolina. The South had a way of exiling those who threatened the fixed Southern patterns of race and economics. Over the years many exiles had left voluntarily. Others, particularly those defeated in politics and without independent wealth, had no real choice. Very well: he would leave North Carolina and the South to work, while he had time, for what he believed in.[24] But he knew that North Carolina and the South would never leave him. Chapel Hill would always be "home," and he would return whenever there was an excuse to do so. If the doors in his home in the South were closed, other doors in his home in the world would open. Of that he was confident.

Part Six

Liberal-at-Large:
1950-1972

20

The United Nations, India, and Pakistan

This keeping by India and Pakistan of their own UN-sponsored international commitments . . . would hopefully become a prophetic and creative part . . . of the people's unresting dream of building a nobler home for all the children in all lands . . . .[1]

—FRANK PORTER GRAHAM (N.D.)

WHEN GRAHAM LEFT THE SENATE IN SEPTEMBER, 1950, it was the first time since he had left his parents' home in 1904 that he had no plans even for the immediate future. Although he was sixty-four, he did not consider retiring, and job possibilities were not long in coming. President Truman proposed to appoint him president of the American Red Cross, but Graham declined. He also asked not to be considered for appointment to the Civil Aeronautics Board or the Federal Trade Commission. All seemed sinecures; Graham wanted a challenge. Then Truman asked him to stand by for consideration as the director of the National Science Foundation. "I had other things in mind," said Graham, "but it has been my policy when the Commander-in-Chief calls or says he would like to call me for a particular post in a critical time, to stand by for the call."[2] While being reviewed by the foundation's board, he turned down offers or possible offers, some of which would have meant double the income of the directorship of the Science Foundation. He was offered membership in a law firm, the associate editorship of a newspaper, the presidency of several institutions of higher learning, and a position with the United Nations Point IV Program dealing with relief and refugee work. The board of the Science Foundation did not recommend Graham as director, however, noting that he was not a scientist. Graham interpreted the opposition as coming from conservative economic groups who disliked his positions on unions and farm cooperatives, as well as from groups that disapproved of his stands on behalf of minorities. "Not willing to start being different for any appointment," he asked the President not to make the appointment if the board of the foundation would not recommend him.[3] There was more than one reason to be disappointed: in the months without a job he and Marian had been forced to cut into the savings they had stored up for the cottage they hoped to build in Chapel Hill.

The Korean War, which had started in June, 1950, had an immediate impact upon the American economy. There was a frantic mobilization of men and materials. In the light of the prevalent belief in Russian involvement in the North Korean invasion, Alaska was viewed as strategically significant because of its proximity to the Soviet Union. A walkout of building trades that would bring the Alaskan defense program to a standstill was imminent. Senator Lester Hunt (D., Wyo.), a member of the Senate Subcommittee on Preparedness, who, with other members of the committee, had visited Alaska in October, 1950, approached Oscar Chapman, secretary of the Interior Department, which had jurisdiction over Alaska, and urged that he plan a labor-management conference. The conference, bringing together thirteen government agencies, was planned for January 21, 1951, at Anchorage, Alaska, with Graham, appointed a consultant to the Department of the Interior, as chairman.

Graham invited a federal judge, a respected citizen of the territory, to deliver an address of welcome; he read a telegram of encouragement (which he had instigated) from George C. Marshall, Secretary of Defense; and he made the keynote address which, according to a newspaper report, "sounded the right note" and "dispelled the fear and won the confidence of the disputants." On the first afternoon Graham met separately with labor, then with management, giving them the opportunity "to get off their chests all their sense of grievances, wrongs and misunderstandings, and also to make constructive suggestions for meeting the problems." As negotiations continued, he gave to each side all the facts available to the other and facilitated direct telephone conversations with the Secretary of Labor in Washington and national union leaders then in session in Miami.

On January 25 management and labor reached an agreement, not on a structure for further negotiations (which was all that had been hoped for), but on all points including wages and procedures to avoid all stoppages of work. The unexpected achievement received high commendation in the Senate. Wayne Morse said "it is one of the best jobs of negotiating in the labor field that I know anything about." And Oscar Chapman, admitting his original pessimism about the outcome of the conference, wrote to Graham, "You went to Alaska as the head of a government team to attack a problem which at the time seemed almost insoluble. In the face of this situation your accomplishment in completing a successful mission has been the more remarkable."[4]

287
——
THE
UNITED
NATIONS,
INDIA,
AND
PAKISTAN

Early the same month Charles E. Wilson, who had become head of the newly created Office of Defense Mobilization, had talked with Graham about a post on his staff. When asked for advice, Graham pointed out that the two most crucial groups for the program were labor and the public. Therefore, the key people on Wilson's staff should be "a person with a background and experience in the field of organized labor and a person with a background and experience in public responsibility."[5] To the dismay of liberals, including Graham, Wilson surrounded himself with businessmen and did not appoint to a major position a single person who could represent labor or the public.[6]

For reasons difficult to discern—perhaps they had to do with the dissatisfaction of liberal senators and labor leaders with Wilson's office—Maurice Tobin, Secretary of Labor, established on March 10 within his department a Defense Manpower Administration with thirteen regional offices. He asked Graham to head the program, and in a simple ceremony on March 21, Graham was sworn in as its first administrator. It was not entirely clear what the work would be, however. During the scant six weeks he was on the job as manpower administrator he spent much of his time "jumping around, attending manpower conferences, North, South, East and West." In both public and private statements he consistently listed six goals for American manpower:

> to prevent a third world war; to win the war in Korea and a third world war if it comes; to lick inflation as a chief threat to our freedom and our power; to aid our allies of the free world against the monstrous threats of totalitarian tyranny which would lock all peoples behind the Iron Curtain, hanging over the prison walls of the police State; to maintain also a high level of civilian production for the economic, social, and spiritual well-being of our own people; to be the bulwark of a stronger United Nations as the chief hope of freedom, justice, and peace on the earth.[7]

On April 5, 1951, Graham received an unexpected call from John D. Hickerson, Assistant Secretary of State for United Nations Affairs. Hickerson asked whether Graham would accept a three-month appointment as United Nations Representative for India and Pakistan in the dispute regarding Kashmir. Since Graham's name had already been approved by President Truman, it could be anticipated that the appointment by the seven-member United Nations Security Council would come following nomination by the United States and the United Kingdom. Graham was not familiar with the Kashmir dispute beyond what he had read in the press, that both India and Pakistan claimed Kashmir and might well go to war over it. He had had no previous experience in South Asia, but he was interested in international peace and the United Nations, and he felt that he had been successful in one previous short-term appointment for the United Nations. He agreed to talk with Hickerson the following week.

When Graham went to the State Department across from the White House, Hickerson was not alone in awaiting him. Before the visit ended, he had seen Secretary of State Dean Acheson and Assistant Secretary of State for Near Eastern Affairs George C. McGee, as well as South Asian specialists. All stressed the importance of the Kashmir dispute in the quest for peace in South Asia. Hickerson explained that the appointment would be made in accordance with the March 30 Security Council resolution that authorized United Nations personnel to try again, after repeated failures, to effect a demilitarization in Kashmir. Pakistan had accepted the resolution; India had not but had reluctantly agreed to consult with the United Nations representative. In view of past failures to resolve the conflict, it was clear that the ability and personality of the representative would play a major role in narrowing the issues in dispute and in bringing about demilitarization or agreement upon a demilitarization plan. The representative was expected to visit South Asia and report to the Security Council within three months.[8]

It was the kind of challenge Graham loved. He secured a three-month leave from the Department of Labor and accepted the offer. The fact that he would have the chance to work closely with Andrew Cordier, a friend from graduate school days, was an added incentive. Cordier, chief administrator in the Secretary-General's office, would assist in securing the representative's immediate staff of six persons. Hickerson explained that the salary would likely be $14,000 net, tax-free, and could be as much as $25,000 when perquisites were added.

289

THE
UNITED
NATIONS,
INDIA,
AND
PAKISTAN

On April 30 the Security Council, over the objection of Jacob Malik of the Soviet Union, appointed Graham United Nations Representative for India and Pakistan, a post corresponding to that of an assistant secretary-general.

By the time of his appointment Graham had learned about the complexity of the problem. First there were the voluminous United Nations documents and State Department memoranda to read, then he was scarcely into those materials before he felt the need for books on India and Pakistan and Kashmir. So off went requests to the Library of Congress and the United Nations library as well as to bookstores. It was exciting and depressing reading, impossible to assimilate in full.[9]

India had a history and culture rich beyond belief: probably no other peoples could match the subtle complexities of Indian life and thought. They were an ancient people who had assimilated many alien cultures before the Muslim invasion of the thirteenth century, when the Delhi Sultanate began. The Muslims were the only invading peoples who were not absorbed into Indian social and political life. They had, at least as seen by many Muslims, brought to India and developed a vastly different religious, social, and political culture.

In the fourteenth century Kashmir had been conquered by the Muslims, and the population had been converted to Islam. Five centuries later, in 1819, the Sikhs, a militant religious sect in northwest India, had "liberated" the region from Muslim rulers with the assistance of a Hindu prince, and not long after had rewarded the prince, Haja Gulab Singh, by giving him control over Jammu, an area south of Kashmir. Toward mid-century the British had conquered the Sikhs, and once again Gulab Singh was on the winning side. Again he was rewarded: despite the fact that the majority of Kashmiris were Muslim, as they had been since the fourteenth century, the British delivered all of Kashmir to a Hindu, declaring by the 1846 Treaty of Kashmir that it was to belong "forever, an independent possession, to Maharajah Gulab Singh and the heirs male of his body."[10]

It was almost a century before a political consciousness, stimulated by the neighboring All-India National Congress, emerged among the Kashmiri people. In 1931 a revolt was led by the young Sheikh Mohammad Abdullah, who was immediately imprisoned by the Hindu ruler and who in the following years, whether in jail or out, was a key figure in the many twists and turns of Kashmiri politics. In February, 1947, after years of the Indian struggle for independence, the British announced that they would grant independence to India by June, 1948, and that Viscount Mountbatten, Supreme Allied Commander for Southeast Asia, would be responsible for the peaceful transition. Mountbatten arrived in Delhi in late March. Rapidly assaying the volatile situation, in less than three months he made three fateful recommendations that were accepted by Indian and British leaders. First, the transfer of power would be on August 15, 1947, rather than awaiting 1948. Second, the country would be divided into a Muslim Pakistan and a secular (though predominantly Hindu) India, with the former receiving 17.5 percent of the national assets, the latter 82.5 percent. Third, the independent princely states, constituting 45 percent of the land area of the subcontinent, could accede to either nation or remain independent. By Independence Day almost all the princely states had joined one of the nations, thus creating, despite the partition, inclusive political unities greater than South Asia had ever known.[11]

When, in August, 1947, the Maharajah of Kashmir did not decide to join either India or Pakistan, political struggles intensified within the region. Rumors of the sufferings and killings caused by partition in the neighboring Punjab reached Kashmir and seemed for some to foretell Kashmir's own fate. There was no way to assess the human tragedies in the Punjab; but the largest migration of refugees in human history was taking place, with some ten million people in flight, Muslims to Pakistan, Hindus and Sikhs to India. Trainloads of massacred Muslims would arrive in Pakistan; trainloads of dead Sikhs or Hindus in India. How many died by violence was unknown: the claims went up to a million, but relief workers on the scene estimated that it was between one and two hundred thousand. Besides the killing, there were other deaths from disease, exposure, and hunger, which were a natural consequence of the migrations.[12]

As in the case of India and Pakistan, the Kashmir problem was compounded of religious, cultural, social, and political factors. The conflict, which had been smouldering for years, flared up in September, 1947, when some two thousand Muslim tribesmen from the northwest invaded Kashmir, burning, killing, maiming, and raping. They proclaimed the establishment of a free ("Azad") Kashmir. The Maharajah frantically appealed to India for help; but Lord Mountbatten, now the governor-general of India, insisted that no military help could be given unless the Maharajah signed an instrument of accession to India as required by the procedures for transfer of power in the partition agreement. This was done on October 26; and the following day Mountbatten accepted it "conditional on the will of the people being ascertained as soon as law and order were restored." The accession only brought into the open the deep conflict between the longing of both Pakistan and India for Kashmir. The open conflict meant that Pakistani and Indian armies faced each other in Kashmir across the recently established boundaries.[13]

291

THE
UNITED
NATIONS,
INDIA,
AND
PAKISTAN

The United Nations Security Council, in response to a complaint from India written January 1, 1948, established on January 20 a commission to investigate the facts and "to exercise mediatory influence"; and on April 21 it reaffirmed its action. The first meeting of the United Nations Commission for India and Pakistan convened in Geneva June 15, 1948, and in July it proceeded to South Asia. On August 13 it adopted unanimously the first of the two resolutions that would form the basis for all further United Nations action in the dispute. The first resolution established a cease-fire, defined truce agreements, and concluded that "the Government of India and the Government of Pakistan reaffirm their wish that the future status of the State of Jammu and Kashmir shall be determined in accordance with the will of the people."

India accepted the resolution; Pakistan also accepted, but with so many qualifications that the commission viewed its answer "tantamount to rejection." Disappointed, the commission continued its work and, returning to Geneva in September, prepared another resolution, which was accepted by both Pakistan and India and was adopted by the Security Council on January 5, 1949. This resolution stated specifically that "the question of the accession of the State of Jammu and Kashmir to India or Pakistan will be decided through the democratic method of a free and impartial plebiscite." Provision was made for the appointment of an international plebiscite administrator, for a truce agreement, and for military forces that would make the plebiscite possible.[14]

The two resolutions gave hope that the dispute would be solved.

It seemed to be only a matter of working out details. The commission returned to the subcontinent in February to finish its work. At the United Nations, an administrator of the plebiscite was appointed. Hopes and expectations for a settlement were destroyed with an interpretation made by India, which was unacceptable to Pakistan, regarding the disposal of military forces in Kashmir. By September the commission concluded, with despair, that its work was ended. In a report critical of India, it recommended that the problem be turned over to one person as a mediator and, should mediation fail, proposed arbitration on those technical points that would make a plebiscite possible.[15]

General A. G. L. McNaughton of Canada, president of the Security Council, was requested by the council to investigate and make proposals. He saw the problem as a straightforward military one, as it might have been if the resolutions had been accepted in clear and complete good faith. Thus his proposals were military, suggesting means toward the reduction of forces that would make possible a fair plebiscite. Pakistan accepted his proposals with minor modifications; India submitted amendments that amounted to an entirely different proposal. It was another failure.[16]

In March, 1950, the Security Council decided to designate a United Nations Representative for India and Pakistan, whose responsibility would be the elimination of obstacles that were preventing the implementation of previous resolutions for the plebiscite. Sir Owen Dixon, judge of the High Court in Australia, was appointed on April 13. Dixon saw the problem as a matter of implementing a recognized legal contract. He found upon arrival in New Delhi and Karachi that the situation had "strange features," since both parties had agreed to a plebiscite but in almost eighteen months had taken not a single step to make it possible. Dixon proposed means to the agreed-upon end. When those proposals were rejected, usually by India, he proposed other means, but was ultimately forced to conclude:

> In the end, I became convinced that India's agreement would never be obtained to demilitarization in any such form, or to provisions governing the period of the plebiscite of any such character, as would in my opinion permit the plebiscite being conducted in conditions sufficiently guarding against intimidation, and other forms of influence and abuse by which the freedom and fairness of the plebiscite might be imperiled.

FIGURE 45. Dr. Graham, U. N. Representative for India and Pakistan, meets with Prime Minister Nehru in New Delhi. Left to right: Petrus J. Schmidt, Dr. Graham's Principal Secretary; Dr. Graham; Jawaharlal Nehru; I. S. Chopra, Chief of Protocol, Government of India; and General Jacob L. Devers, Dr. Graham's Military Adviser.
United Nations, (from Government of India)

FIGURE 46. Dr. Graham meets with Sheikh Abdullah, Premier of Kashmir, in Srinagar. Left to right: Sheikh Abdullah, Dr. Graham, General Jacob L. Devers (background), and Mr. P. J. Schmidt. *United Nations*

FIGURE 47. Dr. Graham presents his report on the Kashmir question to the Security Council in January, 1952. Left to right: Dr. Graham; Sir Gladwyn Jebb, United Kingdom; Mr. Ernest A. Gross, United States; and Jose Carlos Muniz of Brazil. *United Nations*

FIGURE 48. Representatives of India and Pakistan shake hands after the meeting of the Security Council. Left to right: Sardar J. S. Malik, Head of India's delegation; Dr. Graham; and Sir Zafrulla Khan, Head of Pakistan's delegation. *United Nations*

FIGURE 49. At United Nations Headquarters in May, 1952. Left to right: Dr. Graham; Thomas J. Watson, Jr., President of International Business Machines Corp.; Trygve Lie, Secretary-General of the United Nations; and Paal Berg, former Chief Justice of the Supreme Court of Norway. *United Nations*

FIGURE 50. Dr. Graham is photographed in Karachi in 1958 with delegates to a Seminar on "Teaching about the UN." *United Nations*

FIGURE 51. Mme. Vijaya Lakshmi Pandit, sister of Prime Minister Nehru of India, talks with Dr. Graham and V. K. Krishna Menon. *United Nations*

FIGURE 52. Dr. Graham and President Sukarno of Indonesia in Karachi, 1958. *Southern Historical Collection, UNC Library*

FIGURE 53. Dr. Graham is met by M. J. Desai, Secretary, Commonwealth Relations, at the Palam Airport in New Delhi, January 12, 1958. *Southern Historical Collection, UNC Library*

FIGURE 54. Sign posted on a store front in Kashmir.
Southern Historical Collection, UNC Library

FIGURE 55. Prior to the meeting of the Security Council on the Kashmir question, Dr. Graham talks with U Thant, acting Secretary-General of the UN, and Carlos Salamanca of Bolivia. *United Nations*

FIGURE 56. Observers at the Security Council meeting on the Kashmir question, February 1, 1962. Dr. Graham, center, was not called upon to speak.
Southern Historical Collection, UNC Library

FIGURE 57. Dr. Graham and Dr. Nikolai T. Fedorenko of the USSR following the Security Council's adjournment of discussion on the Kashmir question, March 20, 1964. *United Nations*

FIGURE 58. Dr. Graham, Francis Winslow, and Kemp Battle during a television presentation, June 11, 1962.

Southern Historical Collection, UNC Library

And he asserted, "There is, I believe, on the side of India a conception of what ought to be done to ascertain the real will of the people which is not that tacitly assumed by me. Doubtless it is a conception which Pakistan does not share."[17]

In reading the United Nations documents, Graham's interest in mediation was aroused. He had recently returned from successful mediation of the difficult labor-management dispute in Alaska; he had been successful in his brief foray in Indonesia and with the National Mediation and War Labor boards. But it was clear that he would be dealing with a problem in mediation more tangled, more intractable than any he had worked with before. Pakistan and India did not openly share any discernible common interest upon which to base an agreement. Moreover, their mental characteristics were very different: Pakistan exhibited the Muslim mind, with its love of logic and clear distinctions; India largely displayed the Hindu mind, where all realities can merge together to the extent that the most evident contradictions are not, in the totality, viewed as contradictions.[18]

When Graham was appointed United Nations Representative, there began two years of feverish activity. For those two years his time was nearly consumed by the Kashmir problem, and during the rest of his life it remained a primary preoccupation. Until his fifth report to the Security Council on March 27, 1953, all other interests were subordinated to his United Nations responsibility. He never lost contact with the committees and causes on behalf of human welfare with which he was connected, but his social activism and public speaking were severely limited. Even the time he cherished most, that which he spent with Marian, was curtailed by travel and study. It was Marian, then, who arranged the move in the summer of 1951 from their Washington apartment on Massachusetts Avenue to a two-room suite in the Commodore Hotel in New York, and the move in April, 1952, to an apartment in the Fairfax Hotel on East 56th Street, which Graham described as "a strangely quiet nook in the middle of this thunderous city."[19]

Graham chose a young North Carolina law professor, William B. Aycock, as his personal representative; but he trusted Andrew Cordier's recommendations for the remainder of his staff. Miguel Marin, associated with the Kashmir problem through his work as United Nations staff member on the Commission for India and Pakistan, was Graham's political and legal adviser, and General

293

THE
UNITED
NATIONS,
INDIA,
AND
PAKISTAN

Jacob L. Devers of the United States Army was his military adviser. Throughout the two years the work was essentially a cooperative effort. Marin formulated most of the political and legal issues, and the personal representatives, first Aycock and then Elmore Jackson (appointed in 1952), gave emphasis to personal and moral relations in the negotiations.

From Graham's sessions with his staff and his reading of the United Nations documents, he was able to see the major problems. India and Pakistan had taken immovable positions that somehow had to be worked around before serious talks could even begin.[20] India resolutely refused any wording which suggested that Pakistan was on an equal basis with India in the Kashmir dispute. It insisted that one of the chief problems was the failure of the United Nations to point to Pakistan as an aggressor, and it would not accept what seemed essential steps for a fair plebiscite: replacing the pro-India Kashmir government with a temporary coalition or neutral government and replacing Indian forces with a United Nations armed force. Finally, India would not accept arbitration of any points whose resolution was necessary for a vote. Pakistan, in the weaker position, had accepted most of the suggestions from the previous United Nations commission and representatives but would not budge on certain military matters. Pakistan refused to withdraw its forces from Kashmir until an agreement had been reached concerning Indian withdrawals, and it refused to work toward the disbanding of the Azad Kashmir forces until after the implementation of the truce agreement of the 1948 resolution.

Seeing these irreconcilable differences, Graham suggested that he and his staff develop some specific points for possible agreement that would not mention any of the adamant positions of either side. These points, prepared by the time they left for South Asia in late June, 1951, would not be mentioned in the first conversations. They would be injected gradually into the discussions in the hope that preliminary agreements could be reached as they talked with each side, agreements that could later lead step-by-step to a solution of the major problems. This was Graham's way of mediating, and it led to some preliminary successes. It also led to confusion. As Nehru pointed out to his parliament, when Graham arrived in Delhi, "he did not even once refer to the Security Council's resolution. It was as if the resolution was not there."[21] But even the confusion helped Graham focus the Indian and Pakistani minds on points on which they might agree.

295

——

THE
UNITED
NATIONS,
INDIA,
AND
PAKISTAN

If he had learned much about the dispute and the disputing nations from his reading and his staff consultations, all that he had previously learned was burned into his mind by what he saw, read in the newspapers, and heard from government officials after his arrival in Karachi and New Delhi. Both cities are on the edge of deserts; and in both cities for weeks prior to the arrival of the rains, usually in early July, the heat and airborne sand grind away the flesh and spirit.

Graham and his staff arrived at Karachi the morning of June 30. The temperature when they stepped off the plane at nine o'clock was, for that time of year, a comfortable ninety degrees. (It would sink to eighty-four degrees on Graham's first night in Pakistan.) As he was driven in the government's car into the city, Graham was distracted by seeing the people and their poverty. Karachi in 1947 had been a city of 300,000; now, with an influx of Muslim refugees, especially from Bombay and western India, it had swollen to more than a million. The huts and hovels along the road were unbelievable to Graham. They represented the indomitable will of the Pakistanis to survive.

That will, expressed in newspapers and by government officials, was both frightening and dignified. The government, like the city, had been created almost from nothing. Yet beginning with the universally respected Prime Minister, Liaquat Ali Khan, upon whom Graham called on the afternoon of his arrival, and continuing with all the other government officers, the determination and fear and suspicion were manifest. The fear was of India; the specific charges were of Indian army concentrations along the Punjab border. The suspicion was that India was out to destroy Pakistan, that Kashmir was a part of this plot, and that India would never acquiesce in a fair resolution of the Kashmir problem. If what he heard from government officials was not clear enough, the newspapers shouted Pakistani convictions. Not long before his arrival the World Muslim Conference had met in Karachi urging all Muslim governments to support the cause of Kashmir and Pakistan; the Grand Mufti of Jerusalem had visited Azad Kashmir, calling for *jehad*, a holy war. The press fueled the determination and fear and suspicion with daily insults against India. It was a shaken, enlightened Frank Graham who left Karachi for New Delhi on the morning of July 2.

Stepping off the plane at the Palam Airport at ten o'clock was like stepping into an oven with the temperature already above

100 degrees. The drive into New Delhi was again an education. Graham saw fewer people than in Karachi, since Delhi's refugees, he was told, were located in another section of the city. The landscape was barren; emaciated cows roamed aimlessly; but the tree-shaded streets, the expansive lawns, and the imposing Mughal-style secretariat buildings contrasted sharply with the crowded streets and makeshift government buildings of Karachi.[22]

The first afternoon, there was an appointment with the Prime Minister, Jawaharlal Nehru, at the Rashtrapati Bhawan, the President's Home and center for welcoming important foreign guests. Conversations with Indian officials were at first restrained, since India had been insistent upon not recognizing the United Nations resolution that formed the basis of Graham's visit. But what Graham heard from the Indians and read in the press was the mirror-image and echo, somewhat softened in tone, of what he had heard and seen in Karachi. Suspicion, fear, bitterness, and determination were pervasive. The talks initially concerned the basic resolutions of 1948 and 1949, which both nations had agreed to; and since both had accepted a plebiscite as the final way to resolve the issue, talk led by degrees into discussion of the major obstacles to a vote. There were specific matters of interpretation to be dealt with. During the next two months, as the team visited with Pakistani and Indian officials in Karachi, Srinagar, the capital of Kashmir, and New Delhi, those differences of interpretation were to reappear constantly.[23]

Although Graham was careful not to pull any specific recommendations out of his file as though he had proposals in hand when he first arrived, the conversations confirmed what he and his staff had known; therefore, prior to leaving South Asia, it was not difficult to write a letter to both parties proposing twelve points for their agreement.

The first four points were a reaffirmation of what had been agreed to previously: a no-war declaration regarding Kashmir, restraint from hostile statements, continued observation of the cease-fire agreement, and a plebiscite under United Nations auspices to decide the status of Jammu and Kashmir.

Six of the points dealt with demilitarization. A new major proposal was that the demilitarization, rather than taking place by separated, discontinuous steps, should be "effected in a single continuous process." This would be completed within ninety days.

An important point was to specify the number and condition of forces that would remain on either side of the cease-fire line at the end of demilitarization, but Graham left blank the precise number of forces in the hope that proposals from the two sides would provide bases for subsequent negotiations. Any difference regarding the process of demilitarization would be decided by the military adviser to the United Nations Representative.

Three other points dealt with the administration of territory evacuated by the Pakistanis. An organization of local authorities, set up under the surveillance of the United Nations and with the acceptance of the plebiscite administrator, would take charge not later than the final day of demilitarization. The United Nations representative and the plebiscite administrator would have authority regarding the "final disposal" of forces.[24]

To one emotionally outside the dispute, the extraordinarily complex cauldron of issues had cooled into what seemed a reasonable approach toward a resolution of the conflict. Within five days after the proposals were sent on September 7, replies were received: Pakistan, which had everything to gain, substantially accepted all twelve points; India, with much to lose, accepted the first four but found serious problems with the remaining eight. It was less than Graham had hoped for, but it was something.

On September 12 he left South Asia to complete his report in Geneva. He made his oral report to the Security Council on October 18, requesting that the council authorize him to continue the negotiations. This the council readily did; so he went to Paris for further talks. In his second report on December 18, followed by an oral statement to the council on January 17, 1952, he was able to report further progress: India had acceded to four more points. Again, because he could point to some progress, he requested additional time for negotiation; again the council readily agreed. The debate in the United Nations was marred only by the vituperation of the Russian delegation, led by Jakob Malik, who accused Graham of being a "tool of the Pentagon" and claimed that the entire process was an Anglo-American plot to subvert Kashmir with the aim of creating a military base for aggression.[25]

Graham spent the month of February in Paris conferring with Indian and Pakistani diplomats. In March he was again in South Asia conferring with both sides. The Indians had presented the greatest obstacle to the acceptance of Graham's twelve proposals,

297

—

THE
UNITED
NATIONS,
INDIA,
AND
PAKISTAN

so Graham spent the larger amount of time in talks with government officials in New Delhi. But that caused Pakistan to be fearful that Graham's next report would favor India. The report, presented to the Security Council in Geneva on April 22, did not favor India but was a summary of conversations with both governments, which had ended in failure. Graham's optimistic belief that the conflicts could be resolved, given good will on both sides, may have led him to minimize the failure. He suggested that the two nations enter into direct negotiations under United Nations auspices with the stipulation that the conference be limited to one month.[26]

The talks began on August 19 at the League of Nations Palace in Geneva. For a week the representatives of the two countries sat at the same table; then, when the conflicts became irrepressible, they began to meet separately with Graham. The negotiating method had been successful before in many a labor dispute and in Indonesia.[27] On September 7 Graham wrote Marian that he was continuing his reading about the history of the peoples "for some understanding and background." He concluded:

> We are deadlocked again. When the way is tough I think of you and you come to my side in your prayer to help. Whatever else we fail in we must not lose our faith in the people, in their good faith in wanting a solution and in an elective solution through the ballots of the people rather than the bullets of armies.[28]

The talks ended inconclusively on September 11; Graham reported the failure to the United Nations on October 11. Still he refused to admit defeat and, pointing to the urgency of the problem, recommended that the talks be resumed. The Security Council once more agreed. These talks began in Geneva on February 4, 1953, and lasted for two weeks. When a recommendation based on the talks was referred to the two governments, both rejected it. On March 27 Graham had to admit another failure. This time he recommended that the United Nations representative be withdrawn from the negotiations and that the prime ministers of the two countries be urged to enter into direct conversations.[29] It was to be exactly five years before he would make another report to the Security Council.

Jawaharlal Nehru and Mohammed Ali, the current prime minister of Pakistan, met in Karachi for three days in July and again in New Delhi for three days in August. The beginning was auspicious: they reported that the talks were "frank and cordial," that they had discussed Kashmir and other outstanding problems between their countries, and that "both Prime Ministers were actuated by a firm resolve to settle these problems as early as possible, peacefully and cooperatively, to the mutual advantage of both countries."[30] Whatever the influence of Graham and the United Nations had been, it seemed for a moment that the prime ministers not only might resolve the major problem of Kashmir but might develop cooperation between the two nations; and the initial private correspondence between the two confirmed this possibility. But on November 10 Nehru wrote a personal letter to Mohammed Ali expressing apprehension at the news of a possible military pact between the United States and Pakistan. He followed this with an official letter on December 9 stating that such a pact would "affect the major questions we are considering and, more especially, Kashmir." An American-Pakistan pact would destroy the possibility of resolving the Kashmir problem, he said, since that entire problem had thus far foundered on the question of how much demilitarization was required before the plebiscite, but "in fact, it becomes rather absurd to talk of demilitarization, if Pakistan proceeds in the reverse direction with the help of the United States."[31]

The military pact between the United States and Pakistan was announced in November, 1953. It was immediately obvious that for the foreseeable future there would be no solution of the Kashmir problem. Whether that pact was for Nehru and the Indian government a reason or an excuse for becoming recalcitrant on the issue of Kashmir it is impossible to know. In any case, the cold war policies of the United States, policies that had been initiated by liberals, were a partial cause of the collapse of the negotiations. This fact was recognized at the time in the State Department. The deputy director of the Division for South Asian Affairs informed Elmore Jackson (who immediately passed the word to Graham) that Nehru's anxiety over the United States' arms aid to Pakistan meant that India would not enter into serious negotiations to settle the Kashmir dispute. Probably "the ultimate solution of the Kashmir problem would be an international boundary along the lines of the present cease-fire lines."[32]

The helplessness of the United Nations in dealing with the political problem of Kashmir was evident by the spring of 1954. For

299

THE
UNITED
NATIONS,
INDIA,
AND
PAKISTAN

three years the case disappeared from the United Nations agenda, and during that time, though Graham remained the United Nations Representative for India and Pakistan, no progress was made. Then, in February, 1957, the council requested its president for that month, Gunnar Jarring of Sweden, to "examine with the Governments of India and Pakistan any proposals which, in his opinion, are likely to contribute towards the settlement of the dispute."[33]

Unfortunately Graham was not formally notified of this usurpation of his responsibilities; the first time he heard the news was through gossip in the halls. His secretary, Daisy Lippner, later said it was the only time in all the years they were together that she saw him angered or provoked. Graham went to Pierson Dixon, the British delegate who had been a key person in the Jarring assignment, to complain. A staff member reported to Lippner, "I have never seen your boss that way before. He really told him off right."

When, shortly thereafter, the case came up in the council, members one by one praised Graham for his work. Graham then spoke of the nature of the India-Pakistan problem and the possibilities for its resolution. As Lippner left the council chamber, two United Nations guards spoke to her. "That's the kind of man we need in the United Nations," said one. "We need more like him who can talk of the human things about people and about their needs." And the second guard continued the theme. "We don't need so much this going back to Article 1, Section 5 where everything becomes so complex the person is lost."[34]

Jarring visited both India and Pakistan. India reported that it would take no further steps because, it maintained, Pakistan had not fully implemented basic sections of the original 1947 agreement; Pakistan insisted it had implemented those sections. Jarring recommended that this issue be arbitrated, a term he subsequently recognized as unfortunate, since what he was proposing was "a determination of certain facts which, in the Indian view, were incontrovertible." India refused, so once more failure was reported to the Security Council.[35]

Later in 1957 the council requested that Graham make another attempt. He visited South Asia in February and March of 1958, trying to breathe new life into old negotiations. He proposed that the two countries reaffirm their good will and the basic principles of the cease-fire agreement, initiate specific steps toward holding a plebiscite, and meet once more at a high level conference under United Nations sponsorship. Pakistan agreed, but India refused on the grounds that Pakistan was the aggressor and had not fulfilled its pledges. But, Graham told the Security Council, the government of India had informed him that "they have been and are anxious to promote and maintain peaceful relations with Pakistan . . . and that they firmly adhered to their determination to pursue paths of peace, while placing their faith in the United Nations and its Charter."[36]

301

THE
UNITED
NATIONS,
INDIA,
AND
PAKISTAN

After 1958, Graham, as the United Nations Representative for India and Pakistan, was essentially a man with an office but without a job. He continued to study the problem; he continued to write and rewrite proposals that he thought should be considered by the two nations; he continued to rework "A Summary Review of the Mediatory Reports of the United Nations in the Kashmir Situation," which included further recommendations and also included his resignation.[37] He viewed the report as a magnum opus; but he was never called upon to deliver it. The refusal of the United Nations to face the problem of Kashmir by calling upon him to state the facts and issues as he saw them pushed him closer to despair than he had ever been. Again and again, tirelessly, he approached the presidents and other members of the Security Council and suggested that he be invited to make the report. The invitation never came. What was worse, when the Security Council debated the Kashmir issue in 1962 and again in 1965 during the India-Pakistan War, he was not asked to speak to the council.[38] He proposed to Ralph Bunche, Undersecretary-General, and to U Thant, Secretary-General of the United Nations, that he resign. They both asked him to remain, and he acquiesced. All the while he became more and more restive; and in March, 1965, he felt he had to plead with and justify his actions to U Thant:

In view of the present crises in the United Nations I have wondered when will develop the best time for carrying out my wishes (to make my final report and resign).

At your convenience, in the midst of all your heavy burdens and recurring crises, I would appreciate very deeply having your advice and the advice of your Secretary-General who has special responsibility in the Kashmir case.

Meantime I have continued speaking up for the United Nations in many parts of the country. My secretary has roughly estimated that during recent years I have made more than 1500 talks on the United Nations in 43 states. For these talks, of course, I do not charge an honorarium but when honoraria nevertheless are provided they are immediately passed on to the United Nations for the Children's Fund.[39]

The position as United Nations Representative for India and Pakistan, which had begun as a three-month appointment in 1951, stretched out into a nineteen-year job until Graham's resignation from the United Nations in 1970 for reasons of health. His loyalty to the United Nations was such that as long as his superiors requested that he remain, nothing could force him to resign. Repeatedly he conferred with Bunche, and less often with Hammerskjold and later U Thant, about resigning. Always they expressed the wish that he stay on the job, though it was never precisely clear that the wish was tied exclusively to his potential usefulness in the India-Pakistan dispute. During the many years that the Kashmir issue was quiescent, he might have drawn his paycheck and stayed at home awaiting the call for his report from the Security Council. Instead, his compulsive habits of work caused him to continue studying the India-Pakistan situation and rewriting his report, though it was never published. But the major part of his time was given to the educational, or propaganda, work of the United Nations within the United States. For a number of years he was chairman of the United Nations Speakers Bureau.[40]

Despite the fact that he was not a polished orator and tended to ramble in his remarks, Graham was among the most popular and certainly the most used of United Nations officials on the lecture circuit. He was especially appreciated by university groups, by organizations of students and women and labor, and by churches. In fact, his admirers were the very persons in whom he had so great a confidence. In the talks, which by the time of his retirement numbered more than 2,000, he refused to speak directly about the Kashmir situation, but he did speak emphatically about the indispensable aspects of the United Nations. He believed and repeatedly insisted that in a number of specific occasions the United Nations had prevented the outbreak of war, a war that might have engulfed the world, and he advocated a continuation of the political activities of the United Nations as the best guarantee of avoiding a nuclear conflict. He saw the economic and humanitarian work of the United Nations to be, in the long run, of yet greater importance, since he believed that work would meet fundamental human needs of the underprivileged nations and individuals.

303

THE
UNITED
NATIONS,
INDIA,
AND
PAKISTAN

In spite of the obvious frustrations and failure in his work as Representative for India and Pakistan, he never expressed the despair he often came close to feeling. Hopelessness was alien to his nature. Indeed, he even continued to express confidence in the people of India and Pakistan, and never placed blame where others might have placed it, perhaps even where it belonged. The closest he came was in his unpresented, unpublished final report, where he commented that "Pakistan accepted and India rejected most of the basic proposals of the several United Nations mediators for resolving this deadlock." But he insisted that his own twelve proposals were "neither pro-India nor pro-Pakistan, but are pro-United Nations." He concluded with "A Summary of Faith and Hope in the Great People of India and Pakistan," which expressed the belief typical of his enthusiastic advocacy of the United Nations:

The agreed peaceful settlement of the Kashmir dispute would make possible the desperately needed more generous provisions for (1) family planning; (2) sound general education adapted to the needs of the people; (3) technical training; (4) modern scientific agricultural methods; (5) well-balanced economic production; (6) better health and well-being of the people in the cities and in the hundreds of thousands of rural villages where three-fourths of the people live, struggle, and hope for a better day.

This keeping by India and Pakistan of their own UN-sponsored international commitments for a cease-fire, a truce and a plebiscite, would hopefully become a prophetic and creative part of the larger structure and moral substance of the people's unresting dream of building a nobler home for all the children in all lands in the great adventure of the human spirit through the United Nations for freedom, justice and peace, under law, and human brotherhood, under God, in this age of mortal peril and immortal hope for all peoples on the earth as the home of the family of man.[41]

Always the enthusiast, he spoke the convictions of his heart. They were the dreams of freedom, dreams that had been stirred in his childhood, clarified by his youth, and confirmed by his experience. They were a liberal's dreams that were not to become real, certainly not in his lifetime.

21

The Ideals of the American Revolution

The ideals of the American Revolution have gone around the world and have come home again....[1]
—FRANK PORTER GRAHAM (1961)

DURING THE YEARS THAT HE WAS WITH THE United Nations, Frank Graham's basic attitudes were both simplified and enlarged, becoming more intense and inclusive. Previously he had been forthright in action and speech; but his actions had been primarily mediatorial, beginning with a principle and attempting to compromise opposing positions without sacrificing the principle. In this process his most fundamental beliefs had been in people and the powers of persuasion. His speech, while direct, had embodied and expressed sympathy for honestly held views different from his own, unless they were anti-democratic. His unique action and speech were primarily the manifestation of temperament; but they were also modified by the fact that he had represented a state institution and therefore felt restraint upon his personal behavior. After 1950 both were changed, freeing him to be even more direct in his activity, more plain in his speech.

His defeat for the United States Senate did not alter significantly his personality, but it had a discernible effect upon his temperament. Though he at times made painful reference to the treatment of Marian in the campaign, he never discussed his defeat. Still, his friends believed that his rejection by his own people had left deep wounds that only further battles could heal. One obvious consequence was the introduction of the lengthy "Farewell Statement" into the *Congressional Record*. That detailed defense, so untypical of his public or private self, was psychologically freeing: henceforth he would not hesitate to defend his record when called upon to do so, even at times taking the initiative in wanting people to know how he had participated with others in democratic causes.

His departure from the South was also instrumental in enlarging his personal freedom. At the time of his defeat, his secret preference had been to remain in Chapel Hill to teach in the University.[2] This preference arose naturally from his self-image as a teacher, which he had never lost. It also came from the facts that for almost half a century Chapel Hill had been home, that he and Marian had a small lot on the edge of the campus on which they planned to build a small house, and that at the age of sixty-three, he was close to the normal University retirement age. But he felt that, because he had recently been president, it was inexpedient for him to stay in Chapel Hill; and for this reason he mentioned his desire to no one, not even to Marian.

Graham's new freedom, his simplified and enlarged beliefs, led him, during the remaining twenty-two years of his life, into battles that sometimes appeared to others as minor but in his view were of major importance. They were important because they were the expression of the return of "the ideals of the American Revolution to the house of its fathers." He wanted to do his share in welcoming those ideals home, for Chapel Hill and North Carolina and the South were still home to him, even though he felt he must live elsewhere.

Early in 1952, while he was preoccupied with the tangled India-Pakistan problem, Graham learned that the Orange Presbytery in North Carolina had established a judicial commission to examine "the general situation" of the Chapel Hill Presbyterian Church, and that the commission had the authority to remove the church officers and the minister. Graham was one of those officers. He had been an active member of the Chapel Hill church since shortly after his graduation from college in 1909. Every Sunday he was in Chapel Hill, unless he was ill, he was in church. The church was important to him, so he saved as much time as he could spare from his United Nations responsibilities to prepare a defense of it. Any fair commission, he believed, would be convinced by the true facts.

The occasion for the creation of the commission was the petition of twenty-six persons, only six of whom were members of the church, to establish a new Presbyterian church in Chapel Hill. When Graham learned who the six were, he knew that the concerns were not church order and doctrine, as stated in the initial stages of the inquiry, but that they grew out of the social liberalism

305

THE
IDEALS
OF THE
AMERICAN
REVOLUTION

of the church. And he believed that one issue was at the heart of the trouble. That issue was race.[3]

The church had a long Southern liberal tradition. The tradition had taken on new vitality in 1940 when Charles M. Jones, a minister in his early thirties, had come to the church. Jones and Graham quickly found an affinity for one another, and through the years they developed working relations in which each gave the other understanding, support, and freedom. Both were social activists, but while Graham was always careful to work within existing laws and social customs, Jones was willing to go further. The recognition by Graham that his minister frequently did what he, with his institutional loyalties and responsibilities, was not always free to do was but another factor in intensifying his loyalty to the church and its ideals as embodied in his minister.

In early 1944, in a regular meeting of students for Sunday morning breakfasts at the church, the suggestion was made that some friends at the North Carolina College for Negroes in Durham be invited to breakfast and worship. Six Negroes accepted; breakfast was served, and they attended church without special seating arrangements. Two powerful taboos had been broken: Negroes and whites had eaten and worshiped together in a white church. With the taboos broken, students frequently brought Negroes to Friday evening sessions, sometimes with Jones's encouragement and always with his consent. Less frequently, Negroes attended Sunday morning worship. This was too much for some communicants, who openly expressed disapproval to the minister. He countered that the church would not be true to the teachings of Jesus if it should let color, creed, or race keep anyone from its fellowship. Church officers had a series of meetings to study the problem. A majority would have voted for Jones's unequivocal position, but the small session refused to accept a motion to that effect when it knew that the motion would have passed by only one vote. Francis Bradshaw, a professor of philosophy, then presented a statement, which was approved, that entrusted "the matter to the conscience and judgment of the minister, who has heard all the discussion sympathetically." For the benefit of those who had raised the issue, the statement said that "the minister is fully aware of the factors involved in the situation and . . . we trust ourselves to his informed and conscientious leadership."

Graham was not at that meeting on May 8, 1944, but when he read the statement, he was incensed and phoned Jones immediately.

"Charlie, that statement leaves you in a place where you don't have any integrity as far as the church is concerned. We can't do that to you. Why don't the three of us get together this evening and work that over?"

307

——

THE
IDEALS
OF THE
AMERICAN
REVOLUTION

Bradshaw, Jones, and Graham met at the church. The document they worked out, which later passed more decisively than the original statement, was largely Graham's. It bore his mark by insisting that the church take leadership in interracial relations, in admitting Negroes to the church while not encouraging them to desert their own churches, and in expressing the need for gradual adjustments with due regard for the laws of the state.[4]

There was no place in the University or in commercial restaurants in Chapel Hill where interracial groups could eat together in the forties, so the Chapel Hill Presbyterian Church, under the leadership of Jones, became known as the place where interracial meetings would always be welcome. Gradually other churches in the community opened their facilities to Negroes. Encouraged by the stand his church had taken, Jones expanded his interracial activities on the local, regional, and national scene. In 1948 four Negro and four white "freedom riders," traveling through the South to test integration on interstate buses after the Supreme Court had nullified the laws requiring segregation, were arrested in Chapel Hill. A fight between the riders and some local cab drivers was narrowly averted. Jones was called to the scene because of his known interest, and he offered the riders shelter in the Presbyterian manse. After nightfall the cab drivers stoned the house, and threats were made by telephone that it would be burned.[5] Graham was one of the first people to offer support. After the riders had left, Jones and his wife, Dorcas, upon the advice of Graham and others, decided that it would be better for them and their family to leave town for a few days until tempers died.[6]

It was natural to believe, then, that race was the primary concern of the six members who petitioned for the Presbytery to establish a new church. Those six had for years been troubled by Jones's racial position. The investigating commission insisted that race was not the issue, however. During six months of listening to Jones's sermons, reviewing church procedures, and interviewing the elders, the commission members never introduced the question of race. But for those, including Graham, who were convinced that race was the problem, it was difficult to deal with the situation on the basis of doctrinal and procedural matters. It was especially difficult for the minister, since the commission never made specific charges against him or gave him the chance to state his case.

When Graham first received news of the impending investigation and the general nature of the charges, he consulted with John Bennett and Henry Pitt Van Dusen of Union Theological Seminary in New York to get recommendations of books on Christian doctrine, social ethics, and the history of the Church, especially Presbyterianism.[7] He wanted to make a representation to the commission members, who were mainly ministers, in their own terms.

Following its investigation, the commission reported late in 1952 that they "found it difficult to ascertain the exact nature of Mr. Jones theological convictions" yet admitted that he was "deeply loved by the vast majority of the active officers and members. ... There are those who frankly consider him an embodiment of Jesus." That, apparently, was not sufficient; the commission asked for the resignation of Jones and all the church officers because they had not been scrupulously faithful to Presbyterian doctrine and practices. (Phillips Russell, an officer of the church, said, "If Jesus were to preach in the Church they would ask him to resign on the grounds that although he might be a good Christian he wasn't Presbyterian enough.") The minister and officers refused to resign, and in December, in a secret ballot, the congregation voted by a ratio of 10 to 1 to ask the commission to withdraw its demands. The commission withdrew the demand for the officers' resignations but told Jones to "resign or be fired."[8]

Graham flew down to speak to the Presbytery. He began by recognizing the values in the commission's report, pointing out that as a result of its investigation, recommended changes had already been made in the rules, rituals, and practices of the church. He then spoke of the faith of the church and the significance of historic Presbyterianism and described the nature of Jones's ministry. That, he thought, clearly took care of all the commission's explicit complaints; so "if these do not meet the situation then there is something more than doctrine, rules and ritual behind the situation." To the issue of race he spoke directly, reviewing the history of the church's racial policies and setting the problem in a larger context.

> In the worldwide struggle for the loyalties and souls of men between Christianity and the spiritual forces of freedom on the one side, and totalitarianism and tyranny on the other side, Charles Jones is in

the front lines as an evangelist of Jesus Christ, preaching and ministering, humbly, joyously, and unafraid. In correcting his and our faults let us not strike him down.[9]

309

——

THE
IDEALS
OF THE
AMERICAN
REVOLUTION

The commission struck. On March 1 it dismissed Jones because "the interest of religion imperatively demands it." In May the synod condemned the confidential evidence collected by the commission and ordered a new hearing, and the 1953 General Assembly ordered a trial if Jones wanted one. Graham urged Jones to stick it out. Jones requested a trial before the entire synod, since the Presbytery, which had already rendered its verdict, could hardly be a fair tribunal. Unless the issue of race could be brought into the open before new judges, there was no hope. The Presbytery refused. Jones resigned from the Presbyterian ministry.[10]

Graham's attitude toward Negro-white relations was not changed by his Senate defeat largely on issues of race, by his departure from the South, or by his work in the United Nations. What did change Graham's stand on race was the Supreme Court decision of May 17, 1954.

Graham was ready for that decision. On May 12, 1954, five days before the opinion was rendered, Graham wrote to James Dombrowski refusing an invitation to join the Southern Education Fund, an organization directly descended from the Southern Conference for Human Welfare, which had collapsed in 1948:

> I am concentrating such time as I have from my United Nations duties in working through the churches as one of the most basic approaches to the problem of racial injustice and discrimination. Also in several talks I have made in North Carolina and elsewhere I have made a plea for the abolition of segregation in the churches and for acceptance of the decisions of the United States Supreme Court.[11]

The Supreme Court's assertion of May 17, "We conclude that in the field of public education the doctrine of 'separate but equal' has no place," was for Graham a conclusion to be accepted; to one who had always advocated life within the law, the simple judgment "It is so ordered" had the ring of finality.[12] Within a week he sent Clarence Poe a long statement advocating compliance with the decision of the court.[13] Other Southerners also spoke out immediately; but within a brief time their voices became muted. Frank

Graham was one of the few Southerners of stature who in private conversation and public address consistently advocated obedience to the Supreme Court decision as the law of the land.

His views were expressed in countless speeches, and there was consistency in what he said wherever he spoke, North or South. Sometimes the problem of segregation and the public schools was only a brief portion of a speech dealing with another major social issue; sometimes the problem constituted the full substance of a speech. Always he placed the immediate problem in a larger setting of history and the contemporary world, of religion as well as law. In was as though past history and present world struggles for freedom culminated in the decision of the court, which Graham saw as having values which all persons could recognize, no matter how much they might disagree with the specific decision. He spoke of the "inner moral value" in helping America in its struggle for freedom and equality for all its people.[14]

Within a few months Graham brought together his views in an article published in the *Virginia Quarterly Review* and subsequently reprinted and circulated throughout the South by the Fellowship of Southern Churchmen.[15] It is typical Graham writing—inclusive in scope, rambling in style. Even the involved title is Grahamesque: "The Need for Both Wisdom and Good Faith: Two Suggestions for Procedures in Carrying Out the Supreme Court's Decision Against Segregation." But there was no mistaking the theme: The abolition of segregation in the public schools is now the law of the land and must be obeyed. The "two suggestions" of the title appear in a single paragraph, and they represent typical Graham attempts to take into account social realities. Long before the court issued its second decree of obeying the law "with all deliberate speed," Graham suggested that integration should progress by grades, "beginning with the elementary grades," because "the younger the person the less the prejudice." The second suggestion was to abolish segregation first in the geographic areas where there were fewest blacks, since conflict between the races seemed to correlate with the ratio of blacks to whites. Thus,

> steps in complete integration would then more wisely and faithfully proceed, north to south, from the Border, Upper and Southwestern South to the Deep South, and from the mountain counties West to the Piedmont and to the Mississippi bottomlands and from

the mountain counties east to the Piedmont and to the coastal plains.[16]

311

THE
IDEALS
OF THE
AMERICAN
REVOLUTION

To Graham the decision of 1954 was a decision for the integration of public schools. Many Southerners, including Graham's friend Judge John Parker, argued that the Supreme Court had not required integration but only the abolition of segregation. This argument paved the way for "freedom of choice" doctrines and other delaying tactics. To Graham the implications of the decision were obvious: The states had no alternative but to integrate the public schools. And he was convinced that once the plain issues were understood, Southerners would rise to the occasion:

> In a pleasant land under a southern sun between the Chesapeake and the Gulf, a friendly folk will, we trust, in their dreams and programs work out together the integration of the public schools. . . .
> In the free minds and loyal hearts of millions of southern people of both races will live and grow the unfulfilled teachings of our religion, the struggles of freedom for a higher freedom, and the faith of the American dream with a message of hope and brotherhood in this age of suspicion and fear.[17]

When Southern governments, both state and local, thwarted the court decision, when the federal government was inactive until forced to uphold the law, as in Little Rock in September, 1957, Graham became disappointed in the faltering drive toward integration. He continued to work for integration, however, especially through the church and other organizations. He insisted that "with due regard for the stages in time and place, there must be no retreat but rather a wise and progressive fulfillment of the law of the land." When Representative Brooks Hays, the moderate from Arkansas, was defeated by a racial campaign, Graham was "stricken low" by knowing once more that "the race issue can set the woods on fire and will run its course with devastating power for a time."[18] But he encouraged Hays not to lose heart.

Increasingly he placed his hopes in the leadership of Negroes he had known for years, such as Channing Tobias and Benjamin Mays, and in that of Martin Luther King. These men

> valiantly struggle forward without sacrifice of convictions or compromise of principles, yet stand for enlightenment and understanding, non-violence, love and brotherhood, as really both the

fastest and most enduring way for the fulfillment of our religious faith and democratic hopes.[19]

Graham was psychologically prepared, then, for the student sit-ins that began in Greensboro in January, 1960. He immediately began to incorporate reference to the sit-ins in his speeches, not as a major part of the speech, but a simple statement occurring in a larger theme of freedom. With his great confidence in students and his belief in their non-violent methods, which were shaking communities throughout the South, he made a straightforward affirmation:

> The southern youth movement in the lawful petitions for the same service for the same price did not have its democratic origin in Moscow, but in Carpenter's Hall, Philadelphia on the fourth of July 1776 and its farther head waters are in the Judean Hills where the carpenter's son taught and died for the equal freedom and dignity of all people as children of one God and brothers of all people.[20]

These same words were spoken over and over again in more than forty states, ten of them in the South. Most people who came to hear Graham were encouraged by his affirmations; some were offended. When he spoke in April, 1961, at Winthrop College in South Carolina, a cross was burned on the lawn of the home at which he was staying. The South Carolina General Assembly passed a resolution condemning the college for inviting Graham and prohibiting him from speaking in a state-controlled college again.[21] The race issue had again "set the woods on fire" and was running its course with devastating power. It had become a matter not only of the freedom to eat or travel or be educated in unsegregated facilities, but of the freedom to speak.

On the final day of its biennial session in 1963, the North Carolina legislature passed a law forbidding state institutions of higher education to allow any person to speak who was a "known member of the Communist Party," advocated "the overthrow of the Constitution," or had ever pleaded the Fifth Amendment to the United States Constitution. Similar laws were rejected that year by seven other state legislatures; and North Carolina became the only state in the nation with a "speaker ban law." The legislature acted efficiently: the bill had not been considered by any committee, the rules of both houses were suspended, and the law was enacted in a total of nineteen minutes, four minutes in the House, fifteen in the more deliberative Senate. William Friday, president of the University, heard about the bill for the first time just as it was being introduced. He rushed the thirty miles from Chapel Hill to Raleigh to appeal for a delay; but the bill was law before he was halfway to the capital.[22]

313

THE
IDEALS
OF THE
AMERICAN
REVOLUTION

Although the bill was law, the University administration believed it such a bad law it assumed that quiet rational persuasion would convince the next legislature that it should repeal the act. The general opinion was that the law had been vindictive, arising from racial demonstrations by students and a few faculty members.[23] Earlier that spring some students and faculty members at North Carolina State University in Raleigh, including Allard Lowenstein, who at that time was an assistant professor of political science, had joined in a march for racial justice. Five days prior to the introduction of the bill, Lowenstein and others had joined in a demonstration at the Sir Walter Hotel, the residence of many legislators.

The law struck at Graham's most cherished beliefs about a free university. Immediately upon hearing about the bill, he telephoned friends at the University, in the legislature, and in the public life of North Carolina to discover what had happened, to express dismay, and to insist that the law must be repealed. The University must either be free or not a university. For more than four years, whenever he was invited to speak in North Carolina, he always spoke vehemently against the speaker ban law.[24] He made more public addresses against the law than did any other person.

The speeches were invariably cast in the same context and emphasized the same points. The context was that of history: the history of the University and its struggles in the twentieth century for freedom; the history of the American ideal; the history of individuals who, living or dead, had contributed to the life of freedom in the nation and state. He emphasized that the law clearly violated the Bill of Rights, unwisely prevented students from hearing all points of view, and unnecessarily took responsibility from students, faculty, and administrators who were best able to defend democracy in the University.

The 1965 legislature did nothing about the bill. Late in the session, Governor Dan Moore announced the appointment of a commission that would study the problem and make recommendations to a special session. The faculty, seven hundred and thirty of whom had publicly protested the law, were dismayed. So, too, were the students and Graham. It was the students who did something about it. Student leaders led by Paul Dickson III, who had just been elected president of student government on a platform pledged to open forums, decided that their rights could be protected only by a court decision. Initiating an ad hoc student organization to change the law, the leaders conferred with McNeill Smith, a leading lawyer in the state and a close friend of Graham's. Plans were made to take the matter to court.

The Governor's commission met over a period of weeks and listened to lengthy testimony. It made its report November 2, 1965, recommending that the legislature direct the boards of trustees of state institutions to adopt policies and regulations regarding the appearance of Communists and Fifth Amendment pleaders, further suggesting that the appearance of such speakers should be "infrequent." The special session duly adopted the face-saving recommendations. Even before the legislature modified the law, however, the boards of trustees of the state institutions had adopted new policies turning over responsibility for oversight to the administrators of the individual campuses.[25]

Graham was indignant. Those who would ask University administrators, faculty, and students to accept a policy they considered wrong for the sake of gaining the world, he asserted, "are asking for all our state colleges and universities to sell their souls, with the result that in the long run they lose both their souls and the world." In his horror that North Carolina was the only state that prohibited or limited open forums, he came as close as he ever did in his entire life to criticizing publicly the trustees of his University: "It is my faith in the Trustees that they do not mean to say to state institutions of higher learning, that these institutions are to have academic freedom provided they do not exercise real academic freedom."[26]

With the change in policy, the students and McNeill Smith were plagued with the problem of whether they should still take the matter to court. On the surface it appeared that what they had asked for had been granted—the sole responsibility for invitation to speakers would be located in the individual universities and colleges. But that responsibility would not belong to the students or the faculties but to the administrators. What was much worse was that the new law and trustees' policy seemed to say, as Graham put it, "You can have academic freedom so long as your use of it is 'infrequent.'" They decided to press the court case.[27]

315

THE
IDEALS
OF THE
AMERICAN
REVOLUTION

In January, 1966, the Students for a Democratic Society at Chapel Hill announced plans to have two speakers on the campus: Herbert Aptheker, the Communist historian, and Frank Wilkinson, who had pleaded the Fifth Amendment before a California legislative committee. Governor Moore, maintaining that the invitations were intended to create controversy for the sake of controversy, asserted that it would be illegal to approve the invitations until the new rules had been formally adopted. They were adopted February 28, and the students planning the court case—including, in addition to Dickson, the presidents of the YMCA, the YWCA, the Carolina Political Union, and the Carolina Forum and the editor of the *Daily Tar Heel*—immediately renewed the invitations to Apthteker and Wilkinson. Chancellor J. Carlyle Sitterson, accepting the recommendation of a faculty-student committee, refused to permit the speakers to appear.

They came anyway. When they began to speak on University property, the speakers and the students sponsoring the program were charged by a local police officer with violating the law and were threatened with arrest if one word was spoken. They moved a few feet beyond the campus and, on a public street, addressed the crowd, which was gathered in a festive mood. Later, when Sitterson granted approval for two Communist scholars from Moscow and Prague to speak at the University, the students planning the court case again requested Sitterson for permission for Aptheker and Wilkinson to speak. Again Sitterson refused. The student plaintiffs filed suit in federal court, claiming that their constitutional rights had been violated.[28]

The case proceeded through the courts with deliberate speed, taking inordinate hours of the time of administrators, state lawyers, private lawyers, and students. When Frank Graham learned that the case would be heard by a three-judge panel consisting of federal judges Clement F. Haynsworth, Edwin M. Stanley, and Algernon L. Butler, he immediately got in touch with McNeill Smith. "It might help you to know," he said, "that Algernon Butler is the nephew of Marion Butler, the U.S. senator at the turn of the century. He was invited to speak at the University, but he was a dangerous Republican, so the president said he couldn't come. A group of students then fought a battle on behalf of academic freedom.

And we won. The judges on your panel personally know all those students: John J. Parker, who became a federal judge; Walter Stacy, who became chief justice of the State Supreme Court; Kemp Battle, that great lawyer; and me. At the right time, when you are talking about the importance of academic freedom and its history in the University, it wouldn't hurt to slip these little facts in." Smith included the story in his final summation.[29]

The law had been passed in nineteen minutes. Four and a half years later, two years after the suit had been filed by students, the three-man court unanimously ruled the law "unconstitutional because of vagueness."[30] Graham's faith in youth was again confirmed.

It was not surprising to his friends that, long after he might have retired, Frank Graham continued to engage in battles on behalf of the rights of blacks and students. His sensitivity toward those who were obviously discriminated against and who were disadvantaged was well known. Not so well known was his sensitivity to the hidden poor, to those disadvantaged to whom society was blind.

In his concern that the South, in becoming industrialized, should avoid the mistakes of Old and New England, he had tried since the twenties to be alert to those dispossessed by regional progress. In the thirties, largely through the studies of the South at Chapel Hill and the courageous efforts to organize a Southern Tenant Farmers Union in the deep South, he had become painfully aware of the rural poor, especially the almost three million sharecroppers in the sixteen Southern states. Late in the decade he joined Eleanor Roosevelt, Norman Thomas, black union leader A. Philip Randolph, Senator Paul Douglas, and New York Mayor Fiorello La Guardia in organizing a "National Sharecroppers Week" to support the embattled Southern Tenant Farmers Union and to raise money for clothing, food, and medicine for displaced Southern tenant farmers. The annual fund-raising weeks had continued until the establishment, in 1943, of the National Sharecroppers Fund, which publicized the plight of the rural poor in the South. In 1948 the fund began publishing an annual report on the conditions of small farmers throughout the nation; and this report, providing the basis for a legislative program in which Graham engaged, soon became recognized as the definitive statement about America's small farmers and farm workers. It was never pleasant reading.[31]

Graham, one of the founders of the fund, was always active on its board; and in 1953 he was elected chairman. For more than sixteen years, until his retirement from the chairmanship in 1969, he worked closely with Fay Bennett, the energetic executive secretary, in shaping the programs that attempted to make Americans sensitive to the unbelievably harsh conditions of their own farm poor. He was, for the often harried and discouraged fund staff and board members, a guide and inspirer, a lobbyist and publicist.[32]

As chairman of the National Advisory Committee on Farm Labor, he was discouraged to learn that a reporter brushed off the 1959 Washington hearings of the conference as a futile activity, with the description of Eleanor Roosevelt and others as "some do-gooders trying to do something about some no-gooders." He was not troubled about being called a "do-gooder," but he was bothered that anyone should be referred to as a "no-gooder." "As part of our Judaic-Christian faith and historic Americanism no people are to be rightfully classified as 'no-gooders.'" But the judgment set him thinking, and he decided that, from the historical perspective, the appellation really gave hope to those it insulted. For it was the "no-gooders" of the past who had created some of the most significant institutions, institutions to which the strongly conservative side of Graham gave unquestioned loyalty. The "no-good" servants, slaves, and lowly people of the Roman Empire became the Church Universal, which with "all its faults and frustrations" he saw as "one of the most beneficent organizations of the modern world"; the medieval "no-good" serfs became the middle class, who organized the Commons of England, the Third Estate of France, the corporate enterprises and professional societies; the "no-good" industrial workers of the nineteenth century, choosing to organize and help themselves, became a dominant force for social legislation, universal education, and universal suffrage. The hopeful lesson was clear to him: "The remnants of disinherited agricultural workers, migrants, colored and colonial people of the world, are on the march for the fulfillment of the teachings of our religion and the principles of our democracy."[33]

In that one sentence he summarized the lessons he had learned from his religion and from the continuing American revolution, lessons he had helped take around the world and had always tried to bring home.

317

THE
IDEALS
OF THE
AMERICAN
REVOLUTION

22

Life with Marian
and the Return Home

Here in Chapel Hill among a friendly folk . . .
traditions grow with ivy on the historic buildings
and the moss on the ancient oaks. Friendships
form here for the human pilgrimage.[1]
—FRANK PORTER GRAHAM (1931)

IN CONNECTION WITH ALL THE ACTIVITY OF FRANK
Graham's sixteen years with the United Nations in New York,
there remains the question of what happens to a small-town Southerner, for whom life had always been personal, when he is trans-
planted to a huge, impersonal city. The answer for Graham was to
keep life personal.

His office on the tenth floor of the United Nations Secretariat and
the Grahams' small apartment two blocks away were vastly different from the gracious South Building and the president's home
in Chapel Hill. At the office, letters were dictated and telephone
calls were made; they almost always dealt with a cause close to
Graham's heart and always included the familiar personal note.
He replied carefully to the many requests that came for information or advice. Some of his letters, especially those dealing with
the University of North Carolina, would run to thirty or more
pages. But with the time available to him and with his compulsion
to keep busy, it was not requests alone to which he responded.
When he learned of a newspaper attack upon him, he would now
often answer the attack with a letter to the editor. When a speech
of his was printed, he would send a copy to Wayne Morse, hinting
that it might be worth placing in the *Congressional Record*, and a
number were published there. When the United Automobile
Workers celebrated their twenty-fifth anniversary, a letter of "congratulations and challenge, personal affection and general hope"

went to Walter Reuther. When Paul Douglas had a conflict with the American Medical Association over a cancer drug, Graham wrote to Douglas supporting his advocacy of a fair test. There was far more than the business at hand in these letters. There was the continual re-establishment of personal contact. There was also a reminder of crusades shared in the past, and at times, a defense of positions Graham had taken.[2]

319

—

LIFE
WITH
MARIAN
AND THE
RETURN
HOME

Even the most personal letters were normally related to social problems. In 1967, when the Vietnam controversy swirled about the adamant Secretary of State, Dean Rusk, there was widespread publicity about the marriage of Rusk's daughter to a black. When Graham, a friend of Rusk's since the Indonesian negotiations, saw a picture of the wedding party, he wrote a letter marked "personal":

> Dear Dean,
>
> This little note is simply to express my admiration for the equanimity and dignity with which you and Mrs. Rusk, as parents of the lovely bride, and Mr. and Mrs. Smith, as parents of the handsome groom, met the situation incident to the marriage of two noble spirited people.
>
> Without pretense of establishing a precedent or custom, it is the right of persons as individuals to make the most sacred choices of their life companions. Blessings upon them and may happiness be theirs in all the years to come.
>
> In them and all of you America stood four square to all the winds that blow.
>
> Whatever be the differences that develop among your friends, or the burdens which overload your robust shoulders, or the storms that beat upon your devoted head, there should only be admiration for the inner resources of spirit, revealed in the faces and calm assurance of you and your wife on that occasion.[3]

Individuals visited Graham every day he was in New York; and all were cordially received. He did not want his secretary, Daisy Lippner, to protect him from difficult people, even from those she considered crackpots. Once an emotionally disturbed woman got by her and into Graham's office. Although he had other engagements, he sat patiently, listening, occasionally making a comment. When Mrs. Lippner later remonstrated with him, he said, "You just have to treat these people with kindness. You never know when a simple push might knock them over completely."[4]

Upon receiving a letter from an Arthur Beltone, who claimed to be "an anvil for adversity," Graham told his secretary, "Send him ten dollars." "But," she objected, "he didn't ask you for any money." "Any man who is an anvil for adversity is bound to be in need of money." The ten dollars was sent. A short time later another letter came with the name "Arthur Henry Beltone" engraved in beautiful letters on the stationery. "Look," Mrs. Lippner told Graham, "he took your ten dollars and bought some new stationery. His stationery is a lot better than yours."

Graham had a way of making life personal throughout the United Nations building, as the many who visited and talked with him well knew. There was a young Jamaican elevator operator to whom Graham would always speak, asking how he was getting along and how his family was. His family was trying to get into the United States, but all doors seemed closed. Upon checking the story, Graham wrote his congressional representative, not asking for anything special for the young man but pointing out that rightfully his wife and child should be able to follow him to the States. Shortly thereafter they came. When he heard that the young man's mother was in Jamaica, Graham wrote another letter; she, too, came to New York. Several years later the mother died; and Graham received a black, engraved announcement of a death and funeral signed with a name he did not immediately recognize. After repeated inquiries, Graham discovered that the sender was the Jamaican. Graham asked his secretary how to get to the Bronx, went there, and found the funeral home in time for the service. The Jamaican later reported that Graham was the only white person and the only person from the United Nations at the funeral.[5]

Graham had long since developed a habit of going to funerals. It was for him a Southern, human custom that was both obligation and privilege upon the death of a friend. Funerals were an occasion for saying "good-bye" and "hello," for seeing old friends, for recalling the past, for gaining insights into its meaning and foresight for the future. (When Willis Smith died in office in June, 1953, Graham flew to Raleigh to attend the funeral and sat on the back pew of the Edenton Street Methodist Church.)[6] He was often asked to speak at memorial services for state, national, or international figures; and he always took that responsibility seriously, trying through study and inquiry to understand the essential values of the person's life, attempting to convey that what he had been and done would live beyond him. In September, 1961, the death of Dag Hammarskjold had special significance for Graham. At the memorial service at Town Hall Graham expressed a fore-

boding about the future of the United Nations. "It is our faith
. . . that the wreckage of his plane shall not mean the wreckage of the United Nations; and that we here highly resolve
that [the United Nations civil servants killed in service] shall not
have died in vain."[7] Later, in 1962, there was the funeral of Eleanor
Roosevelt; and in 1963 that of John F. Kennedy.

321
—
LIFE
WITH
MARIAN
AND THE
RETURN
HOME

"In religion," Graham had said early in his New York years,
"I am a Presbyterian, in politics I am a New Deal–Fair Deal–
Stevensonian Democrat, and as a student I have been interested in
history, classical and renaissance humanism, modern sciences and
social sciences."[8] His financial contributions confirmed those interests. He and Marian made pledged contributions to four churches: the Presbyterian, Community, and Chapel of the Cross Episcopal in Chapel Hill and St. Bartholomew's Episcopal in New
York; and they made occasional contributions to many other
churches as well. He contributed regularly to the Democratic presidential campaigns and to the Democratic Party in North Carolina. He continued membership in well over a hundred and fifty
organizations, mostly liberal and directed toward specific causes.
He served on the boards of many and contributed anywhere from
ten to fifty dollars a year to almost all.[9]

By the mid-sixties his accumulated savings were less than ten
thousand dollars and his life insurance less than twenty thousand.[10]
His indifference to personal financial interests remained with him
throughout his life, yet he was meticulous about such things as not
using business or official postage for personal mail. It was typical
that after making a speech at Mars Hill College he wrote his host,
"I find I was paid $3.48 above my travel expenses and am therefore
enclosing a check for that amount."[11] And after attending a labor
conference in the North Carolina mountains, he wrote a union
friend in Washington who had organized the conference: "I owe
somebody 20¢ which I borrowed to complete a telephone call
from the pay station. I borrowed it from a man who was sitting on
the porch of the building which faces the pay telephone station.
Will you please find out who it was and pay him the 20¢. I am
enclosing herewith two dimes for this purpose. Please also thank
my unnamed friend."[12]

It was Marian who took care of their banking, of their homes,
and of him in his frequent illnesses. During his New York years
Graham continued to have almost annually an illness, usually
respiratory, that kept him in bed for from two to four weeks.

Sometimes when Frank was away on extended trips, Marian would visit her sister in Hillsborough. They tried to keep in close touch, though Frank was often careless about remembering to tell exactly where he would be. "Well," she once wrote in a note to his office, "you certainly have me guessing by your mysterious phone number! If I didn't have complete faith in you, I might think you were up to some mischief."[13]

Their friends knew that it was a solid marriage. It was obvious that Frank and Marian admired and cared for each other; so it was recognized that their reticence about personal feelings was the other side of the secret tenderness in their relations. They had no children. As with many happy couples who focus love upon each other, they became, in many ways, alike. Friends enjoyed seeing and talking with Marian. Her sister, admiring her courage and poise, said that "she is as unselfish, as selfless, as any one I know."[14]

Marian had her own moral sensitivity and strength of conscience. Not all Frank's political loyalty and convictions could persuade her to vote for Willis Smith. And there were times, she readily confessed, when she thought people should be condemned for their unethical behavior. "But," she added, "I cannot think of a single time when I heard Frank condemn another individual. I do not know that he would ever have called any person an enemy. He just didn't think in those terms."[15]

Frank not only relied upon the steadfastness of Marian, but he came to see in her the embodiment of all he believed in. At Christmas, 1965, he wrote a poem, "To Marian," and published it anonymously in the county newspaper serving Hillsborough and Chapel Hill. Six months later he borrowed $900 to have the poem printed for private circulation.[16] The poem confirms Frank Graham's love for Marian, but it shows a silent love that he was incapable of expressing clearly. When he tried to capture it in a poem, he connected it with all the social causes in which he believed and which she supported. He found in her the reminder that "man is human and divine," and he stated that "the spirit of Christ is in her heart." He also saw that she had both the common and universal touch: she "sympathizes with frailties common to all/ Yet lifts our sights beyond the enclosing wall/ Of status, region, culture, race and creed."

Marian died on April 27, 1967, in New York. Her funeral was held in the Chapel of the Cross, directly across the street from their former home in Chapel Hill. In responding to those who expressed sympathy, Graham, who had returned to New York immediately after the funeral, could not refrain from mentioning social beliefs and causes to which they were both dedicated:

323

LIFE
WITH
MARIAN
AND THE
RETURN
HOME

> She gave selflessly to me and to countless others the quiet blessing of a life whose inner resources came from the deep humility of her deep spiritual faith.
>
> People to her were individual persons and children of God and brothers of all. This sense of human brotherhood was deepened here in her work in the Union Settlement, Everybody's Thrift Shop, and the Woman's Division of St. Bartholomew's Church, and more than a decade of our years at the United Nations.
>
> ... Her home and her heart were always open to all who came.[17]

Against the advice of his physician, who for several years had been urging retirement, Graham refused to cancel scheduled commencement addresses. So he returned to North Carolina again and again: on May 28 he spoke at Guilford College, on May 31 at Wagram High School, and on June 6 at John Graham High School in Warrenton, where sixty-three years before he had gone to John Graham's school. The strain was too much; on June 16 he had a heart attack. During the period of his hospitalization he confessed, in a rare private reference, that Marian's death "still cuts to the heart."[18]

A simple phrase written to Carlyle Sitterson on October 26 reveals where his heart was and had always been: "I am writing you this little note to say that I am on my way home."[19]

For more than thirty years Frank and Marian had dreamed of building a cottage on their property in Chapel Hill, but it was not to be. Rather, his sister, who had made his first home near the University, also made his last, establishing him in November, 1967, in an apartment in her home. Kate and Shipp Sanders had built a two-story house in quiet Gimghoul Forest in 1938. Shipp had been a professor of Latin in the University, and following his death Kate had continued to make her home in Chapel Hill. The back door of her house opened near the end of a lane and provided easy access to the flower gardens, neighbors, and town. The front of the neat brick house overlooked a long, sloping, ivy-covered yard, an infrequently traveled road, and across the road, deep woods. The garage was remodeled for Frank's bedroom and bath, and a living room was added between the garage and the kitchen. His living room was lined to the ceiling with bookshelves. The disarray among the books and magazines, which were in continual use, the scattering of papers on tables, and the comfortable chairs and sofa were as expressive of Frank's personality as, at the opposite end of the house, the immaculate, formal, but hospitable living room was expressive of Kate's. As often as possible he took walks in Chapel Hill, and in his own small apartment he continued his pilgrimage by daily reading, the continual rewriting of his United Nations report, the many visits of friends, and his recurring ill-nesses.[20]

He read the *New York Times* as soon as it arrived each day; and he renewed the habit he had begun in childhood of reading the Raleigh *News and Observer*. He followed journals of opinion and interpretation, including the *Nation, New Republic, Foreign Affairs,* and *Christianity and Crisis.* His reading of books was for the most part limited to those dealing with contemporary affairs, especially those relating to India and Pakistan, problems of war and peace, and national political and social matters. He carefully read the reports that came from the many organizations to which he belonged, paying particular attention to anything arriving from the United Nations, the University, or the National Sharecroppers Fund, or dealing with labor unions and the South.

Graham, at eighty-one, kept in touch with the world not only through his reading but also through work with his secretary, Sally Coe. For several years she came each day to take dictation, but as illness intermittently disabled Graham, she came only when he had special work. With her assistance, he continued to rework his United Nations report on India and Pakistan in the hope that someday he would be asked to present it to the Security Council. He gave her numerous speeches, still written in his cumbersome, square-lettered, but now shakier, hand. Frequently he dictated letters to friends or to others who had written to congratulate him or to request his judgment on a specific matter. The letters, those he wrote and received, almost invariably expressed a warm greeting and usually related to a current political or social development. But the personal touch was always present. And the telephone was used day and night to encourage action for a social cause, to talk about the University, to console a friend, or simply to keep intact the human bond.

Since Graham had an enormous capacity for friendship, many visitors gave special joy and sustenance to his last years. Groups of students often asked to see him, and he received them enthusiastically. Because his room could accommodate comfortably only three or four people, whenever a larger group came, they would meet in Kate's living room. There the students would sit on the floor, crowded about him, and engage in lively discussion about whatever problem of the day was dominant. It was like the Sunday evenings when he had been president of the University, and he again delighted in listening and responding to students. There were, during these years, student disturbances throughout the country over Vietnam, civil rights, and the rigidities of higher education. Many students had become far more radical than Graham, but despite open disagreement on some methods of effecting change, he never lost touch with them.

325

LIFE
WITH
MARIAN
AND THE
RETURN
HOME

He found delight, too, in the parties honoring him. Sometimes these brought together friends from his student days or colleagues who had taught with him in the University. More often they were planned by a coterie of younger friends who continued to give expression to ideals they had learned in part from him. They included Al Lowenstein, an ardent battler for civil rights in the South and in Africa, an active participant in national politics, and a leader in the "Dump President Johnson" movement; Joel Fleischman, Provost for Urban Affairs at Yale University; Jimmy Wallace, a political science professor noted for his environmental crusades; John Sanders, formerly student body president and now head of the Institute of Government; and Anne Queen, who as secretary of the University YM-YWCA continued as much as any other person the Graham tradition of directly inspiring students to become involved in struggles for freedom. A wide spectrum of people of all ages and professions was brought together at those parties. The lives of all had in some way been affected by Graham.

It was, however, the visits of individuals that meant most to him. In the course of the conversations, whether lasting minutes or hours, there were rapid shifts among three focal points. One focal point was the area of immediate concern to the visitor, whether University politics or teaching, political campaigns or the environment, race relations or international affairs. Graham spoke wistfully of the United Nations and the completed, confidential, yet dormant report on India and Pakistan. A second focus of conversation was the battles of the past in which Graham and the visitor had shared. Every visit ended with Graham requesting the visitor to take greetings to specific people; and, more and more, he would suggest that particular people be asked to visit him.

Frequently, in remembering past battles, Graham would express the wish that his visitor "help set the record straight." Then, with remarkable memory of detail—a memory reinforced and slightly altered by repeated retelling—Graham would recount the inside story. The stories dealt with University affairs prior to and during his presidency; with Southern—especially North Carolinian—political, economic, and social history, and with race; with the Indonesian negotiations. (He refused to talk about the Pakistan and Indian problem, however.) In recounting the events he always emphasized the essential contributions of others. He was reverting to his early profession of historian, desiring that the scope of history in which he had been involved be reported accurately. But more than that, he was reminding himself, as well as his visitor, of past achievements, of some real and solid accomplishments in helping to shape a freer society. Remembering past achievements was a necessary way for him to deal with the society of the late sixties and early seventies, which was not the free society for which he and his liberal friends had fought for so many years.

The turbulent world erupted daily in Graham's small living room in Gimghoul Forest, as it did in homes throughout the nation. Graham's life had spanned two world wars, and he had witnessed social change and violence unequaled in any similar time span in history. Despite the violence, Graham, like many Americans, had believed that the changes of the first two-thirds of the century were for the better. He had believed that the future of the nation, as of the world, belonged to democratic liberalism. The placid fifties had seemed to confirm this optimism, and the sixties had begun with intensified hopes. The war in Vietnam made everything different.

When, in retirement, Frank Graham walked the familiar gravel-packed sidewalks of Chapel Hill and visited with friends, when he continued his interests and activities, and when he became increasingly confined to his small apartment because of illness, many of the institutions and causes he had believed in for so long had either been transformed through violence or had disappeared from public view.

Graham, as an advocate of black freedom and equality, had in the late fifties and early sixties heartily endorsed, at serious personal risk, the nonviolent law-breaking of Martin Luther King. But he was not prepared for the inflammatory rhetoric and violence of the black militants who soon appeared, nor for the unplanned urban riots. Such violence might have beneficial results, he felt, but it was contrary to all he stood for and, if unabated or victorious in its stated aims, would lead to the destruction of the love that was both the cause and fulfillment of liberalism.

327

LIFE
WITH
MARIAN
AND THE
RETURN
HOME

And the Democratic Party was clearly in disarray. The problems had been evident before 1968, but up to that time they had been interpreted as typical Democratic brawling. The convention of 1968 destroyed any illusion that what was manifesting itself in internal conflicts was anything but an infective chaos that would end in defeat. The disarray of the Chicago convention was all the more fascinating to Graham, as he watched it on television, because one of the agents of the disarray was Al Lowenstein. Graham was, and remained throughout the 1968 campaign, an ardent supporter of his friend Hubert Humphrey; and it was not lost on him that the defection of liberals led to the defeat of Humphrey and the election of Richard Nixon.

Within higher education, too, there was no calm. The disruption in the universities that had begun at the University of California in 1964 reached the Ivy League with violence and repression at Columbia in 1968. Deploring the Columbia rioting, Graham had confidence in the ultimate outcome, since his friend from graduate school and United Nations days, Andrew Cordier, had become acting president of Columbia in early 1969. Graham believed he would work with peaceful democratic skills to restore a decent order. But the violence at Columbia and the disruption of campuses at the very best universities in the nation—at Harvard and Dartmouth, at Yale and Princeton—were shocks difficult to absorb for one whose whole life in higher education had been built upon academic freedom.

There were major changes also in the nation's attitudes and social policies toward the poor. For a moment in the mid-sixties, with the flash of the Great Society program, it seemed that the resources of the nation would focus upon problems of poverty. Then, far more suddenly than they had come into view, the poor seemed to disappear from public sight and conscience.

It was the same with the American view of the developing nations, who constituted a kind of "underdog" for whom Graham had always had special feeling. From the mid-forties to the mid-sixties there had been much concern in the United States, as in Europe, for these peoples. That concern had always been linked with self-interest; but to Graham the concern was the expression of a liberal humanitarianism, the culmination of centuries of education in social conscience. The idealism reached its apex in the public mind with the creation of the Peace Corps in 1961. Then, in the late sixties, the violence of Vietnam and the turbulence within the United States obscured the sight of other nations in dire need.

It was during his retirement years that those nations with which Graham had been involved in international negotiations came to disaster. In Indonesia in the mid-sixties an estimated 400,000 people were killed in a civil struggle. In the area of the world other than the South that now mattered most to Graham, in Pakistan and India, that which many had feared and the most pessimistic had predicted happened. West Pakistan's suppression of equality and freedom in East Pakistan was the direct cause of at least a million deaths and the evacuation of ten million refugees into India. Graham had given almost twenty years of his life to the hope of a peaceful settlement of the conflict over Kashmir, and his hope was not entirely destroyed until 1971 when, on December 16, Pakistan surrendered to India and independent Bangladesh began an uncertain future.

The institutions in which Graham had believed and for which he had worked were moved by the chaotic sixties toward a diffusion of purpose or impotence. The familiar structures and methods, the old personnel and ideals, were not able to meet the human needs beneath the social tremors. The United Nations, the Democratic Party, the University, the church, and the labor unions all faced institutional crises. Black Power violence conflicted with his liberal view of race relations.

It was obvious to Graham, as he tried to keep up with the world from his apartment in Chapel Hill, that the causes to which he had given so much of his life were in trouble. Many other liberals were led to despair, but Graham never gave any indication to friends that he believed any long-term battles for freedom could be lost. In his last years, when the social scene became more violent, the social voices more strident, and his own body increasingly wracked with pain, his friends noticed that he openly reaffirmed the political, social, economic, and educational principles, the moral and religious ideals, that had been his life. He continued to have faith in liberal causes and in people, especially youth.

The confidence in youth, in its moral idealism, enthusiasm, and courage—in the very qualities he had never outgrown—was the final hold he had amid the death of so much and so many. As he lived into his eighties, it was natural that more and more of his friends died; and they died when what they stood for was most needed. It was more than a personal need, since their departure was simultaneous with a demise of liberalism.

The disturbances in society and the deaths of so many friends came during long periods of complex, intermittent, and then total, physical disability. Following the death of Marian, his body caught up with him and there was no bouncing back, first from mild heart attacks and then from pneumonia.

After he returned to Chapel Hill, the illnesses were unpredictable. First there was a heart disorder; then months of good health; and suddenly the respiratory ailments would recur. In 1969 these were accompanied by shingles, and from that moment he was in almost constant pain. If he took medication to ease the pain, it would affect his digestion and he would be laid low for days. When his friends visited him, they would often find him in bed or reclining in his bathrobe on the sofa, encased in soft pillows. He would mention his ailments without dwelling on them, and though he frequently admitted to being in pain, he made light of it. He never complained to Kate. Once she heard him fall and rushed to his room to find him on the floor trying to get up, unable to do so, and laughing at his helplessness.

Graham went to the hospital for the last time in mid-January, 1972. Lying in a small single room at the end of a corridor, he received visitors and, frequently with his eyes closed, discussed events of the day and sent personal messages to friends. He was encouraging about his own condition and expected to be out of the hospital in a few days. One visitor, skeptical of Graham's optimistic appraisal, stopped by the hall desk on his way out to get a physician's judgment. Six interns were working in the area, in the hospital Graham had been instrumental in building. Not one knew him or anything about his condition. "The doctor taking care of him is off duty just now," said one.

329
—
LIFE
WITH
MARIAN
AND THE
RETURN
HOME

Vance Barron, minister of the Chapel Hill Presbyterian Church, was one of the last people to talk with Graham. At one point the conversation turned to speculation about life in outer space. The idea was intriguing to Graham, but even in his imaginative flights he could not escape the moral and religious perceptions that had come in his first years at home. There might well be other forms of life on other planets, he agreed. But whatever they might be, "they cannot know anything higher about God than we know, because God has revealed his love to us, and there cannot be anything higher than 'God is love.' "[21]

He died quietly on February 16, 1972. The funeral was held the next day in the Chapel Hill Presbyterian Church with a University memorial service the same afternoon. He was buried beside Marian under a dogwood tree in the Chapel Hill cemetery. On the stone, beneath their names, were carved words they together had chosen: "They had faith in youth and youth responded with their best."

Sources

1. MANUSCRIPT COLLECTIONS

The Frank P. Graham Papers in the Southern Historical Collection of the Wilson Library at the University of North Carolina is the indispensable manuscript collection. Partially catalogued, it contains considerable materials from all periods of Graham's life, particularly since 1930. The University Files, also in the Southern Historical Collection, contain official records of the University of North Carolina, including personal materials relating to Graham. The North Carolina Collection, also in the Wilson Library, has an extensive Frank Porter Graham file. The Alumni Office of the University at Chapel Hill and the Jackson Library at the University of North Carolina at Greensboro have files dealing with Graham.

The North Carolina Conference for Social Service in Raleigh has materials dealing with social problems in North Carolina and with Graham's work in that organization. Materials relating to the Southern Conference for Human Welfare have been deposited with the Tuskegee Institute Library and, to a lesser extent, with the Arnette Library, Atlanta University. The United States Archives has documents relating to Graham's work on the National Defense Mediation Board and the War Labor Board. The United States Department of State has materials dealing with the role of the United States and of Graham in the development of Indonesian independence. The most important United Nations documents dealing with Graham's work are to be found in the Security Council Official Records and the Official Records of the Good Offices Committee.

2. INTERVIEWS

Four tape-recorded interviews were held by the author with Frank Graham in New York from June 21, 1960, through June 24, 1960. An additional six lengthy recorded interviews were held at Nags Head, N.C., from August 8, 1960, through August 13, 1960. Participating in the Nags Head interviews were Kemp D. Battle and Francis Winslow, in addition to the author.

Transcripts have been made of recorded interviews which the author had about Graham with R. Mayne Albright, William B. Aycock, Henry Brandis, Laura Weill Cone, Jonathan Daniels, Marian Graham, Robert B. House, Charles Jones, Allard K. Lowenstein, Clarence Poe, D. Hiden Ramsey, Hubert Robinson, Otho Ross, John W. Umstead, and M. T. Van Hecke. There were also group interviews with some of

Graham's Raleigh High School students and with the Charlotte Philosophy Club, whose members had close association with Graham.

The author had access to transcripts of television interviews, taped June 9, 1962, through June 12, 1962, in which Graham was questioned by R. Mayne Albright, Warren Ashby, William B. Aycock, Kemp D. Battle, Henry Brandis, Jonathan Daniels, Joel Fleishman, William C. Friday, Robert B. House, Mrs. Jeff Johnson, Charles Jones, Henry Patterson, Anne Queen, Hubert Robinson, Terry Sanford, Mrs. Kerr Scott, Claude Teague, James Wallace, Fred Weaver, Stuart Willis, and Francis Winslow. The interviews, under the direction of John Ehle, have been deposited in the North Carolina Collection of the Wilson Library at Chapel Hill.

The author has had personal interviews or conversations with Mrs. James Rowland Angell, Henry T. Belk, Fay Bennett, Albert Coates, Andrew W. Cordier, William H. Davis, Eugenia Withers Doar, Paul H. Douglas, Edward K. Graham, Jr., Hattie Graham, Marian Graham, Mary Graham, Mrs. Thomas Hayes, Mrs. Charles C. Hooke, D. Edward Hudgins, Elmore Jackson, Herschel Johnson, Vera Largent, Mrs. Albert Lathrop, Mrs. Daisy Lippner, L. P. McLendon, H. L. Mitchell, Wayne L. Morse, Mary Armand Nash, Frederick L. Patterson, Claude Pepper, Mrs. Franklin D. Roosevelt, Otho Ross, Dean Rusk, Mrs. Shipp Sanders, J. Maryon Saunders, Norman Thomas, Mrs. C. W. Tillett, Gertrude Weil, Herman Weil, Paul Whitaker, Louis R. Wilson, and Francis E. Winslow.

3. OTHER INDIVIDUAL SOURCES: DOCUMENTATION AND CORRESPONDENCE

The following people have provided materials from personal or office files: Fay Bennett, Mrs. L. L. Bernard, Francis O. Clarkson, Marian B. Folsom, Mary Graham, Hattie Graham, Robert B. House, Charles Jones, Edward S. Lanier, Daisy Lippner, L. P. McLendon, J. Covington Parham, Jr., Clarence Poe, William G. Pollard, Jr., Hubert Robinson, Otho Ross, John Sanders, J. Maryon Saunders, Mack Swearingen, Claude Teague, Mrs. C. W. Tillett, Gertrude Weil, Paul Whitaker, Louis R. Wilson, and Francis E. Winslow.

The following provided information in correspondence: Arthur J. Altmeyer, E. Osborne Ayscue, Sr., Harding Bancroft, John Bennett, Barry Bingham, Mrs. James Boyd, Francis Bradshaw, Shephard Bryan, Francis O. Clarkson, T. E. Clemmons, Kenneth Douty, Mark Ethridge, Mrs. Frances Fawcett, Marion B. Folsom, Robert Goodwin, Virgil M. Hancher, G. Maurice Hill, Phillip Jessup, George McT. Kahin, Howard Kester, Thomas J. Lassiter, Herbert H. Lehman, Frank W. McAllister, Mrs. P. P. McCain, Benjamin E. Mays, Francis Pickens Miller, Broadus

Mitchell, Raymond D. Moley, H. C. Nixon, Thomas Parran, William G. Pollard, Sidney Reitman, George M. Stephens, George W. Taylor, Herman Wells, and Leo R. Werts.

4. GRAHAM'S WRITINGS

The 1946 edition of the University of North Carolina *Publications of the Faculty* lists eighty-two addresses, articles, and reports by Graham. References to Graham in the major periodical guides identify additional published articles. In addition, more than one hundred and fifty unpublished items by Graham, usually addresses in typescript or mimeographed, have been located. The *Congressional Record* and United Nations documentary sources contain other writings by Graham.

5. NEWSPAPERS AND PERIODICALS

The *New York Times* is the indispensable source for the life of any public figure in the twentieth century. It was carefully checked for all items relating to Graham and to causes with which he was associated. Special attention was given to the files of the Raleigh *News and Observer*, the *Chapel Hill Weekly*, the *Tar Heel* (later the *Daily Tar Heel*), the student newspaper at the University of North Carolina at Chapel Hill, and the University of North Carolina *Alumni Magazine*. The *New Republic* and the *Nation* were examined not only for references to Graham but also for interpretations of liberal programs in which he was involved. The *Greensboro Daily News* and the *Charlotte Observer* were examined for special events.

Notes

Abbreviations used in notes

CR   *Congressional Record*
DTH   *Daily Tar Heel* (or *TH: Tar Heel*)
GDN   *Greensboro Daily News*
NCC   North Carolina Collection
NCCSS   North Carolina Conference for Social Service
NDMB   National Defense Mediation Board
NYT   *New York Times*
PP   President's Papers (in University Archives, Manuscripts Department, UNC Library)
RECS   *Report on Economic Conditions of the South*
RNO   Raleigh *News and Observer*
SHC   Southern Historical Collection
SCHW   Southern Conference for Human Welfare
SCOR   United Nations Security Council Official Records
WLB   War Labor Board
UA   University Archives, Manuscripts Department, UNC Library

The Graham interviews are identified by number as follows

FPG 1   June 21, 1960, New York, N.Y.
FPG 2   June 22, 1960, New York, N.Y.
FPG 3   June 23, 1960, New York, N.Y.
FPG 4   June 24, 1960, New York, N.Y.
FPG 5   August 8, 1960, Nags Head, N.C.
FPG 6   August 9, 1960, Nags Head, N.C.
FPG 7   August 10, 1960, Nags Head, N.C.
FPG 8   August 11, 1960, Nags Head, N.C.
FPG 9   August 12, 1960, Nags Head, N.C.
FPG 10 August 13, 1960, Nags Head, N.C.

PART ONE

Years of Preparation, 1886–1920

General background information for Part One is found in Wilbur J. Cash, *The Mind of the South* (New York: Alfred A. Knopf, 1941); W. T. Couch, ed., *Culture in the South* (Chapel Hill: University of North Carolina Press, 1935); Hugh T. Lefler and Albert Ray Newsome, *North Carolina: The History of a Southern State* (Chapel Hill: University of North Carolina Press, 1973), esp. pp. 503–98; George B. Tindall, *The Emergence of the New South, 1913–1945* (Baton Rouge: Louisiana State University Press, 1967), esp. pp. 1–353; Louis R. Wilson, *The University of North Carolina, 1900–1930* (Chapel Hill: University of North Carolina Press, 1957); C. Vann Woodward, *Origins of the New South, 1877–1913* (Baton Rouge: Louisiana State University Press, 1951), esp. pp. 107ff. (The books by Tindall and Woodward are volumes X and IX, respectively, in *A History of the South*, ed. Wendell H. Stephenson and E. Merton Coulter.)

In Chapter 1, the information about Graham's boyhood is taken primarily from interviews with Graham, Hattie Graham, Mary Graham, Kate Graham Sanders, and Mrs. James Rowland Angell (née Katherine Sloan). Information about Alderman and McIver is found in Rose Howell Holder, *McIver of North Carolina* (Chapel Hill: University of North Carolina Press, 1957), esp. chs. 8 and 9; *Charles Duncan McIver: Memorial Volume* (Greensboro: n.p., n.d.); Dumas M. Malone, *Edwin A. Alderman: A Biography* (New York: Doubleday, Doran, 1940). Data about Charlotte is from Isaac Erwin Avery, *Idle Comments* (Charlotte: Stone, 1912); D. A. Tomkins, *A History of Mecklenburg County and the City of Charlotte, from 1740–1903* (Charlotte: *Charlotte Observer*, 1903), 2 vols.

In Chapter 2, essential sources are interviews with FPG, Kemp D. Battle, Francis E. Winslow, John Umstead; *TH* for 1905–9; Edward Kidder Graham, *Education and Citizenship and Other Papers*, ed. Louis R. Wilson (New York: Putnam, 1919); Archibald Henderson, *The Campus of the First State University* (Chapel Hill: University of North Carolina Press, 1949); Louis R. Wilson, *The University of North Carolina, 1900–1930* (Chapel Hill; University of North Carolina Press, 1957).

Essential material for Chapter 3 is from interviews with Robert B. House, FPG, Kemp D. Battle, Francis E. Winslow, John W. Umstead, and FPG's Raleigh High School students; *TH*, 1912–1915, 1919–1920. Louis R. Wilson, *The University of North Carolina, 1900–1930* (Chapel Hill: University of North Carolina Press, 1957) gives a good account of the development of the University under Francis Preston Venable (Book II, pp. 43–178) and E. K. Graham (Book III, pp. 179–294).

1. The Door Opens (pp. 3–13)

1. George William Russell, "Germinal," in *Selected Poems* (London: Macmillan, 1935), pp. 160–61.

2. FPG 1; Edwin A. Alderman, "Memorial Address," in *Charles Duncan McIver*, pp. 138–39.

3. Malone, *Edwin A. Alderman*, pp. 23–24; Henry M. Wagstaff, *Impressions of Men and Movements at the University of North Carolina* (Chapel Hill: University of North Carolina Press, 1950), pp. 68–69.

4. Malone, *Edwin A. Alderman*, pp. 38–40; Holder, *McIver*, pp. 90–91.

5. R. D. W. Connor, ed., *North Carolina: Rebuilding an Ancient Commonwealth* (Chicago: American Historical Society, 1928), III: 504; "Portrait of the Grand Old Man of Education is Unveiled," *Charlotte Observer*, January 30, 1927.

6. Tomkins, *History of Mecklenberg*, I: 158, 169, 176–79; interview with Mary and Hattie Graham, July 20, 1960.

7. Interview with Mrs. James Rowland Angell, June 24, 1960.

8. Interview with Mary and Hattie Graham, July 20, 1960; interview with Kate Graham Sanders, January 7, 1972; Mary Graham to author, n.d.

9. FPG 1.

10. FPG 1; *Charlotte Observer*, January 30, 1927.

11. FPG 1; Avery, *Idle Comments*, p. 27.

12. FPG 1.

13. Interview with Mary and Hattie Graham, July 20, 1960.

14. Robert B. House, "John Graham, Teacher," *Warrenton Record* (date illegible); Lizzie Wilson Montgomery, *Sketches of Old Warrenton* (Raleigh: Edwards and Broughton, 1924), pp. 126–28; Robert B. House, *The Light That Shines, Chapel Hill—1912–1916* (Chapel Hill: University of North Carolina Press, 1964), pp. 213, 215–16; FPG 1; interview with Kemp D. Battle, August 8, 1960. See also references to John Graham in Manly Wade Wellman, *The County of Warren, North Carolina, 1586–1917* (Chapel Hill: University of North Carolina Press, 1959).

2. A Breath of Freedom (pp. 14–31)

1. Edwin A. Alderman in University of North Carolina *Record* III (October 1899): 3, quoted in Wilson, *University*, p. 38.

2. FPG 1.

3. University of North Carolina *Catalog, 1904–1905;* FPG 1.

4. Henderson, *Campus*, passim; FPG 1.

5. E. K. Graham, "The College and Human Need," in *Education and Citizenship*, pp. 137–47. This address was made in 1915 but newspaper accounts of addresses to freshmen indicate similarities through the years. The 1905 address was reported in the *Tar Heel*, September 29, 1905: "Professor E. K. Graham strikingly portrayed the lasting benefit to the individual himself and to others of effective, consecrated service."

6. *TH*, September 29, 1905.

7. *TH*, October 5, 1905.

8. Ibid.

9. *TH*, March 2, 1910.

10. Interview with Kemp D. Battle and Francis E. Winslow, August 8, 1960; Thomas Wolfe, *Look Homeward Angel* (New York: Charles Scribner's Sons, 1952), p. 423.

11. *TH*, September 20, 1906 and 1905–7 issues passim; FPG 1.

12. *Yackety Yack* (senior yearbook of the University of North Carolina) IX (1909): 40.

13. *TH*, June 11, 1908; interview with Kemp D. Battle, August 8, 1960.

14. FPG 1.

15. FPG 10.

16. *TH*, October 3, 1907; FPG 10.

17. *Yackety Yack*, p. 40.

18. Interview with Otho Ross, June 20, 1960. A slightly different version appears in Otho Ross, "The Decision that Changed the University," unpublished ms., author's files.

19. Interview with John W. Umstead, June 7, 1960.

20. FPG record in Office of Registrar, University of North Carolina; *TH*, 1908–9 issues passim, e.g., February 3, 1908, March 19, 1908, June 11, 1908.

21. *TH*, November 28, 1908.

22. Ibid., January 14, 1909.

23. Ibid., March 26, 1910; see March–April issues passim.

24. Interview with John W. Umstead, July 7, 1960; *TH*, June 5, 1909.

25. *TH*, February 4, 1909.

26. FPG 10.

27. Woodrow Wilson, *Robert E. Lee: An Interpretation* (Chapel Hill: University of North Carolina Press, 1924), pp. v–vi, 40–41. The address is also in Woodrow Wilson, *College and State: Educational, Literary and Political Papers (1875–1913)*, ed. Ray Stannard Baker and William E. Dodd (New York: Harper, 1925), II: 64–82.

28. Woodrow Wilson, *Robert E. Lee*, p. 2.

29. Ibid., p. 41.

30. Ibid., p. 40.

31. Ibid., pp. 40–41.

32. FPG 10.

33. Edward K. Graham, "Higher Education and Business," in *Education and Citizenship*, pp. 113–22.

34. FPG, "The State and the University," address on Class Day, May 29, 1909, SHC. Also in *TH*, June 5, 1909.

35. *Yackety Yack*, p. 67.

36. Ibid., p. 40.

37. FPG 10.

38. *TH*, March 26, 1910, April 23, 1910, and 1909–10 issues passim.

39. Interviews with Laura Weill Cone, March 5, 1959, and Francis E. Winslow, August 8, 1960.

40. *Yackety Yack*, p. 345.

3. The Discovery of History (pp. 32–43)

1. Woodrow Wilson, *Robert E. Lee: An Interpretation* (Chapel Hill: University of North Carolina Press, 1924), pp. 41–42.

2. FPG 10; interview with Raleigh High School students, October 29, 1960.

3. "Last Will and Testament, Class of 1911, Raleigh High School," SHC.

4. FPG to Eugene E. Barnett, September 5, 1910, and February 12, 1912, SHC.

5. Kemp D. Battle to author, June 20, 1967; Francis E. Winslow to author, June 21, 1967, and July 28, 1967.

6. FPG 2; Wilson's acceptance speech is in Woodrow Wilson, *College and State: Educational, Literary and Political Papers*, ed. Ray Stannard Baker and William E. Dodd (New York: Harper, 1925), II: 474.

7. FPG 2.

8. *TH*, March 11, 1915, and 1913–15 issues passim.

9. Interview with Robert B. House, June 30, 1960.

10. Cf. *TH*, February 1915.

11. FPG 2; the title of FPG's master's thesis is "Carl Schurz in the Liberal Republican Movement of 1872," typescript, 32 pp.

12. FPG 2.

13. Wilson address to the Senate, January 1, 1917, in Woodrow Wilson, *The New Democracy: Presidential Messages, Addresses and Public Papers (1913–1917)*, ed. Ray Stannard Baker and William E. Dodd (New York: Harper, 1926), II: 413–14.

14. FPG 2.

15. Wilson Declaration of War speech, April 2, 1917, in Wilson, *New Democracy (1917–1924)*, I: 14–16.

16. FPG 2; FPG to (illegible), July 4, 1932, and July 8, 1932, SHC.

17. FPG made this remark in many speeches.

18. Wilson, *University of North Carolina*, pp. 413–14.

19. Ibid., pp. 310–12.

20. Ibid., p. 532.

PART TWO

Time of Trials, 1920–1931

General background material for Part Two can be found in the files of NCCSS, SHC, and NCC. Also important are Wilbur J. Cash, *The Mind of the South*; Virginia Wooten Gulledge, *The North Carolina Con-ference for Social Services: A Study of Its Development and Methods*, (n.p., 1942); Samuel Huntington Hobbs, Jr., *North Carolina: Economic and Social* (Chapel Hill: University of North Carolina Press, 1930); and George B. Tindall, *The Emergence of the New South—1913-1945*, esp. pp. 184-390.

A principal source for Chapter 4 is the full account of the 1920-1921 campaign for education found in Louis R. Wilson, "Campaign for Higher Education in North Carolina: Summary of Papers," unpublished mss., 1932, NCC. Additional information in FPG, "An Epic in Democracy and Progress," University of North Carolina *Alumni Review*, April 1921, pp. 229-34, and *Alumni Review* for 1920-21, passim; and R. D. W. Connor, "North Carolina's Crisis in Higher Education," a series of three articles in *RNO*, December 26-28, 1920. (Opposite the December 26 article was a full-page advertisement signed by A. M. Scales, General Director of the Association for the Promotion of Education in North Carolina, headed "Rich Beyond Measure in Wealth and Natural Re-sources North Carolina Stands Today Educationally Bankrupt.") Files of Judge Francis O. Clarkson given to the author contain much valuable information. For FPG's Chicago and London periods, two privately written memos have been indispensable: Mack Swearingen, "Frank," and Lois MacDonald, "Frank P. Graham in London, 1924-25.)"

Important sources for Chapter 6 are Samuel Huntington Hobbs, Jr., *North Carolina: An Economic and Social Profile* (Chapel Hill: Univer-sity of North Carolina Press, 1958); Liston Pope, *Millhands and Preach-ers: A Study of Gastonia* (New Haven: Yale University Press, 1942); and Jennings J. Rhyne, *Some Cotton Mill Workers and Their Villages* (Chapel Hill: University of North Carolina Press, 1930).

4. The Discovery of a Cause (pp. 47-61)

1. R. H. Tawney, *Religion and the Rise of Capitalism* (New York: Harcourt, Brace and World, 1926), p. 286.

2. *GDN*, September 23, 1920. The writer of the editorial was probably Gerald W. Johnson.

3. Wilson, *Campaign for Higher Education*, pp. 6-8.

4. Ibid., pp. 8-9.

5. *UNC Alumni Review* IX, no. 2 (November 1920): 46-48.

6. Wilson, *Campaign for Higher Education*, pp. 10-11; see also *Alum-ni Review* issues from vol. IX, no. 3, through vol. IX, no. 7 (December 1920-April 1921). Most of the editorials were written by Wilson, FPG, and Lenoir Chambers.

7. Files of Judge Francis O. Clarkson; letters from FPG to unidenti-

fied correspondents, October 28, 1920, December 20, 1920, and March 21, 1921; FPG 3.

8. FPG 3.

9. Wilson, *Campaign for Higher Education*, passim.

10. FPG 3.

11. Swearingen, "Frank," pp. 4–5; FPG 2.

12. Swearingen, pp. 7–8; FPG 2.

13. Swearingen, pp. 1–2, 11–12.

14. Ibid., pp. 10–11.

15. Mack Swearingen to author, July 25, 1959.

16. FPG 2; the terms of the Amherst Fellowship are described in the *Amherst College Bulletin, 1970–1971*, pp. 187–88.

17. FPG 2.

18. FPG 3.

19. Swearingen and MacDonald memos; Elizabeth Fawcett to author, July 28, 1960.

20. Swearingen, "Frank," pp. 14–15.

21. See Swearingen and MacDonald memos; FPG 2.

22. Tawney, *Religion*, pp. 63, 287. FPG's copies of Tawney's *Religion and the Rise of Capitalism* and *Equality* are heavily marked throughout with considerable underlining of passages and comments in the margins. Frequently FPG's books have markings on the first few chapters only. See Ross Terrill, *R. H. Tawney and His Times: Socialism as Fellowship* (Cambridge: Harvard University Press, 1973).

23. FPG 3.

24. Suzanne Cameron Linder, *William Louis Poteat: Prophet of Progress* (Chapel Hill: University of North Carolina Press, 1966), pp. 37–38, 105–25; Norman F. Furniss, *The Fundamentalist Controversy, 1918–1931* (New Haven: Yale University Press, 1954), p. 95; FPG, "Evolution, the University and the People," *Durham Morning Herald*, March 2, 1925. See also *RNO* and *GDN* of same date. Wilson, *University of North Carolina*, pp. 511–13.

25. Swearingen, "Frank," pp. 15–16.

26. FPG 2; Thomas Wolfe to Benjamin Cone, July 27, 1929, in *The Letters of Thomas Wolfe,* ed. Elizabeth Nowell (New York: Scribner's, 1956), p. 192.

5. History Taught and Lived (pp. 62–70)

1. FPG, "The University and the Press: An Address Delivered at the Newspaper Institute at Chapel Hill," January 13–15, 1926, typescript, pp. 8–10, SHC.

2. FPG to Eugene Barnett, February 12, 1912, SHC.

3. Swearingen, "Frank," p. 9. Notebooks and other first drafts by FPG in SHC also reveal his methods of research and writing. It was apparently a method consistently employed. Interview with Marian Graham, June 20, 1960.

4. FPG 3; interviews with R. Mayne Albright, July 21, 1960; Eugene E. Pfaff, November 1, 1970.

5. FPG to Mrs. Robert Lassiter, April 24, 1930, NCCSS.

6. FPG, "The University and the Press," p. 4.

7. Ibid., pp. 8, 10.

8. Data about the Citizens' Library Movement in NCCSS; FPG to Harriet Herring, August 18, 1928, NCCSS; FPG to Mrs. W. T. Bost, October 13, 1928, NCCSS.

9. FPG to Josephus Daniels, October 13, 1928, NCCSS.

10. FPG to Anne Pierce, February 8, 1929, NCCSS.

11. FPG to J. C. M. Vann, December 11, 1929, NCCSS.

12. FPG to E. W. Knight, December 2, 1929, NCCSS.

13. NCCSS files for 1929.

14. NCCSS files; see esp. resolutions passed at annual conferences.

15. *Social Service Quarterly* I (April-June, 1913): 1; NCCSS files for 1927, 1928, 1929.

16. FPG, "The Old South and the New Industrialism," address to NCCSS, February 13, 1927.

17. FPG to Robert M. Hanes, March 21, 1929, SHC.

18. J. Maynard Keech, *Workmen's Compensation in North Carolina, 1929–1940* (Durham: Duke University Press, 1942), pp. 13–18; Gulledge, *North Carolina Conference*, p. 36.

19. FPC 3; Gulledge, *North Carolina Conference*, pp. 36–39; NCCSS files, esp. resolutions of July 3, 1925, February 10, 1927, February 28, 1929, and April (n.d) 1930.

6. Industrial Revolution and a New Bill of Rights (pp. 71–81)

1. FPG to Nell Battle Lewis of *RNO*, n.d., 1929, SHC.

2. The statistics are from Hobbs, *North Carolina*, passim; see also the 1930 edition.

3. Quoted in Pope, *Millhands*, p. 214.

4. Ibid., p. 214; Hobbs, *North Carolina* (1930 edition), p. 148; Rhyne, *Some Cotton Mill Workers*, p. 89. (0.3% of the workers were 10–13 years of age); Cash, *Mind of the South*, pp. 270ff.

5. Files of NCCSS; FPG to State Commissioners of Labor of Rhode Island, Massachusetts, New York, Pennsylvania, Virginia, Illinois, South Carolina, Georgia, February 9, 1929, SHC.

6. FPG to Nell Battle Lewis of *RNO*, n.d., 1929, SHC.

7. Pope, *Millhands*, p. 240.

8. Ibid., pp. 222–23. The story of the effigy told to the author by Louis R. Wilson; a variant report appears in Tindall, *Emergence of the New South*, p. 344.

9. The best account of the strike is in Pope, *Millhands*, pp. 207–30. Briefer reports are in Irving Bernstein, *The Lean Years: A History of the American Worker* (Boston: Houghton, Mifflin, 1960), pp. 20–28; Tindall, *Emergence of the New South*, pp. 344–47; and a more partisan account in Thomas Tippett, *When Southern Labor Stirs* (New York: Cape and Smith, 1931), pp. 76–108. Editorial from *Gastonia Gazette*, June 8, 1929, quoted in Pope, *Millhands*, p. 272.

10. *RNO*, June and July, 1929 issues passim.

11. *RNO*, July 28, 1929.

12. Cf. Pope, *Millhands*, and Tippett, *When Southern Labor Stirs.*

13. Weimar Jones, "Southern Labor and the Law," *Nation* CXXXI (July 2, 1930): 16 .

14. The original of the "Industrial Bill of Rights" is in SHC.

15. Henry L. Sloan to FPG, February 13, 1930, SHC.

16. Bernard M. Cone to FPG, February 5, 1930, SHC.

17. *Southern Textile Bulletin*, August 29, 1929, p. 13; February 6, 1930, p. 15; April 10, 1930, p. 22; April 17, 1930, pp. 30–31.

18. FPG to Kemp D. Battle, November 18, 1920, SHC. On December 7, 1929, FPG wrote to David Clark, editor of the *Southern Textile Bulletin*, correcting Clark's errors and reporting openly FPG's activities on behalf of labor. Attached to the typed letter was a handwritten note: "I wish you would print this whole letter in approximately the same place as your statements about my attendance at the labor conference. I think this is due as a matter of clarity and fairness. With best wishes to you, Harry Hill and Junior Smith." The letter was rewritten December 10, 1929, but apparently was never sent to Clark.

19. David Clark letter dated January 31, 1930, SHC.

20. Clyde R. Hoey to FPG, December 30, 1929, SHC.

21. Bernard M. Cone to FPG, February 5, 1930, SHC.

22. Tyre Taylor to FPG, February 6, 1930, SHC.

23. Ibid.

24. FPG, "An Interpretation of the Statement," February 1930, SHC; FPG to Dr. John Wright, January 18, 1930, SHC.

25. FPG to Kemp D. Battle, February 18, 1930, SHC.

26. NCCSS files, 1930.

27. FPG to W. W. Peele, March 15, 1930, NCCSS.

28. FPG to C. O. Kuester, March 15, 1930, NCCSS.

29. FPG, Presidential Address, Annual Meeting of NCCSS, Charlotte, N. C., April 14, 1930, NCCSS.

1. FPG, "The Deficit, the Debt, the Depression and the Stakes of the People," an address delivered before the North Carolina Press Association, Morehead City, N.C., July 23, 1931, typescript, pp. 9–10.

2. *RNO*, February 21, 1930; *DTH*, February 21, 1930, February 22, 1930.

3. William deB. MacNider to FPG, February 25, 1930, SHC.

4. Louis Graves, *Chapel Hill Weekly*, February 28, 1930.

5. FPG to Mrs. W. T. Bost, March 20, 1930, NCCSS.

6. Elizabeth Sloan Graham to FPG, n.d., 1930, SHC.

7. *Chapel Hill Weekly,* May 9, 1930.

8. Interview with Otho Ross, July 20, 1960. Also in Otho Ross, "The Decision that Changed the University," unpublished ms., author's files.

9. Henry Sloan to FPG, April 8, 1930, SHC.

10. Charles W. Tillett to Kemp D. Battle, n.d., SHC; see also Charles W. Tillett to FPG, March 30, 1930, SHC; FPG to Charles and Gladys Tillett, April 8, 1930, NCCSS.

11. Charles W. Tillet in statement circulated to University of North Carolina Board of Trustees, n.d., 1930, SHC.

12. FPG to F. O. Clarkson, June 4, 1930, SHC, is representative of many telegrams.

13. Interview with Kemp D. Battle, August 8, 1960.

14. Minutes of the University of North Carolina Board of Trustees, June 9, 1930, SHC; *Chapel Hill Weekly*, June 13, 1930.

15. *RNO*, June 10, 1930; interviews with Otho Ross, June 20, 1960, and Kemp D. Battle, August 8, 1960. The author was skeptical of the legend that FPG had sincerely done everything possible to oppose his election and even at the last minute tried to avoid the presidency. A careful examination of available records and critical questioning of those who had direct knowledge of the events did not reveal any action on his part indicative of wanting the position. Those supporting him were thoroughly convinced of the sincerity of his opposition to their efforts.

16. Interviews with Hubert Robinson, June 24, 1959, July 9, 1960; Marian Graham, June 20, 1960; FPG to Kemp D. Battle, July 18, 1936; Charles W. Tillett, July 18, 1936, SHC; FPG papers in SHC for 1930.

17. "UNC Maintenance Appropriate Expenditures, 1923–24 to the Present," December 28, 1959, prepared for the author by Claude Teague from the North Carolina Budget.

18. FPG to Tyre Taylor, August 13, 1930, SHC.

19. FPG to John W. Umstead, May 26, 1931, SHC; FPG to Mary Hyman, May 23, 1931, SHC; see also other letters, e.g., FPG to Otho Ross (mimeo), April 4, 1931, SHC.

20. Tyre Taylor to FPG, January 3, 1931, SHC.

21. *RNO*, January 30, 1931, June 9, 1931.

22. *RNO*, January 30, 1931; FPG, "Statement to the Appropriations Committee," January 19, 1931, typescript, 13 pp., SHC.

23. *Chapel Hill Weekly*, April 9, 1931.

24. FPG mimeographed letters, April 4, 1931, SHC.

25. FPG to Senator Lee Gravely, April 20, 1931, SHC.

26. FPG to Representative J. Dolph Long, April 20, 1931, SHC. See also FPG, "The Deficit, the Debt, the Depression and the Stakes of the People," p. 4; FPG, "Statement to the Appropriations Committee," SHC.

27. *RNO*, May 29, 1931.

28. FPG to Harry W. Chase, July 9, 1931, SHC.

29. FPG to Gerald W. Johnson, July 17, 1931, SHC.

30. Howard W. Odum to O. Max Gardner, April 6, 1931, SHC.

31. Sixteen professors are listed in an undated memo, "Sample of Men Who Have Received Offers Elsewhere," with FPG handwritten note, "There are others," SHC; FPG to Representative J. Dolph Long, April 21, 1931, SHC.

32. FPG to Dean William C. Russell, December 5, 1931, SHC.

33. Ibid.

34. FPG, "The University Today," inaugural address as President of the University of North Carolina, November 11, 1931, typescript, pp. 27–29.

35. Ibid., pp. 30–31.

36. Ibid., p. 32.

37. Ibid., p. 33.

38. Interview with Mrs. James Rowland Angell, June 24, 1960.

39. *GDN*, November 12, 1931.

40. Ibid.

PART THREE

University President and Southern Liberal, 1931–1940

Background sources providing the most helpful perspectives for the author for Part Three, 1931–1940, were Wilbur J. Cash, *The Mind of the South*; Gunnar Myrdal, with Richard Sterner and Arnold Rose, *An American Dilemma: The Negro Problem and Modern Democracy* (New York: Harper, 1944); Howard W. Odum, *Southern Regions of the United States* (Chapel Hill: University of North Carolina Press, 1936); Arthur M. Schlesinger, Jr., *The Age of Roosevelt* (Boston: Houghton, Mifflin, 1957–1960), vol. I, *The Crisis of the Old Order* (1957); vol. II, *The Coming of the New Deal* (1958); vol. III, *The Politics of Upheaval* (1960); Charles G. Sellers, Jr., ed., *The Southerner*

as *American* (Chapel Hill: University of North Carolina Press, 1960);
George B. Tindall, *The Emergence of the New South, 1913–1945*, esp.
pp. 318–649; C. Vann Woodward, *The Burden of Southern History*
(Baton Rouge: Louisiana State University Press, 1960).

The basic facts for Chapter 8 were provided in interviews with FPG
and Marian Graham, who are not responsible for the interpretations of
the data they provided. As secondary sources many individuals provided
the author with their views of the personalities of FPG and Marian
Graham and their relations with each other. The references to Hillsboro and Nags Head, like previous references to Chapel Hill, are derived
largely from the author's visits. (Incidentally, the spelling of the name
"Hillsboro" employed in this book reflects the off-again, on-again history
of that name. It was originally "Hillsborough" in colonial times; by the
early twentieth century it had been shortened to "Hillsboro"; then in
1965 it was returned to its original form. Current practice omits the apos-
trophe in Nags Head.)

The discussion of University consolidation in Chapter 9 relies in part
on David A. Lockmiller, *The Consolidation of the University of North
Carolina* (Raleigh: University of North Carolina, 1942), and Louis R.
Wilson, *The University of North Carolina Under Consolidation, 1931–
1963: History and Appraisal* (Chapel Hill: University of North Carolina
Consolidated Office, 1964). For the author's interpretations the most
important sources were FPG 7, 8, 9 and the FPG and University Papers
in SHC.

Basic materials for Chapter 12 are found in *Report on Economic Conditions of the South, Prepared for the President by the National
Emergency Council* (Washington, D.C.: Government Printing Office,
1938), 64 pp.; SCHW files at Tuskegee Institute and Atlanta University;
and general background materials for Part Three. A good account of
SCHW is Thomas Krueger, *And Promises to Keep: The Southern Conference for Human Welfare, 1938–1948* (Nashville: Vanderbilt University Press, 1967). Morton Sosna, *In Search of the Silent South* (New
York: Columbia University Press, 1978) has excellent material on Southern liberals with a major chapter on Howard W. Odum. George B.
Tindall, *The Ethnic Southerners* (Baton Rouge: Louisiana State University Press, 1976) also has an important chapter on Odum.

8. At Home in the President's House (pp. 99–107)

1. FPG, "The University Today," p. 32.

2. Interviews with Hubert Robinson, June 24, 1959; Kate Sanders,
January 7, 1972; D. C. MacRae to FPG, August 5, 1943, SHC.

3. University of North Carolina *Alumni Magazine*, January 4, 1936,

pp. 9, 26; Cecil Johnson, "The Day they Turned Fukusata Loose," *Chapel Hill Weekly*, February 27, 1972.

4. Lenoir Chambers to FPG, n.d., 1929, NCCSS.

5. FPG to Francis E. Winslow, July 30, 1931, SHC.

6. FPG to Mrs. Francis E. Winslow, August 3, 1931, SHC.

7. FPG 2 (though the quoted statement was made many times to friends).

8. Conversations with Marian Graham's family in Hillsboro; interview with Hubert Robinson, June 24, 1959.

9. FPG 2; Nettie Sue Tillett to author, n.d.

10. *GDN*, July 22, 1932; interview with Marian Graham, June 20, 1960.

11. Interview with Hubert Robinson, July 9, 1960.

12. Interview with Marian Graham, June 20, 1960.

13. The anecdote was repeated in literally hundreds of speeches by FPG almost invariably as an analogy of the troubled world pressing upon America.

14. Francis Pickens Miller to author, March 24, 1961.

15. FPG to Wendell Willkie, November 6, 1940, SHC.

16. Interview with Marian Graham, June 20, 1960.

9. The New University of North Carolina (pp. 108–23)

1. FPG, "The University Today," p. 32.

2. Lockmiller, *Consolidation*, passim; Wilson, *University Under Consolidation*, pp. 6–7.

3. R. B. House to Leslie Weil, November 26, 1930, PP. ("If he were pressed for an opinion right now he would be decidedly opposed to any consolidation.")

4. FPG 7.

5. Lockmiller, *Consolidation*, p. 34; *RNO*, March 4, 1931.

6. Lockmiller, *Consolidation*, pp. 40–42.

7. George A. Works in Minutes of University of North Carolina Board of Trustees, July 11, 1932, p. 4, SHC.

8. Lockmiller, *Consolidation*, pp. 45–49.

9. Ibid., pp. 53–54; Trustees Minutes, July 11, 1932.

10. Julius I. Foust to FPG, October 21, 1932, PP.

11. FPG to Kemp Lewis, July 2, 1932, PP.

12. David Clark to E. C. Brooks, July (n.d.) 1932.

13. Julius I. Foust to FPG, October 21, 1932, PP.

14. FPG to Julius I. Foust, November 1, 1932, PP.

15. FPG to Leslie Weil, November 9, 1932, PP.

16. Leslie Weil to FPG, November 2, 1932, PP.

17. Josephus Daniels to FPG, November 7, 1932, PP.

18. FPG to N. A. Townsend, September 15, 1932, PP.

19. FPG to Mrs. Charles Doak, December 31, 1932, PP.

20. FPG 7, 8.

21. Ibid. Correspondence between FPG and Julius I. Foust confirms this interpretation. See esp. Graham files in Jackson Library, University of North Carolina at Greensboro.

22. FPG 7, 8.

23. Willard B. Gatewood, Jr., *Eugene Clyde Brooks, Educator and Public Servant* (Durham: Duke University Press, 1960), pp. 266–67; FPG 9; *RNO*, November 21, 1933, November 25, 1933.

24. O. Max Gardner to Clarence Poe, n.d., 1933, SHC.

25. FPG 8, 9.

26. Randall Thompson to FPG, June 6, 1933, PP.

27. FPG 9.

28. FPG 8.

29. See the "Act of Consolidation," in Lockmiller, *Consolidation*; George A. Works, Trustees Minutes, July 11, 1932, UA.

30. Trustees Minutes, July 11, 1932.

31. FPG 8; Trustees Minutes, May 30, 1935, UA.

32. FPG, "The Question of Consolidation," *RNO*, May 17, 1936.

33. Lockmiller *Consolidation*, pp. 86–88, 100.

10. University Crusades and Crises (pp. 124–40)

1. FPG, "The University Today," p. 32.

2. Ibid.

3. *Literary Digest* XIV (October 15, 1932): 22–23; *RNO*, September 9, 1932; *GDN*, September 9, 1932; *New York Evening Post*, September 8, 1932, quoted in Barry Feinberg and Ronald Kraslis, *Bertrand Russell's America, 1896–1945* (New York: Viking, 1973), p. 120.

4. FPG to George Tracy Cunningham, August 26, 1932, SHC.

5. Cf. letters to FPG, June through September, 1932, SHC.

6. FPG to Birmingham, Alabama, editor, September 16, 1932, SHC.

7. FPG to Rev. Albea Godbold, September 12, 1932, SHC.

8. FPG to Rev. Theodore Partrick, September 17, 1932, SHC; FPG to C. O. Kuester, October 4, 1932, SHC.

9. FPG to Tom Glasgow, October 4, 1932, SHC.

10. FPG to Roger Baldwin, October 4, 1932, SHC.

11. FPG to Mrs. Jessie Kenan Wise, December 8, 1932, SHC.

12. Bernard M. Cone to FPG, February 5, 1930.

13. FPG 8; *RNO*, September 30, 1933.

14. New York *Herald Tribune*, October 1, 1933.

15. See FPG correspondence October-November, 1933, SHC.

16. FPG to Durham Medical School alumni, November 1, 1933, PP.

17. FPG to Gov. O. Max Gardner, July 31, 1931, PP.

18. Professor Louis O. Katsoff to author in 1948.

19. FPG to Josephus Daniels, September 7, 1933, PP.

20. *Chapel Hill Weekly*, November 13, 1931.

21. Interview with Cecil Johnson, May 8, 1963.

22. *NYT*, November 20, 1930, p. 3.

23. A. H. Upham, ed., *National Association of State Universities, Transactions and Proceedings*, XXVIII (1930): 148–62; ibid., XXXIII (1933): 105. See also Abraham Flexner, *Universities, American, English, German* (New York: Oxford University Press, 1930), pp. 64–66, 206.

24. Howard J. Savage et al., *American College Athletics for the Carnegie Foundation for the Advancement of Teaching*, Bulletin 23 (New York: Carnegie Foundation for the Advancement of Teaching, 1929), pp. xx–xxi; see also supplementary report by Howard J. Savage, John T. McGovern, and Harold W. Bentley, *Current Developments in American College Sport*, Bulletin 26 (New York: Carnegie Foundation for the Advancement of Teaching, 1931).

25. Savage, *American College Athletics*, p. 265.

26. FPG 9; for details of plan see Upham, *National Association of State Universities*, XXXII: 204ff, XXXIII: 105ff.

27. FPG 9.

28. Trustees Minutes, November 1935, UA.

29. *NYT*, November 24, 1935, p. 12.

30. *RNO*, January 12, 1936, January 24, 1936.

31. FPG 9; *RNO*, December 13, 1935.

32. FPG to Foy Roberson, January 24, 1936, SHC.

33. Trustees Minutes, January 31, 1936, UA; "Statement by President Frank P. Graham to the Board of Trustees with Regard to the Proposed Supplementary Athletic Regulations," n.d., printed, 4 pp, PP; *RNO*, February 1, 1936.

34. See correspondence in FPG papers, January through May, 1936, SHC; *RNO*, February 1, 1936.

35. *RNO*, February 5, 1936, February 6, 1936, February 8, 1936.

36. See, e.g., *RNO*, February 13, 1936 (quoting Clark's letter in full), February 14, 1936, February 16, 1936.

37. James Bryant Conant to FPG, January 4, 1936; James Rowland Angell to FPG, January 2 and 21, 1936; Ernest H. Lindley to FPG, January 3, 1936; Lotus D. Coffman to FPG, January 22, 1936, PP; "Statement by President Graham to the Faculty," typescript, n.d., 8 pp. SHC.

38. William E. Dodd to FPG, February 23, 1936, PP.

39. *RNO*, December 12, 1936; see also *RNO*, December 13, 1936, December 14, 1936; *GDN*, December 22, 1936; University of North Carolina Faculty Council Minutes, December 7, 1936.

40. Herman G. James, ed., *National Association of State Universities, Transactions and Proceedings*, XXXVI (1938): 228.

41. Joseph Y. Barnett to FPG, January 28, 1936, PP; FPG 9; R. B. House to FPG (confidential memorandum), January 28, 1936, PP.

42. Jack Pool to FPG, October 8, 1936, PP.

43. FPG to Jack Pool, October 12, 1936, PP.

44. FPG to unidentified correspondent, October 1936, PP.

45. *RNO*, February 3, 1936. The incident was reported in various state newspapers, e.g., *RNO*, February 2, 1936; *RNO*, February 5, 1936, reported 48 students had been suspended with the investigation "practically ended."

46. Questionnaire sent by Alumni Office, February 1936; Phillips Russell to FPG, February 25, 1936, PP.

47. *RNO*, February 24, 1936; *New Republic* LXXXVI (March 11, 1936): 122–23.

48. Josephus Daniels to FPG, March 4, 1936, PP; Joseph L. Morrison, *Josephus Daniels: The Small-d Democrat* (Chapel Hill: University of North Carolina Press, 1966), p. 186.

49. FPG to Mrs. Julius W. Cone, April 30, 1936, PP; cf. letters from Kemp D. Battle to FPG, March 7, 1936, and April 22, 1936, PP.

50. Charles W. Tillett to FPG, April 18, 1936, May 25, 1936, SHC; see also frequent letters from Tillett to various persons, SHC; and memos of M. T. Van Hecke to Charles W. Tillett, May 25, 1936, PP; Robert B. House to Charles W. Tillett, May 26, 1936, PP; J. W. Harrelson to Charles W. Tillett, May 29, 1936, PP.

11. Social and Economic Justice (pp. 141–50)

1. FPG, "The University Today," p. 24.

2. FPG address to Southern Summer School for Workers in Industry, June 17, 1932, SHC.

3. Gen. Hugh S. Johnson to FPG, October 9, 1933, PP; Minutes of the University of North Carolina Board, October 14, 1933; FPG to Gen. Hugh S. Johnson, October 16, 1933, PP.

4. FPG address delivered before Code Authority Meeting, Constitution Hall, Washington, D.C., March 5, 1934, Release No. 3626, National Recovery Administration.

5. Interview with Clarence Poe, July 21, 1960.

6. FPG to Nell Battle Lewis, February 21, 1933, PP.

7. FPG, "Memorandum for Consideration by the Comptroller of the University with Regard to the Three Units of the University and Their Relation to the NRA Program," September 20, 1933, typescript, PP.

8. *RNO*, September 7, 1934.

9. *GDN*, September 8, 1934.

10. *RNO* editorial, "A Man Stands Up," September 10, 1934; cf. reports in state newspapers, September 7 through 23, 1934, when the end of the strike was reported.

11. *NYT*, November 11, 1934, p. 1; November 5, 1934, p. 3; Edwin E. Witte, *The Development of the Social Security Act* (Madison: University of Wisconsin Press, 1962), p. 51.

12. A good account of "The Hundred Days" is in Arthur M. Schlesinger, Jr., *The Age of Roosevelt*, pp. 1–23.

13. Schlesinger, *Age of Roosevelt*, pp. 303–4.

14. Franklin D. Roosevelt, "Presidential Message to the Congress Reviewing the Broad Objectives and Accomplishments of the Administration, June 8, 1934" (H. R. Doc. 397, 73d Cong., 2d. Sess.), in Robert B. Stevens, ed., *Statutory History of the United States: Income Security* (New York: Chelsea House, 1970), pp. 60–64. (A prefatory note, pp. 59–60, places the message in context.)

15. "Executive Order Establishing the Committee on Economic Security and the Advisory Council on Economic Security," June 29, 1934, Executive Order 6757, in Stevens, *Statutory History*, pp. 64–65.

16. An excellent account of the origins of the Social Security Act is found in Witte, *Development of the Social Security Act*.

17. FPG, "The Road to Recovery and Security," in *Security* (Washington, D.C.: Committee on Economic Security, December 1934), p. 17.

18. Witte, *Development of the Social Security Act*, pp. 43–44.

19. Franklin D. Roosevelt, "Security of the Nation," in *Security*, p. 2.

20. Frances Perkins, "The Task that Lies Ahead," in *Security,* pp. 5–9; FPG, "The Road to Recovery and Security," in *Security*, p. 16.

21. Conclusion of the author in interpreting data. For an account of the difficulties the Cabinet Committee on Economic Security had with the Advisory Council, see Theron F. Schlabach, *Edwin E. Witte, Cautious Reformer* (Madison: State Historical Society of Wisconsin, 1969), pp. 122, 126, 138; Witte, *Development of the Social Security Act*, pp. 54ff.

22. Paul Douglas, *Social Security in the United States* (New York: McGraw-Hill, 1938), pp. 50–51; see also pp. 28–129; Abraham Epstein, "Our Social Insecurity Act," *Harper's* CLXXII (December 1935): 55–66.

23. Witte, *Development of the Social Security Act*; Arthur J. Altmeyer to author, September 15, 1962.

24. *Economic Security Act, Hearings Before the Committee on Finance, United States Senate, 74th Cong., 1st Sess. (S1130)* (Washington, D.C.: Government Printing Office, 1935), pp. 291–317.

25. Ibid., p. 314.

26. *NYT*, August 15, 1935, p. 1.

27. *The Advisory Committee on Education: Report of the Committee* (Washington, D.C.: Government Printing Office, 1938), pp. i, iii.

28. Ibid., pp. 194–221.

29. FPG, "Address on Federal Aid to Education," May 7, 1938, SHC. He did not cite instances.

30. Ibid.

31. Katherine Lackey to R. C. Lawrence, May 24, 1939, SHC.

32. FPG 5.

12. A More Democratic South (pp. 151–68)

1. FPG, "The University Today," p. 20.

2. *RECS*, overleaf, p. 1; Lowell Mellett to FPG, June 25, 1938, PP; the classical study of the Southern region is Odum, *Southern Regions*.

3. *RECS*, p. 1. The phrase "the nation's number one economic problem" was used for the first time by President Roosevelt in a letter to members of the Conference on Economic Conditions of the South, July 5, 1938.

4. *NYT*, July 10, 1938, p. 2.

5. *NYT*, August 13, 1938, p. 1, August 21, 1938, sec. IV, p. 6. *RECS* was printed in full in *NYT*, August 13, 1938, pp. 4–6.

6. *RECS*, p. 8.

7. Ibid., pp. 9–16, 45–48.

8. Ibid., pp. 21–24.

9. Ibid., pp. 25–28.

10. Ibid., pp. 29–32.

11. Ibid., pp. 49–52, 57–60.

12. Ibid., p. 5; FPG, "The University Today," p. 20.

13. For North Carolina Conference for Social Service see Gulledge, *North Carolina Conference*; for Southern Policy Committee see *Southern Policy*, Report of the Southern Policy Conference in Atlanta, April 25–28, 1936, (n.p., n.d.); for Southern Tenant Farmer's Union see Tindall, *Emergence of the New South*, pp. 416–24, with accompanying bibliography.

14. *Report of the Proceedings of the Southern Conference for Human Welfare*, Birmingham, Ala., November 20–23, 1938, 32 pp.

15. Louise O. Charlton, SCHW *Report*, pp. 3–6; officers elected are listed on p. 7.

16. FPG to Louise O. Charlton, November 8, 1938, SHC. Acceptance speech, in SCHW *Report*, pp. 26–29.

17. FPG opening address, in SCHW *Report*, p. 29.

18. "To the Board Members of the Southern Conference for Human Welfare" (memo), n.d., SHC.

19. *NYT*, November 23, 1938, p. 23; details of resolutions in SCHW *Report*, pp. 13–22.

20. FPG to L. A. Crowell, Jr., December 22, 1938, SHC; *GDN*, November 4, 1938; Carl Thompson et al to FPG, November 24, 1938 (telegram), SHC.

21. Lucy Randolph Mason to FPG, November 24, 1938, SHC; Louise O. Charlton to FPG, November 26, 1938, SHC.

22. Lucy Randolph Mason to FPG, December 6, 1938, SHC.

23. Mark Ethridge to FPG, November 30, 1938, SHC.

24. Howard W. Odum to Mark Ethridge, December 6, 1938, SHC.

25. FPG to Mark Ethridge, December 20, 1938, SHC.

26. *GDN*, November 25, 1938; *NYT*, November 26, 1938, p. 5, November 28, 1938, p. 2; see *NYT*, November 24, 1938, p. 33; Krueger, *And Promises to Keep*, p. 65.

27. Minutes of the Executive Committee, SCHW, February 7, 1939, SHC; FPG to Stanton Smith, October 16, 1939, PP; FPG to Barry Bingham, November 13, 1939, PP.

28. Howard Kester to Francis P. Miller, March 19, 1939, PP; Rob F. Hall to Joseph Gelders, November 9, 1939, PP; Jack F. Talbert to Josephine Wilkins, October 19, 1939, PP; FPG to H. C. Nixon (telegram), November 19, 1939, PP; H. C. Nixon to FPG, November 20, 1939, PP; FPG to Howard Kester, December 1, 1939, PP; Howard Kester to FPG, December 11, 1939, PP.

29. R. B. Hanes in Dombrowski file in FPG papers, dated June 17, 1944, SHC.

30. FPG to H. C. Nixon, December 2, 1939, PP.

31. H. C. Nixon to FPG, January 17, 1939, PP; Francis Pickens Miller to author, March 24, 1961.

32. FPG to Mark Ethridge, April 7, 1940, PP; FPG to Barry Bingham, July 30, 1940, PP; FPG to Mrs. Franklin D. Roosevelt, June 1, 1940, PP.

33. FPG to Howard Kester, December 1, 1939, SHC. In the midst of the controversy FPG said, "I have been accustomed to being called all sorts of names for trying to take seriously the teachings of Jesus in religion, Jefferson in politics, W. H. Hamilton, May, Keezer, Mitchell and Veblen in economics, and Woodrow Wilson in international organization. I have not in my own mind and heart found it necessary to go outside of the American traditions and the Christian religion to find all and much more that I can hope to achieve in my own small way." FPG to Joseph Gelders, January 15, 1940, SHC.

34. FPG to Joseph Gelders, January 15, 1940, SHC, is representative of the many letters he wrote on this issue.

35. FPG to H. C. Nixon, December 2, 1940, SHC, is representative.

36. Howard Kester to FPG, December 11, 1930, SHC; see also Kester to Francis Pickens Miller, March 19, 1939, SHC.

37. FPG to Lucy Randolph Mason, November 16, 1939, PP; Lucy Randolph Mason to FPG, November 10, 1939, PP.

38. Press release, Chattanooga Conference, March, n.d., 1940.

39. Julian La Rose Harris to FPG, January 25, 1940, PP.

40. Clark Foreman to FPG, March 20, 1940, PP.

41. W. T. Couch to FPG, April 12, 1940, PP.

42. Marc Friedlaender to Representative Carl Durham, February 12, 1949, SHC; FPG to William Mitch, April 21, 1955, SHC.

43. William Mitch to FPG, April 25, 1955, SHC.

44. Quoted in Walter Gellhorn, "Report on a Report of the House Committee on Un-American Activities," *Harvard Law Review* LX (October 1947): 1226.

45. This may seem a different conclusion from that of Krueger, *And Promises*, p. 59, who asserts "the meeting had been harmonious, except for a brief, bitter conflict over the convention's resolutions on foreign policy." In the light of the collapse of SCHW less than a decade later the "brief, bitter conflict" has special significance. FPG at the time, unable to separate domestic and foreign policies, recognized its significance, though he was optimistic concerning the ultimate outcome. See FPG to Eugene E. Pfaff, June 3, 1955, SHC; Yelverton Cowherd to FPG, December 28, 1955. The letters of 1955, like the earlier letters of 1949, represent efforts on FPG's part to "set the record straight."

46. George Stoney to FPG, April 29, 1940, PP.

47. Lucy Randolph Mason to FPG, May 8, 1940, PP; FPG to Howard W. Odum (telegram), June 15, 1940, PP; Howard W. Odum to FPG (telegram), n.d., PP; FPG to Barry Bingham, July 30, 1949, PP.

48. Barry Bingham to FPG, May 27, 1940, PP.

49. FPG to Frank McAllister, July 11, 1942, PP.

PART FOUR

Triumphs, 1940–1949

The most helpful sources for Chapter 15 are United Nations, *Security Council Official Records and Official Records of the Good Offices Committee*. Background material with some documentation is found in "Work of the United Nations Good Offices Committee in Indonesia" (Washington, D.C.: Department of State Publication 3108, March 14, 1948), 14 pp. FPG, "Report to the United Nations on Indonesia," February 17, 1948, 10 pp., mimeo, is also helpful. Other basic sources the author found especially valuable: J. Foster Collins, "The United Nations and Indonesia," *International Conciliation* (New York: Carnegie Endowment For International Peace, March 1950), no. 459; Louis Fischer, *The Story of Indonesia* (New York: Harper, 1959); George

McT. Kahin, *Nationalism and Independence in Indonesia* (Ithaca: Cornell University Press, 1952); Alastair M. Taylor, *Indonesian Independence and the United Nations* (Ithaca: Cornell University Press, 1960); Charles Wolf, Jr., *The Indonesian Story: The Birth, Growth, and Structure of the Indonesian Republic* (New York: John Day, 1945). Taylor's is a particularly excellent study.

The essential document on civil rights in Chapter 16 is *To Secure These Rights, the Report of the President's Committee on Civil Rights* (Washington, D.C.: Government Printing Office, 1947). The files of the *Southern Conference for Human Welfare* provide essential information. The detailed investigations of FPG reported fully in Federal Bureau of Investigation documents are important in relation to the charges regarding communism and, to a lesser extent, to activities concerning civil rights. While the press, especially the *Daily Tar Heel*, the state newspapers, and the *New York Times*, report fully Graham's public activities, the most important source of information is the FPG files, Southern Historical Collection.

13. "The Central Issue is Human Liberty" (pp. 171–91)

1. FPG, "Southport Petroleum Co. and the Oil Workers International, Local 449, CIO," June 5, 1943, in *National War Labor Board Reports* (Washington, D.C.: Bureau of National Affairs), VIII: 2898–CS–D.

2. Winston Churchill, *The Second World War*, vol. II, *Their Finest Hour* (Boston: Houghton-Mifflin, 1949), p. 118.

3. FPG, "American Aspects of the Crisis in Democracy," address at Williamstown Institute, August 28, 1935, typescript, SHC.

4. FPG, "The Challenge of Totalitarian Dictatorship to Religion, Freedom and Democracy in the Modern World," address at Williamstown Institute, August 29, 1938, pp. 5–6, typescript, SHC.

5. FPG, "Democracy and the Second World War," in William Allen White, ed., *Defense for America* (New York: Macmillan, 1940), p. 107.

6. FPG to Mrs. Franklin D. Roosevelt, June 1, 1940, SHC.

7. FPG, "The University and National Defense," convocation address, September 27, 1940, *Alumni Review* supplement, 1940, p. 3.

8. Ibid., p. 4.

9. *RNO*, March 20, 1941; cf. *NYT*, March 20, 1941, p. 1.

10. *CR* LXXXVII, pt. 3 (April 15, 1941): 3128.

11. *NYT*, March 20, 1941, p. 1.

12. *NYT*, March 20, 1941, p. 20.

13. General accounts of NDMB in Rose M. Stein, "Big Steel and the Union Shop," *Nation* LIII (October 4, 1941): 306–8; "Storm Over NDMB," *Time* XXXVIII (September 8, 1941): 13–14; "New Mediation Board," *Time* XXXVIII (December 1, 1941): 17.

14. For good accounts of William H. Davis see *Survey Graphic* XXX (November 1941): 547–51; John Chamberlain, "Will Davis of the War Labor Board," *Fortune* XXV, no. 3 (March 1942): 70ff. See also Ann Victoria Adler, "The National Defense Mediation Board: Its Creation, Activities and Termination" (M. A. Thesis, UNC–Chapel Hill, 1932).

15. FPG, "Policies and Experiences on the War Labor Board," in *Southern University Conference*, New Orleans, April 17–19, 1947, pp. 137, 199. The description of FPG's work on NDMB is taken primarily from this source, pp. 135–49.

16. *NYT*, November 12, 1941, p. 1.

17. Ibid., November 23, 1941, p. 1.

18. Interview with Senator Wayne L. Morse, August 5, 1959.

19. *NYT*, December 9, 1941, p. 1.

20. Ibid., December 12, 1941, p. 29.

21. Ibid., December 18, 1941, p. 1.

22. Ibid.

23. *National War Labor Board Termination Report* (Washington, D.C.: Government Printing Office, 1942), II: 49.

24. Executive Order 9017, January 12, 1942.

25. *NWLB Termination Report*, I: 12.

26. FPG 4; interviews with Senator Wayne L. Morse, August 5, 1959; Charles M. Jones, April 18, 1961.

27. Dexter M. Keezer, "Observations on the Operations of the War Labor Board," *American Economic Review* XXXVI, no. 3 (June 1946): 233–57. In July 1945 the Board employed 2613 persons full time, 1162 part time, and 618 persons without pay. Interviews with William H. Davis, December 3, 1962; M. T. Van Hecke, June 30, 1960; see John Chamberlain, "Will Davis"; Allan R. Richards, *War Labor Boards in the Field* (Chapel Hill: University of North Carolina Press, 1953).

28. Keezer, *Observations*, pp. 233–34.

29. *WLB Termination Report*, III: 58405. Dissenting opinion of AF of L members to Case No. 13–279; statements and reply opinions, October 28, 29, 30, 1943.

30. Interview with Senator Wayne L. Morse, August 5, 1959.

31. Keezer, *Observations*, p. 233; see James MacGregor Burns, *The Lion and the Fox* (New York: Harcourt, Brace, 1965), p. 462.

32. FPG, "Humble Oil and Refining Co. and the Oil Workers International Union, Local No. 316, CIO," April 1, 1944, *WLB Reports*, XV: 111–1919–D.

33. FPG, "Southport Petroleum Co. and the Oil Workers International Union, Local 44, CIO," June 5, 1943, *WLB Reports*, VIII: 2898–CS–D.

34. Ibid.

35. Interview with Senator Wayne L. Morse, August 5, 1959.

36. *WLB Termination Report.*

37. Joseph Shister, "The National War Labor Board: Its Significance," *Journal of Political Economy* LIII, no. 1 (March 1945): 54–56. See also Robert G. Dixon, Jr., "Public Power and Critical Labor Disputes," *The Journal of Politics* XIII, no. 4 (November 1951): 511–35; Herman Feldman, ed., "Labor Relations and the War," *Annals of the American Academy of Political and Social Science* CCXXIV (November 1942); FPG, "Union Rights in Wartime," *New Republic* CVI (June 29, 1942): 884–87.

38. Felix Frankfurter to FPG, August 15, n.d, SHC.

39. FPG to Edward K. Graham, January 30, 1943, SHC; interview with Robert B. House, June 30, 1960.

40. Wilson, *University Under Consolidation*, pp. 108–10.

41. FPG to J. S. Lewis, Jr., October 8, 1942, SHC.

42. William deB. MacNider to FPG, July 14, 1942, SHC.

43. *RNO*, May 27, 1944.

44. Minutes of University of North Carolina Board of Trustees, October 2, 1944, UA.

45. Charles W. Tillett to FPG, June 3, 1944, SHC.

46. FPG to President Franklin D. Roosevelt, October 9, 1944, PP; *NYT*, November 4, 1944, p. 1, November 14, 1944, p. 1, November 16, 1944, p. 15.

47. *NYT*, November 28, 1945, pp. 19–20; President Harry S Truman to FPG, December 27, 1945, PP.

48. *NYT*, January 13, 1946, pp. 1, 5–8.

14. A People's Movement for Medical Care (pp. 192–206)

1. FPG, "Address at Dedication of the Medical Center," Chapel Hill, 1953, SHC. Reprinted as "A Challenge to the Medical Schools and the Medical Profession," *Pediatrics* XIII (January 1954): 92–102. An introduction by Lytt I. Gardner gives a brief account of the development of the Medical Center.

2. *RNO*, January 8, 1946.

3. Wilson, *University Under Consolidation*, pp. 161–64.

4. FPG 9.

5. FPG 9; Wilson, *University Under Consolidation*, p. 100.

6. Wilson, *University Under Consolidation*, pp. 102–3.

7. *RNO*, March 28, 1947.

8. FPG 5, 6.

9. Wilson, *University of North Carolina*, pp. 13–14, 98–103.

10. FPG 5, 6; Upham, *National Association of State Universities*, XXXIII (1935): 69.

11. FPG 5, 6.

12. Upham, *National Association of State Universities*, XXXIV (1936): 31.

13. FPG 5, 6.

14. Ibid.

15. Minutes of University of North Carolina Board of Trustees, January 31, 1944, UA.

16. J. Melville Broughton, *Public Addresses, Letters and Papers* (Raleigh, 1951), pp. 478–81; *North Carolina Medical Journal* V, no. 3 (March 1944): 105.

17. *RNO*, October 15, 1944; The Commission on Hospital and Medical Care, *To All the People of North Carolina* (Raleigh, 1944).

18. Interview with Paul Whitaker, April 10, 1961.

19. FPG 5, 6; interview with Paul Whitaker, April 10, 1961; *North Carolina Medical Journal* VI, no. 2 (February 1945): 108ff.

20. *North Carolina Medical Journal* VI, no. 3 (March 1945): 177; ibid., no. 4 (April 1945): 217–19.

21. FPG 5, 6.

22. *RNO*, February 16, 1947.

23. R. Gregg Cherry, *Public Addresses and Papers* (Raleigh, 1951), pp. 36–41.

24. *RNO*, January 8, 1946; interview with Paul Whitaker, April 10, 1961.

25. Medical Care Commission, *Report for 1945–1949* (Raleigh, 1950); see also *Official Report of the Medical Care Commission on the Expansion of the Medical School of the University of North Carolina* (Raleigh, 1947).

26. Interview with Paul Whitaker, April 10, 1961.

27. *RNO*, September 20, 1946.

28. FPG 5, 6; FPG to Louis R. Wilson, December 11, 1961, SHC; *RNO*, August 8, 1946; Wilson, *University Under Consolidation*, pp. 208–9; Senator Lister P. Hill to FPG, August 5 (?), 1946.

29. Interview with L. P. McLendon, February 20, 1959.

30. Medical Care Commission, *Report*; Wilson, *University Under Consolidation*, pp. 205–7; *North Carolina Medical Journal* VII, no. 10 (October 1946): 570; Ibid., no. 12 (December 1946): 671.

31. Interview with Paul Whitaker, April 10, 1961.

32. FPG 5, 6.

33. *Journal of the American Medical Association* XIII (August 17, 1946): 1281; see also pp. 1282–83.

34. FPG 5, 6.

35. *RNO*, February 3, 1947.

36. *RNO*, February 14, 1947.

15. Independence for Indonesia (pp. 207–23)

1. FPG, "Report to the United Nations on Indonesia."

2. Log of Hubert Robinson.

3. UN doc. S/459, August 1, 1947.

4. UN doc. S/525, August 26, 1947.

5. Taylor, *Indonesian Independence*, p. 55.

6. *NYT*, October 2, 1947, p. 10.

7. See basic sources above.

8. Taylor, *Indonesian Independence*, pp. 49–50; interview with Herschel V. Johnson, June 17, 1959.

9. Interviews with Dean Rusk, June 23, 1960; Henry Brandis, July 21, 1960.

10. Interview with Dean Rusk, June 23, 1960.

11. Interview with Henry Brandis, July 21, 1960.

12. Paul Van Zeeland, "Report to the United Nations," *SCOR*, February 17, 1948.

13. "Interim Report of the GOC to the Security Council," UN doc. S/AC.10/79 and S/AC.10/SR.1 (December 31, 1947).

14. FPG, "Statement to the United States Senate," April 5, 1949, *CR* XLV: 3921–22, quoted in Taylor, *Indonesian Independence*, p. 400.

15. *NYT*, October 26, 1947, p. 1: John W. Henderson, *Area Handbook for Indonesia* (Washington, D.C.: Government Printing Office, 1970), pp. 9–16, 77 and passim.

16. Interview with Henry Brandis, July 21, 1960; Taylor, *Indonesian Independence*, p. 66. Batavia later became Djakarta.

17. Taylor, *Indonesian Independence*, pp. 68–77   .

18. FPG reported publicly on the invitation and his response at various times, e.g., a student UN conference in New York, April 1955; George McT. Kahin to author, August 24, 1960. *Current Biography, 1947* (New York: H. W. Wilson) is the source for Sukarno's height; *Current Biography, 1951*, for FPG's. (His height as reported in the college yearbook may have been exaggerated.)

19. *NYT*, November 2, 1947, p. 1; interview with Henry Brandis, July 21, 1960.

20. *NYT*, December 9, 1947, p. 21; Taylor, *Indonesian Independence*, pp. 77–78. Fischer, *Story of Indonesia*, pp. 102ff., provides a journalistic, biased account.

21. Van Zeeland's analysis is in UN doc., Annex 1, S/AC.10/SR.49, December 25, 1947, quoted in Taylor, *Indonesian Independence*, pp. 79–80; see reports of Taylor's interview with FPG, p. 82. FPG memorandum providing bases for settlement is Annex 2 in S/AC/10/SR.49, December 22, 1947.

22. Text of message, S/AC/10/75 and 75/Corr. 1; text also in UN doc.,

S/649, February 10, 1948, p. 70; quoted in "Work of UN GOC," p. 8.

23. Ibid.

24. Taylor, *Indonesian Independence*, pp. 84–86.

25. Interview with Henry Brandis, July 21, 1960.

26. *New York Herald Tribune*, January 10, 1948, quoted in Taylor, *Indonesian Independence*, p. 88.

27. Interview with Henry Brandis, July 21, 1960; Fischer, *Story of Indonesia*, pp. 103–6.

28. *NYT*, January 19, 1946, p. 10; *USS Renville*, S/AC.10/Conf.2/SR 4, January 17, 1948.

29. FPG, "Report to the UN," February 17, 1948.

30. UN Security Council, 248th Meetings, *SCOR*, February 17, 1948.

31. *NYT*, February 14, 1948, p. 6.

32. Log of Hubert Robinson.

16. Civil Rights and Communism (pp. 224–39)

1. *DTH*, January 14, 1949.

2. *NYT*, October 30, 1947, p. 1; *To Secure These Rights*, passim.

3. *To Secure These Rights*, p. 166.

4. Ibid., passim., esp. pp. 151–78.

5. Ibid., pp. 166–67.

6. Kate Burr Johnson to FPG, February 26, 1929; FPG to Kate Burr Johnson, February 25, 1929, NCCSS.

7. Charlotte Hawkins Brown to FPG, April 27, 1934, PP; see also FPG address to Commission on Interracial Cooperation, Richmond, Va., December 8, 1931, SHC.

8. L. E. Austin to FPG, July 5, 1938, SHC.

9. Pauli Murray to FPG, January 17, 1939, PP.

10. FPG to Pauli Murray, February 3, 1939, PP.

11. Walter White to FPG, February 11, 1939, PP.

12. E.g., F. A. Middlebush to FPG, January 9, 1939, PP; H. C. Byrd to FPG, February 1, 1939, PP.

13. FPG to F. A. Middlebush, January 18, 1939, PP.

14. FPG to H. C. Byrd, February 19, 1939, PP.

15. Rufus Clement to FPG, March 30, 1939, PP; Leo Favrot to FPG, May 10, 1939, PP.

16. FPG to James R. McCain, May 17, 1939, PP.

17. FPG 5; FPG to L. P. McLendon, May 1, 1951.

18. Howard K. Beale to FPG, May 14, 1943, SHC.

19. FPG to Howard K. Beale, May 29, 1943, SHC; see also John W. Nason to FPG, November 11, 1942, SHC.

20. Interview with Charles M. Jones, April 18, 1961.

21. FPG, "Southport Petroleum and the Oil Workers International,

Local 449, CIO," June 5, 1943, in *National War Labor Board Reports* VIII (Washington, D.C.: Bureau of National Affairs): 2898-CS-D.

22. Howard C. McKinney to FPG, July 17, 1943, SHC; see FPG correspondence for 1942–1945, SHC.

23. Pauli Murray to FPG, June 20, 1944, PP.

24. FPG to Frederick B. Patterson, April 18, 1944, PP.

25. *DTH*, December 2, 1945.

26. Interview with Allard K. Lowenstein, April 18, 1961.

27. FPG press release on Student Assembly, December 9, 1945, PP.

28. FPG to Walter White, May 29, 1946, PP.

29. Author's files. The original announcement of the recital with FPG's handwritten statement on reverse was given to the author, with an oral account of the session, by J. C. Herrin.

30. Interview with Charles M. Jones, October 30, 1958.

31. U.S., Congress, House, Committee on Un-American Activities, *Report on Southern Conference for Human Welfare*, Union Calendar No. House Report 592, 80th Congress, 1st session, 1947, see esp. pp. 6, 17; also in *CR* XCIII, pt. 6 (June 16, 1947): 7066–71; *NYT*, June 15, 1947, p. 44.

32. *CR* XCIII, pt. 6 (June 16, 1947): 7065.

33. Ibid., p. 7066; *NYT*, June 17, 1947, p. 5.

34. Roger Baldwin to Clark Foreman, May 19, 1942, SHC; see SCHW files in FPG papers, SHC.

35. SCHW news release, March 6, 1945, SHC.

36. Louise O. Charlton to Clark Foreman, March 21, 1946, copy with handwritten note to FPG, SHC.

37. E.g., FPG to Ada M. Field, August 14, 1947, SHC.

38. Director of FBI to U.S. Attorney General, October 7, 1946; see also *Charlotte Observer*, *GDN*, *RNO*, August 13, 1940.

39. Director of FBI to U.S. Attorney General, October 7, 1947. The Clark speech to the Charlotte Lions Club, "Communism and Socialism at Chapel Hill," had been previously reported in an FBI investigative report, August 10, 1943, pp. 5, 7.

40. Tom Pridgen to FPG, May 6, 1940, SHC; see *Charlotte News*, May 12, 1940.

41. Trustees Minutes, June 1940.

42. *Alumni Review*, June 1940; reported in FBI investigative report, November 1, 1947, file no. 116–1489, pp. 22–23.

43. *GDN*, September 21, 1953.

44. *GDN*, December 1, 1954, April 11, 1955, December 25, 1962.

45. *CR* LXXXVII, pt. 8: 8461–62. It is not clear what the "documentary proof" was. The first major FBI investigation was initiated by J. Edgar Hoover the following year, July 15, 1942. FPG was thoroughly

investigated three times, with many minor investigations. In addition to factual information about FPG's activities and statements, the FBI reports have considerable information from named and unnamed informants. A report of October 13, 1955 (FBI File No. 100–23300), stated that previous investigations had developed substantially the same information that "Dr. Graham was associated with numerous liberal-type organizations including several listed by the Attorney General. No evidence was developed, however, that he was a member of or was in any way affiliated with the Communist Party. To the contrary, investigation determined that Graham took an opposite stand to the Communist Party line on many issues and was attacked publicly by known Communists in those instances." On April 3, 1949, FPG's secretary compiled a list of 221 committees "on which Graham has served, or sponsored, or signed statements for, or contributed to in any way." (Author's files.) A number of committees are, in fact, omitted from this list.

46. Walter Gellhorn, "Report on a Report of the House Committee on Un-American Activities," *Harvard Law Review* LX (October 1947): 1193–1234.

47. *NYT*, January 13, 1949, p. 1. The Lewis broadcasts were January 11, 12, 13, 14, 17, and 25, 1949. They are quoted in full in the FBI reports.

48. See letters from William G. Pollard to FPG ("Oak Ridge File"), FPG papers for 1949–1950, SHC.

49. *NYT*, December 21, 1948, p. 20.

50. *NYT*, January 13, 1949, p. 1.

51. FPG to Fulton Lewis, Jr. (telegram), January 12, 1949, SHC. Mr. Lewis quoted most of the telegram in his broadcast of January 13.

52. *DTH*, January 11, 1949, January 12, 1949, January 13, 1949.

53. *DTH*, January 14, 1949.

54. *NYT*, January 14, 1949, p. 5.

55. *NYT*, January 30, 1949, p. 17.

56. *CR* XCV, pt. 1: 814–18.

57. Ibid., p. 1809.

58. Ibid., p. 1810.

PART FIVE

The Hazards of Politics, 1949–1950

For Chapter 17, *The Congressional Record*, 81st Congress, 1st and 2d Sessions, contains essential documents. An interview with Jonathan Daniels was helpful regarding FPG's appointment to the Senate. Interviews with Senators Paul Douglas and Wayne L. Morse, and with Allard K. Lowenstein, were particularly helpful in providing insights into

FPG's style as senator. William White, *Citadel* (New York: Harper, 1957) is a good, popular account of the Senate as an institution.

Materials provided by John Sanders and interviews with Allard Lowenstein provided indispensable data on the senatorial campaign described in Chapter 18. J. Covington Parham, Jr., "The North Carolina Democratic Senatorial Primary of 1950," Senior Thesis, Princeton University, 234 pp., 1952, was especially helpful in providing a sense of structure of the campaign. Mr. Parham's thesis deservedly was awarded the C. O. Joline Prize in American Political History.

Background materials for Chapter 19 are in Robert H. Carr, *The House Committee on Un-American Activities, 1945–1950* (Ithaca: Cornell University Press, 1952); Harold W. Chase, *Security and Liberty: The Problem of Native Communists* (Garden City: Doubleday, 1955); *CR*, 81st Congress, 2d Session; and Richard R. Rovere, *Senator Joe McCarthy* (New York: Harcourt, Brace, 1959).

17. Southerner and Senator (pp. 243–56)

1. FPG, first Senate speech, *CR* XCV, pt. 7 (July 20, 1949): 9799.

2. Interview with Jonathan Daniels, July 28, 1960.

3. Television interviews, FPG with Jonathan Daniels, Mrs. Kerr Scott, Mrs. Jeff Johnson, June 12, 1962, NCC.

4. Interview with Jonathan Daniels, July 28, 1960.

5. *RNO*, March 23, 1949; *GDN*, March 23, 1949; *NYT*, March 23, 1949, p. 1.

6. *CR* XCV, pt. 3 (March 23, 1949): 2997; *NYT*, March 24, 1949, p. 1.

7. *CR* XCV, pt. 3 (March 23, 1940): 3000–3001.

8. Ibid., p. 3001.

9. Ibid., p. 3001–2.

10. Ibid., pp. 3004–5.

11. *RNO*, March 28, 1949; *DTH*, March 28, 1949.

12. *RNO*, March 30, 1949.

13. White, *Citadel*, esp. pp. 27–94.

14. *CR* XCV, pt. 3 (March 29, 1949): 3322; ibid. (April 5 and 6, 1949), pp. 3927, 4073, 4877–78; Kahin, *Nationalism and Independence in Indonesia*, pp. 419–20; Taylor, *Indonesian Independence*, pp. 211–12.

15. FPG to Secretary of State George C. Marshall, December 3, 1949, SHC; Kahin, *Nationalism and Independence in Indonesia*, chs. 11, 13, pp. 320–25, 391 ff.

16. FPG to Acting Secretary of State Robert Lovett, January 10, 1950, SHC.

17. FPG 4.

18. *CR* XCV, pt. 3 (April 6, 1950): 3990–94.

19. Ibid. (April 5, 1950, April 6, 1950), pp. 3839–48.

20. Ibid. (April 6, 1949), pp. 3991, 4004.

21. Interview with Marian Graham, June 20, 1960; log of Hubert Robinson, April 3, 1949, April 20, 1949.

22. *CR* XCV, pt. 4 (May 2, 1949) : 5426–27; Ibid., pt. 5 (May 12, 1949) : 6077; interview with Marian Graham, June 20, 1960; Senator Wayne L. Morse, August 5, 1959; *RNO*, May 21, 1950.

23. *CR* XCV, pt. 7 (July 20, 1949) : 9799.

24. Ibid., p. 9800.

25. Ibid., XCVI, pt. 1 (February 2, 1950) : 1342.

26. See Alonzo L. Hamby, *Beyond the New Deal: Harry S Truman and American Liberalism* (New York: Columbia University Press, 1973), p. 236.

27. *NYT*, June 3, 1949, p. 1.

28. *CR* XCV, pt. 9 (August 24, 1949) : 12132; ibid., pt. 11 (October 13, 1949) : 14397ff.; ibid. (October 15, 1949) : 14691–93.

29. *CR* XCVI, pt. 1 (January 26, 1950) : 954; ibid., pt 2 (February 28, 1950) : 2479ff; ibid, pt. 4 (April 5, 1950) : 4725.

30. Ibid., pt. 4 (April 5, 1950) : 4798–99; *NYT*, June 17, 1950, p. 1.

31. *NYT*, June 17, 1950, p. 1; *RNO*, June 17, 1950.

18. Campaign Ordeal (pp. 257–71)

1. *RNO*, June 22, 1950.

2. *RNO*, February 1, 1950.

3. Interview with Allard K. Lowenstein, April 18, 1961; *RNO*, February 1, 1950.

4. See state newspapers, esp. *Charlotte Observer*, *RNO*, and *GDN* for February and March, 1950. Smith quoted in papers March 23, 1950.

5. Material in author's files supplied by John Sanders; also in Parham, "The North Carolina Democratic Primary."

6. Interview with Allard K. Lowenstein, April 18, 1961.

7. Cf. *CR* XCVI, pts. 1–5 (February through April, 1950); ibid., pt. 5 (May 5, 1950) : 6445, 6490.

8. *RNO*, May 13, 1950.

9. Interview with Allard K. Lowenstein, April 18, 1961; Paul H. Douglas, *In the Fullness of Time* (New York: Harcourt, Brace, Jovanovich, 1972), pp. 240–41. Senator Douglas reported he and his wife had known three "political saints": FPG, Jerry Voorhis, and Herbert Lehman.

10. Interview with Allard K. Lowenstein, April 18, 1961.

11. *RNO*, May 16, 1950.

12. *RNO*, May 22, 1950.

13. *RNO*, May 23, 1950.

14. Author's files on Senate campaign.

15. Ibid.

16. *RNO*, June 1, 1950.

17. *RNO*, May 29, 1950.

18. *NYT*, June 1, 1950, p. 4.

19. *RNO*, June 2, 1950.

20. *RNO*, June 2, 1950.

21. *RNO*, June 6, 1950; see "North Carolina on Trial," editorial, June 8, 1950.

22. *RNO*, June 7, 1950.

23. *GDN*, June 8, 1950.

24. Author's files; *RNO*, June 14, 1950.

25. Interview with Allard K. Lowenstein, April 18, 1961.

26. *RNO*, June 18, 1950.

27. *RNO*, June 20, 1950, June 22, 1950.

28. *RNO*, June 14, 1950, June 21, 1950.

29. Author's files.

30. *RNO*, June 14, 1950.

31. *RNO*, June 18, 1950.

32. Parham, "The North Carolina Democratic Primary," passim, esp. pp. 166ff. The material on Baldwin is on pp. 168–69. Both Parham and Sanders have an extensive collection of campaign leaflet propaganda, both official and unofficial.

33. *RNO*, June 21, 1950.

34. Interview with Allard K. Lowenstein, April 18, 1961.

35. *GDN*, June 26, 1950.

36. *GDN*, June 26, 1950.

37. *NYT*, June 27, 1950, p. 1.

38. *GDN,* June 27, 1950.

39. Author's files; see also SHC.

19. Beyond Defeat (pp. 272–82)

1. FPG, "Farewell Statement" in *CR* XCVI, pt. 11 (September 22, 1950): 15470–79.

2. Interviews with Jonathan Daniels, July 28, 1960, Senator Wayne L. Morse, August 5, 1959, Allard K. Lowenstein, April 18, 1961; *RNO*, July 13, 1950; *NYT*, July 13, 1950, p. 1; Paul Douglas, *In Fullness,* p. 241.

3. Rovere, *Senator Joe McCarthy*, pp. 125ff.

4. *NYT*, February 12, 1950, p. 5.

5. Rovere, *Senator Joe McCarthy*, pp. 125, 128, and passim.

6. Ibid., pp. 34–39, 267–68; *CR* XCVI, pt. 9 (August 10, 1950): 12145; *Nation* CLXXI (September 9, 1950): 14533ff.

7. *CR* XCVI, pt. 11 (September 11, 1950): 14533ff.

8. Douglas, *In Fullness*, pp. 306–8. ("To oppose the bill would mean being labelled pro-Communist. It was with heavy hearts that Humphrey and I conferred together just before the roll call and decided that as a practical matter we would vote for the bill. Only seven voted 'no'. After twenty years I have come to feel that their names should be inscribed on a roll of honor, and that I had done the wrong thing," p. 307); *NYT*, September 23, 1950, p. 6.

9. Hamby, *Beyond the New Deal*, pp. 411–15.

10. September 23, 1950, p. 6.

11. Quoted in "Liberals Outsmarted," *Nation* CLXXI (September 23, 1950): 260.

12. Zechariah Chafee, Jr., to FPG, October 4, 1950, SHC.

13. Vol. XXIX, no. 12 (September 22, 1950): 20–1.

14. *CR* XCVI, pt. 11 (September 22, 1950): 15556.

15. *NYT*, September 24, 1950, p. 1; Douglas, *In Fullness*, p. 309; *CR* XCVI, pt. 11 (September 22, 1950): 15520–21.

16. *CR* XCVI, pt. 11 (September 23, 1950): 15726.

17. E.g., ibid., pt. 10 (August 30, 1950): 13847.

18. Ibid., pt. 17, Appendix, pp. A 6774–75.

19. Ibid., pt. 11 (September 22, 1950): 15470–79.

20. Ibid., pp. 15470–71.

21. Ibid. (September 23, 1950): 15728–30.

22. Ibid., p. 15730.

23. Interviews with Allard K. Lowenstein, April 18, 1961, Marian Graham, June 20, 1960.

24. Francis Pickens Miller to author, March 24, 1961. ("The tragedy of political life in the South is that its best sons when defeated in the arena are forced to leave. It's a system of ostracism even more cruel than the old Grecian system because no time limit is set.")

PART SIX

Liberal-at-Large, 1950–1972

Primary documents are found in the UN Security Council Official Reports and in the Reports of the United Nations Commission for India and Pakistan and the United Nations Representative for India and Pakistan. Many of the documents are in K. Sarwar Hasan, ed., *Documents on the Foreign Relations of Pakistan: the Kashmir Question* (Karachi: Pakistan Institute of International Affairs, 1966). Other particularly helpful background sources are Norman Brown, *The United States and India, Pakistan, Bangladesh* (Cambridge: Harvard University Press, 1972) and Josef Korbel, *Danger in Kashmir* (Princeton: Princeton University Press, 1954).

20. The United Nations, India and Pakistan (pp. 285–303)

1. FPG, "A Summary Review of the Mediatory Reports of the United Nations in the Kashmir Situation as the Introduction to and the Basis of the Recommendations which Conclude this Report," unpublished mimeo, n.d., SHC.

2. FPG to Raymond B. Allen, December 14, 1950, SHC.

3. FPG to Kemp D. Battle, March 10, 1951, SHC.

4. *Washington Post*, March 12, 1951; FPG to Senator Lester Hunt, February 19, 1951, SHC; Senator Wayne L. Morse to FPG, February 10, 1951, SHC; Oscar Chapman to FPG, n.d. (received February 23, 1951), SHC; FPG to Mrs. James Rowland Angell, February 12, 1951, SHC. ("It was good to see the parties themselves take responsibility in the critical situation and work out agreements satisfactory to both sides.")

5. FPG to Charles E. Wilson, January 13, 1951, SHC.

6. Hamby, *Beyond the New Deal*, pp. 446–50.

7. FPG, "Testimony before the Senate Appropriations Committee," April 19, 1951, SHC; see also FPG to Ralph McGill, June 6, 1951, SHC; FPG to Mrs. J. Melville Broughton, May 21, 1951, SHC; FPG to H. L. Griffin, March 22, 1951, SHC.

8. Mr. Nickerson to Mr. Wainhouse (State Dept. memo), April 10, 1951, April 12, 1951.

9. Interview with Daisy Lippner, June 23, 1960.

10. Korbel, "The Forgotten Nation," ch. 1 of *Danger in Kashmir*, pp. 3–24; Brown, *United States and India*, pp. 179–82.

11. Korbel, "The Struggle Begins," ch. 3 of *Danger in Kashmir*, pp. 44–72; Brown, *United States and India*, pp. 159–60; Alan Campbell-Johnson, *Mission with Mountbatten* (New York: Dutton, 1951), pp. 17–166.

12. Brown, *United States and India*, pp. 160–61. One of the most informative and sensitive eyewitness accounts is Penderel Moon, *Divide and Quit* (Berkeley: University of California Press, 1972). Moon's estimate of the number killed is in a "Note on Casualties," p. 293.

13. Brown, *United States and India*, p. 184; Campbell-Johnson, *Mission with Mountbatten*, p. 225; K. Sarwar Hasan, "Instrument of Accession of Jammu and Kashmir," October 26, 1947, *Documents*, pp. 58–62.

14. Representative of India to President of Security Council, January 1, 1948, S/628; Resolution adopted by UN Security Council, November 20, 1948, S/654; Resolution adopted April 28, 1948, S/726; Resolution adopted by UNCIP, August 13, 1948, S/100, para. 75; Resolution adopted by UNCIP, January 5, 1949, S/1196, para. 51.

15. Korbel, "The UN Commission at Work," ch. 6 of *Danger in Kashmir*, pp. 118–64

16. Idem, "The United Nations Representatives," ch. 7 of *Danger*

in Kashmir, pp. 165–97; proposals made by the President of the Security Council, Gen. A. G. L. McNaughton, December 22, 1949, SCOR, 5th Yr. Supplement for January-May, 1950, pp. 4–6.

17. Resolution adopted by the UN Security Council, March 14, 1950, S/1469; Report submitted by UNRIP, Sir Owen Dixon to the Security Council, September 15, 1950, S/1791 incorporating S/1791/Add. 1.

18. FPG reports reveal an appreciation for the history and culture of India and Pakistan. The judgments expressed here are those of the author based upon two years in India and Pakistan and a reading in Hindu and Moslem culture.

19. Interview with Marian Graham, June 20, 1960; FPG to Gordon Gray, May 10, 1952, SHC.

20. FPG, "A Summary Review"; cf. Korbel, *Danger in Kashmir*.

21. Quoted in Korbel, *Danger in Kashmir*, p. 188.

22. The descriptions of the drives into the two cities are based upon the author's visits to Karachi and New Delhi. The temperatures for Karachi and New Delhi are from *Hindustan Times*, August 3, 1951.

23. Korbel, *Danger in Kashmir*, p. 183; Lord Birdwood, *A Continent Decides* (London: Hale, 1953), p. 249.

24. The proposals first appear in identical letters from UNRIP to the Prime Minister of India, Jawaharlal Nehru, and the Prime Minister of Pakistan, Liaquat Ali Khan, September 7, 1951, S/2375, SCOR, 6th Yr. Special Supplement, no. 2, Doc. S/2375, Annex 2, pp. 26–28; replies, ibid., pp. 28–33.

25. FPG, "First Report of Dr. Frank Graham," S/2365, October 15, 1951; FPG, "Dr. Frank Graham's Statement to the Security Council," S/Pv 564, October 18, 1951; FPG, "Dr. Frank Graham's Statement to the Security Council," S/Pv 570, January 17, 1952, S/2448, SCOR, Supplement, January-March, 1952.

26. *NYT*, March 1, 1952, p. 4, March 6, 1952, p. 3, March 9, 1952, p. 2, April 6, 1952, p. 3; see as representative of many *NYT* editorials praising FPG that on April 28, 1952, p. 8; FPG, "Third Report of Dr. Frank Graham," S/2611, April 22, 1952.

27. *NYT*, August 19, 1952, p. 4, September 1, 1952, p. 6.

28. FPG to Marian Graham, September 7, 1952, SHC.

29. *NYT*, October 11, 1952, p. 2, December 24, 1952, p. 3, February 19, 1953, p. 6, February 20, 1953, p. 4, April 1, 1953, p. 4; FPG, "Fourth Report of Dr. Frank Graham," S/2783, September 19, 1952; FPG, "Dr. Frank Graham's Statement to the Security Council," S/Pv 605, October 10, 1952; FPG, "Fifth Report of Dr. Frank Graham," S/2967, March 27, 1953.

30. Hasan, "Negotiations Between India and Pakistan," ch. 10, *Documents*, pp. 327–60.

31. "Letter of Prime Minister of India Addressed to the Prime Minister of Pakistan," November 10, 1953, and December 1, 1953, in Hasan, "Negotiations," pp. 340–44.

32. Elmore P. Jackson to FPG (memo), April 20, 1954, SHC.

33. Draft Resolutions, Amendments, and Resolutions Adopted By the Security Council, February 21, 1957, S/3787, S/3798, S/3793, SCOR, 12th Yr. Supplement, January-March, 1957, pp. 7–9.

34. Interview with Daisy Lippner, June 21, 1960.

35. "Report Submitted by the President of the Security Council for the Month of Feb., 1957," Gunnar Jarring, April 20, 1957, SCOR, 12th Yr. Supplement, April-June, 1957, pp. 13–16.

36. "Resolution Adopted by the Security Council," December 2, 1957, S/3922, SCOR, 12th Yr. Supplement, October-December, 1957, pp. 21–22; "Resolution Submitted by UNRIP to the President of the Security Council," March 28, 1958, S/3984, SCOR, 13th Yr. Supplement, January-March, 1958, pp. 41–45.

37. FPG, "A Summary Review."

38. Interview with Allard K. Lowenstein, April 18, 1961.

39. FPG to Ralph J. Bunche, February 28, 1964, SCH; FPG to His Excellency U Thant, March 25, 1965, SHC.

40. Interview with Daisy Lippner, June 21, 1960.

41. FPG, "A Summary Review," esp. pp. 49, 53, 55, 67.

21. "Ideals of the American Revolution" (pp. 304–17)

1. FPG, personal note to friends, April 12, 1961, SHC.

2. FPG to N. J. Newman, February 17, 1961.

3. "Deplore Secrecy in the Jones Case," *Christian Century* CLXX (March 4, 1953): 245; "Presbyterian U. S. Commission Fires Chapel Hill Pastor," *Christian Century* (March 11, 1953), p. 277; Henry Ruark, "Orange Presbytery vs. Jones," *Christian Century* (March 18, 1953), pp. 319–20; Jay Jenkins, "Around the U.S.A.: Disturber of the Peace," *Nation* CLXXVII, no. 6 (August 8, 1953): inside cover; "Pastor vs. Presbytery," *Time* LXI (February 23, 1953): 53.

4. "A Consideration of the Church and the Racial Problem by the Elders, March-June, 1944," n.d., printed, author's files; interview with Charles M. Jones, April 18, 1961.

5. Interview with Charles M. Jones, April 18, 1961.

6. Ibid.

7. John Bennett to author, August 4, 1960.

8. Jay Jenkins, "Disturber of the Peace."

9. FPG, "Summary by Frank P. Graham of His Written and Spoken Statements on the Case of the Chapel Hill Presbyterian Church, Late 1952 and Early 1953," n.d., 18 pp., printed, SHC.

10. Interview with Charles M. Jones, April 18, 1961.

11. FPG to James Dombrowski, May 12, 1954, SHC.

12. *"Brown* v. *Board of Education of Topeka, Kansas,"* 347 US 483, May 17, 1954, in *U. S. Supreme Court of the United States, October Term, 1954,* Book 99, Lawyer's Edition, ed. Ernest H. Schopler (Rochester: Lawyers Cooperative Publishing, 1955), pp. 1083, 1105–6.

13. FPG to Clarence Poe, May 26, 1954, SHC.

14. See FPG addresses for this period, SHC.

15. FPG, "The Need for Wisdom: Two Suggestions for Carrying Out the Supreme Court's Decision Against Segregation," *Virginia Quarterly Review* XXXI, no. 2 (Spring 1955): 192–212. The reprint enlarged the title to "The Need for Both Wisdom and Good Faith," etc.

16. Ibid., p. 208.

17. Ibid., p. 210.

18. FPG to Representative Brooks Hays, December 1, 1958, SHC.

19. Author's files.

20. Personal multigraphed note FPG sent to friends who had written about the Winthrop College incident, April, n.d., 1961, SHC.

21. *NYT,* April 5, 1961, p. 24.

22. *RNO,* June 26, 1963; "Academic Freedom, Futile Ban on Ideas," *Time* LXXXV, no. 24 (June 11, 1965): 74–77.

23. Conversation with McNeill Smith and James Medford, July 15, 1977.

24. FPG, "A Talk by Frank Graham at the Invitation of the Student Leaders of North Carolina State University in Raleigh," October 2, 1965, SHC; *CR* CXIII, pt. 6 (June 19, 1967): 16318–23.

25. "Speaker Ban: State Assembly Kills Law Denying Forum to Communists, UNC's Status is Believed Safe," *Science* CL (November 26, 1965): 1141, 1194. Other accounts include: "Academic Casualty," *New Republic* CLIII (July 10, 1965): 10; and Kenneth L. Penegar, "Who's for Academic Freedom," *New Republic* CLIII (December 4, 1965): 15–17. It is instructive that the most complete reporting in a national journal throughout the history of the controversy is to be found in *Science.*

26. "Graham Speaks for Academic Freedom," February 18, 1966, SHC.

27. Interview with McNeill Smith, July 15, 1977.

28. "Speaker Ban Controversy is Revived at UNC," *Science* CLII (April 9, 1966): 50–52.

29. Interview with McNeill Smith, July 15, 1977.

30. *RNO,* February 20, 1968.

31. "The Next Five Years: A RAF Working Paper," Rural Advancement Fund (Charlotte: National Sharecroppers Fund, October 1976).

32. "Frank Porter Graham, NSF Chairman 1953–1969," *Rural Advance* VI, no. 1 (Summer 1972): 3–4.

33. FPG speech at National Sharecroppers Fund Conference, Bricks, N.C., November 1962, SHC; cf. FPG, "People Who Are Poor," *AFL-CIO American Federationist*, June 1958, pp. 13–14, 31.

22. Life with Marian and the Return Home (pp. 318–30)

1. FPG, inaugural address, 1931, SHC.

2. Interviews with Daisy Lippner, June 21, 1960, McNeill Smith, July 15, 1977; FPG to Louis R. Wilson, December 11, 1961, 22 pp., SHC; FPG to L. P. McLendon, February 23, 1962 (incomplete at 54 pp.), SHC; FPG to Herb Sites, November 19, 1960, SHC; FPG to Walter Reuther, June 8, 1961, SHC; FPG to Wayne L. Morse, May 9, 1961, SHC; FPG to Paul Douglas, December 11, 1963, SHC.

3. FPG to Dean Rusk, September 19, 1967, SHC.

4. Interview with Daisy Lippner, June 21, 1960; cf. correspondence: FPG to Matthew Tolbin, Daisy Lippner to Matthew Tolbin, 1966, SHC.

5. Interview with Daisy Lippner, June 21, 1960.

6. *RNO*, June 29, 1953.

7. FPG, "A Talk at the Hammarskjold Memorial Service," September 24, 1961, SHC; reprinted in various places including *GDN*, October 1, 1965.

8. FPG to Marvin Singleton, October 4, 1956, SHC.

9. See FPG files for 1965 ("Contributions"), SHC.

10. FPG files (1966, Box 1, "Life Insurance Data"), SHC.

11. FPG to James J. Jordan, n.d., 1967, SHC.

12. FPG to Ben Segal, October 19, 1956, SHC.

13. Marian Graham to FPG, March 12, 1966, SHC.

14. Mrs. J. Cheshire Webb, quoted in *RNO*, June 5, 1942.

15. Interview with Marian Graham, June 20, 1960.

16. *The News* (of Orange County), January 13, 1966. ("The following anonymous contribution was submitted in recognition of Mrs. Frank P. Graham currently convalescing from a recent illness in New York.")

17. FPG to friends, May 16, 1967, SHC.

18. See FPG files for 1967, SHC.

19. FPG to J. Carlyle Sitterson, October 26, 1967, SHC.

20. The descriptions and judgments are the author's based upon visits and conversations in 1968–72 with FPG, Kate Graham Sanders, and friends of FPG.

21. Vance Barron at FPG funeral, February 17, 1972, partially quoted in Tom Wicker, "Death of a Man," *NYT*, February 20, 1972, sec. E, p. 13.

Index